Creative AI Tools and Ethical Implications in Teaching and Learning

Jared Keengwe
University of North Dakota, USA

IGI Global
PUBLISHER of TIMELY KNOWLEDGE

A volume in the Advances in Educational Technologies and Instructional Design (AETID) Book Series

Published in the United States of America by
IGI Global
Information Science Reference (an imprint of IGI Global)
701 E. Chocolate Avenue
Hershey PA, USA 17033
Tel: 717-533-8845
Fax: 717-533-8661
E-mail: cust@igi-global.com
Web site: http://www.igi-global.com

Library of Congress Cataloging-in-Publication Data

Names: Keengwe, Jared, 1973- editor.
Title: Creative AI tools and ethical implications in teaching and learning / Edited by Jared Keengwe.
Description: Hershey, PA : Information Science Reference, [2024] | Includes bibliographical references and index. | Summary: "The book provides information on the potential of AI tools and applications in traditional face-to-face, blended, and online education. Further, the book examines the pedagogical models/design, constraints, and opportunities for innovative use of AI in teaching and learning"-- Provided by publisher.
Identifiers: LCCN 2023038634 (print) | LCCN 2023038635 (ebook) | ISBN 9798369302057 (hardcover) | ISBN 9798369302095 (paperback) | ISBN 9798369302064 (ebook)
Subjects: LCSH: Artificial intelligence--Educational applications. | Artificial intelligence--Moral and ethical aspects. | Blended learning. | Critical pedagogy.
Classification: LCC LB1028.43 .C74 2024 (print) | LCC LB1028.43 (ebook) | DDC 371.9--dc23/eng/20230818
LC record available at https://lccn.loc.gov/2023038634
LC ebook record available at https://lccn.loc.gov/2023038635

This book is published in the IGI Global book series Advances in Educational Technologies and Instructional Design (AE-TID) (ISSN: 2326-8905; eISSN: 2326-8913)

British Cataloguing in Publication Data
A Cataloguing in Publication record for this book is available from the British Library.

Advances in Educational Technologies and Instructional Design (AETID) Book Series

Lawrence A. Tomei
Robert Morris University, USA

ISSN:2326-8905
EISSN:2326-8913

Mission

Education has undergone, and continues to undergo, immense changes in the way it is enacted and distributed to both child and adult learners. In modern education, the traditional classroom learning experience has evolved to include technological resources and to provide online classroom opportunities to students of all ages regardless of their geographical locations. From distance education, Massive-Open-Online-Courses (MOOCs), and electronic tablets in the classroom, technology is now an integral part of learning and is also affecting the way educators communicate information to students.

The **Advances in Educational Technologies & Instructional Design (AETID) Book Series** explores new research and theories for facilitating learning and improving educational performance utilizing technological processes and resources. The series examines technologies that can be integrated into K-12 classrooms to improve skills and learning abilities in all subjects including STEM education and language learning. Additionally, it studies the emergence of fully online classrooms for young and adult learners alike, and the communication and accountability challenges that can arise. Trending topics that are covered include adaptive learning, game-based learning, virtual school environments, and social media effects. School administrators, educators, academicians, researchers, and students will find this series to be an excellent resource for the effective design and implementation of learning technologies in their classes.

Coverage

- Curriculum Development
- Higher Education Technologies
- Instructional Design
- Educational Telecommunications
- E-Learning
- Social Media Effects on Education
- Online Media in Classrooms
- Digital Divide in Education
- K-12 Educational Technologies
- Virtual School Environments

IGI Global is currently accepting manuscripts for publication within this series. To submit a proposal for a volume in this series, please contact our Acquisition Editors at Acquisitions@igi-global.com or visit: http://www.igi-global.com/publish/.

The Advances in Educational Technologies and Instructional Design (AETID) Book Series (ISSN 2326-8905) is published by IGI Global, 701 E. Chocolate Avenue, Hershey, PA 17033-1240, USA, www.igi-global.com. This series is composed of titles available for purchase individually; each title is edited to be contextually exclusive from any other title within the series. For pricing and ordering information please visit http://www.igi-global.com/book-series/advances-educational-technologies-instructional-design/73678. Postmaster: Send all address changes to above address.

Titles in this Series

For a list of additional titles in this series, please visit: www.igi-global.com/book-series

Transforming the Language Teaching Experience in the Age of AI
Galip Kartal (Necmettin Erbakan University, Turkey)
Information Science Reference • copyright 2023 • 328pp • H/C (ISBN: 9781668498934) • US $230.00 (our price)

Dynamic Curriculum Development and Design Strategies for Effective Online Learning in Higher Education
Kelley Walters (Western Governors University, USA)
Information Science Reference • copyright 2023 • 320pp • H/C (ISBN: 9781668486467) • US $215.00 (our price)

Developing Skills and Competencies for Digital and Green Transitions
Patricia Ordóñez de Pablos (The University of Oviedo, Spain) Mohammad Nabil Almunawar (School of Business and Economics, University of Brunei Darussalam, Brunei) and Muhammad Anshari (School of Business and Economics, University of Brunei Darussalam, Brunei)
Business Science Reference • copyright 2023 • 367pp • H/C (ISBN: 9781668490891) • US $250.00 (our price)

Artificial Intelligence Applications Using ChatGPT in Education Case Studies and Practices
Muhammad Shahzad Aslam (School of Traditional Chinese Medicine, Xiamen University Malaysia, Malaysia) and Saima Nisar (School of Computing, UUM College of Arts and Sciences, University Utara Malaysia, Sintok, Malaysia)
Information Science Reference • copyright 2023 • 234pp • H/C (ISBN: 9781668493007) • US $215.00 (our price)

Using Assistive Technology for Inclusive Learning in K-12 Classrooms
Jeremy Bell (University of Louisiana, Monroe, USA) and Timothy Gifford (Movia Robotics Inc., USA)
Information Science Reference • copyright 2023 • 280pp • H/C (ISBN: 9781668464243) • US $215.00 (our price)

The Impact and Importance of Instructional Design in the Educational Landscape
Christie F. Calhoun (Jacksonville State University, USA)
Information Science Reference • copyright 2023 • 295pp • H/C (ISBN: 9781668482087) • US $215.00 (our price)

Global Perspectives on Effective Assessment in English Language Teaching
Miguel Fernández Álvarez (Universidad Politécnica de Madrid, Spain) and Amanda Lira Gordenstein Montes (Northeastern Illinois University, USA)
Information Science Reference • copyright 2023 • 287pp • H/C (ISBN: 9781668482131) • US $215.00 (our price)

Handbook of Research on Innovative Frameworks and Inclusive Models for Online Learning
Jared Keengwe (University of North Dakota, USA)

IGI Global
PUBLISHER of TIMELY KNOWLEDGE

701 East Chocolate Avenue, Hershey, PA 17033, USA
Tel: 717-533-8845 x100 • Fax: 717-533-8661
E-Mail: cust@igi-global.com • www.igi-global.com

Table of Contents

Detailed Table of Contents

In the vital context of education, the application of artificial intelligence (AI) to assessments necessitates a nuanced examination of the boundaries between ethically permissible and impermissible practices. In this chapter, the authors applied a systematic literature mapping methodology to scour extant research, so as to holistically structure the landscape into explicit topical research clusters. Through topic modelling and network analyses, research mapped key ethical principles to different assessment phases in a triadic ontological framework. The chapter looks to provide researchers and practitioners the insights into the ethical challenges that exist across an end-to-end assessment pipeline.

The use of artificial intelligence (AI) is becoming widespread in educational settings including schools. It has the potential to support teaching and learning across all subjects. The focus of the chapter is to explore how it can be used to support literacy development. In understanding use by teachers, the TPACK model is investigated. This is then followed by a focus on the teacher's role and the importance of teacher training. The focus then moves to AI and literacies. As part of this section, digital story writing and AI is investigated as well as special and inclusive education. This section concludes with a focus on assessment and feedback. The ethical use of AI is an important consideration and is an area that is currently engaging researchers and educators. This aspect is investigated. To conclude the chapter, areas of future research are discussed.

The impact of technology and its advancements has proliferated in all the sectors of the economy, including the education sector. The integration of technology into the education sector is very evident from the teaching pedagogy and strategies followed by educational institutions worldwide. The concept of blended learning has gained much attention due to its multifaceted nature; as it includes blending traditional face to face teaching with the use of online and electronic media. As the integration of technology requires huge amounts of student data to be processed, it can also lead to ethical dilemmas and concerns due to its sensitive and confidential nature. This chapter focuses on the various dimensions of technological integration in the education system and its practical implications on enhancing student learning and engagement. In order to provide a road map for future research on developing an education model that can improve learning and teaching experiences, the article also addresses key hurdles, ethical issues, and potential risks of integrating AI for education.

This chapter explores the impact of the development and implementation of the ChatGPT language model on the traditional framework of Bloom's taxonomy of learning stages. Through examination of data and case studies, the study argues that the advanced natural language processing capabilities of ChatGPT have led to a shift away from the linear, hierarchical model of Bloom's taxonomy, towards a more dynamic and fluid approach to knowledge acquisition and application. The results of the study suggest that the incorporation of ChatGPT and similar language models into education and training programs may lead to more effective and efficient learning outcomes.

This chapter presents a comprehensive exploration of the transformative influence of generative AI tools in education. It examines the personalized learning experience enabled by AI, the role of AI tools as virtual tutors, content creation aids for educators, and their application in language learning and communication enhancement. Additionally, the chapter delves into the ethical implications associated with AI integration, including data privacy, fairness, and transparency. Practical strategies for responsible AI adoption are proposed, encompassing guidelines for ethical usage and educator training. The chapter concludes by highlighting the vast potential of AI-powered education while underscoring the significance of ethical considerations in its implementation. It encapsulates the evolution of AI in education and foresees a future where learners are empowered through dynamic and personalized educational experiences.

The role of AI in education is not doubtful. This chapter critically explores the potential benefits, challenges, and implication of integrating AI game activities in educational settings. It underlines how Al algorithms are vital in promoting critical thinking, problem solving skills, and knowledge retention among learners. Moreover, this chapter also discusses the utilization of simulation, virtual reality, and interactive narrative in Al- driven gaming activities to amplify active engagement and foster a deeper understanding of complex concepts. Additionally, the chapter explores how Al games have the capacity to enhance collaborative leaning, foster social interaction, and facilitate the growth of essential skills needed in the of 21st- century. The chapter addresses the crucial topics of ethics concerns, safeguarding data privacy, and promoting inclusivity. Furthermore, it underscores the potential of AI game activities in addressing the evolving requirements of learners in the digital age and equipping them for a technology-driven future.

Preface

Educators, researchers, and stakeholders across the globe find themselves at a pivotal crossroads, navigating the uncharted terrain of AI's role in teaching and learning while grappling with its ethical implications. It is within this context that the anthology *Creative AI Tools and Ethical Implications in Teaching and Learning* takes form, offering a comprehensive exploration of the multifaceted dimensions of AI in education.

This book provides a rich tapestry of chapters, each meticulously crafted to deepen your understanding of AI's transformative potential and its ethical boundaries. The chapter contributors have collaborated to offer insights into a broad spectrum of topics, from the practical applications of AI in traditional classrooms to its dynamic role in online and blended learning environments. They delve into the nuances of designing AI-based classroom activities and explore the promising realm of open AI in education. The also uncover the creative potential of AI in education, offering imaginative approaches to AI integration, including innovative activities, designs, and development strategies.

As editor, I have embarked on a quest to unravel the myriad opportunities and challenges that AI brings to the educational domain. The primary goal is to shed light on the ethical underpinnings, pedagogical insights, and practical wisdom necessary for harnessing the potential of AI tools in diverse educational settings. To this end, this book underscores the importance of responsible AI practices and provides a framework of ethical guidelines for educators and administrators to navigate this transformative journey with integrity. Further, it delves into the world of learning analytics, educational data mining, and machine learning, offering insights into how these technologies can shape the future of education. The 13 chapters of the book also explores the practical applications of AI, such as AI game activities and the utilization of generative AI tools like ChatGPT to enhance teaching and learning experiences. The critical dimension of student assessment in the context of AI is thoroughly examined, providing educators with tools to rethink traditional evaluation methods.

Chapter 1 provides a theoretical foundation for objective debates surrounding the implementation of AI in education. It addresses the sensationalism that often surrounds AI and its potential benefits and harms. The chapter emphasizes the importance of ethical philosophy and sociology in guiding future practices, setting a new paradigmatic sufficiency for ethical AI integration.

Chapter 2 introduces AI in higher education, discussing its tools, resources, and positive contributions to learning. It also addresses the ethical concerns related to students' unethical use of AI, particularly chatbots. The chapter explores how faculty education in AI can promote positive innovation while mitigating ethical issues and presents a real-world course redesign using AI best practices.

In Chapter 3, the authors conduct a systematic literature mapping to explore the ethical challenges in AI-based assessments. They map ethical principles to various assessment phases and offer a comprehensive overview of the ethical considerations in educational assessments, providing valuable insights for researchers and practitioners.

Chapter 4 delves into the role of AI in supporting literacy development, focusing on teacher practices and the importance of teacher training. It explores AI's potential in literacy education, addressing ethical concerns. The chapter concludes by identifying areas for future research in the intersection of AI and literacy development.

Chapter 5 explores the integration of technology and AI in education, particularly in the context of blended learning. It discusses practical implications and ethical concerns related to the use of AI to enhance student learning and engagement. The chapter highlights key hurdles and potential risks while proposing strategies for responsible AI adoption.

Chapter 6 examines the impact of ChatGPT on traditional Bloom's Taxonomy of Learning Stages. It argues that ChatGPT's natural language processing capabilities have led to a shift in how knowledge acquisition and application are approached. The chapter discusses the implications for learning outcomes in education and training programs.

Chapter 7 explores the transformative influence of generative AI tools in education. It discusses their role in personalized learning, virtual tutoring, content creation, and language learning. The chapter addresses ethical implications, data privacy, and offers practical strategies for responsible AI adoption, emphasizing the significance of ethical considerations.

Chapter 8 critically examines the potential benefits, challenges, and ethical implications of integrating AI game activities in educational settings. It emphasizes how AI-driven gaming can promote critical thinking, collaboration, and essential skills among learners while highlighting ethical concerns and data privacy safeguards.

Chapter 9 explores the utilization of ChatGPT and generative AI tools in education, with a focus on the differences between developing and developed countries. It discusses the skill gaps in adopting these tools and their implications for education and development in developing countries.

Chapter 10 reviews the applications of ChatGPT in higher education, emphasizing its impact on student essays and research production. It highlights the need for pedagogical changes to adapt to ChatGPT and explores challenges, risks, and ethical considerations, suggesting innovative approaches to its use.

Chapter 11 provides an overview of the ethical concerns surrounding AI in education and across various sectors. It proposes a model with strategies for various stakeholders involved in ethical AI use, based on the socio-technical theory. The chapter addresses the challenges associated with AI ethics and offers guidance for responsible deployment.

Chapter 12 examines the usage of chatbots in higher education, focusing on their potential to improve student engagement and learning outcomes. It explores the consequences and benefits of integrating chatbots, underpinned by Vygotsky's sociocultural theory and the Ranganathan law of library science.

Chapter 13 critically analyzes and synthesizes literature on ethical guidelines for AI in education. It discusses approaches to ensure effective and ethical AI use, implications for educational stakeholders, and the need for clear policies, ongoing training, and regular evaluations to uphold ethical standards in AI integration.

These chapters collectively provide a comprehensive exploration of AI in education, addressing its theoretical foundations, practical applications, ethical considerations, and potential impacts on teaching and learning. To ensure a responsible and ethical integration of AI, this book rigorously examines issues related to bias, misinformation, and equitable access.

This book is not just for scholars and researchers; it is for educators, administrators, students, and all stakeholders invested in the present and future of education. Whether you are a teacher educator seeking innovative pedagogical approaches or a student curious about the ethical considerations surrounding AI, this book offers valuable insights.

I encourage readers to engage with the chapters presented here, to reflect on their own teaching practices, and to contribute to the ongoing dialogue surrounding AI and education. I hope that the diverse perspectives presented herein will inspire conversations, spark ideas, and ultimately empower educators and learners alike to navigate the intricate intersection of AI and education.

I extend my gratitude to the authors, reviewers, and the publishing team for their invaluable contributions in bringing this book to fruition. It is my belief that this collection of chapters will serve as a valuable reference and guide for educators and researchers navigating the evolving landscape of education, the integration of AI and the underlying ethical contemplation.

Jared Keengwe
University of North Dakota, USA

Chapter 1
Hyperbole or Hypothetical?
Ethics for AI in the Future of Applied Pedagogy

Catherine Hayes
https://orcid.org/0000-0003-3870-2668
University of Sunderland, UK

ABSTRACT

Debates and sensationalized presentations of artificial intelligence (AI) across the media and in scientific and industrial contexts have shaped public perception of its potential benefits; but the profound potential for harm ought to be acknowledged. This chapter provides a theoretical insight into how AI can be objectively debated amidst the hyperbole surrounding its implementation and the potential for the inaccessible to be made accessible over forthcoming months and years. A new level of paradigmatic sufficiency in terms of underpinning future practice with due regard for the ethical philosophy and sociology within which it will be based.

INTRODUCTION

'By their very nature, heuristic shortcuts will produce biases, and that is true for both humans and artificial intelligence, but the heuristics of AI are not necessarily the human ones.'

(Daniel Kahneman, b. 1934)

This chapter will consider applied ethics in the context of pedagogical practice in relation to the potential impact of Artificial Intelligence (AI) in education and other societal infrastructures such as the military and health and medicine. The extent to which AI has been progressively integrated into society over the last three years, has exponentially increased media and scientific debates of what is and what might be, if all we are to believe about AI is realised (Bareis & Jatzenbach, 2022). As with any landmark paradigmatic shift in society's use of and access to technological advance, the widespread introduction

DOI: 10.4018/979-8-3693-0205-7.ch001

of AI has both positive and negative aspects which can be harnessed for both human progression and decimation (Mikalef et al, 2022).

Initial debates surrounding AI focused predominantly on their functionalist capacities to reduce the complexity and challenge of largely physical tasks, where algorithmic decision making could be used as an adjunct support to mundane and burdensome human work (Mirbabaie et al 2022). This has now progressed to the widespread cognitive debates as to how AI can address tasks which before, seemed impossible and largely inaccessible, in terms of the decision-making processes necessary to undertake them (Madhav & Tyagi, 2022).

One of the key aspects of these debates is how humanity has often designed AI in human form, to the extent technological artefacts are often perceived as robots with a high degree of sentient ambition (Owe and Baum, 2021). It is often thought AI can compete for cognitive advantage rather than simply being a design artefact used to extend the reach of humanity's applied intellect (Mele, & Russo-Spena, 2023; Yamin, et al, 2021). This has led to widespread hyperbole that AI somehow has the capacity to override human cognition and that its capacity for extended algorithmic thinking may eventually pose a huge threat to mankind, alongside offering some of the greatest technological developments of our age (Cools, Van Gorp & Opgenhaffen, 2022).

Unlike other technological advances whether the choice to engage with them was always an option, AI poses a wider societal issue where that choice may no longer be possible, should the self-advancement of algorithmic decision making pose an overriding threat to humanity in terms of speed and capacity for action (Igna & Venturini, 2023). As such the ethical principles of AI are factors that all organisations now must contemplate so that the integration of ethical practice becomes a societal norm in terms of the use of AI in practice. Beyond an anthropological perspective, social ethics and the philosophies underpinning them all impact upon the capacity of organisational decision making and how AI may remain fully controllable and where the algorithms within which it operates may be constructively aligned with those affective attributes of humanity, that as a society, we would wish to promulgate, rather than any degree of negativity (Henin & Le Métayer, 2021).

Whilst every organisational infrastructure operated by humans is designed on principles of altruism, equity and equality, the integration of AI poses several questions which necessitate critical reflexivity of the situated nature of their use within highly sensitive contexts such as healthcare, law, and education, all of which can have the potential for an inordinate impact on society as it is currently known (Cheng, Varshney, & Liu, 2021). Perhaps then it is rather an issue with the design of AI rather than implementation, which ought to serve the hyperbole and hypothesising that surround it (Bareis & Jatzenbach, 2022).. This chapter will also explore how the social implications of AI are being posited, often sensationalised as a threat to humanity, rather than being framed in something humanly designed that ought to remain within the control of its maker, transparent in terms of capacity to undertake complex decision making and which most importantly is accountable for every individual action made in terms of design and programming (Novelli, Taddeo & Floridi, 2023).

The aims of the chapter are threefold, namely, to consider global ethics and the impact that AI could potentially have in terms of increasing societal inequalities in terms of existing infrastructure; to provide an insight into the developmental and progressive use of AI across organisational infrastructures such as global medicine and health and the military; finally to embed the concept of ethical AI and the potential for its praxis across all areas of its integration.

THE WIDENING GAPS OF SOCIETAL INEQUALITY

Geopolitically there are several ethical debates around the role of AI (Palomeres et al, 2021). A collective sense of global responsibility necessitates ensuring not only accountability but a huge degree of reassurance that the use of AI in practice will not be of detriment to humanity in any way. In those developing countries where technological advances have not yet reached the stage of development of their Western counterparts, this poses a huge risk of adding further and widening gaps of societal inequality, where the impact of AI may still be felt but remain under the control of other nations (Haluza & Jungwirth, 2023).. Being able to functionally adapt to the use of emergent technology still predominantly remains the preserve of developed nations so from an ethical perspective the use of AI as an adjunct to human experience rather than a replacement for it is essential if we are not to lose sight of global public well-being amidst global societal interest in novel approaches to technological development (Farrow, 2021; Floridi & Cowls, 2022).

GLOBAL ETHICS AND COLLECTIVE SOCIETAL RESPONSIBILITY

The irony of developing a metric framework of accountability for issues of ethical transparency, accountability, equity, and trust, is not lost on a world where the functional role of AI has far reached implications for address than those encountered in typical industrial, commercial, and educational contexts. In issues of human endeavour where predicting the future capacity and capability of AI as functionally autonomous, there are several issues of explanation which remain a challenge to justify in 21st Century developmental progress (Colaner, 2022). One of the main issues in terms of ontological and epistemological justification of AI is the lack of any apparent philosophical or theoretical underpinning for its use. Usually in the context of applied research, it is possible to provide a degree of constructive alignment, where ethical praxis is a primary and relatively predictable issue (Zhang et al, 2021). Global responsibility for a concept which has the potential to have universal impact, despite there not necessarily being a global capacity to support, sustain and ethically evaluate, is one which impacts beyond one facet of human infrastructure and pervades them all (Khogali & Mekid, 2023). Perhaps most significantly it is the degree of agency that AI occupies, which is of greatest concern to humanity and our human tendencies to frame AI as insentient threats to humanity, which have caused the greatest concerns and misunderstandings of what the ethical implications of AI might be (Hwang & Park, 2020).

Beyond the technological challenges of functional AI in relation to its capability development lies the justification of man to permit its widespread inception to the digital community. Formal policy and practice initiatives have been driven by global conferences, which in their earliest years focused largely on the fundamental positive impact that AI could bring, and which largely preceded the research literature which has provided an inferential insight into what the impact of widespread AI introduction might constitute for global civic futures on both a personal and professional level (Floridi & Cowls, 2022). Leading in this arena is the UNESCO Recommendation on the Ethics of Artificial Intelligence, which using an array of Delphi methodologies have drawn on the specific expertise of specialists in the field of AI to operationally define and frame the nature of ethical frameworks and praxes in the field ought to be. In theory, human attributes and characteristics are relatively understandable choices within the consensus of those with specialist expertise within AI. However, what is more concerning is how binary decision making, without sentience or conscience can become of the preserve of man-made machines, which have no capacity for tacit discernment in relation to the binary decision-making processes that underpin the algorithms controlling them and enabling them to process a greater degree of digital information than any human has capacity for.

The temporal fact that AI does not need to eat, sleep, or have any of the human 'baggage' that human capital is certain to have, ensures that progress can be made at an astonishing pace and to a level which may not have been anticipated before (Makridakis, 2017). As with any model of ethical praxis, key principles have been devised to ensure that the concepts of beneficence, non-maleficence, autonomy, justice, and explication are central to the use of ethical AI (Prem, 2023). Where the greatest challenges with this lie, though, is the fact that AI is not sentient, does not have a conscience, so in instances where automated decision making is advocated, the ethical use of AI has even greater ramifications, especially in relation to the justification of human decision making in its use (Floridi & Cowls, 2022; Mantello et al, 2023). The operational use of AI in practice is what has maintained a strategic focus on functional usage and the practicalities of system design (Peeters et al, 2021).

THE CULTURE AND CONTEXT OF AI ETHICS IMPLEMENTATION

Global cultural differences pose one of the greatest threats to the ethical management of AI, particularly in instances of competition (Humble, 2023). Not all use of AI will be altruistic and there are clear advantages to be gained in being able to win the race for supremacy in AI development and implementation (Qiao-Franco & Bode, 2023). Where specific ethical values are missing due to historical and local cultures then the justification of state intervention with AI may be lie beyond public questioning (Elliott, 2019). Across non-democratic countries there may even be a perceived benefit to autocratic leaders of being able to assert authority and surveillance with AI that has never been possible before (Zeng, 2020; Zuiderwijk, Chen & Salem, 2021; Young et al, 2021). It is in instances like this that human rights of privacy are destroyed, yet justified by the ideology that control of the state and state intervention is for human benefit. Any propositions to introduce global ethical frameworks of governance and accountability must first consider how best these cultural differences can be reconciled amidst such a degree of diversity, so that a universal set of principles can be agreed (Visivizi, 2021).

The whole concept of privacy is a relatively Westernized concept. Other nations value state intervention where collective control leads to individuals being responsible for their place and position in society (Döring, 2019) Not only does this link to ethics but more significantly, in countries such as China, is an integral part of morality, where moral behaviour has been an instrumental focus of attention for thousands of years prior to the introduction of AI (Nichols, 2022). Liberalist Western democracies have presented the need for individual autonomy at all costs. The rise of AI implementation has raised new questions of just how possible universal regulation of such systems can be. With such differences in state infrastructure, it is virtually impossible to see how AI ethics and governance and regulation can possibly become operational under such differences in contextual and situational specificity. Where philosophy underpins the justification of human rights, then across different global stages, this can be radically different (Zajda & Vissing, 2022).

MECHANISMS OF ACCOUNTABILITY IN PROFESSIONAL PRACTICE

Technological emergence and machine learning continue to revolutionize societal life and will soon become existentially embedded as adjunct mechanisms of intellectual decision making, upon which we become dependent (Bareis and Katzenbach, 2022). The ethical implications of this within health and medicine cannot be overlooked, since AI, is insentient. It may be capable of making active choices via strategically designed algorithmic programming, but it has no conscience with which to couple binary or even complex decision-making processes (Islam et al, 2022). Whilst scenarios such as this are usually the preserve of Hollywood movies, the implications for humanity, lie in the degree of control and algorithmic decision making that these machines are permitted (De Bruijn, Warnier & Janssen, 2022; Nader et al, 2021). Ethical complexity is even greater when we consider that any subjective or emotive intelligence can be removed from decisions where life and death can be at stake, for instance within policing, the military or indeed medical and surgical intervention (Miller, 2022). It is where autonomous AI is introduced that the situated context of its use must be contemplated, acknowledged, and accounted for (Alter, 2022). When faced with humanoid robots, which deliver AI this becomes even more of issue, since our cognitive capacity to perceive them as 'real' instead of the machines they are, is an issue (Finkel & Krämer, 2022). We have given non sentient objects, the characteristic of humanity, yet are surprised at our reaction to just how realistic they can appear (Sweeney, 2022).

Since ethical practice is based on our capacity to recognise the potential risks that AI may pose to humanity. It is the metacognitive processes of meaning making which differentiates the highly nuanced characteristics of man from the decision making itself (Ganapini et al, 2023). Searching for meaning, in this sense is central to human consciousness and arguably more importantly conscience. Being able to bind algorithms to specific parameters of focused operational practice, is straightforward in terms of ethical praxis (He, 2022). Where it becomes steadily more contentious is in instances where the intellectual capacity of AI is released within parameters of practice which also incorporate social contexts and social interaction (Chen, Sun & Wang, 2022). From an economic perspective, it is AI's potential to impact positively on areas such as enhanced productivity, the elimination of human error and the potential for more specific surgical intervention, which offer most (Goralski and Tan, 2020). It is the transparency of decision making which is imperative to ensure that man always remains in control of ongoing algorithmic processing, since if AI is permitted to iteratively improve itself without oversight and reaches decision making capacity beyond man's knowledge and scope of ethical practice, then it can be hypothesized that the disconcertment characterizing Hollywood's portrayal of AI could indeed become an unwelcome reality (Brewer et al, 2022). This would entail the AI adding algorithmic decision-making processes into originally human designed algorithms for the purposes of iterative improvement, regardless of the ongoing need for ethical praxis. It is also this potential that constitutes much of the hyperbole and media panic around just what AI might represent in terms of existential threat and how this might be best managed in the context of technological evolution (Harper, 2021).

ETHICAL EDUCATION AND THE FUTURE AGENCY OF AI IMPLEMENTATION

Since the progressive developmental work in AI operationalisation and implementation forms the basis for future work in the field, the need to educate and provide an insight into the agentic power necessary to manage the ethical implications of AI has never been greater (Nyholm, 2020). Beyond the functional implications of introducing emergent technologies across society, the impact and meaning making of AI on people's lives ought also to be considered so that mitigation of co-existing dangers, alongside the irrefutable benefit of AI can be accounted for and organisations held accountable for in terms of formal governance processes (Smith, 2021). Education and skills training via the embedding of strategic pedagogical intervention across curricula will become a central mechanism of ensuring due regard for the ethical implications of AI and potentially a means of harnessing strategic frameworks which safeguard aspects of professional and workforce praxis, where AI may pose complex implications It is the widespread coverage of AI implementation which means that its use is no longer a proactive choice for society, rather something which has been progressively incorporated and at the same time exploited by those who wish to harness it for reckless and illegal activity (Dauvergne, 2021).

In terms of corporate responsibility though, there remains active debate over whether, the military, for example, ought to be given intellectual and operational rights to AI for autonomous use in algorithmic decision making which lacks any bias and as such any conscience in relation to the potential outcome of it, when the primary objective of its mission is simply to reach the completion of a task (Shaw et al, 2019). Issues of data protection and the use of AI algorithms to collate specific information and identify all members of society pervade all use of the technology in practice. Where ethical issues are most apparent however is that AI has the potential to override the innate epistemic bias and positionality which provides the unique decision-making skill of every individual in terms of their rights, capacities, and capabilities (Araujo et al, 2020). Justification of AI within everyday society is frequently legitimised based on the accuracy with which technology can now make complex decisions from algorithmic processing, which outweighs the capacity, capability, and speed with which a human counterpart every could. In addition to this, we see a challenge to human existentialism in that any aspect of subjectivity raised by epistemic positionality and the consequent personal bias this perpetuates can be eliminated with AI.

The complex ambiguity here is that from an ethical and moral perspective, since this technology is man made, then the responsibility for what AI can do to humanity also has to be an embedded and integral part of AI design, justification, and evaluation, and the 21st Century must be educated to reflect this (Holmes et, 2021). Failing to do so could be catastrophic for the potential of what AI may progress to become and man's ability to maintain ultimate control of AI capacity and capability (Benbya, Davenport & Pachidi, 2020). As AI becomes further embedded into everyday society it is complacency which needs to be avoided as there is an educational and pedagogical responsibility to ensure that iterative generations of AI users, developers and entrepreneurs maintain absolute accountability for the emergent technology, which will inevitably be such a part of humanity's future. Ultimately, the situated and contextual nature of AI's use will determine how best algorithmic decision making can be continually monitored to ensure that whilst society is progressively developed, ethical complexities of its use can be addressed at source and with ease.

THE EXISTENTIAL THREAT OF ARTIFICIAL GENERAL INTELLIGENCE (AGI)

Artificial General Intelligence (AGI) is the term applied to a theoretical version of AI which can surpass human intellect and undertake complex decision-making processes at speeds not possible in terms of cognitive function (Helm et al, 2020). Whether AI is an existential threat to humanity remains one of contention in the media, not least because those who invented it are now calling for a measured pause in its developmental progression and have released formal statements warning that AI could potentially pose a greater threat to humanity than nuclear weapons or further global pandemics. Whilst these statements are regarded as the hyperbole of the super-rich or super invested. Whilst all scientists are aware of the need for ethical praxis in relation to technological advancement it is the routine use of AI which is causing greatest concern. Being clear evidence on the positive impact of it within fields such as medicine, in the context of drug discovery, health and education is imperative (Rajpurkar er al, 2022). Whilst AI use is purposeful and direct, the evolution of AI systems continues to astonish even those who have been instrumental in its invention (Samuel, 2023). Whether certain sectors of society should be given agency in relation to the use of AI is contentious, particularly the military, where exploitation of AI systems could pose an existential threat (Federspiel et al, 2023).

One of the commonest areas for concern, however, is the current use of AI chatbots such as ChatGTP, which are an active source of bias and the spread of potential misinformation (Najafali, 2023). Alongside this is the issue of whether human resources can be replaced by AI as a mechanism of economic savings and whether AI can produce written content, which can actively compete or surpass the capabilities of humans under any given circumstance (Alvero, 2023). In terms of explanation, it is the neural capacity of AI which demonstrates clear similarity to human neurological function. Deep learning is the process by which information is processed and learning takes place. By moving beyond the superficial mechanisms of data evaluation that initial computers could be programmed to undertake, it is the prospect of machine learning which can be developed to algorithmically perform reasoning and discernment, which is an issue, particularly in relation to the short time taken for developmental process with AI systems to be made (Zhang, Zhu & Su, 2023). Whilst presently AI is not sentient, larger debates exist around the notion of consciousness when AI develops significantly and has a far higher degree of sophistication in relation to its evolution.

MILITARY ETHICS AND AUTONOMOUS WEAPONRY

A fundamental discriminating feature of autonomous weaponry and its potential deployment by the military is the ethical responsibility of placing the decision to discern whether to kill or not to kill, being legitimized by a technological algorithm (Pereira, 2019). One key issue is that it cannot be guaranteed that autonomous weaponry will remain the preserve of regulated military praxis. This AI can also be harnessed by terrorists, state proponents of repression and dictators, whose agendas are far from the democratic empowerment of humanity (McKendrick, 2019). Since these progressive developments are often iterative by nature and incremental by functional design, each enhancement of their capability does not remain a topical political cause for concern, and as such ensures that informed consensual debate with the societies upon these autonomous weapons systems could impact, is not happening. An additional implication of this, is that the global markets for AI weaponry, continue to increase, with demand outstripping demand at a pace of acquisition which is incomparable with any other previous weaponry (Sauer, 2021). International security is thus threatened by the potential of error, criminal hacking, and algorithmic dysfunction, which could lead to mass loss of life and an unknown level of devastation.

The introduction of international law on the regulated use of advanced weaponry across the world is one potential mechanism of mitigating the risk of this happening however this needs to occur with a high degree of expedience if timing of regulation (Werthner et al, 2023). The threat posed to democratic society by the largescale introduction of autonomous weaponry continues to grow in sync with the rate of proliferation of the systems used for their operationalization. Since the systems can operate remotely, the potential of terrorists to preserve their anonymity and consequently their arrest and detainment, means their attractiveness in terms of a weapon of choice, is growing exponentially. Terrorist capacity and capability with AI autonomous weapons also has the potential to accelerate quickly since the technology used within AI defence systems is fiscally less obtainable since it needs to discern between targeted approaches to ensure targets are engaged with expedience and safety, which necessitates more expensive functional components. Whilst this represents a true dystopia, in terms of the potential for individual and collective slaughter, in the hands of despotic, authoritarian dictators, this represents a mechanism of disempowering humanity and stripping away human rights as we currently recognise them (Fontes et al, 2022).

AI can become a tool in changing sociocultural norms, where surveillance becomes a norm rather than an instance of exceptional security measure. The concept of an AI arms race poses significant questions regarding the ethical development of autonomous weaponry since the pace of development is also happening amidst the competition to be the first and be the best in terms of arms acquisition. This speed may well detract from the need to ascertain AI's safety both during military intervention and the impact on humanity if this is potentially overlooked in favour of winning an arms race (Armstrong, Bostrom & Shulman, 2016). Ultimately human intellect needs to assert authority over AI at any given time, to be able to intervene in instances where risk needs to be mitigated with immediate effect. Without globally agreed policy and practice directives the impact of AI being able to retain agency could pose a threat to global safety, regardless of their state ownership. Those countries whose cultural heritage is firmly rooted in the control of populations may be more inclined to align political strategy with the potential for thresholds of escalation in AI decision making, which bypass collective humanitarian need in favour of an ongoing means of population control (Kile, 2013). In terms of mediating risk where advanced AI weaponry could potentially act autonomously by bypassing algorithmic instruction or have some degree of systems failure where human intervention is impossible, the ethical constraints of using military artificial intelligence are significant. Since this is a possibility all military intervention always necessitates an absolute degree of human control, however the greatest dilemmas will occur if the AI becomes progressively more capable of advanced decision making prior to human's being able to keep up with their speed of action.

Ethical education in the use of operationalising AI military weaponry will be essential to ensure the contextualised and situated nature of both weapons' deployment and use (Amoroso & Tamburrini, 2020). This will involve extensive simulation training and an assurance that military staff always remain in agentic control of the technological equipment, to ensure both humanitarian and personal safety (Pizzi, Romanoff & Engelhardt, 2020). Alongside the potential risks of integrating AI into military operations, it is also necessary to consider the exceptional advantages that these systems offer, in preference to potentially sacrificing troops within terrains which are hazardous due to geography, topography or sheer physical danger (Masakowski, 2020). The potential of operating machinery remotely, ensures that even in instances where multifaceted decision making needs to take place, in the most dangerous military events, forces will have the opportunity, via AI, to make decisions which are acutely responsive, timely and which no longer endanger human life.

ETHICAL PRACTICE IN HEALTH AND MEDICINE

Since empathy and ethics are two of the fundamental philosophies underpinning the medical relationship between doctors and patients and that the two belie the trust within active dialogue in assessment, diagnosis and medical management, the use of AI within medical practice has implications for trust, reliability, and compassion (Hatherley, 2020). Since AI is not sentient but offers high degrees of functional reliability and validity via deep neural networks in the context of diagnosis and assessment, it is not difficult to see how AI is currently very much a valued adjunct to human medical practice, rather than as alternative or replacement of this (Salahuddin et al, 2022).

Within the context of medical and surgical practice technological development has meant an exponential increase in data collection, analysis, and reporting (Liu et al, 2022). Many of the deep learning techniques now possible because of AI deep learning capacity to not only manage data but effectively interpret it due to its capacity to recognise data based on having previously been exposed to the same or similar forms of it. This represents the potential of removing human bias and subjective decision making in the functional interpretation of results which can be undertaken with far greater efficiency and expediency than humans (Dwivedi, et al 2021). This is indeed a marked improvement for the productivity of the medical workforce but its impact on the relationships between it and the patients it serves remains, yet, largely unexplored. Within the United Kingdom, where the National Health Service (NHS) has become a victim of its own success in terms of an infinite need for resources but a finite resource pot from which to fund the assessment, diagnosis, and management of patients from the cradle to the grave, this represents an important opportunity for not only more accurate and valid medical praxis but also increased efficiency in the process (Haug & Drazen, 2023).

It remains something of an irony that whilst longevity has, over the last half century increased, recent events have ensured that these statistics are now in reverse, especially with more advanced technological diagnostic support and intervention mechanisms than there have ever historically been. Acceptance of technology by the public in the context of an infrastructure where they have been acclimated to being able to have absolute trust in human compassion and empathy, is another core aspect of why being able to ensure quality and standards is imperative (Schneiderman, 2020). Historically these levels of quality standards have been rooted in the need for the validity and reliability of AI in terms of diagnostic capacity (Larson et al, 2021). In terms of the ethics of healthcare where all risk must be mitigated and accounted for. Since the algorithmic capacity of AI cannot be 100% guaranteed, but nor can the mitigation of the human risk of error, it is about ascertaining the modality which offers best levels of accuracy and ensuring that ethical practice is maintained by ensuring that regardless of how purposeful AI may be, it is certainly only an adjunct support to the qualified medical staff who make use of them in clinical settings (Aslam and Hoyle, 2022).

Collective global efforts to reach agreement on the regulation of AI, in terms of its integration across both high income and developing nations is still far off where it ought to be in terms of any ethical consensus surrounding AI (Uunona & Goosen, 2023). This is further complicated by race wars which have ensued in the light of global conflict where state players are competing to outwit their enemies and civilian lives are often tokenistically protected in the name of war (Taddeo et al, 2021). The address of the sociocultural impact of AI across global societies is one which remains a core issue for the roll out of AI based decision making algorithms in practice. Also separated by heuristics and the fiscal implications of new technology use, the potential for the gap between those low-income countries who are not yet able to develop a national AI infrastructure and those who are becoming adept at it, to widen global inequalities, is a major cause for ethical concern (Nordling, 2019).

VIRTUE ETHICS AND ANTHROPOLOGICAL VIRTUE WITH AI

Criticisms that organisations harnessing ethical praxis in relation to environmental justice within the context of AI usage are not unfounded in terms of the potential processes and outcomes being adopted at the front line of industrial, commercial, and academic institutions (Hickman & Petrin, 2021). What is necessary for address is the potential difference between the ideology of ethical responsibility and its practical implementation in work-based practice. One major concern is that if ethics is commodified and packaged as something tokenistically delivered by educators in abstraction from progressive technological emergence, that the tripartite relationship between technological advancement, power and social justice can effectively become meaningless and in some way diminished in terms of pragmatic impact and proactive conscientiousness (Burrell & Fourcade, 2021).

Where knowledge comes from in terms of ongoing research of AI development and how AI ethics ought to be shaped therefore, is something stymied by standardized learning packages which are delivered (Birhane, 2021; Schiff 2021). One outcome of this is the potential debate that rather than commodifying ethics and permitting them to exist in abstraction from the use of AI, is that as an anthropological virtue, they ought to be an embedded part of professional practice and intrinsic epistemic positionality, so that tacit assumption and concerns about deviation from acceptable practice can be identified as part of an ongoing process. (Avnoon, Kotliar & Rivnai-Bahir, 2023).

CONCLUSION

Amidst the communities of practice that constitute expertise in AI on a personal and professional level, ethics has not been an historical element of operational praxis, which is attributable to relative need, rather than the need for proactive choice. Within the 21st Century progressive development of AI, though, ethics has become central to the capacity of the discipline of computing and technology to ensure social justice and a temporal regard for the future of humanity with AI playing an ever-increasing role across so many disciplines and societal infrastructures. This chapter has considered the emergent role of AI across societies, from commerce, industry, and education to spirituality and existentialism. Whilst it is impossible to conclusively predict what the future of AI across these infrastructures will be, what can be accounted for is human responsibility for the scope of its potential reach and impact. Education of existing and forthcoming generations of society will be instrumental in ensuring that the progressive implementation of AI across societies is subject to rigorous regulation and stringent regard for accountability and responsibility of use. Whilst there will always remain the opportunity for rogue non-state jeopardy in terms of AI misuse, the core principles of ethical AI use will be shaped and adapted to the sociocultural perspectives of members states for whom the ethics of AI is a priority.

The hyperbole of whether AI will autonomously and objectively override human decision making, remains a debate which both sensationalises and highlights the once unimaginable capacity of AI within the contexts of medicine, health and the military and also the inevitable inequity that AI will exacerbate between the West and developing nations.

How regulatory frameworks can be designed as a mechanism of consensus building across global society and its representatives remains an ongoing challenge. What is clear however is that ethical praxis must become instrumental rather than a conceptual commodity, which can be packaged to accompany education in computing, engineering, and technology over forthcoming decades. This chapter has illustrated how the progressive development from the use of AI in the manufacturing and industrial centres across the world represents an important opportunity to harness potential predictable complications and implications of AI use. To embed competence and AI literacy necessitates the active uptake of educational contexts to integrate AI literacy alongside core signature pedagogies such as Mathematics and English Language. The very possibility that AI can develop to have superhuman intelligence and far outpace humanity's intellect means embedding ethical contingency within all AI systems is imperative. When potential knowledge of the future remains entirely predictive and inferential it is these degrees of ethical contingency, which provide a haven for transparency and accountability, which ought to frame AI moral and ethical praxis.

REFERENCES

Alter, S. (2022). Understanding artificial intelligence in the context of usage: Contributions and smartness of algorithmic capabilities in work systems. *International Journal of Information Management*, *67*, 102392. doi:10.1016/j.ijinfomgt.2021.102392

Alvero, R. (2023). ChatGPT: Rumors of human providers' demise have been greatly exaggerated. *Fertility and Sterility*, *119*(6), 930–931. doi:10.1016/j.fertnstert.2023.03.010 PMID:36921837

Amoroso, D., & Tamburrini, G. (2020). Autonomous weapons systems and meaningful human control: Ethical and legal issues. *Current Robotics Reports*, *1*(4), 187–194. doi:10.100743154-020-00024-3

Araujo, T., Helberger, N., Kruikemeier, S., & De Vreese, C. H. (2020). In AI we trust? Perceptions about automated decision-making by artificial intelligence. *AI & Society*, *35*(3), 611–623. doi:10.100700146-019-00931-w

Armstrong, S., Bostrom, N., & Shulman, C. (2016). Racing to the precipice: A model of artificial intelligence development. *AI & Society*, *31*(2), 201–206. doi:10.100700146-015-0590-y

Avnoon, N., Kotliar, D. M., & Rivnai-Bahir, S. (2023). Contextualizing the ethics of algorithms: A socio-professional approach. *New Media & Society*, 14614448221145728. doi:10.1177/14614448221145728

Bareis, J., & Katzenbach, C. (2022). Talking AI into being: The narratives and imaginaries of national AI strategies and their performative politics. *Science, Technology & Human Values*, *47*(5), 855–881. doi:10.1177/01622439211030007

Benbya, H., Davenport, T. H., & Pachidi, S. (2020). Artificial intelligence in organizations: Current state and future opportunities. *MIS Quarterly Executive*, *19*(4).

Birhane, A. (2021). The impossibility of automating ambiguity. *Artificial Life*, *27*(1), 44–61. doi:10.1162/artl_a_00336 PMID:34529757

Burrell, J., & Fourcade, M. (2021). The society of algorithms. *Annual Review of Sociology*, *47*(1), 213–237. doi:10.1146/annurev-soc-090820-020800

Chen, J., Sun, J., & Wang, G. (2022). From unmanned systems to autonomous intelligent systems. *Engineering (Beijing)*, *12*, 16–19. doi:10.1016/j.eng.2021.10.007

Cheng, L., Varshney, K. R., & Liu, H. (2021). Socially responsible AI algorithms: Issues, purposes, and challenges. *Journal of Artificial Intelligence Research*, *71*, 1137–1181. doi:10.1613/jair.1.12814

Colaner, N. (2022). Is explainable artificial intelligence intrinsically valuable? *AI & Society*, 1–8.

Cools, H., Van Gorp, B., & Opgenhaffen, M. (2022). Where exactly between utopia and dystopia? A framing analysis of AI and automation in US newspapers. *Journalism*, 14648849221122647. doi:10.1177/14648849221122647

Dauvergne, P. (2021). The globalization of artificial intelligence: Consequences for the politics of environmentalism. *Globalizations*, *18*(2), 285–299. doi:10.1080/14747731.2020.1785670

De Angelis, L., Baglivo, F., Arzilli, G., Privitera, G. P., Ferragina, P., Tozzi, A. E., & Rizzo, C. (2023). ChatGPT and the rise of large language models: The new AI-driven infodemic threat in public health. *Frontiers in Public Health*, *11*, 1567. doi:10.3389/fpubh.2023.1166120 PMID:37181697

De Bruijn, H., Warnier, M., & Janssen, M. (2022). The perils and pitfalls of explainable AI: Strategies for explaining algorithmic decision-making. *Government Information Quarterly*, *39*(2), 101666. doi:10.1016/j.giq.2021.101666

Döring, H. (2019). Public perceptions of the proper role of the state. In *The State in Western Europe Retreat or Redefinition?* (pp. 12–31). Routledge. doi:10.4324/9781315037479-2

Dwivedi, Y. K., Hughes, L., Ismagilova, E., Aarts, G., Coombs, C., Crick, T., Duan, Y., Dwivedi, R., Edwards, J., Eirug, A., Galanos, V., Ilavarasan, P. V., Janssen, M., Jones, P., Kar, A. K., Kizgin, H., Kronemann, B., Lal, B., Lucini, B., & Williams, M. D. (2021). Artificial Intelligence (AI): Multidisciplinary perspectives on emerging challenges, opportunities, and agenda for research, practice and policy. *International Journal of Information Management*, *57*, 101994. doi:10.1016/j.ijinfomgt.2019.08.002

Elliott, A. (2019). *The culture of AI: Everyday life and the digital revolution*. Routledge. doi:10.4324/9781315387185

Farrow, E. (2021). Mindset matters: How mindset affects the ability of staff to anticipate and adapt to Artificial Intelligence (AI) future scenarios in organisational settings. *AI & Society*, *36*(3), 895–909. doi:10.100700146-020-01101-z PMID:33223620

Federspiel, F., Mitchell, R., Asokan, A., Umana, C., & McCoy, D. (2023). Threats by artificial intelligence to human health and human existence. *BMJ Global Health*, *8*(5), e010435. doi:10.1136/bmjgh-2022-010435 PMID:37160371

Finkel, M., & Krämer, N. C. (2022). Humanoid robots–artificial. Human-like. Credible? Empirical comparisons of source credibility attributions between humans, humanoid robots, and non-human-like devices. *International Journal of Social Robotics*, *14*(6), 1397–1411. doi:10.100712369-022-00879-w

Floridi, L., & Cowls, J. (2022). A unified framework of five principles for AI in society. *Machine learning and the city: Applications in architecture and urban design*, 535-545

Fontes, C., Hohma, E., Corrigan, C. C., & Lütge, C. (2022). AI-powered public surveillance systems: Why we (might) need them and how we want them. *Technology in Society*, *71*, 102137. doi:10.1016/j.techsoc.2022.102137

Ganapini, M. B., Campbell, M., Fabiano, F., Horesh, L., Lenchner, J., Loreggia, A., & Venable, K. B. (2023). Thinking fast and slow in AI: The role of metacognition. In *Machine Learning, Optimization, and Data Science: 8th International Conference, LOD 2022,* (pp. 502-509). Cham: Springer Nature Switzerland.

Goralski, M. A., & Tan, T. K. (2020). Artificial intelligence and sustainable development. *International Journal of Management Education*, *18*(1), 100330. doi:10.1016/j.ijme.2019.100330

Haluza, D., & Jungwirth, D. (2023). Artificial Intelligence and Ten Societal Megatrends: An Exploratory Study Using GPT-3. *Systems*, *11*(3), 120. doi:10.3390ystems11030120

Harper, R. H. (2021). AI: The social future of intelligence. In *Routledge Handbook of Social Futures* (pp. 52–58). Routledge. doi:10.4324/9780429440717-4

Hatherley, J. J. (2020). Limits of trust in medical AI. *Journal of Medical Ethics*, *46*(7), 478–481. doi:10.1136/medethics-2019-105935 PMID:32220870

Haug, C. J., & Drazen, J. M. (2023). Artificial intelligence and machine learning in clinical medicine, 2023. *The New England Journal of Medicine*, *388*(13), 1201–1208. doi:10.1056/NEJMra2302038 PMID:36988595

He, Q., Zheng, H., Ma, X., Wang, L., Kong, H., & Zhu, Z. (2022). Artificial intelligence application in a renewable energy-driven desalination system: A critical review. *Energy and AI*, *7*, 100123. doi:10.1016/j.egyai.2021.100123

Helm, J. M., Swiergosz, A. M., Haeberle, H. S., Karnuta, J. M., Schaffer, J. L., Krebs, V. E., Spitzer, A. I., & Ramkumar, P. N. (2020). Machine learning and artificial intelligence: Definitions, applications, and future directions. *Current Reviews in Musculoskeletal Medicine*, *13*(1), 69–76. doi:10.100712178-020-09600-8 PMID:31983042

Henin, C., & Le Métayer, D. (2021). Beyond explainability: Justifiability and contestability of algorithmic decision systems. *AI & Society*, •••, 1–14.

Hickman, E., & Petrin, M. (2021). Trustworthy AI and corporate governance: The EU's ethics guidelines for trustworthy artificial intelligence from a company law perspective. *European Business Organization Law Review*, *22*(4), 593–625. doi:10.100740804-021-00224-0

Holmes, W., Porayska-Pomsta, K., Holstein, K., Sutherland, E., Baker, T., Shum, S. B., ... Koedinger, K. R. (2021). Ethics of AI in education: Towards a community-wide framework. *International Journal of Artificial Intelligence in Education*, 1–23.

Humble, K. (2023). Artificial Intelligence, International Law and the Race for Killer Robots in Modern Warfare. In *Artificial Intelligence, Social Harms and Human Rights* (pp. 57–76). Springer International Publishing. doi:10.1007/978-3-031-19149-7_3

Hwang, H., & Park, M. H. (2020). The Threat of AI and Our Response: The AI Charter of Ethics in South Korea. *Asian Journal of Innovation & Policy*, *9*(1).

Igna, I., & Venturini, F. (2023). The determinants of AI innovation across European firms. *Research Policy*, *52*(2), 104661. doi:10.1016/j.respol.2022.104661

Islam, S. R., Russell, I., Eberle, W., & Dicheva, D. (2022). Instilling conscience about bias and fairness in automated decisions. *Journal of Computing Sciences in Colleges*, *37*(8), 22–31.

Khogali, H. O., & Mekid, S. (2023). The blended future of automation and AI: Examining some long-term societal and ethical impact features. *Technology in Society*, *73*, 102232. doi:10.1016/j.techsoc.2023.102232

Kile, F. (2013). Artificial intelligence and society: A furtive transformation. *AI & Society*, *28*(1), 107–115. doi:10.100700146-012-0396-0

Larson, D. B., Harvey, H., Rubin, D. L., Irani, N., Justin, R. T., & Langlotz, C. P. (2021). Regulatory frameworks for development and evaluation of artificial intelligence–based diagnostic imaging algorithms: Summary and recommendations. *Journal of the American College of Radiology*, *18*(3), 413–424. doi:10.1016/j.jacr.2020.09.060 PMID:33096088

Liu, H., Wang, Y., Fan, W., Liu, X., Li, Y., Jain, S., Liu, Y., Jain, A., & Tang, J. (2022). Trustworthy AI: A computational perspective. *ACM Transactions on Intelligent Systems and Technology*, *14*(1), 1–59. doi:10.1145/3546872

Madhav, A. S., & Tyagi, A. K. (2022). The world with future technologies (Post-COVID-19): open issues, challenges, and the road ahead. *Intelligent Interactive Multimedia Systems for e-Healthcare Applications*, 411-452.

Makridakis, S. (2017). The forthcoming Artificial Intelligence (AI) revolution: Its impact on society and firms. *Futures*, *90*, 46–60. doi:10.1016/j.futures.2017.03.006

Mantello, P., Ho, M. T., Nguyen, M. H., & Vuong, Q. H. (2023). Bosses without a heart: Socio-demographic and cross-cultural determinants of attitude toward Emotional AI in the workplace. *AI & Society*, *38*(1), 97–119. doi:10.100700146-021-01290-1 PMID:34776651

Masakowski, Y. R. (2020). Artificial intelligence and the future global security environment. In *Artificial Intelligence and Global Security* (pp. 1–34). Emerald Publishing Limited. doi:10.1108/978-1-78973-811-720201001

McKendrick, K. (2019). Artificial intelligence prediction and counterterrorism. London: The Royal Institute of International Affairs-Chatham House, 9.

Mele, C., & Russo-Spena, T. (2023). Artificial Intelligence in Services. Elgar Encyclopedia of Services, 356.

Mikalef, P., Conboy, K., Lundström, J. E., & Popovič, A. (2022). Thinking responsibly about responsible AI and 'the dark side'of AI. *European Journal of Information Systems, 31*(3), 257–268. doi:10.1080/0960085X.2022.2026621

Miller, G. J. (2022, March). Artificial Intelligence Project Success Factors—Beyond the Ethical Principles. In *Information Technology for Management: Business and Social Issues: 16th Conference, ISM 2021, and FedCSIS-AIST 2021 Track,* (pp. 65-96). Cham: Springer International Publishing.

Mirbabaie, M., Brünker, F., Möllmann, N. R., & Stieglitz, S. (2022). The rise of artificial intelligence–understanding the AI identity threat at the workplace. *Electronic Markets, 32*(1), 1–27. doi:10.100712525-021-00496-x

Nader, K., Toprac, P., Scott, S., & Baker, S. (2022). Public understanding of artificial intelligence through entertainment media. *AI & Society*, 1–14. doi:10.100700146-022-01427-w PMID:35400854

Nichols, R. (2022). The cultural evolution of Chinese morality, and the essential value of multi-disciplinary research in understanding it. In The Routledge International Handbook of Morality, Cognition, and Emotion in China (pp. 19-37). Routledge. doi:10.4324/9781003281566-3

Novelli, C., Taddeo, M., & Floridi, L. (2023). Accountability in artificial intelligence: What it is and how it works. *AI & Society*, 1–12. doi:10.100700146-023-01635-y

Owe, A., & Baum, S. D. (2021). Moral consideration of nonhumans in the ethics of artificial intelligence. *AI and Ethics, 1*(4), 517–528. doi:10.100743681-021-00065-0

Palomares, I., Martínez-Cámara, E., Montes, R., García-Moral, P., Chiachio, M., Chiachio, J., Alonso, S., Melero, F. J., Molina, D., Fernández, B., Moral, C., Marchena, R., de Vargas, J. P., & Herrera, F. (2021). A panoramic view and swot analysis of artificial intelligence for achieving the sustainable development goals by 2030: Progress and prospects. *Applied Intelligence, 51*(9), 6497–6527. doi:10.100710489-021-02264-y PMID:34764606

Peeters, M. M., van Diggelen, J., Van Den Bosch, K., Bronkhorst, A., Neerincx, M. A., Schraagen, J. M., & Raaijmakers, S. (2021). Hybrid collective intelligence in a human–AI society. *AI & Society, 36*(1), 217–238. doi:10.100700146-020-01005-y

Pereira, L. M. (2019). Should I kill or rather not? *AI & Society, 34*(4), 939–943. doi:10.100700146-018-0850-8

Pizzi, M., Romanoff, M., & Engelhardt, T. (2020). AI for humanitarian action: Human rights and ethics. *International Review of the Red Cross, 102*(913), 145–180. doi:10.1017/S1816383121000011

Prem, E. (2023). From ethical AI frameworks to tools: A review of approaches. *AI and Ethics, 3*(3), 1–18. doi:10.100743681-023-00258-9

Qiao-Franco, G., & Bode, I. (2023). Weaponised artificial intelligence and Chinese practices of human–machine interaction. *The Chinese Journal of International Politics, 16*(1), 106–128. doi:10.1093/cjip/poac024

Salahuddin, Z., Woodruff, H. C., Chatterjee, A., & Lambin, P. (2022). Transparency of deep neural networks for medical image analysis: A review of interpretability methods. *Computers in Biology and Medicine, 140*, 105111. doi:10.1016/j.compbiomed.2021.105111 PMID:34891095

Samuel, J. (2023). *Response to the March 2023 'Pause Giant AI Experiments: An Open Letter.'*

Sauer, F. (2021). Lethal autonomous weapons systems. In *The Routledge Social Science Handbook of AI* (pp. 237–250). Routledge. doi:10.4324/9780429198533-17

Schiff, D. (2021). Out of the laboratory and into the classroom: The future of artificial intelligence in education. *AI & Society, 36*(1), 331–348. doi:10.100700146-020-01033-8 PMID:32836908

Shaw, J., Rudzicz, F., Jamieson, T., & Goldfarb, A. (2019). Artificial intelligence and the implementation challenge. *Journal of Medical Internet Research, 21*(7), e13659. doi:10.2196/13659 PMID:31293245

Shneiderman, B. (2020). Bridging the gap between ethics and practice: Guidelines for reliable, safe, and trustworthy human-centered AI systems. [TiiS]. *ACM Transactions on Interactive Intelligent Systems, 10*(4), 1–31. doi:10.1145/3419764

Smith, H. (2021). Clinical AI: Opacity, accountability, responsibility and liability. *AI & Society, 36*(2), 535–545. doi:10.100700146-020-01019-6

Sweeney, P. (2022). Trusting social robots. *AI and Ethics*, 1–8. PMID:35634257

Uunona, G. N., & Goosen, L. (2023). Leveraging Ethical Standards in Artificial Intelligence Technologies: A Guideline for Responsible Teaching and Learning Applications. In Handbook of Research on Instructional Technologies in Health Education and Allied Disciplines (pp. 310-330). IGI Global. doi:10.4018/978-1-6684-7164-7.ch014

Visvizi, A. (2021). *Artificial intelligence (AI): Explaining, querying, demystifying*. Artificial Intelligence and Its Contexts: Security, Business and Governance, 13-26.

Werthner, H., Stanger, A., Schiaffonati, V., Knees, P., Hardman, L., & Ghezzi, C. (2023). Digital Humanism: The Time Is Now. *Computer, 56*(1), 138–142. doi:10.1109/MC.2022.3219528

Yamin, M. M., Ullah, M., Ullah, H., & Katt, B. (2021). Weaponized AI for cyber attacks. *Journal of Information Security and Applications, 57*, 102722. doi:10.1016/j.jisa.2020.102722

Young, A. T., Amara, D., Bhattacharya, A., & Wei, M. L. (2021). Patient and general public attitudes towards clinical artificial intelligence: A mixed methods systematic review. *The Lancet. Digital Health, 3*(9), e599–e611. doi:10.1016/S2589-7500(21)00132-1 PMID:34446266

Zajda, J., & Vissing, Y. (Eds.). (2022). *Discourses of globalisation, ideology, and human rights* (Vol. 14). Springer. doi:10.1007/978-3-030-90590-3

Zeng, J. (2020). Artificial intelligence and China's authoritarian governance. *International Affairs, 96*(6), 1441–1459. doi:10.1093/ia/iiaa172

Zhang, B., Zhu, J., & Su, H. (2023). Toward the third generation artificial intelligence. *Science China. Information Sciences, 66*(2), 1–19. doi:10.100711432-021-3449-x

Zhang, Y., Wu, M., Tian, G. Y., Zhang, G., & Lu, J. (2021). Ethics and privacy of artificial intelligence: Understandings from bibliometrics. *Knowledge-Based Systems*, *222*, 106994. doi:10.1016/j.knosys.2021.106994

Zuiderwijk, A., Chen, Y. C., & Salem, F. (2021). Implications of the use of artificial intelligence in public governance: A systematic literature review and a research agenda. *Government Information Quarterly*, *38*(3), 101577. doi:10.1016/j.giq.2021.101577

ADDITIONAL READING

Aung, Y. Y., Wong, D. C., & Ting, D. S. (2021). The promise of artificial intelligence: A review of the opportunities and challenges of artificial intelligence in healthcare. *British Medical Bulletin*, *139*(1), 4–15. doi:10.1093/bmb/ldab016 PMID:34405854

Bistron, M., & Piotrowski, Z. (2021). Artificial intelligence applications in military systems and their influence on sense of security of citizens. *Electronics (Basel)*, *10*(7), 871. doi:10.3390/electronics10070871

Devagiri, J. S., Paheding, S., Niyaz, Q., Yang, X., & Smith, S. (2022). Augmented Reality and Artificial Intelligence in industry: Trends, tools, and future challenges. *Expert Systems with Applications*, *207*, 118002. doi:10.1016/j.eswa.2022.118002

Haenlein, M., & Kaplan, A. (2019). A brief history of artificial intelligence: On the past, present, and future of artificial intelligence. *California Management Review*, *61*(4), 5–14. doi:10.1177/0008125619864925

Hagendorff, T. (2021). Forbidden knowledge in machine learning reflections on the limits of research and publication. *AI & Society*, *36*(3), 767–781. doi:10.100700146-020-01045-4

Kaminski, M. E. (2023). Regulating the Risks of AI. *Forthcoming. Boston University Law Review. Boston University. School of Law*, 103.

Kaur, D., Uslu, S., Rittichier, K. J., & Durresi, A. (2022). Trustworthy artificial intelligence: A review. *ACM Computing Surveys*, *55*(2), 1–38. doi:10.1145/3491209

Kazansky, B., & Milan, S. (2021). "Bodies not templates": Contesting dominant algorithmic imaginaries. *New Media & Society*, *23*(2), 363–381. doi:10.1177/1461444820929316

Maibaum, A., Bischof, A., Hergesell, J., & Lipp, B. (2022). A critique of robotics in health care. *AI & Society*, *37*(2), 1–11. doi:10.100700146-021-01206-z

Medaglia, R., Gil-Garcia, J. R., & Pardo, T. A. (2023). Artificial intelligence in government: Taking stock and moving forward. *Social Science Computer Review*, *41*(1), 123–140. doi:10.1177/08944393211034087

KEY TERMS AND DEFINITIONS

Agency: The capacity for action or intervention producing a particular effect.

Algorithm: An algorithm is a process or set of rules to be followed in decision-making or other problem-solving operations, especially by computing technology.

Autonomous Weapons: A classification of military systems which has the independent ability to search for, identify and engage strategic targets based upon pre-programmed constraints and restrictions.

Epistemic Bias: The lens of subjective interpretation which influences systematic research practice due to failing to acknowledge or detail the ideals of human impartiality and value-freedom which may potentially be influencing it.

Existentialism: The philosophy of the nature of human existence as determined by capacity and capability for free will and free choice.

Hacking: The gaining of illegal, unlawful, or unofficially unauthorised access to data within the context of computing and technology.

Reliability: The extent to which a research instrument can repeatedly provide the same results in temporally separated incidences of measurement.

AI Safety: AI safety pertains to the interdisciplinary field which prevents the misuse, accidental or otherwise, or other consequences which could be the resultant outcome of an AI system.

Sentient/Sentience: Sentience is the capacity of a being to experience feelings and sensations.

Validity: Is the state of being officially true or legally acceptable.

Chapter 2
Using Artificial Intelligence Ethically and Responsibly:
Best Practices in Higher Education

Luanne M. Amato
https://orcid.org/0000-0003-1403-4343
Holy Family University, USA

Christine Schoettle
Holy Family University, USA

ABSTRACT

Within the 21st century technology explosion, higher education is facing its greatest challenge to managing students' ethical conduct in completing course assignments. This challenge, known as artificial intelligence (AI), is also one of higher education's greatest assets. This chapter will introduce AI, explain its tools and resources, and its positive contribution to education. It will also identify how students are using chatbot resources unethically, which has become a topic of concern for faculty, with the increased usage and inability to detect plagiarism. The chapter will also explain how faculty education in AI can promote the positive aspects of AI innovation and at the same time help to mitigate student ethical issues. The chapter will showcase an actual course redesign using AI best practices. Finally, the chapter will identify future research needed to explore how AI innovations partnered with course design can increase student learning while ensuring attention to ethical standards.

INTRODUCTION

Artificial intelligence (AI) in the form of a chatbot is a powerful change agent that bolsters a human's capacity to solve complex problems (Abdous, 2023). AI tools such as ChatGPT, BingAI, and Chatsonic, to name a few, are freely available with a simple search on Google. Chatbots provide ease in conducting research and help to automate tasks. However, these resources, without the proper understanding and usage parameters, can also put academic integrity at risk (Honorlock, 2023). In a recent BestColleges

DOI: 10.4018/979-8-3693-0205-7.ch002

survey, 43% of undergraduate students surveyed use AI tools, and over half of those students (51%) admit to using AI tools specifically for cheating. Also identified in the survey was the lack of faculty engagement in discussing AI resources with their students about how to utilize them to avoid cheating (Welding, 2023).

Chatbot resources are born from AI, based on algorithms, and are considered the best of current emerging technology. The main benefit for higher education students when using chatbots is the ability to simulate a human's response to any question using AI resources found in machine learning, natural language understanding, and natural language processing (Shweta, 2022). Chatbots provide positive results for timely completion of assignments, but since AI output is not always reliable and students are copying and pasting without revision, plagiarism is cited as a critical problem and a chief outcome of college students' use of AI technology.

This chapter will explain how, instead of prohibiting the use of AI tools, educators become proficient in understanding how to utilize these tools to support student learning outcomes, especially since AI resources offer strategies that improve cognitive ability and promote interactive learning ("How ChatGPT and Other AI Tools Can Maximize the Learning Potential," 2023; Liu et al., 2022). The use of these tools also provides faculty with a professional development opportunity to recognize and appreciate the value of AI technology and increase their skill in course design and course execution. Faculty who understands and embrace AI innovation offer their students a better learning opportunity that is applicable to real world applications and be able to provide insights into the importance of ethical behavior. According to Stachowicz and Amann (2020), to successfully use AI for positive outcomes for students and faculty, educators must "rethink, retrain, and redesign" (p 1).

This chapter has four objectives:

- Introducing AI in the form of chatbots and explaining its practical applications in higher education.
- Providing information on the rise of plagiarism on college campuses, how AI has contributed to the problem, and explaining how bolstering ethics training can act as a solution to deter cheating practices.
- Demonstrating the use of best practices in applying AI resources to an actual redesign of a higher education course.
- Identifying research needed going forward to add to the literature on how to evaluate and validate best practices in integrating AI into course design and to educate the students on the ethical principles involved in plagiarism.

BACKGROUND

AI applications, specifically in the form of chatbots, have burst onto the educational scene with students seemingly having the upper hand in understanding and using the technology to support their learning, not always in an ethical manner. Educators are lagging behind in recognizing the value of AI chatbots, due to their resistance to learning about yet another technological innovation that has the potential to upend their standardized course design and increase their workload. Research outcomes report that faculty resistance to adoption of new technology is a significant barrier to successful implementation of software designed to increase learning outcomes. In a recent study that tested the successful implementation of accounting software, 93% of faculty in this study admitted to engaging as inhibitors, rather than innovators (Watty et al., 2016).

The increase in plagiarism in tertiary learning is directly linked to AI chatbots. It is commonly known that using AI technology will provide students with a quick response that mimics their actual writing style when completing an assignment; however, what is not generally known is how the use of AI technology violates an integrity code. Students who are confronted with cheating allegations when assignments are found to be created using AI, express confusion, especially when there are no formal ethical standards that specifically relate to AI tools (Barnett, 2023).

It is important for faculty to become proficient in how to understand and use AI tools in course design. Educators, by developing this expertise, have a perfect opportunity to utilize AI to alleviate and demonstrate realistically how to utilize and integrate chatbot outputs, while exposing the ethical challenges created by the technology. Finally, faculty can act as a change agent by promoting the positive aspects of best practices with integration of AI into their coursework.

ARTIFICIAL INTELLIGENCE

The phrase "what hath God wrought", first uttered with the invention of the telegraph (Dixon Jr., 2023) was also quoted by Charles Francis Adams, the son of John Quincy Adams, when expressing his dire predictions and negative response to the newly constructed trans-continental railroad. Despite his first misgivings and in later years, Charles became president of the Union Pacific Railroad and a champion for change. Changes that impact long existing societal practices have a long tradition of challenge before acceptance (Dixon Jr., 2023).

AI is a transformative technology, is limitless in its applications, and is the 21st century embodiment of global change. AI tools are based on an algorithm that peruses text in the form of books and articles and converts them into a language that is correct in grammar, structure and meaning, within a meaningful context. When a request is inputted into an AI service, for example ChatGPT, the response is generated from pattern identification and statistical analysis. Based on the requestor's need, data can be manipulated to create an output that is not always authentic, especially in audio and visual media (Dixon Jr., 2023). Since adaptation of AI tools and resources has become standard practice in many industries, it is important that education incorporates the skill in using this technology, as graduates will be faced with AI in their careers.

Artificial Intelligence in Higher Education

Today, business firms, small, large, domestic, and international, embrace and promote AI to improve customer experience. AI tools and resources are numerous. Examples of simple and well-known applications for business are found in Alexa, Siri, and Hey Google, with the more complex applications found in iPhone apps, maps and search engines, and self-driving technology, to name a few (Barret et al., 2019; Essien et al., 2021). Taking the lead from the business arena, higher education institutions look to AI to improve their customer service experience by aiding with admissions applications, course planning, financial aid form filings, and unlimited access to virtual campus tours (Barret et al., 2019). AI is credited with improving communications between students, staff, and faculty early in the preregistration and subsequent onboarding process. This service helps to ensure that any prospective or committed student who encounters the complexities of tertiary school admissions can easily locate the proper channel to find a solution. In addition, sophisticated AI data analysis can identify at-risk students for failing or dropping out early in their academic career thus allowing for early intervention strategies to mitigate these issues and promote persistence. Using AI as a communication strategy allows colleges and universities to showcase high efficiency standards which can bolster enrollment, retention, and graduation rates (Barret et al., 2019).

There is a dark side to utilizing AI tools in the classroom that is creating anxiety for administrators and faculty. AI in the form of chatbots easily produces seemingly authentic outputs that, in actuality, produce finished products with a high degree of inaccurate information, especially with references that are not actually associated with the assignments (Dixon Jr., 2023). Students are willing to gamble that teachers will not closely review the authenticity of the submitted information. The use of AI chatbots are flooding the academic hallways by providing services that offer agility and time savings in completing course assignments but threaten ethical standards oftentimes through lack of understanding. As a result, although AI positively impacts the academic organization's recruitment and retention statistics, the student and faculty experience are a mixed blessing.

Artificial Intelligence and the Student Experience

Nelson Mandela stated, "education is the most powerful weapon which you can use to change the world" (Jain & Shetty, 2022, p. 1083). This quote underscores the benefits to obtaining a tertiary degree. In recent years, colleges and universities have recruited from a variety of demographics and cultures, from the traditional high school graduate to the senior retiree, who can opt for educational access across a variety of course access modalities of face-to-face, asynchronous, synchronous, and blended or hybrid. Within this mix of people, place and content delivery systems are also the challenges and barriers that stem from accommodations for students with physical or mental disabilities.

Persistence to graduation is a critical issue facing those enrolled in an advanced degree program. The yearly dropout rate for colleges and universities is 40%, with a four-year graduation rate of 41%. A majority of students will leave between their first- and second year, citing work life balance, cultural disparities, financial constraints, and academic pressure as reasons for their decision to drop out (Bouchrika, 2023). Therefore, when students are provided with tools to help ease the burden of completing assignments timely and effectively, many will embrace the solution without investigating the validity of the resource.

For the student, AI offers an opportunity to complete their assignments in time, albeit not always accurately. The chatbot, in response to prompts about the assignment requirements, has successfully mastered completed outputs in many different areas, such as writing essays, responding to test questions, creating jokes, music, screenplays, resumes, and cover letters, and in the field of technology creating code and debugging it (Honorlock, 2023). For those technological neonates, there is now a plethora of information available to coach even the most unsavvy student on successful usage of the AI chatbot for an assignment. Although students are aware of inaccuracies when using AI, they are willing to risk discovery because of the time savings in completing their course work. However, when a student uses fraudulent means to complete their education, the effectiveness of their knowledge decreases and their ability to master critical thinking is impaired (Ison, 2018).

Artificial Intelligence and the Faculty Experience

Educators across the world recognize that AI technology is creating broad-based changes at all levels from kindergarten to advanced degrees. Andreas Schleicher initiator of global educational platforms for policymakers and researchers that educate on innovation in practice, is credited with insights with his quote "innovation in education is not just a matter of putting more technology into more classrooms; it is about changing approaches to teaching so that students acquire the skills they need to thrive in competitive global economies" (Essien et al., 2021, p. 72)

A major impediment to successfully dealing with the increasing student use of AI tools is faculty resistance to change, especially when adopting new technologies. The pandemic of 2019-2021 clearly demonstrates the instructional challenges from the lack of competency in online teaching when educators were forced to switch to a curriculum totally executed online, even though most tertiary learning institutions have adopted a multitude of online course offerings pre pandemic. Although access to education through online learning has become the norm, there is a lack of mandatory professional development to assist teachers in adapting their course work plans to an online format. This adaptation is not accomplished through a copy over of an on-campus course curriculum but requires a specialized knowledge in course design integrated with a learning management system (LMS). Today, the adoption of AI tools and resources mirrors the pandemic experience with online learning.

Embracing the change that technology adoption requires for faculty is a critical challenge for academic administrators. Within the theory of reasoned action, the technology acceptance model posits that an educator's motivation to adopt a new technology is linked to positive perceptions of usefulness of the technology, organizational support, and ease of adaptability (Siegel et al., 2017). Acceptance is also linked to faculty's time constraints in preparing course work that supports the new technology (Wang et. al., 2021).

Additionally, it is important to mention that educators' lack of knowledge about applying innovative software technology is increasing the culture of suspicion especially when grading student course work. The lack of knowledge on how to apply technology ethically has led to a significant rise of ethical issues surrounding academic integrity, while adding another frustrating element of challenge and suspicion as part of assignment review (Ison, 2018).

ARTIFICIAL INTELLIGENCE AND ETHICS

Plagiarism is defined as the use of text or ideas without proper citation (Eaton, 2023). Plagiarism and other forms of cheating are a global concern for faculty and administrators in higher education (Ison, 2018). Issues of cheating have always been a concern for educators, but the recent increase of plagiarism incidents on college campuses is an outcome of the pandemic and the evolution of AI software to a more user-friendly version. During the pandemic and 100% online learning, students could complete assignments and take tests with little or no oversight (Wong, 2020).

Prior to AI resources becoming popular, the availability of the Internet and a plethora of information available in a milli-second from a myriad of sources, students used the Web site cut and paste method to complete research requirements quickly. However, if a writing assignment was challenged, it was easy to expose the cut-and-paste method by a simple Google search. It is often difficult to detect when chatbots are used for plagiarism, since the AI software used to create the chatbots is continually refined to avoid detection (King, 2023). The rise in plagiarism has also uncovered the lack of quality education into what exactly constitutes an ethics violation, and faculty's inconsistent requirement for use of source-checking writing tools, for example APA and MLA writing standards. As a result, students are primed to easily adapt to the user-friendly and invisible chatbot for completing assignments.

In addition to the availability of technology for plagiarism, it is important to note that cultural context can affect a student's attitudes towards cheating. In the United States and Western Europe, competition, economic inequality, and an individualistic culture that focuses on achievement as a barometer for personal success are viewed as reasons to support ethical shortcuts. India, a significant contributor to scholarship through dissertations and research, reports experiencing increasing ethical issues when reviewing student submissions and China also reports having an "academic integrity problem" (Ison, 2018, p. 295). However, it is argued that although there are cultural mores, ethics is an individual's choice, and, with the availability and low risk of exposure linked to economic pressures to succeed, there is a significant increase in the global incidence of ethical violations (Ison, 2018).

Strategies for Using Artificial Intelligence

AI tools and resources are changing the educational landscape, and the traditional lesson plan that is continually utilized for every class, in every semester, is no longer a viable option. This technology boom is forcing educators to become creative in course design and lesson planning. Instead of employing detective skills to track the misuse of this technology, faculty can use AI as an asset to the planning and execution of a course redesign and educate students on how to use the technology effectively and ethically.

Strategies to Mitigate Cheating

The quality of education is lessened when students engage in cheating. AI has increased student opportunities for undetectable cheating, but there are strategies for faculty to discourage ethical violations. They include requirements for citations and references that are validated, nontraditional essay writing, active learning strategies, ethics education, and the use of plagiarism checking software (King, 2023).

Although chatbots are sophisticated software that are continuously revised to avoid detection, they are not completely impervious to exposure. One major chatbot error involves the incorrect application of citation and reference for sources. When faculty require the use of APA or MLA in their writing requirements, a simple check of sources from the reference list will uncover a disparity. Checking sources is also helpful since currently AI software is not able to distinguish between reliable sources and those not sanctioned for valid research (Dixon Jr., 2023).

Another exposure tool is an understanding of the authentic voice of the student. Chatbots are not generally used for writing assignments that require an emotional component, expressed opinion or an ethical consideration. They are inexact in interpretation of feelings as they are not designed to mimic human feelings (Rehman, 2022). Other writing strategies are:

- Assignments that require demonstration of learning objectives (e.g., oral presentations, group projects, and hands-on activities).

- Rough draft of assignments that allow for a chatbot submission. Students will be prompted to revise the chatbot submission with updated research information.

Student education into ethical use of AI technology can also be a strong weapon against cheating. Student writing that originates from a chatbot tool is accurate and usually undetectable, with students, in some cases, not aware that a chatbot generated paper is considered cheating (McEwen, 2023). There are simple strategies to guide students to the ethical use of AI tools and resources which include:

- Using AI resources as a search engine to initiate research.
- Using AI resources for generating review questions and clearer explanations for topics under discussion.
- Using AI resources to start the story for the topic under discussion (i.e., finding additional references to add to and validate the AI output).
- Formal education on plagiarism and ethical violations with learning outcomes demonstrated through testing or other types of assignments.

Finally, higher education offers self-check assistance through plagiarism checkers to detect misuse of AI. For example, Turnitin is a widely used plagiarism checker that can be embedded into a school's LMS, and most recently in response to an upsurge in the use of AI for writing assignments, offers checklists and rubrics to help instructors create and grade assignments that lessen the risk of plagiarism.

Strategies for Course Design

One of the best tools for faculty to address plagiarism issues fueled by AI chatbots is to utilize the technology when designing course learning objectives and assignments. Mollick and Mollick (2023) published guidelines to help instructors appreciate the value of using AI software in designing courses. These guidelines list instructional practices where AI chatbots provide a wider breadth of information to better inform the students about the learning outcomes of an assignment. The practices easiest to implement are:

- **The Use of Examples When Teaching Complex Concepts**: AI can quickly provide a significant number of detailed examples based on the instructional need.
- **The Use of Multiple Explanations That Fit Different Learning Styles and Aptitudes to Explain a Concept**: AI can quickly provide explanations from 1) multiple perspectives, 2) simplification of ideas, and 3) step-by-step approach after input provides the type of audience receiving the information. This approach considers learning style and level of understanding thus producing an output that is easy to decipher.
- **Development of Low-Stake Testing:** It challenges student learning but does not frustrate because of intensity. Low-stake testing is considered practice and meant to reinforce learning by having students demonstrate what they know, without the rigidity of a labeled midterm or final exam. AI can generate low-stake tests from lecture notes and provide an answer key for easy grading and feedback. One complaint about testing is that, many times, the test is graded and there is little or no feedback about the errors. AI reduces the time needed to create these tests, leaving more time for feedback.

- **Assessment of Student Learning:** AI offers an assessment of student learning outcomes based on input from students who are responding to an instructional prompt. Some questions that are used for this strategy are: What was the most important idea or concept covered in class today? Why do you think this idea is important? What is the most difficult class concept so far? What did you struggle to understand? What concept or problem would you like to see explored in more detail? These questions use student opinion blended with input about the lesson into an AI tool. For example, AI can determine the most important learning outcomes for the lesson, provide more explanation, and then students are free to add their own ideas (Angelo & Cross, 2012; Mollick & Mollick, 2023).

Importantly, the faculty and administrative populations have raised concerns about integration of AI into a higher education curriculum. They are:

- Rapid growth of AI technology and having the expertise to understand and provide training.
- Budgetary constraints, since new technologies come with a hefty price tag.
- Lack of expertise in data analytics for the decision-making process involved in acquiring and using AI tools and resources (Inside Higher Ed, 2023).
- Lack of buy-in from traditionalist faculty who are averse to the use of any type of technology.

Concerns About Artificial Intelligence

Geoffery Hinton, former vice president and engineering fellow at Google, is considered a founder of modern AI. Hinton expressed concerns about the development of AI resources which include:

- AI intelligence can parallel and possibly supersede human intelligence.
- The inferior quality of information produced from AI software and, if unchecked, the spread of this misinformation. The risks associated with misinformation extend to a wide range of industries utilizing AI to expand their knowledge. Examples include healthcare (cancer screening), forecasting (weather predictions), and impacting the sorting function used in the postal service (Dixon Jr., 2023).

Privacy issues are another source of concern when using AI tools and resources. As individuals or businesses input data into AI, this information becomes available in the public domain. It is recommended that education and training, and the placing of appropriate safeguards precede AI usage (Dixon Jr., 2023).

COURSE REDESIGN WITH ARTIFICIAL INTELLIGENCE INTEGRATION

The authors of this chapter have redesigned an existing course utilizing AI best practices and ethics education, which was piloted in the Fall 2023 semester. The college course, CMIS 220 Management of Information Systems, is an introductory course usually taken in the first year. The course is a blend of directed writing assignments based on the textbook chapters assigned for each week, interspersed with demonstration assignments that reflect an understanding of the Microsoft 365 applications of PowerPoint and Excel. The authors selected this course for redesign chiefly because its resources did not support

Universal Design for Learning (UDL). UDL requires that all students can access instructional materials in a format best suited to their learning style and abilities. Prior to the redesign, the course relied heavily on written explanations even for complex tasks found in the Microsoft Excel functions. Students were required to peruse documents and illustrations for assistance in completing the assignments. In addition to inclusion of UDL criteria, the authors used the redesigned course to incorporate AI tools to provide faculty with a roadmap to integrate AI best practices in design, creation of assignments, and ethics training.

Table 1. also located in the Appendix - consists of tools to support faculty and students that use AI to ensure ethical submission and support UDL principles.

This course redesign is an outcome of an institutional grant which requires research into the results of the pilot redesign and a report of the findings. When the course concludes, we as the researchers will host a focus group for the six professors teaching the course and ask for insights into the value of AI for the course plans, assignments, rubrics, and any other uses of AI tools initiated during the semester. Table 2 identifies the list of questions discussed during the focus group.

At the same time, students will be asked to voluntarily participate in an Institutional Review Board approved survey to gauge their perception of improvement in learning outcomes using AI especially for ethics training. Table 3 provides the online survey presented to students who voluntarily agreed to participate.

An outside information technology administrator will compile the results through Qualtrics to assure student anonymity. The results gleaned from the instructors' focus group and student surveys will help to validate best practices using AI in the classroom. The grant also requires that, based on the course outcomes, the university offers a formal professional development program in AI to be delivered to all faculty in the next academic year.

CONCLUSION

The 21st century academic landscape is besieged with innovative technology designed to ease the rigors of learning through better practices in accessibility, course design, and research. AI resources, as part of this innovative revolution, promote outcomes as a double-edged sword, with negative consequences as

Table 1. AI Tools and Resources Utilized in the Redesign of CMIS 220

Faculty resources	Student resources
Inclusion of a literature review of articles related to AI, origins, best practices, and its contribution to unethical practices.	Detailed instructions on how to download and use a chatbot for the class.
Lesson planning based on submitting text chapter outcomes covered each week to ChatGPT and adapting output to faculty's individual preferences.	Formalized ethics training that requires a competency-based quiz with a passing score of 95% required.
All assignments are graded using rubrics constructed as a blend of AI generated algorithms and instructor preferences. Rubrics used in this course were applied to assignments of writing, discussion board, excel problems, and PowerPoint presentations.	Writing assignments with instructions on using chatbots ethically. Instructions require that students first research the topic on ChatGPT or other chatbot resources, submit the output, and, using additional sources, revise the chatbot output and include real life examples that demonstrate the topic.
End of course focus group with six instructors to determine the effect of AI integration and ethics training. Focus group questions created using AI ChatGPT.	End of course survey to gauge the students' reaction to the open use of AI tools within a course. Survey questions created using AI ChatGPT

Table 2. Focus Group Questions Designed by ChatGPT

Criteria	Questions
Overall experience	How would you describe your overall experience with this course? In what ways do you believe AI resources enhanced or detracted from the teaching and learning experience?
Content and relevance	How effectively did the AI resources align with the course content and learning objectives? Did the AI resources offer new perspectives or insights that traditional materials did not?
Student engagement	Were there any challenges or barriers that students encountered when interacting with AI resources?
Pedagogical impact	How did the integration of AI resources affect your teaching methods or instructional approach?
Technical aspects	How user-friendly were the AI tools or platforms you used? Did they require significant technical skills to navigate?
Assessment and feedback	Were you able to utilize AI rubrics for evaluating student progress or providing timely feedback? If yes, how effective was this approach?
Professional development	How has your experience with AI resources influenced your perspective on integrating technology into future courses?
Future implementation	Would you consider using AI resources again in future courses? Why or why not? Are there specific improvements or enhancements you would like to see in AI resources to better support teaching and learning?
Student perspectives	Have you gathered any feedback from students regarding their experiences with AI resources? If so, what were their observations and opinions?

Table 3. Student Survey Designed by ChatGPT

Survey statements
1. The instructions for using AI tools were clear and understandable.
2. The incorporation of AI resources enhanced my understanding of course concepts.
3. AI tools improved my overall learning experience in this course.
4. The use of AI resources positively impacted my engagement with the course material.
5. The integration of AI resources made the course content more interesting and relevant.
6. The AI tools and platforms used in the course were user-friendly and intuitive.
7. I would like to see more courses incorporate AI resources to enhance the learning experience.
8. I am aware of the ethical considerations associated with the use of AI resources in this course.
9. The AI-supported rubrics provided a fair and accurate evaluation of my knowledge reflected in the grading.
10. Please provide any additional comments or suggestions regarding your experience with AI resources in this course.

Note. Likert scale: 1 = strongly disagree, 2 = disagree, 3 = neutral, 4 = agree, and 5 = strongly agree.

part of the output. Currently, there is a lack of literature to support faculty and administrators in how to befriend innovation to promote integrity, guarantee student success, and increase marketability within the post-graduation job market. Educators can mitigate the negative effects by focusing on the positive aspects of AI, which can only be accomplished through faculty's awareness and education in best practices with a sound and enforceable standard for ethical codes of conduct.

REFERENCES

Abdous, M. (2023, March 21). How AI is shaping the future of higher ed. *Inside Higher Ed.* https://www.insidehighered.com/views/2023/03/22/how-ai-shaping-future-higher-ed-opinion

Agata Stachowicz-Stanusch. (2019). *Management and Business Education in the Time of Artificial Intelligence: The Need to Rethink, Retrain, and Redesign.* Information Age Publishing.

Andreas Schleicher - Director for the Directorate of Education and Skills. (n.d.). OECD. https://www.oecd.org/education/andreas-schleicher.htm

Angelo, T. A., & Cross, K. P. (2012). *Classroom assessment techniques.* Jossey Bass Wiley.

Barnett, S. (2023, January 30). ChatGPT is making universities rethink plagiarism. *Wired.* https://www.wired.com/story/chatgpt-college-university-plagiarism/

Barret, M., Branson, L., Carter, S., DeLeon, F., Ellis, J., Gundlach, C., & Lee, D. (2019). Using artificial intelligence to enhance educational opportunities and student services in higher education. *Inquiry, 22*(1), 1–11.

Bouchrika, I. (2023, June 28). *College dropout rates: 2023 Statistics by race, gender & income.* Research.com. https://research.com/universities-colleges/college-dropout-rates

Dixon, J. H. B. Jr. (2023). Artificial intelligence— "What hath God wrought.". *The Judges' Journal, 62*(3), 37–39.

Eaton, S. E. (2023, March 4). Artificial intelligence and academic integrity, post-plagiarism. *University World News.* https://www.universityworldnews.com/post.php?story=20230228133041549

Essien, A., Chukwukelu, G., & Essien, V. (2021). Opportunities and challenges of adopting artificial intelligence for learning and teaching in higher education. In M. B. Ali & T. Wood-Harper (Eds.), *Fostering communication and learning with underutilized technologies in higher education* (pp. 67–78). Information Science Reference/IGI Global., doi:10.4018/978-1-7998-4846-2.ch005

Honorlock. (2023). *Preventing AI content tools in higher.* Issuu. https://issuu.com/honorlockonlineproctoring/docs/preventing_ai_content_tools_in_higher_education

How ChatGPT and other AI tools can maximize the learning potential of your case-based classes. (2023, June 1). HBSP. https://he.hbsp.harvard.edu/how-chat-gpt-can-maximize-your-case-based-classes.html

Inside Higher Ed. (2023). Emerging technology and AI. *Inside Higher Ed.* https://www.insidehighered.com/sites/default/files/2023-06/2023-IHE-Emerging-Technology-and-AI_.pdf

Ison, D. C. (2018). An empirical analysis of differences in plagiarism among world cultures. *Journal of Higher Education Policy and Management, 40*(4), 291–304. doi:10.1080/1360080X.2018.1479949

Jain, V., & Shetty, A. S. (2022). Digital competence among schoolteachers across gender. *Turkish Online Journal of Qualitative Inquiry, 13*(1), 1083–1089.

King, M. R. (2023). A conversation on artificial intelligence, chatbots, and plagiarism in higher education. *Cellular and Molecular Bioengineering*, *16*(1), 1–2. doi:10.100712195-022-00754-8 PMID:36660590

Liu, L., Subbareddy, R., & Raghavendra, C. G. (2022). AI intelligence chatbot to improve students' learning in the higher education platform. *Journal of Interconnection Networks*, *22*(Supp02), 1–17. doi:10.1142/S0219265921430325

McEwen, R. (2023, January 22). Academic papers written by AI get a solid B — but is it cheating? *The Toronto Star*. https://www.thestar.com/opinion/contributors/2023/01/22/academic-papers-written-by-ai-get-a-solid-b-but-is-it-cheating.html

MollickE. R.MollickL. (2023) Using AI to implement effective teaching strategies in classrooms: Five strategies, including prompts. doi:10.2139/ssrn.4391243

Rehman, S. (2022, June 29). *Challenges in chatbot development*. IDETA. https://www.ideta.io/blog-posts-english/challenges-in-chatbot-development-chatbot-strategy

Shweta. (2022, August 21). What is a chatbot? Everything you need to know. *Forbes*. https://www.forbes.com/advisor/business/software/what-is-a-chatbot/

Siegel, D., Acharya, P., & Sivo, S. (2017). Extending the Technology Acceptance Model to Improve Usage & Decrease Resistance toward a New Technology by Faculty in Higher Education. *The Journal of Technology Studies*, *43*(2), 58–69. doi:10.21061/jots.v43i2.a.1

Wang, Y., Liu, C., & Tu, Y.-F. (2021). Factors affecting the adoption of AI-based applications in higher education: An analysis of teachers' perspectives using structural equation modeling. *Journal of Educational Technology & Society*, *24*(3), 116–129.

Watty, K., McKay, J., & Ngo, L. (2016). Innovators or inhibitors? Accounting faculty resistance to new educational technologies in higher education. *Journal of Accounting Education*, *36*, 1–15. doi:10.1016/j.jaccedu.2016.03.003

Welding, L. (2023, March 13). Half of college students say using AI is cheating. *Best Colleges*. https://www.bestcolleges.com/research/college-students-ai-tools-survey/

Wong, J. (2020, October 25). Post-secondary students call for changes to online exam rules as cheating concerns rise. *CBC*. https://www.cbc.ca/news/canada/post-secondary-assessment-integrity-proctoring-1.5767953

ADDITIONAL READING

Corrigan, C., Asakipaam, S., Kponyo, J., & Luetge, C. (Eds.). (2023). *AI ethics in higher education: Insights slfrom Africa and beyond*. Springer International Publishing. doi:10.1007/978-3-031-23035-6

D'Agostino, S. (2023, June 5). How AI tools both help and hinder equity. *Inside HigherEd*. https://www.insidehighered.com/news/tech-innovation/artificial-intelligence/2023/06/05/how-ai-tools-both-help-and-hinder-equity?utm_source=Inside+

Gannon, K. (2023, May 22). Why calls for a "return to rigor" are wrong. *The Chronicle of Higher Education.* https://www.chronicle.com/article/why-calls-for-a-return-to-rigor-are-wrong

Kim, J., & Maloney, E. (2020). *Learning innovation and the future of higher education.* John Hopkins University Press. doi:10.1353/book.71965

McMurtrie, B. (2023, May 26). Teaching: Are professors ready for AI? *The Chronicle of Higher Education.* https://www.chronicle.com/newsletter/teaching/2023-05-25

Schroeder, R. (2023, May 24). Steps to take while AI chat bots mature. *Inside HigherEd.* https://www.insidehighered.com/opinion/blogs/online-trending-now/2023/05/24/steps-take-while-ai-chat-bots-mature

KEY TERMS AND DEFINITIONS

Chatbot: A computer software program that simulates human conversations.

ChatGPT: An AI chatbot brand that mimics human responses.

Institutional Review Board: A peer group that reviews research studies to ensure that they meet ethical standards, follow institutional procedures, and protect all participants from harm.

Learning Management System (LMS): A digital learning platform used to manage course requirements.

Pandemic: COVID 19 epidemic that forced the closing of all academic institutions for in class instruction. All course work was moved to the online environment.

Turnitin: Software that higher education institutions use to check for ethical violations in writing assignments.

Universal Design for Learning (UDL): An approach to teaching that affirms the need for equality for all students when accessing educational materials, and includes accommodations for learning style, culture, and disabilities.

Chapter 3
Ethical Considerations for Artificial Intelligence in Educational Assessments

Tristan Lim
https://orcid.org/0000-0002-2645-5383
Nanyang Polytechnic, Singapore & Singapore Management University, Singapore

Swapna Gottipati
Singapore Management University, Singapore

Michelle L. F. Cheong
https://orcid.org/0000-0002-3192-3452
Singapore Management University, Singapore

ABSTRACT

In the vital context of education, the application of artificial intelligence (AI) to assessments necessitates a nuanced examination of the boundaries between ethically permissible and impermissible practices. In this chapter, the authors applied a systematic literature mapping methodology to scour extant research, so as to holistically structure the landscape into explicit topical research clusters. Through topic modelling and network analyses, research mapped key ethical principles to different assessment phases in a triadic ontological framework. The chapter looks to provide researchers and practitioners the insights into the ethical challenges that exist across an end-to-end assessment pipeline.

INTRODUCTION

Artificial intelligence in education (AIED) is the machine mimicry of human-like consciousness and behavior to achieve educational goals, through the use of technology that allows digital systems to perform tasks commonly associated with intelligent beings.

DOI: 10.4018/979-8-3693-0205-7.ch003

Of the three pillars of education, assessment exists as an important component, alongside pedagogy and curriculum (Hill and Barber, 2014). Within the AIED domain, Chaudhry and Kazim (2022) scoured the landscape and concluded that assessment is one of the four key sub-domains in AIED, alongside learning personalization, automated learning systems, and intelligent learning environments. In an educational context, assessment refers to '*any appraisal (or judgment or evaluation)... of work or performance*' (Sadler, 1989). The infusion of artificial intelligence (AI) in assessments has grown significantly in recent years. Research on assessments related to digital education in the higher education landscape showed that AI and adaptive learning technologies have tripled between 2011 to 2021 and is likely to surpass immersive learning technologies as a prime research area in the near future (Lim, Gottipati and Cheong, 2022, p. 5). Among stakeholders, there is a consensus positive view that "*AI would provide a fairer, richer assessment system that would evaluate students across a longer period of time and from an evidence-based, value-added perspective*" (Luckin, 2017).

Infusion of AI in assessments also brings along its own set of concerns. AI implementation comes with technical and operational issues relating to system implementation. Arguably, these challenges have relatively lesser grey areas to contend with, than the complication of navigating the parameters and boundaries of ethics. Evaluators, as practitioners of assessments, will need to acknowledge, respect, and uphold ethical principles that may plague the implementation of an AI-based assessment.

The objective of this chapter is to examine the landscape of AI-related ethical issues for educational assessments, through the lens of a systematic literature mapping approach. A systematic literature mapping study is a study concerned with the mapping and structuring of a topical research area, the identification of gaps in knowledge, and the examination of possible research topics (Petersen, Vakkalanka and Kuzniarz, 2015).

This chapter investigates the following research questions:

RQ1: Where do the studies that discuss ethical issues relating to AI-based assessments arise from?
This question looks at where the studies discussing ethical issues relating to AI-based assessments arise from, studies patterns arising from exploratory data analysis, and seeks to provide recommendations (if any).

RQ2: What are the main AI use cases relating to assessments?
This question looks at AI applications in different areas of assessments, and how dominantly each AI application areas are featured in related studies.

RQ3: What are the main ethical issues arising from the AI implementations relating to assessments?
This question looks at the key ethical principles related to AI applications in assessments, and how dominantly each ethical principles are featured in related studies.

RQ4: What are the key themes of the systematic literature map?
This question looks to identify key themes of the systematic literature map, and draw up a framework to visualize and generalize the key themes for researchers and practitioners.

Through a systematic meta-analysis of existing literature, this chapter helps: (i) understand and consolidate knowledge regarding what was previously explored relating to AI-based assessment methods and their interconnected ethical issues, (ii) provide an integrated inquiry into the association of the ethical problems faced, and (iii) identify potential future research topics in the field.

The study identified five key research archetypical themes, with presence across the system layers of cognitive, information and physical domains of an AI-based assessment pipeline, namely: (i) AI system design and check for assessment purposes; (ii) AI-based assessment construction and rollout; (iii) data stewardship and surveillance; (iv) administration of assessments using AI systems; and (v) AI-facilitated assessment grading and evaluation. Ten AI ethics principles epitomize the key ethics considerations across each of the five research themes; each manifesting varying levels of importance.

We hope the findings of this chapter can provide researchers and practitioners the insights into the application methods of AI in assessments, especially in terms of their intertwined ethical challenges and how these challenges may be addressed, for follow up studies.

The remainder of the chapter is organized as follows: (i) the *Background and Literature Review* section introduces the background of AIED, in relation to ethics and assessments, supported by a survey of the state-of-the-art; (ii) the *Methodology* section discusses the systematic literature mapping approaches undertaken, explains the machine learning methods utilized, discusses research validity and repeatability issues, and highlights limitations to the research; (iii) the *Findings* section presents the tables and graphic visualizations from charting, coding, topic modelling, and network analyses, and provides in-depth analyses of the data.; (iv) the *Discussion* section aims to generalize the results into key themes that can be used by practitioners and researchers, and discuss practical and theoretical implications of the findings; and last but not least, (v) the *Conclusion* section summarizes the key findings, impact, and closes with proposed future work that can be studied by practitioners and researchers.

BACKGROUND

AIED

Depending on the context in educational technology-related papers, the term 'AI' in education is commonly used broadly and interchangeably with the term 'adaptive learning technology', and to some extents 'learning analytics', 'educational data mining', 'educational data science', 'teaching analytics', 'data-driven decision-making in education', and 'big data in education' (Romero and Ventura, 2020).

It is useful to note that 'intelligence' in AI exists as a continuum. Chassang et al. (2021) describes how AI can be mapped into Bloom's taxonomy of learning, with 'Crystallized Intelligence' describing lower order thinking skills and 'Fluid Intelligence' describing higher order thinking skills. The former includes mainly supervised learning (or target-based prediction), with "*encoding capacity, middle-long term memory and ability to access memorized data in a logical way*", while the latter includes a higher level of intelligence abstraction, with "*the ability to solve new problems, use logics in new situations and identify patterns without necessarily having the prior experience of similar information or problems*".

AIED is a superset that encompasses terms such as educational data mining or learning analytics, depending on its specific use cases (Fig. 1). Educational data mining is relatively more focused on the technological challenges of developing and applying data mining techniques in education. For instance, the use of educational data mining that involves developing a natural language processing algorithm to compare different word embeddings on text similarity in open-ended quiz responses is a use case of AI described as Crystallized Intelligence. On the other hand, learning analytics is more focused on the educational challenges of data-driven decision-making, through the use of predictive models. For instance, the use of learning analytics applying the abstract reasoning abilities of neural network to generalize assessment feedbacks will be a use case of AI described as Fluid Intelligence. There are many

Figure 1. Relationship between educational data mining and learning analytics within AIED

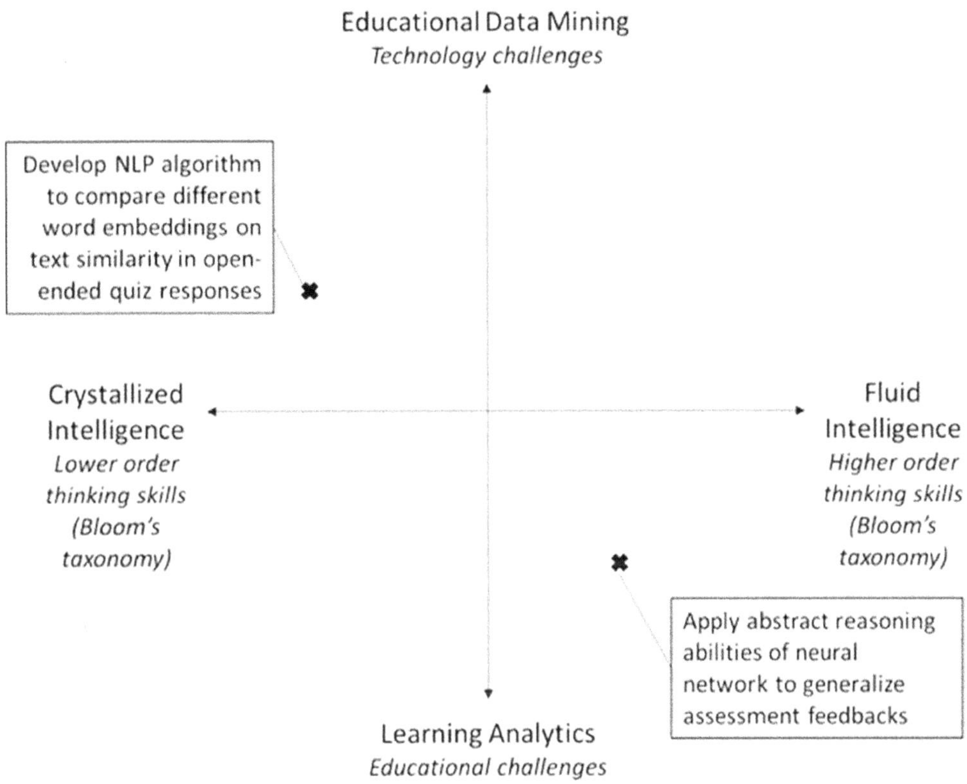

other use cases of AI, including visual data analytics for AI-integrated communication dashboards and recommender systems for formative assessment questions etc.

From a technology point of view, under the sub-fields of AI are machine learning, and in turn, deep learning and reinforcement learning. Machine learning is a field of inquiry that seeks to understand and create methods to leverage on data and learn to make decisions. Deep learning leverages on a class of machine learning methods (specifically neural networks) to identify representation elements of a data-set, so as to learn features and perform tasks. Reinforcement learning seeks to utilize machine learning methods for intelligent agents to take actions in an environment to optimize some notion of reward.

A multitude of learning techniques and algorithms exist under each of these sub-fields. For instance, collaborative analytics refers to machine learning procedures performed to measure metrics tied to interdependent student relationships to predict collaboration dynamics in group assessments. A use case in Martinez-Maldonado et al. (2021) used natural language processing techniques, including a latent semantic analysis algorithm, to study the progression of collaborative critical thinking skills using online forum data. This computer-supported collaborative learning research, was underpinned by theoretical model of communities of enquiry, positing that meaningful learning on online forums occur when there exist high levels of social, cognitive and teaching presence.

Generative AI models, which are designed to create new content or simulations, are increasingly being explored in educational settings. These models can generate personalized learning materials, simulate complex scenarios for assessment, and provide adaptive feedback, bridging the gap between traditional assessments and dynamic, individualized learning experiences.

AIED has grown tremendously in research intensity in recent years. It was observed that there was a significant increase in the number of research papers cited in Google Scholar; research publications increased from 1,739 papers in the decade of 1990 to 1999, to 22,060 papers in the most recent decade ending this year, representing more than twelve folds of increase.

AIED and Ethics

At present, although AI has yet to achieve comparability mimicking human levels of consciousness, it is still of urgent and paramount importance to consider ethical issues in AI applications, including AIED.

Aside from concerns regarding infringement of relevant laws and AI crimes (Sibai, 2020), ethical threats may exist, for instance, in the forms of systemic inequality and discrimination against marginalized learner groups in AI-driven assessments. Chaudhry and Kazim (2022) emphasizes that "*risks of AI going wrong have increased significantly for all stakeholders including, ed-tech companies, schools, teachers and learners.... a lot more work needs to be done on ethical AI in learning contexts to mitigate these risks.*" Prioritizing ethics is crucial to ensure the wellbeing of students, educators and other stakeholders involved in AIED.

Ethics is branch of philosophy. At its core are the concepts of "good" or "bad", and "right" or "wrong". Ethics is closely tied to the study of values (i.e., axiology) and the study of taste and beauty (i.e., aesthetics). Ethics can be subdivided into three core research areas, which can be further divided into a multitude of sub-branches. These three core research areas are, namely:

- *Metaethics:* Study of the nature (i.e., moral ontology), meaning (i.e., moral semantics), and the scope and knowledge to defend or support (i.e., moral epistemology) moral judgments.
    - *Moral ontology*: This investigates the nature of moral judgments. For instance, applying moral relativism in moral ontology, we may ask the question: "*Is the right or wrong of plagiarism necessarily contextualizable to societal conventions?*"
    - *Moral semantics*: This evaluates the meaning and implications to the meaning of moral judgment. For instance, applying ethical naturalism in moral semantics, it may hold that the cognitivist ethical proposition of "*ensuring fairness in assessments is an ethically good act*" may be reducible and supervene into the natural property of "*maximizing happiness*", as embraced by utilitarianism.
    - *Moral epistemology*: This studies and justifies moral knowledge. For instance, applying ethical rationalism in moral epistemology, the ethical principle of cheating is tied to the moral truths of justice and fairness, which are known by reasoning alone *a priori*.
- *Normative ethics:* Study of the moral rules and standards that guide how individuals, institutions and societies should behave in a moral sense.
    - *Virtue ethics*: This emphasizes the inherent disposition of an individual, and not specific actions. 'Good' in this context is the development of practical wisdom, and the flourishing of individual character and wellbeing. As such, morality becomes a holistic personal development process. Virtual ethics argues that virtuous individuals through good motivations can make good moral choices. However, the downsides are that individuals may not agree on what is good, and the existence of value plurality is reduced.

Here, it can be argued that ethics training for stakeholders implementing assessments in AIED achieves *phronesis* (i.e., acquiring practical wisdom to make 'good' decisions), and is sufficient in itself as an ethics stewardship measure.

- *Deontological ethics*: This emphasizes on an individual's rights and duties, including the presence of natural, absolute rights (i.e., natural rights theory), the presence of human rationality and inviolable moral laws (i.e., Kantian categorical imperative), and the morality of good actors arising from unbiasedness behind a veil of ignorance (i.e., contractualism). 'Good' in this context is the fulfilment and discharge of moral duties. As such, morality is focused on intention and obligation. Deontology argues that clear moral intuition and boundaries exist, even in cross cultural settings, although downsides are the lack of flexibility and possibility of conflict between human rights and moral duties.

Here, ethics should be viewed from the lens of human rights, rationality and unbiasedness. For instance, the right to privacy may be viewed as an inviolable moral standard.

- *Consequentialism*: This emphasizes that the outcome of an action defines the morality of an action. Utilitarianism promotes actions that maximize happiness for the greatest number of people. Intellectualism promotes actions that encourage and cultivate knowledge. Situational ethics promotes *moral particularism,* which focuses on contextualizing actions that seek to engender love. 'Good' in this context is the actions that promote 'ideal' outcomes. As such, morality becomes results focused. Consequentialism argues a practical approach that is multi-perspective and objective, although the downsides may be an over-endorsement of value pluralism and the presence of adverse intended motivation behind an action that may use consequentialism to inappropriately justify their course of action.

Here, in the case of AIED, it can be argued that the impact to the relevant stakeholders should be measured, using appropriate metrics, as an ethics stewardship measure.

- *Applied ethics:* Study of the practical application of philosophical tools to examine and provide solutions to real world morality issues.

This can be applied on scopes of digital ethics, defined as the "*attempt to guide human conduct in the design and use of digital technology*", and in narrower terms, AI ethics, defined as the "*attempt to guide human conduct in the design and use of artificial automata or artificial machines, or computers in particular, by rationally formulating and following principles or rules that reflect basic individual and social commitments and our leading ideals and values*" (Hanna and Kazim, 2021). On the subject of definition, it is useful to highlight the difference between AI ethics and ethical AI. Siau and Wang (2020) clarifies the former as "*principles, rules, guidelines, policies and regulations related to AI*", and the latter as "*AI that performs and behaves ethically*". The former relates to the behavior of humans, whereas the latter relates to the behavior of AI systems.

This chapter does not seek to argue the meta-ethics and normative ethics tied to assessments applying AIED. In this chapter, we take a more practical approach by considering fundamental ethical principles (e.g., fairness and cheating) that inform the design, regulation and the use of AIED in assessments.

These are ethics principles which provide concrete property instantiations of applied ethics, as opposed to abstract moral universals (Stringer, 2018). The chapter makes explicit these principles by describing applied instances of these principles found in existing peer-reviewed literature. In addition, the chapter cites practical solutions and mitigation measures that can be used to uphold these principles. It should be highlighted that while this chapter seeks to provide a generalizable approach to the consideration of AI ethics in assessments, the application in specific domains (e.g., medicine and healthcare) may vary in breadth (e.g., safeguard human safety during assessments in medical field training) and are outside the scope of this research.

From the real-world practical application standpoint, we note that there is a tradeoff between the agenda of advancing the AI technology, and the governance and stewardship of the use of AI in an ethical manner. Many professional and governmental bodies have pushed for responsible AI governance and stewardship. Siau and Wang (2020) identified eight institutions that have drawn up such ethics guidelines to facilitate the adoption, development and embracing of AI, including professional bodies such as the Institute of Electrical and Electronics Engineers (IEEE, 2019), and government bodies, such as the Australian government's Department of Industry, Science and Resources (Australian Government, 2019). Specifically, on the subject of AIED, Nguyen et al. (2022) studied five such relevant guidelines, including UNESCO (2021)'s adoption on AI ethics guidelines with applications on AIED, and European Parliament (2021)'s report on AIED. These said, Siau and Wang (2020) notes that companies and institutions are presently more heavily weighted towards growing AI capabilities, with lower focus on ethical considerations.

Hinderance to the lack of focus on AI ethics in practice could stem from several reasons. Firstly, among nascent studies that investigate this tradeoff, Bessen, Impink, and Seamans (2022) studied the cost of integrating ethics in AI development, from a data management perspective. We note that further AI ethics research on cost-benefit analyses can be useful to help balance this tradeoff, and advance AI ethics governance and stewardship. Secondly, while the present AI ethics guidelines, especially the ones related to AIED studied by Nguyen et al. (2022), seek to address AI ethics issues, we note the lack of specificity on AIED applications, for instance, in assessments. Stahl, Timmermans, and Mittelstadt (2016) shares how ethics discourses should be "*focused on particular technologies to have practical importance*." In turn, Whittlestone et al. (2019) argues that these guidelines are "*not specific enough to be action guiding*." This lack of idiosyncrasy and relevance can deter actionable applications.

To our best knowledge, a systematic literature mapping on ethical dimensions of the application of AI in assessments is lacking. This chapter aims to address the latter to enhance real world adoption in the sub-domain of assessments within AIED.

AIED and Assessment

There are different applications of AI in assessment practices. Sánchez-Prieto et al. (2020) presents a systematic literature review on AI-driven assessments, and subdivided assessments into three themes, namely:

- *Assessment of student behavior:* This includes the contextualization of assessment delivery, and the prediction of assessment outcomes.
- *Assessment of student sentiment:* This includes the personalization of feedbacks, and the analysis of socio-emotional elements.

- *Assessment of student achievement:* This includes the automation of grading, and the categorization or profiling of students using data from assessment performance.

In a similar study, González-Calatayud, Prendes-Espinosa and Roig-Vila (2021) identified thematic uses of AI in assessments, mainly in individual or group adaptive formative assessments, automated grading and personalized feedbacks.

There exist different AI-driven assessment types, such as individual or group cognitive assessments and socio-emotional assessments. In addition, there exist different AI use cases across the assessment development and delivery pipeline, including but not limited to, assessment construction, curation and delivery, proctoring, grading, learning intervention and assistance, and feedback (assessment pipeline). From a technology system perspective, the AI system development pipeline includes "*the decision to start collecting data till the point when the machine learning model is deployed in production*" (Chaudhry and Kazim, 2022).

Different assessment types and areas of the assessment pipeline can be associated with different AI ethical concerns. For instance, in relation to assessment type, a socio-emotional assessment may be constructed in a manner that performs a semestral long behavioral tracking surveillance on learners, resulting in privacy infringement and anxiety disorders among students. In another example, in relation to the assessment pipeline, specifically regarding the design of an AI assessment system, data and/or modelling deficiencies may perpetuate stigmatization of minority group students, resulting in negative learning and psychological impact.

In this chapter, we seek to discuss the ethical dimensions of the application of AI in assessments across the assessment development and delivery pipeline, taking into account different assessment types.

In closing, in this literature review, the discourse on *AIED* provides an overview of the field of inquiry, the discourse on *AIED and ethics* provides the context and scope of ethics considerations within AIED, and the discourse on AIED and assessment looks at the applications of AI in assessment practices. The next section discusses the details of the methodology applied in this systematic literature mapping approach.

METHODOLOGY

In this study, we apply the systematic literature mapping approach. The study was conducted using the research methodology in Kabudi, Pappas and Olsen (2021), building upon the guidelines as proposed by Petersen, Vakkalanka and Kuzniarz (2015). We apply the methodology undertaken by both studies as follows, namely: (i) search and selection, (ii) data extraction, (iii) classification and analysis, and (iv) evaluation of validity.

PRISMA approach, or the *Preferred Reporting Items for Systematic Reviews and Meta-Analyses approach*, was employed as a guideline to conduct the search and selection phase (Moher et al., 2009). In accordance with the recommended methodology as part of the PRISMA-P checklist, details including the eligibility criteria, sources of information, search protocol, research records, data items and synthesis of data are described in the following sub-sections.

NVivo11, EndNote X9 and Excel spreadsheets were used for information organization. Further information extraction, data visualization, and machine learning tools and techniques are described in the following sub-sections.

Search and Selection

As AIED researchers stem from a variety of fields publishing across a wide range of publications, literature search was conducted using Scopus, an interdisciplinary rigorously curated database covering the widest range of disciplines (240 disciplines) relative to similar citation databases, with contents including over 87 million publication items, 1.8 billion cited references, 17 million author profiles, 94,000 affiliation sources and 7,000 publishers. On average, each paper indexed on Scopus has 10% to 15% more citations than similar databases (Elsevier, 2022), which implies a more extensive systematic literature mapping analysis.

The first stage of PRISMA, or the *identification* stage, identifies the possible papers to be considered using the Scopus search engine. The search entry was as follows: *ALL ("Artificial intelligence" AND education AND assessment AND ethics).* This stage identified a corpus of 8,203 papers.

The second stage of PRISMA, or the *screening* stage, looks at excluding inappropriate and unrelated papers. This stage reduced the corpus count to 202. Search applied the following inclusion criteria:

- *Language:* Only articles written in English language were included. This step omitted 67 articles.
- *Keywording:* Only articles with subject-relevant keywords coded by Scopus for indexing purposes (also known as *Indexed Keywords* by Scopus) were included. Subject-relevant keywords includ-

Figure 2. PRISMA: The systematic mapping process

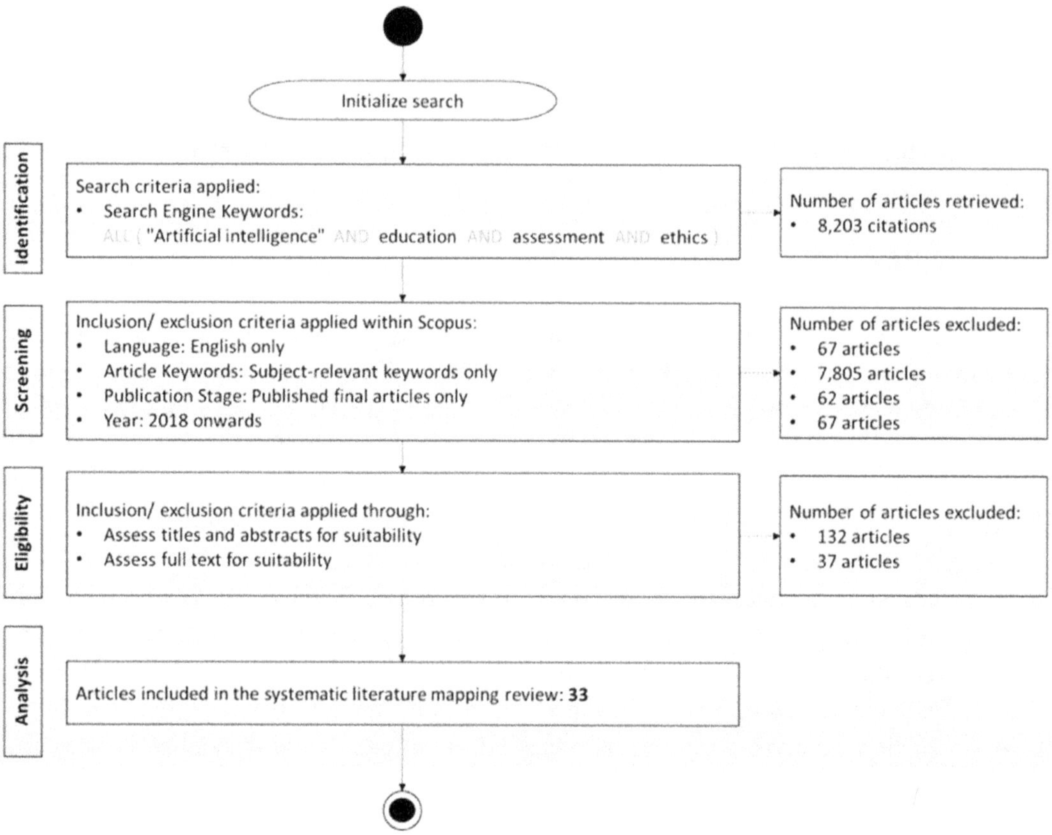

ed, and are not limited to: *Education, University, Higher Education, Learning Environment(s), Learning System(s), E-learning, Online Learning, Education Computing, Intelligent Tutoring System(s), Computer Aided Instruction, Learning Analytic(s), Curricul(a/um), Teaching, Learning, Learning Process(es), Collaborative Learning, Student(s), Academic Performance(s), Ethic(s), Ethical Consideration(s), Ethical Issue(s), Ethical Technolog(y/ies), Fairness, Data Privacy, Trust, Moral(s), Moralit(y/ies), Perception(s).* Excluded keywords included, and are not limited to: *Medical Ethic(s), Bioethic(s), Clinical Stud(y/ies), Patient Simulation(s), Doctor-Patient Relationship(s), Risk Assessment(s), Human Resource Management, Software Engineering, Electronic Assessment(s).* This step omitted 7,805 articles.

- *Publication Stage:* Only peer-reviewed final articles published in scientific venues (e.g., books, journals and conferences) were included, for rigority of selection. This step omitted 62 articles.
- *Year of Publication:* Only articles published in 2018 and beyond were included, to ensure recency of literature. Rigorous peer-reviewed articles would have reviewed key prior related literature within their respective papers. This step omitted 67 articles.

The third stage of PRISMA, or the *eligibility* stage, requires scanning title and abstracts, and full papers to identify relevant eligible articles. This stage yielded a final corpus count of 33 articles. Search applied the following inclusion criteria:

- *Assess Titles and Abstracts for Suitability:* Only relevant titles and abstracts were included. There should be explicit and direct references to the subject matter. This step omitted 132 articles.
- *Assess Full Papers for Suitability:* Only relevant full papers were included. An additional inclusion criterion here was that all articles should have their full text accessible for analysis. This step omitted 37 articles.

A summary of the PRISMA approach is shown in Fig. 2.

Data Extraction

As a citation engine, data in Scopus is highly structured and robustly tagged, delivering metadata for analytical purposes, including (i) author(s), (ii) document title, (iii) affiliation(s), (iv) year, (v) publication, (vi) volume, issue and page source, (vii) citation, (viii) document type, (ix) keywords, and (x) digital object identifier (DOI), among others.

The final pool of 33 primary studies were thoroughly analyzed to answer the research questions of this study (refer to Appendix). Information that was extracted from Scopus included: (i) citation information, such as author(s), title, year, publication, and citation count etc., (ii) bibliographical information, such as affiliation(s), and publisher etc., (iii) abstract, (iv) keywords, and (v) references.

Classification and Analysis

Using the data extracted from Scopus, the study utilized *Tableau Desktop Professional* version 2021.1.20 to perform exploratory data analyses to address RQ1. Tableau platform allows powerful conversion of complex computations into appealing data visualizations.

With the Scopus extracted data, research utilized a corpus analysis platform *CorTexT* (Breucker et al., 2016) to perform text parsing, and a first pass of topic modelling and network mapping, so as to identify major thematic representations of corpuses comprising of Author Keywords and Indexed Keywords. This allowed us to perform machine learning for pattern recognition, utilizing unsupervised text mining techniques on these keywords to identify useful patterns.

Using the Python Library *pyLDAvis* (Sievert and Shirley, 2014), topic modelling generated a topic representation of the keyword corpus' textual fields using the Latent Dirichlet Allocation method, which allowed a visualization of the most relevant words fitting to the topic. Here, each topic was defined as a keyword probability distribution, and each document was defined as a topic probability distribution. Given the total number of topics defined, the topic model was inferred by probabilistically assigning topics to documents, and positioned in 2D according to a multi-dimensional scaling algorithm for visualization purposes.

While topic modelling provided a sense of the latent themes from the underlying keywords, research further performed network analyses to visualize thematic keyword representations in a clustering format, where each keyword was grouped with distinct members, and linked via proximity measures. The Louvain hierarchical community detection algorithm was used (Aynaud, 2020). This algorithm is based on modularity optimization, where the optimal linkage densities are measured, taking into account within-cluster and between-cluster linkages. Louvain algorithm is efficient on large networks.

The first pass of topic modelling and network analyses above allowed the identification of distinct sub-themes of AI application areas and ethical issues. With the key sub-themes of AI application areas and ethical issues identified as a priori, each article was thoroughly evaluated and coded to classify the following: (i) application areas where AI is used in assessments (e.g., assessment curation and personalized feedback etc.), and the (ii) type of ethical issues relevant to AI-based assessments as cited in paper (e.g., fairness and explainability etc.). This would allow us to address RQ2 and RQ3.

The study then undertook a thorough review of the full papers, and provided further analyses to tabulate the following: (i) breakdown of each type of ethical issues identified in each paper (e.g., how explainability of AI systems is an important ethical consideration in assessments etc.), and (ii) breakdown of mitigation and intervention methods for each ethical issue as highlighted in each paper (e.g., applying data sanitization to reduce risk of discriminatory decision making from AI systems etc.).

Using the coded sub-themes of AI application areas and ethical issues, research undertook the second pass of topic modelling and network analyses. The topic modelling and network analyses outputs would be used to guide the identification of the major research themes to address RQ4.

Evaluation of Validity

In the application of systematic literature mapping, it was useful to consider the following types of validity to ensure that the methodology was robustly constructed. These included (i) descriptive validity, (ii) interpretive validity, (iii) theoretical validity, and (iv) generalizability (Petersen and Gencel, 2013). Detailed reporting of the systematic mapping methodology process, including the evaluation of validity, helps improve repeatability of the study.

- *Descriptive validity*

This describes the extent to which there existed objective and accurate observations. To lower the risk of this threat, a data extraction and coding spreadsheet was designed to support data recording. This provided objectification of the data extraction process, and allowed interventive correction to ensure accuracy, if required. As such, this risk was considered under control.

- *Interpretive validity*

This describes, given the data extracted and coded, the validity of the conclusions drawn. A key threat might be researcher biasness. This was alleviated by ensuring that no primary papers authored by the authors were included in the primary papers extracted, which reduced threats in interpretation.

- *Theoretical validity*

This describes the prospect of being able to capture what was purported to be captured. Research looked to ensure that the thematic phenomena identified in the paper represented the patterns of the real world. Scopus provided a strong integration with major publishers, and its wide interdisciplinary focus ensured the lowering of probability of missing key research information. In terms of paper screening, careful curation of keywords, selection of final peer-reviewed papers published in scientific venues, and the recency of literature ensured that the literature reviewed were accurate, peer-reviewed and timely. Extensive in-depth reviews were also made in the full texts to ensure that each paper included were suitable. For quality assessment and to reduce potential biasness, the methodology and data extraction process were checked by an independent external reviewer, with subject matter-relevant background.

- *Generalizability*

This describes the external validity (i.e., generalizability on the basis of repeatability and extendibility of results from this paper to other research), and internal validity (i.e., causal effect between application of AI in assessments and their related ethical issues). In the presence of a wide range of similar ethical discourse on different AI applications, the classification and analysis methodology should not result in major threats for both internal and external validity. However, it is acknowledged that external validity may be influenced by factors such as domain-specificity (Leslie, 2019), cultural differences (Awad et al, 2018), and sample size (Khan et al., 2022), and future studies can help alleviate external validity concerns.

Limitations

Although Scopus is a robust database of digital records for peer-reviewed literature to map and survey specialized scientific areas (e.g., Fahimnia, Sarkis and Davarzani (2015), Rodrigues et al., (2014)), we recognize that Scopus is not the only one available. There are other valid alternatives, including Web of Science, ACM, IEEE Xplore, EBSCO Host, Wiley, SAGE Journals, and Taylor and Francis, among others. Among these databases, there are arguments brought forth by Campedelli (2021) that the degree of overlap between the publication titles in both databases may be closer to 50% to 60%, hence including both databases may have value. However, the discriminant feature that supported the selection of Scopus is that its informative tagging of all papers by professional indexers using Indexed Keywords existed at a higher frequency and provided a richer pool of content for each item, in particular, for textual mining purposes, as compared to Keyword Plus from Web of Science. As a first assessment on this subject matter, this should suffice. For follow up works, it will be useful to consider integrating Web of Science and/or other relevant databases to provide a comprehensive scan of this landscape.

Secondly, throughout this chapter, there were no assumptions made on the intrinsic value of thematic diversity. This work utilizes unsupervised machine learning techniques to search for latent topics embedded in existing literature, and through which seeks to act as a key building block upon which future research can be applied. The study of possible inhibited or dysfunctional states within this thematic diversity, plausibly due to scholarly or technology inertia, or the lack of infrastructure or skills resulting in resistance to state-of-the-art adoption, are outside of the scope of this study. It may be useful for future research to quantify the value of this thematic diversity, in terms of (i) its operationalization impact as a segregable assessment pipeline component, and (ii) the extent to which ethics (or the lack thereof), either in isolation or in combination, impact upon the assessment pipeline component. Drawing from Klinger, Mateos-Garcia and Stathoulopoulos (2020), it may be useful to apply Weitzman (1993)'s economic valuation of ecological diversity, taking into account the cost-benefit analysis of preserving diversity and the threshold below which the archetypical research theme becomes unsustainable.

FINDINGS

This section presents the findings based on an analytical investigation of selected published primary papers identified as relevant to the study.

Research Question (RQ) 1: *Where do the studies that discuss ethical issues relating to AI-based assessments arise from?*

To address RQ1, research undertook exploratory data analyses to explore where the studies discussing ethical issues relating to AI-based assessments arise from.

In Fig. 3, it was noted that, through observing the authors' affiliated departments, the papers emerged from researchers across a wide range of disciplines. About half of the researchers originate from Computer Science and Education departments, with Computer Science leading marginally. The remainder stemmed from eighteen disciplines, ranging from soft pure disciplines such as Language, to hard applied disciplines like Engineering. This suggests that research pertaining to AI-integrated assessments and ethics do not necessary emanate from the Education departments, but from a broad spectrum of disciplines.

In Fig. 4, it was noted that most papers originate from The University of Melbourne, Australia (4); Carnegie Mellon, United States (3); University of Oulu, Finland (3); and University of Eastern Finland, Finland (3). The remainder are institutions that published two papers; the yellow circles denote institutions that published one paper. Papers from The University of Melbourne originated from Law, Psychological Sciences, and Engineering schools. Papers from Carnegie Mellon University originated from the Language Technologies Institute, Eberly Center for Teaching Excellence, and Human-Computer Interaction Institute. Papers from Oulu University originated from the Geography, Chemistry and Education departments. Papers from University of Eastern Finland originated from the Computing and Education Sciences departments. These provided an overview of the disparateness of affiliation and departments.

Subject matter is a complex multi-faceted issue that spans, among others, pedagogy, technology, and psychology domains. Taking cues from present research work, it may be useful for the nature of such

Figure 3. Breakdown of disciplines tied to authors' affiliated department

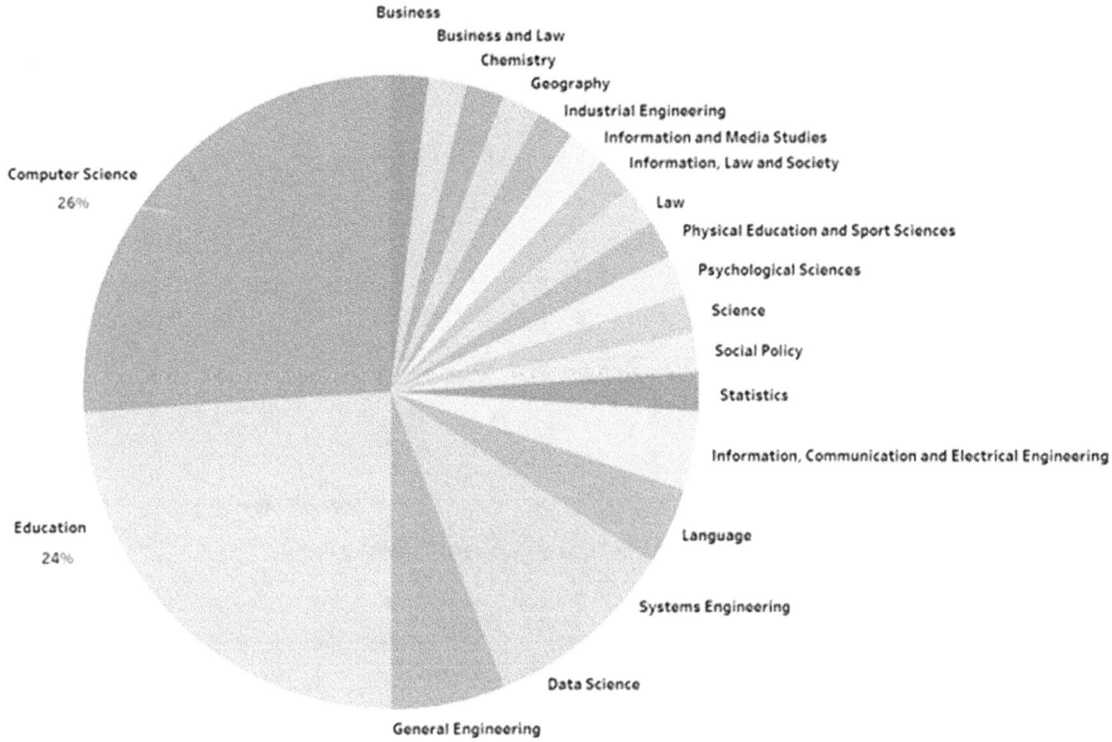

research to have more pluralistic cross-disciplinary collaborations (e.g., computer science, education, social science etc.) in research and development work, to achieve sounder theoretically underpinned methodology approaches and more stakeholder inclusivity (Raji, Scheuerman and Amironesei, 2021).

In Fig. 5, it was noted that the top five countries where the papers originated were the United States, Australia, Brazil, Finland, and Spain (tied at fourth). Bozkurt (2020) found that countries that have historically dominated in educational technology research stemmed from the United States, United Kingdom, and Taiwan. In a different sub-domain in education, ethics-related education, for instance, in the field of healthcare, is also dominated by United States and Taiwan (Andersson et al., 2022). From these lists, aside from the United States which continued to lead in publication numbers, United Kingdom and Taiwan appear to be laggards. There are still room for different countries to play leading roles in this research aspect, as innovators, early adopters and early majority.

In Fig. 6, it was noted that the top publication venues were Computer Science venues, namely (i) 4 conference papers published in Springer's *Lecture Notes in Computer Science (including subseries Lecture Notes in Artificial Intelligence and Lecture Notes in Bioinformatics)*, (ii) 3 conference papers published in Association for Computing Machinery's (ACM) *ACM International Conference Proceeding Series*, and (iii) 3 journal papers published in Institute of Electrical and Electronics Engineers' (IEEE) *IEEE Access*.

As a proportion, 55% of the papers were published in Computer Science venues such as those listed above, 24% were published in Educational Technology venues, such as the *British Journal of Educa-*

Figure 4. Breakdown of affiliated institutions

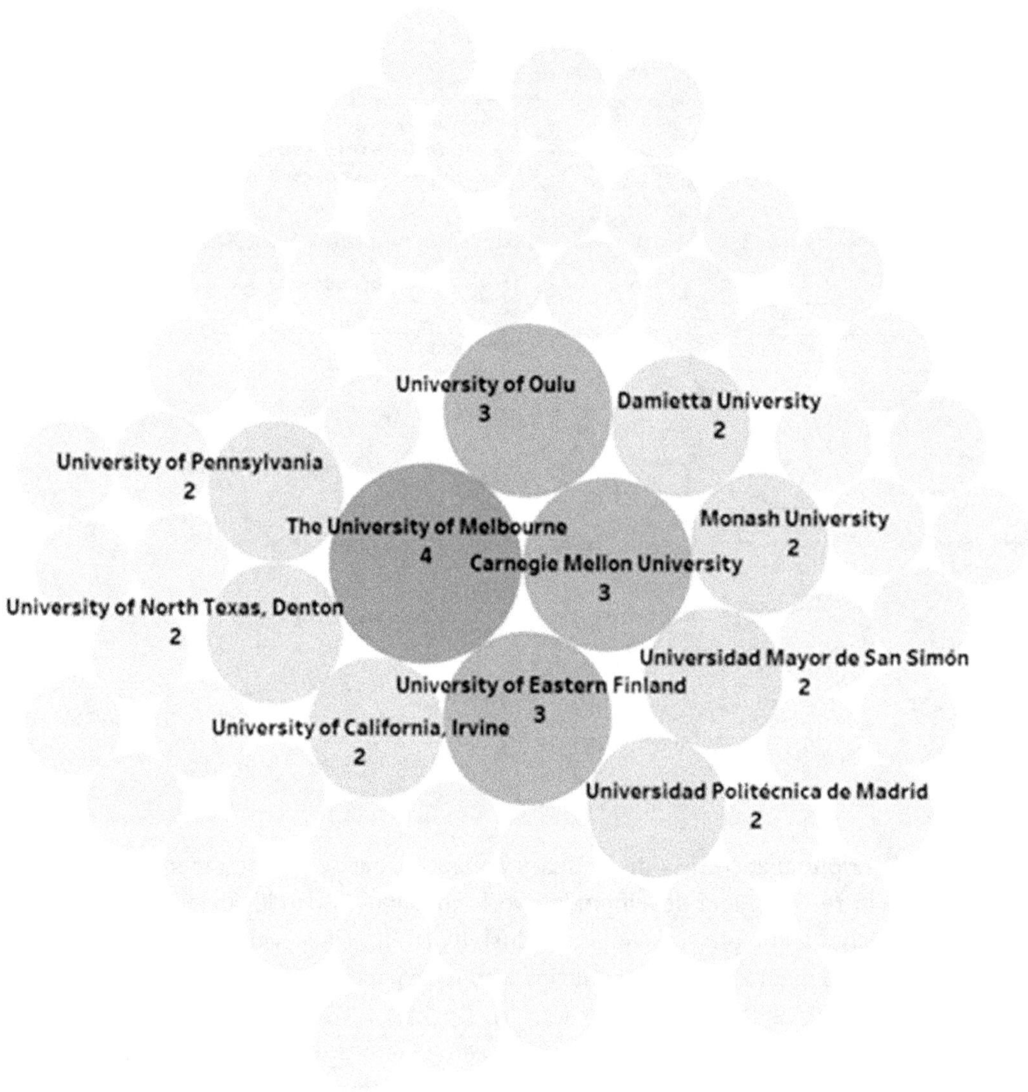

tional Technology, International Journal of Artificial Intelligence in Education, and *Journal of Learning Analytics*; and 15% were published in Education journals (mainly domain-specific education) such as the *International Journal of Information and Communication Technology Education, Journal of Information Systems Education*, and *International Journal of Engineering Education*. This suggests that Computer Science venues play a leading role (and may hold suitable target audience who can and are interested to participate) in the discourse of ethics in AI-based assessment practices.

In summary, the landscape is still at the early phases of the technology adoption curve, with enough room for researchers beyond the education domain. Present research is marginally led by the computer science discipline. However, research in this area is highly interdisciplinary, spanning from soft pure to hard applied disciplines, including but not limited to, education, computer science, educational and technology philosophy and psychology, social policy, and law. When applied on specific domains, it

Figure 5. Breakdown of author locations

Figure 6. Breakdown of publication source

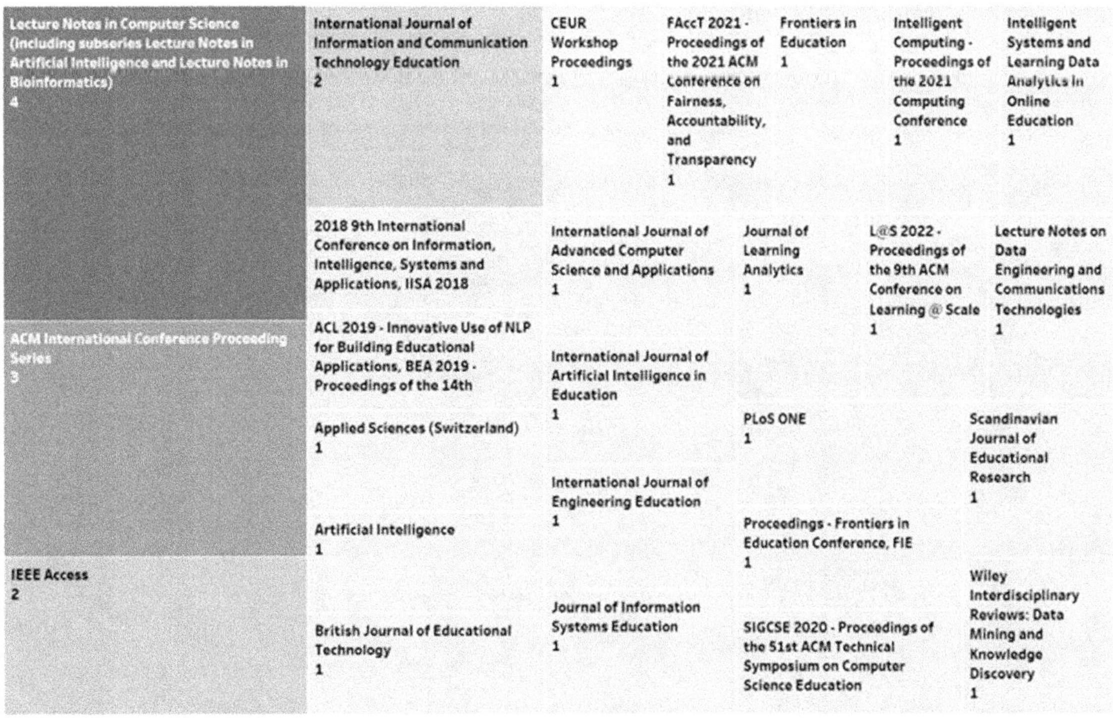

may also involve domain specific knowledge, such as sport science. Hence, a cross-pollination of ideas through inter-departmental collaborations can be highly beneficial to advance in this field.

First Pass of Topic Modelling and Network Analyses

Topic modelling was performed, where the optimal number of topics were generated using a model with the highest topic coherence. Further, we performed network analyses to identify topic clusters. These allowed us to recognize patterns in an unsupervised machine learning approach.

From this first pass of topic modelling, ten latent topics were identified. For instance, in Fig. 7, we observed the latent topic of AI modelling and predictive analytics that might be relatively more closely linked to ethical issues of explainability and fairness. This mirrored well with the network analyses visualization in Fig. 8. Here, we observed a more granular fourteen latent topic clusters, with the clusters of *Modelling*, and *Predictive Analytics and At-Risk Students*, situated in close proximity in the cluster diagram. The higher granularity of the outputs allowed us to identify distinct sub-themes of AI application areas and ethical issues. The top keywords and latent topics of topic modeling are shown in Table 1.

Through the review of the first pass of topic modelling, network analyses outputs, and full paper reviews, the study extensively identified fourteen sub-themes of AI application areas and ten sub-themes of ethical issues. We populate them in Tables 2 and 3, respectively.

Research Question (RQ) 2: *What are the main AI use cases relating to assessments?*

Figure 7. Topic modelling of keyword corpuses

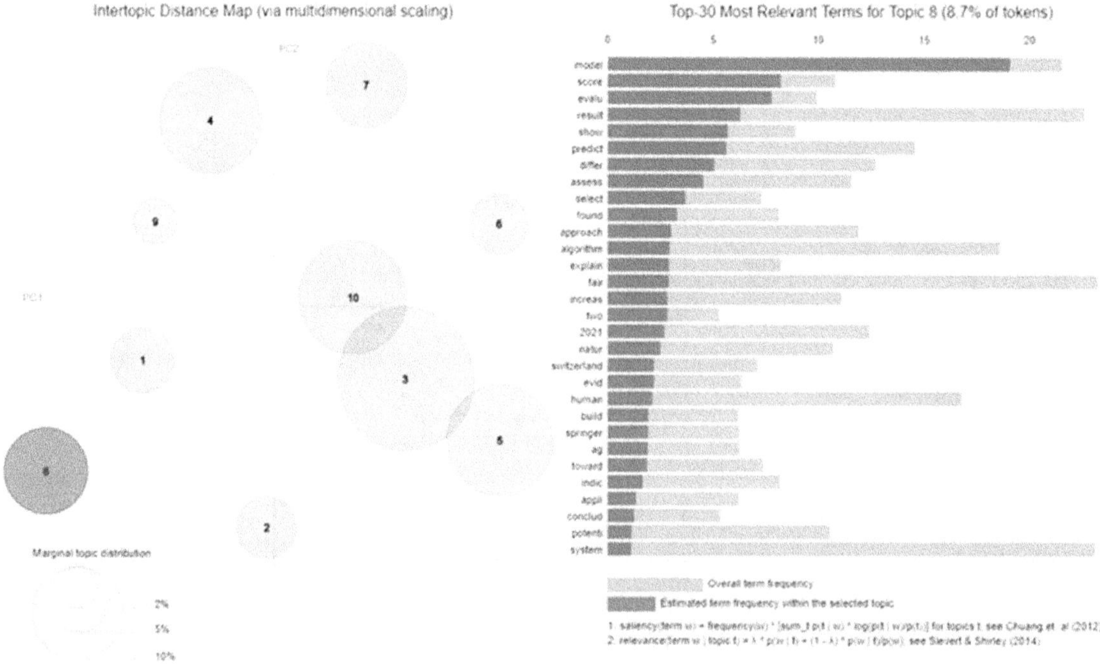

Table 1. First pass of topic modelling: Latent topic and top keywords

Latent Topic	Percentage of Tokens	Top Keywords
Engineering systems	5.0%	Build; Design; Model; Technology; System
Automated grading	14.5%	Feedback; Response; Evaluation; Grading; Automation
Intelligent tutoring and feedback	23.9%	AI; Teacher; Intelligent; Support; Feedback
Predictive analytics and at-risk students	13.0%	Predict; Improve; Support; Measure; Environment
Explainable AI	4.5%	Explainable; Fair; Ethic; Algorithm; Review
Forecasting	4.3%	Forecast; Model; Automation; Learning; Predict
Adaptive robots	4.3%	Adapt; Environment; Tool; Robot; System
Modeling	8.7%	Model; Score; Evaluation; Result; Predict
Security and cheating	2.50%	Privacy; Data; Institution; Risk; Ethics
Assessment tasks	15.10%	Curation; Delivery; Task; Construct; Generate

Figure 8. Network analysis of keyword corpuses

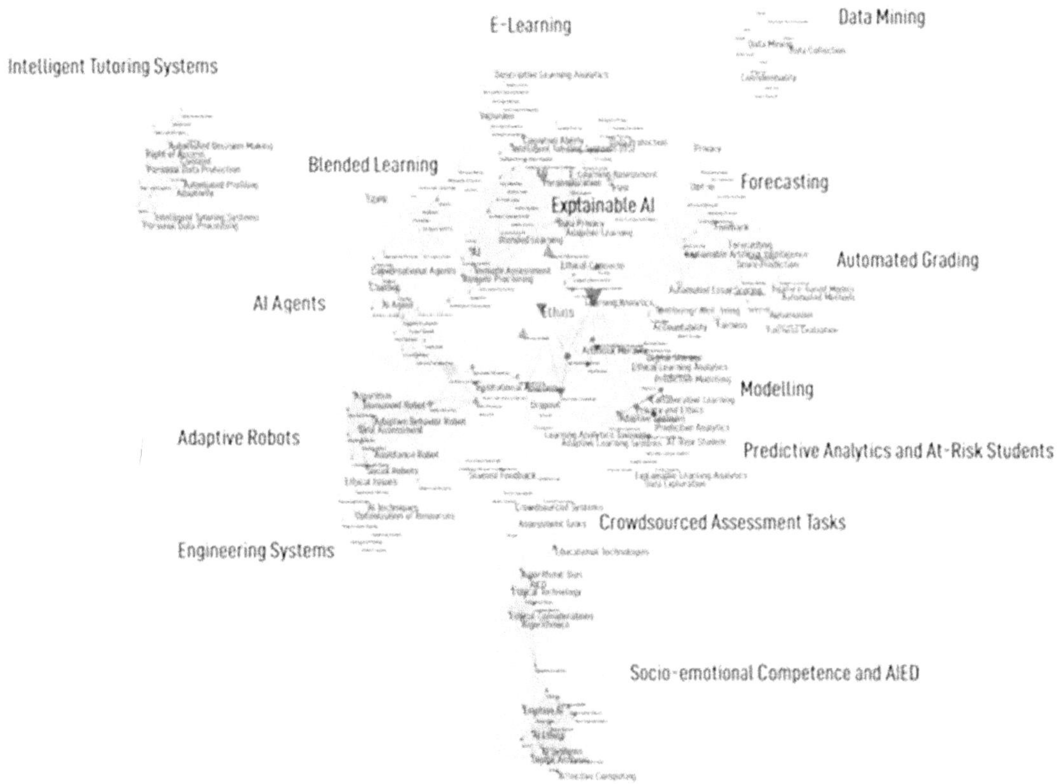

As shown in Table 2, the fourteen sub-themes of AI application areas were, namely:

- *AI-based assessment construction, curation, or delivery*

Table 2. Breakdown of sub-themes of AI application areas by paper

Paper	Applications of AI Related to Assessments														Note
	Construction, curation, or delivery	Socio-emotional assessment	Group assessment	Learning intervention/ assistance	Behavioral tracking	Personalized feedback	Predictive analytics	Teaching evaluation	Grading and response	Proctoring	Authentication and security	Plagiarism detection	Communication dashboard	Autonomous intelligent agent	
Gupta and Chen (2022)	•														- Telegram chatbot @dawebot, an AI-enabled conversational agent, provides formative assessments via multiple choice questions in any subject (Pereira, 2016)
Chounta et al. (2022)	•					•	•								-
Deho et al. (2022)				•			•								-
Shabaninejad et al. (2022)				•		•									-
Nazaretsky, Cukurova and Alexandron (2022)	•			•		•									-
Pontual Falcão et al. (2022)				•		•									-
Merikko et al. (2022)				•		•									-
Khairy et al. (2022)	•														-
Megahed, Abdel-Kader and Soliman (2022)									•						-
Conati et al. (2021)	•														- AI-driven hints on assessments delivered through Intelligent Tutoring System
González-Calatayud, Prendes-Espinosa and Roig-Vila (2021)	•			•		•			•						-
White et al. (2021)					•										- Tracking data of assessment behaviour applied for learning intervention
Ahn et al. (2021)									•						-
Stark and Hoey (2021)		•													-
Papa and Jackson (2021)														•	-

continued on following page

Table 2. Continued

Paper	Applications of AI Related to Assessments														Note
	Construction, curation, or delivery	**Socio-emotional assessment**	**Group assessment**	**Learning intervention/ assistance**	**Behavioral tracking**	**Personalized feedback**	**Predictive analytics**	**Teaching evaluation**	**Grading and response**	**Proctoring**	**Authentication and security**	**Plagiarism detection**	**Communication dashboard**	**Autonomous intelligent agent**	
Kim et al. (2021)						•									-
Litman et al. (2021)									•						-
Casas-Roma and Conesa (2021)				•		•		•	•					•	-
Costas-Jauregui et al. (2021)				•		•							•		-
Elshafey et al. (2021)										•					-
Schneider, Dowell and Thompson (2021)			•												- Application of collaborative analytics in group assessments
Gedrimiene et al. (2020)	•			•		•									-
Kumar and Boulanger (2020)						•	•		•						-
Khosravi, Sadiq and Gasevic (2020)	•														-
Martín Núñez and Lantada (2020)	•			•		•			•						-
Hakami and Hernández-Leo (2020)				•		•		•	•					•	-
Mougiakou, Papadimitriou and Virvou (2019)	•			•		•			•						-
Mayfield et al. (2019)	•			•		•			•						-
Latham and Goltz (2019)	•			•		•									- AI conversational agent - AI-driven hints on assessments delivered through Intelligent Tutoring System
Tlili et al. (2019)	•			•		•									-
Kiennert et al. (2019)										•	•	•			-
Peña-Ayala (2018)	•	•		•		•	•								-
Tlili et al. (2018)	•			•		•		•							-
Total Count	**15**	**2**	**1**	**17**	**1**	**18**	**5**	**3**	**10**	**2**	**1**	**1**	**1**	**3**	
Percentage	*45%*	*6%*	*3%*	*52%*	*3%*	*55%*	*15%*	*9%*	*30%*	*6%*	*3%*	*3%*	*3%*	*9%*	

AI can be a useful tool to:

- construct assessments organically through, e.g., the use of generative AI to generate draft question samples for an assessment practitioner's review (Last and Danon, 2020);
- construct assessments collaboratively through e.g., crowdsourcing of assessment tasks (Ahn et al., 2021); and
- curate and deliver personalized formative assessment (Gupta and Chen, 2022; Heo & Lee, 2019) through e.g., curating multiple choice format formative assessments generated via AI conversational agents (Pereira, 2016).

This form of AI utilization is cited in 45% of the primary studies. This is the third highest cited AI utilization form.

- *AI-based socio-emotional assessment*

AI can be used to:

- assess non-cognitive psycho-emotional behavior qualities, such as persistence and grit, initiative and adaptability etc., through ambient intelligence (Stark and Hoey, 2021; Williamson, 2021); and
- discover socio-emotional patterns that may be predictive of assessment performance (Peña-Ayala, 2018).

This form of AI utilization is cited in 6% of the primary studies.

- *AI-based group assessment using collaborative analytics*

AI can be used to:

- assess collaborative dynamics in group projects through the application of analytics on learners' rich multimodal interaction data; and
- model interdependent relationships to support students' collaboration dynamics through adaptive methods (Schneider, Dowell and Thompson, 2021).

This form of AI utilization is cited in 3% of the primary studies.

- *AI-derived opportunities for learning intervention or assistance*

AI can be useful for:

- identifying and supporting learning intervention opportunities in formative assessments (Shabaninejad et al., 2021; White et al., 2021); and
- providing scaffolding assistance in assessments, e.g., with the help of AI-driven hints through Intelligent Tutoring Systems (Conati et al., 2021; Latham and Goltz, 2019).

This form of AI utilization is cited in 52% of the primary studies. This is the second highest cited AI utilization form.

- *AI-generated personalized feedback*

AI can be a useful tool to personalize feedbacks in terms of:

- clarifying approaches to attempt a new assessment;
- reviewing assessment performance; and/or
- recommending takeaways from assessments to improve learners' demonstration of competence at their current or future workplace (Gupta and Chen, 2022; Merikko et al., 2022).

This form of AI utilization is cited in 55% of the primary studies. This is the highest cited AI utilization form.

- *AI-based predictive analytics*

AI can be a useful tool to predict assessment outcomes, to support educators' focus on learning scaffolding (Chounta et al., 2022; Kim et al., 2021).

This form of AI utilization is cited in 15% of the primary studies. This is the fifth highest cited AI utilization form.

- *AI-based teaching evaluation*

The term '*assessment*' in an educational context is extended to the assessing of educators as a formal evaluation process to review teaching effectiveness and perform in classrooms (Tlili et al., 2018).

This form of AI utilization is cited in 9% of the primary studies.

- *AI-facilitated response and grading*

AI can be a useful tool for:

- adaptive understanding and responding to learners in formative assessments (Khairy et al., 2022); and
- automated grading of structured (e.g., multiple choice questions) and non-structured (e.g., open-ended or essay questions) assessment responses (Litman et al., 2021; Kumar and Boulanger, 2020).

This form of AI utilization is cited in 30% of the primary studies. This is the fourth highest cited AI utilization form.

- *AI-based proctoring*

AI can be a useful tool to proctor on-site (e.g., in classrooms or exam halls) or remotely (e.g., online assessment on Massive Open Online Courses, or MOOCs) to lower the risk of cheating in quizzes and exams (Elshafey et al., 2021).

This form of AI utilization is cited in 6% of the primary studies.

- *AI-based authentication and security gateways for the conducting of assessments*

AI can be used to build authentication and security measures in assessment systems, so that the risk of personal and educational data leakage and exploitation can be lowered (Kiennert et al, 2019).

This form of AI utilization is cited in 3% of the primary studies.

- *AI-backed plagiarism detection in assignment submissions*

AI can be a useful tool to perform plagiarism detections, so that assignment submissions that present someone else's works or ideas without acknowledgement or consent can be detected (Kiennert et al, 2019).

This form of AI utilization is cited in 3% of the primary studies.

- *AI-integrated communication dashboard for assessment outputs*

An AI-integrated communication of assessment outputs can be designed in an inclusive format that promotes:

- clear automated communication and feedback of assessments, accounting for the nuanced sensitivity of communications that may be absent in poorly designed AI-based text generators or audio-visual responses; and
- automation of inclusiveness actions. For instance, for learners with disabilities (such as motor disabilities), there may be an automation of increased time limit catered to complete an assessment (Costas-Jauregui et al., 2021).

This form of AI utilization is cited in 3% of the primary studies.

- *Autonomous intelligent agents for assessment purposes*

This relates to the care given to the design of AI algorithms to create intelligent agents that make autonomous decisions for assessment purposes (Casas-Roma and Conesa, 2021; Hakami and Hernández-Leo, 2020).

This form of AI utilization is cited in 9% of the primary studies.

- *AI-based behavioral tracking for assessment purposes*

AI can be used to track spatio-temporal data of assessment behavior:

- to predict learning intervention opportunities; and/or
- for assessment evaluation purposes (White et al., 2021).

This form of AI utilization is cited in 3% of the primary studies.

Research Question (RQ) 3: *What are the main ethical issues arising from the AI implementations relating to assessments?*

As shown in Table 3, the ten sub-themes of ethical issues were, namely:

Inclusivity

This ethics principle relates to inclusive and accessibility considerations applied to AI systems to meet different student needs in a personalized environment at scale.

- Inclusiveness is concerned about exhibiting empathy towards sensitive learner conditions, such as health, disabilities and learning disorders (e.g., pregnancy, visual handicap, or dyslexia), gender, race, prior education backgrounds (e.g., non-native speakers), and socio-economic backgrounds. In the design of the AI system, actions are taken to respect the diversity of learners and ensure that prejudices, stereotypes, discrimination and biasness do not creep into assessments (Gupta and Chen, 2022; Martín Núñez and Lantada, 2020; Tlili et al., 2019).
- Inclusiveness is concerned about considering the sensitivity of communication and feedbacks generated by AI systems, so that learners are not negatively impacted by AI-generated textual comments or audio-visual responses when they clarify approaches to a new assessment or receive takeaways from completed assessments (Costas-Jauregui et al., 2021).
- Inclusiveness is concerned about lowering the chances of conformity, peer pressure and segregation that may be reinforced because of AI generated decisions, which can negatively impact both educators and learners (Gedrimiene et al., 2022).

This ethics principle is cited in 18% of the primary studies.

Fairness

This ethics principle relates to fair, equitable and appropriate assessment practices that should be perpetuated by AI systems. It is noted that the definition of fairness is plagued with problems of subjectivity, contextualization and cultural-specificity (Hakami and Hernández-Leo, 2020).

- Fairness is concerned about the treatment of data and algorithmic bias to ensure diversity, equity, non-prejudice and non-favoritism towards learners' sensitive attributes, so that needs of minority groups are not disadvantaged or underrepresented. This overlaps with the concept of inclusivity. (Gupta and Chen, 2022; Deho et al., 2022; Megahed, Abdel-Kader and Soliman, 2022; Casas-Roma and Conesa, 2021; Latham and Goltz, 2019; Tlili et al., 2019).
  Tied to this discourse are the ethical concepts of (Mayfield et al., 2019):
  (i) *Allocation harm:* This relates to the equitable distribution of resources of learning, such that the possibility of differential outcome distributions generated by AI systems are minimized.

(ii) *Representational harm:* This relates to the stereotyping biasness perpetuated by data and/or algorithm, resulting in the marginalizing of groups of learners.

- Fairness is concerned about the unintended labelling or profiling of learners, which can affect their learning journey and well-being (Peña-Ayala, 2018).
- Fairness is concerned about, in the context of socio-emotional assessments, how applying universal assumptions on emotional states are harmful, due to different cultural context of emotional interactions and norms (Stark and Hoey, 2021).
- Fairness is concerned about the ad hoc implementation of AI systems, in the absence of:
  (i) standard code of practices and ethics; and
  (ii) befitting monitoring and accounting mechanisms,
  which may impact the implementation of fair, equitable and appropriate assessment practices (Tlili et al., 2018).

This ethics principle is cited in 42% of the primary studies. This is the joint-second highest cited ethical issue, alongside explainability.

Accountability

This ethics principle relates to the responsible discharge of AI ethics when designing and delivering AI systems, depending on the roles and contexts, in a consistent manner. Stakeholders who construct, operate and use AI systems should be accountable for AI systems and decisions.

- Accountability is concerned about the moral obligation for institutions to reflect and act, given that it has access to data that may know and understand how students learn (Costas-Jauregui et al., 2021). Students are data subjects who are not generally able to influence the handling of data in an ethical manner (Gedrimiene et al., 2020).
  Care should be applied when overseeing sensitive data. It was noted that between 2007 and 2011, there were 133 incidents linked to educational institutions unintendedly disclosing sensitive learner information (Stiles, 2012). Such incidents can lead to reputational, legal and/or financial liabilities (Tlili et al., 2018).
- Accountability is concerned about the processes where relevant stakeholders provide reasons and take responsibilities for the actions of decisions influenced by AI algorithms (Hakami and Hernández-Leo, 2020). There should be proper consent, and non-maleficence academic interventions.
  For instance, in the development of AI systems for socio-emotional assessment, designers of AI systems should recognize and be accountable to the fact that there may exist diverse human attitudes to emotions to ensure fairness. Further, AI developers should also be cognizant that care should be applied to the underlying data, as data can be misused and emotions can be harnessed as a social phenomenon (Stark and Hoey, 2021).
- Accountability is concerned about demonstrating compliance with relevant regulations and guidelines (Latham and Goltz, 2019). However, it is noted that there may exist challenges relating to such compliance.
  For instance, there may exist a lack of interoperability of regulatory guidelines on misuse of private information (e.g., European Union and Latin America), and a lack of clarity regarding whether

if the institution or the students own the data that are shared by the students (Costas-Jauregui et al., 2021).

Furthermore, for online courses offered worldwide, informed consent for use of data can be affected by the data protection regulations where the learner is domiciled. This greatly increases the difficulty of compliance efforts (Tlili et al., 2018).

- Accountability is concerned about the availability of avenues for redress that are fair and unprejudiced due to the adverse use of AI systems to account for detrimental individual or societal effects.

This ethics principle is cited in 30% of the primary studies. This is the fourth highest cited AI utilization form.

Accuracy

This ethics principle relates to the reliability and validity of assessments when an AI system is applied. In the presence of possible biasness or errors introduced by data and AI algorithms, which may compromise the reliability and validity of assessments, there should exist measures to establish, log, communicate, diagnose and mitigate the biasness or errors.

- Accuracy is concerned about poor data quality.

  For instance, due to the distributed nature of online learning, data collected may be incomplete or erroneous. Linked to this latter notion is the right for data subjects to check and rectify data collected, so that data inputs are accurate.

  Poor data quality can negatively impact AI-driven decisions (Tlili et al., 2018).
- Accuracy is concerned about inappropriate data inputs.

  For instance, predictive models with imbalanced dataset (e.g., gender) may generate less effective predictions (e.g., for minority gender). The possibility of discriminatory and unfair practice extends to other socio-economic demographical information, such as ethnicity, underrepresented groups etc. (Chounta et al., 2022).

  In another example, in the implementation of collaborative analytics, it is vital to capture multimodal data that best represents and assesses the collaborative interactions of students, otherwise the AI-generated outputs cannot be relied upon (Schneider, Dowell and Thompson, 2021).
- Accuracy is concerned about inaccurate understanding and interpretation of learner responses in assessments.

  For instance, adaptable humanoid robot may not understand or interpret the responses of learners in an oral assessment well. Correct answer rate, if affected by learner's pronunciation or robot's lack of contextual understanding, can affect confidence in the AI system (Khairy et al., 2022).

  Research by Ahn et al. (2021) also showed that automated grading of learners' work, which contains complex data, rich semantic meaning and idiosyncratic and local nuances, may not be well graded by present computational approaches that utilize metrics such as counts of parts of speech and essay length as proxies for writing complexity and quality.

  Further, present systems are generally rigid in formulation of tasks and grading. For instance, the rejection of lexicon and grammar of minority dialects. This limits the choice of tasks, types of acceptable answers and styles of writing (Mayfield et al., 2019).
- Accuracy is concerned about the validity and reliability of an assessment instrument.

Kim et al. (2021) shared that, to allow for shorter assessments in online learning, it is imperative that the question set reduction guided by AI algorithms is done in such a way where the reduced set is able to approximate the original assessment's evaluation of learning. This can help ensure reliability and trust on assessment instrument.

- Accuracy is concerned with the treatment of prediction errors and biases.
  For instance, in the case of cheating detection, the treatment of non-cheating cases that were falsely detected as cheating (or false positives), and cheating cases that were not detected (or false negatives). The false positives and negatives will have to be reduced to improve accuracy rates (Kiennert et al., 2019) .
- Accuracy is concerned about the possibility of inaccurate predictions, due to the "gaming" of AI systems.
  For instance, there exist a possibility for students to modify their behavior and "game" the AI system, when they have the knowledge that they are assessed by the AI system, and the knowledge of the parameters of the AI model. This can create inaccurate AI decisions when assessing students (Tlili et al., 2018).

This ethics principle is cited in 27% of the primary studies. This is the fifth highest cited AI utilization form.

Auditability

This ethics principle relates to the permitting of independent third-party reviewers to audit, analyze and report findings relating to the usage and design of data and AI algorithms in assessments.

Auditability is concerned about the understanding, validating, reviewing and improving of the AI system applied, so that there are appropriate transparency, traceability and utilization of data and AI algorithms, and appropriate validity and reliability of assessment instruments. However, it is noted that challenges may arise if algorithms are proprietary (Tlili et al., 2019; Casas-Roma and Conesa, 2021).

This ethics principle is cited in 9% of the primary studies.

Explainability

This ethics principle relates to the lowering of opacity relating to data, AI algorithms and AI-driven decisions, the justification of its use, and the communication of details in a non-technical easy-to-understand manner to relevant stakeholders (Kumar and Boulanger, 2020; Casas-Roma and Conesa, 2021).

- Explainability is concerned with transparency of the design of AI systems. Transparency is tied to information availability, accessibility conditions, possibility of pragmatic decision-making assistance, and user knowledge (Nazaretsky, Cukurova and Alexandron, 2022).
  It is importance for AI-based assessments to be developed in an explainable and transparent manner to safeguard trust and fairness with human stakeholders. For instance, for AI recommender systems, why are some assessment questions recommended over others (Chounta et al., 2022). "Black-box" AI recommendations, which provide low or no insights into recommendation rationales (Abdi, 2020), may be plagued with biases and confounding problems (Bastani,

Bastani and Kim, 2018; Khosravi et al., 2021), resulting in unjustified actions and discrimination (Papa and Jackson, 2021).

However, it is noted that full transparency may be harmful, as users can "game" the system to their benefit and the detriment of others (Hakami and Hernández-Leo, 2020). Furthermore, challenges may arise from disclosure of proprietary algorithms or trade secrets (Latham and Goltz, 2019).

- Explainability is concerned about the use of explanations to gain insights into the behavior of AI systems.

  Present explainability approaches include global and local approaches. The former synthesizes and uncovers qualities of inputs that affects model behaviors on a global basis, whereas the latter looks to explain the model's behavior to a specific input. Another more recent approach is to leverage on generative capabilities of models to self-explain a human-understandable explanation for input-output responses (Bommasani et al., 2021).
- Explainability is concerned about tradeoffs relating interpretability and complexity of AI systems.

  The design of the AI algorithms may be potentially complex. For instance, for collaborative analytics, the use of interdependent modelling to assess group dynamics and outcomes, may raise challenges on explainability of AI systems. Interdependent models (which looks at students' influences on one another over time) may be significantly more complex than independent models (which looks at students as isolated events). There is a need to assess the trade-off between model complexity and explainability, and ascertain if simpler models are sufficient to model dynamic interdependence (Schneider, Dowell and Thompson, 2021).

  Deho et al. (2022) suggests that interpretable models (e.g., logistic regression) may provide less unfairness as compared to complex fairness-aware models, with robust accuracy results (Kung and Yu, 2020). This supports the notion of using interpretable and explainable models for AI in assessments.
- Explainability is concerned about the absence of theoretical basis to justify the development and use of AI system for assessment purposes.

  González-Calatayud, Prendes-Espinosa and Roig-Vila (2021) cites a lack of pedagogical underpinning and AI training, which affects the meaningful development of assessments with pedagogical reference models when AI is applied.

This ethics principle is cited in 42% of the primary studies. This is the joint-second highest cited ethical issue, alongside fairness.

Privacy

This ethics principle relates to the protection of data subjects against injurious effects from the use of personal information applied in AI systems, without unduly affecting regulatory compliance tied to privacy and restricting AI development.

- Privacy is concerned about the governance of end-to-end data stewardship, including data collection, storage, disclosure, sharing, security and disposal when applied to AI assessments (Chounta et al., 2022).

Kiennert et al. (2019) highlights the importance on the management of sensitive data, such as authentication and biometric samples (e.g., data collected for password, voice recognition, facial recognition and/or keystroke detection). Leakage of these data can cause risk of harm. AI systems should be secure and not vulnerable to tampering.

Stark and Hoey (2021) highlights how individuals are sensitive about data sharing and utilization pertaining to their emotions and emotional expressions. For example, the Facebook emotional contagion study (Kramer, Guillory and Hancock, 2014) were criticized for manipulating emotive content of users.

Safeguarding of trust and confidence in the governance of data stewardship are important for stakeholder security, privacy and risk of harm (White et al., 2021).

- Privacy is concerned about the implementation of fair data stewardship practices such as notice, access, and choice (Mougiakou, Papadimitriou and Virvou, 2019).

Explicit consent should be obtained from data subjects, such that users should be given the right to maintain control over data usage, control the purpose and extent of usage, be granted the option to modify the usage and context, and be given the right to opt in and out of participation. It is noted that consent involving minors can be challenging, as this may require both the students' and their parents' consents (Latham and Goltz, 2019).

Students who wish to join or withdraw from certain AI-influenced activities may be allowed to do so, especially vulnerable groups such as students with learning disorders, language barriers, or students who come from lower socio-economic backgrounds (Gedrimiene et al., 2020). Educator may also exercise the right to opt in or out of participation in AI-driven teaching evaluation (Tlili et al., 2018). The possibility to opt in or out may result in data gaps that can affect accuracy of results and research outcomes, indirectly isolate and reveal outcomes of those who opt in or out, and affect discharge of institutional duty to enhance learning experience for students (Tlili et al., 2019).

Merikko et al. (2022) finds that learners are open to sharing data related to demographics and learning performance, but are apprehensive about sharing when it comes to their online behavior, sensitive or process data. Further, the more personal and granular the data are, the less likely the learners will share them. Furthermore, learners who were not performing well are less likely to share their performance data. This may be tied to help-seeking avoidance, as seeking help may be a sign of weakness and a threat to self-esteem (White and Bembenutty, 2013).

- Privacy is concerned about constant surveillance arising from AI use (Megahed, Abdel-Kader and Soliman, 2022).

There may exist a possibility of violation to individuals' rights to privacy when too much data surveillance exists, especially when data is used beyond academic purposes, for control and surveillance to modify human behavior (Pontual Falcão et al., 2022). Mayfield et al. (2019) discusses the undesirable anxieties and behavioral change related to constant surveillance.

This ethics principle is cited in 55% of the primary studies. This is the highest cited ethical issue.

Trust

This ethics principle relates to the placing of confidence on (i) AI systems and the (ii) provision of data to achieve assessment objectives. The former is a characteristic of the human-machine relationship formed with an AI system. Low trust is largely linked to the lack of human properties (e.g., lack of affect, emotions, pedagogical intuition) in AI systems (Nazaretsky, Cukurova and Alexandron, 2022). The latter is related to the preservation of privacy.

- Trust is concerned about the ability to rely on AI systems to make decisions and provide feedback.
  Pontual Falcão et al. (2022) suggests discomfort among students and educators of AI-driven decision making that involves ranking, sorting and classifying individuals, that may reflect political interests, social values, and risks of omissions or biases.
  In addition, the same paper shares that learners and educators were not confident that incorporating AI in assessments can result in improvements of feedback quality.
- Trust is concerned about the presence of a clear and global consensus of purposes and specifications of AI systems.
  For instance, with regards to socio-emotional assessments, Stark and Hoey (2021) highlights a lack of consensus objective agreement on emotion at a global level as an issue. This is because, in the absence of a consensus, the large variation in the implied social and ethical responsibilities have normative implications for AI systems e.g., while considering ethical values such as accountability and fairness when assessing socio-emotional qualities in learners. This affects trust on AI systems.
- Trust is concerned about the autonomy and control that stakeholders have on AI systems.
  For instance, Pontual Falcão et al. (2022) cites educators' discomfort at lack of autonomy and control due to its use in the appraisal of teaching performance and excessive intrusion in learners' learning routine. Learners may also be worried that their autonomy and independent decision making may be deprived.

This ethics principle is cited in 12% of the primary studies.

Human Centricity

This ethics principle relates to the aim towards upholding human agency, dignity and autonomy, minimization of harm (and when necessary, weighed against a greater good), and equitable distribution of benefits.

- Human centricity is concerned about agency and autonomy of users. This overlaps with the concept of trust.
  Users should not be impacted by profiling, ranking and personalizing derived from AI algorithms. Learning should not be viewed as "*product-oriented learning experiences*" (Duignan, 2020).
  There should be care applied, when it comes to AI algorithm manipulating learner behaviors and emotions (Papa and Jackson, 2021).
  AI systems should not negatively impact a learner's capacity to learn and his/ her level of autonomy to make learning decisions. There should exist a presence of reversible and clear processes, and the possibility to intervene for blocking, termination, correction and erasure (Mougiakou, Papadimitriou and Virvou, 2019).
- Human centricity is concerned about fair allocation of resources.
  Users should not have differential access and availability of technology and resources, such that risk of digital divide and technology exclusion arises. Further, the risk of forming unfair

groups due to classification and profiling should be mitigated, to ensure equitable learning opportunities (Casas-Roma and Conesa, 2021).

- Human centricity is concerned about the states of human wellbeing (e.g., psychological wellbeing and satisfaction). A well-designed AI system should seek to achieve positive states of human wellbeing.

This ethics principle is cited in 12% of the primary studies.

Cheating

This ethics principle relates to dishonest and deceptive learner behavior to violate assessment rules and regulations.

Cheating is concerned about the identification of dishonest and deceptive assessment behaviors through the use of AI-based proctoring and plagiarism detection, both in physical venues and remote assessment platforms (Elshafey et al., 2021; Kiennert et al., 2019).

This ethics principle is cited in 6% of the primary studies.

Second Pass of Topic Modelling and Network Analyses

Next, we utilize the keyword corpuses of fourteen sub-themes of AI application areas and ten sub-themes of ethical issues as an input, to perform the second pass of topic modelling, and network analyses.

Research identified five topical archetypes via topic modelling. For instance, in Fig. 9, we observed the dominant latent topic linked to AI-based assessment construction and rollout aspects. This mirrored well with the network analyses visualization in Fig. 10. In the network analysis diagram, we observed a clear clustering of five topics, with *Assessment Construction and Rollout* similarly dominant in the cluster diagram. The top keywords and latent topics of topic modeling are shown in Table 4.

Understanding of these five key archetypical themes allow researchers and practitioners to breakdown the landscape into clear segments, to decide which area they would like to develop further insights and applications.

DISCUSSION

Morley et al. (2020) emphasizes on the importance of the translation of AI principles into the 'what' and 'how' of implementation. Building on the work of preceding sections, this section discusses actionable insights to make the addressing of AI ethics operable in the real world.

Research Question (RQ) 4: *What are the key themes of the systematic literature map?*

Ontology can be defined as "*an explicit specification of a conceptualization*" (Gruber, 1993), geared towards a "*shared taxonomy of entities*" (Smith and Welty, 2001), as applied in information systems. This is opposed to the philosophical use of the concept of ontology as a nature of reality (Ashok et al., 2022). The investigation of AI systems can be considered a sub-field of information systems.

Table 3. Breakdown of sub-themes of ethical issues by paper

Paper	AI Ethical Issue(s) as Cited in Paper									
	Inclusivity	**Fairness**	**Accountability**	**Accuracy**	**Auditability**	**Explainability**	**Privacy**	**Trust**	**Human centricity**	**Cheating**
Gupta and Chen (2022)	•	•								
Chounta et al. (2022)		•	•	•	•	•	•			
Deho et al. (2022)		•				•				
Shabaninejad et al. (2022)						•				
Nazaretsky, Cukurova and Alexandron (2022)			•			•		•		
Pontual Falcão et al. (2022)							•	•		
Merikko et al. (2022)							•			
Khairy et al. (2022)				•						
Megahed, Abdel-Kader and Soliman (2022)		•					•			
Conati et al. (2021)						•				
González-Calatayud, Prendes-Espinosa and Roig-Vila (2021)						•				
White et al. (2021)							•			
Ahn et al. (2021)				•						
Stark and Hoey (2021)		•	•				•	•		
Papa and Jackson (2021)		•				•			•	
Kim et al. (2021)				•						
Litman et al. (2021)		•		•		•				
Casas-Roma and Conesa (2021)		•			•	•	•		•	
Costas-Jauregui et al. (2021)	•		•				•	•		
Elshafey et al. (2021)										•
Schneider, Dowell and Thompson (2021)	•			•		•				
Gedrimiene et al. (2020)	•		•				•			
Kumar and Boulanger (2020)						•				
Khosravi, Sadiq and Gasevic (2020)			•				•			
Martín Núñez and Lantada (2020)	•						•			
Hakami and Hernández-Leo (2020)		•	•			•			•	
Mougiakou, Papadimitriou and Virvou (2019)							•		•	
Mayfield et al. (2019)		•		•			•			
Latham and Goltz (2019)		•	•			•	•			
Tlili et al. (2019)	•	•	•		•	•	•			
Kiennert et al. (2019)				•			•			•
Peña-Ayala (2018)		•					•			
Tlili et al. (2018)		•	•	•			•			
Total Count	**6**	**14**	**10**	**9**	**3**	**14**	**18**	**4**	**4**	**2**
Percentage	*18%*	*42%*	*30%*	*27%*	*9%*	*42%*	*55%*	*12%*	*12%*	*6%*

Ashok et al., (2022) describes three fundamental domains to conceptually represent the interweaving ethical elements and interrelationships inherent in the design and application of AI in digital technologies. This is theoretically underpinned by ontological frameworks of Ogden and Richards (1923), Popper (1979) and Project and Peirce (1998).

This triadic framework is a modular architecture of an assemblage of technological components that consist of the:

Figure 9. Topic modelling of corpuses involving AI application areas and related ethical principles

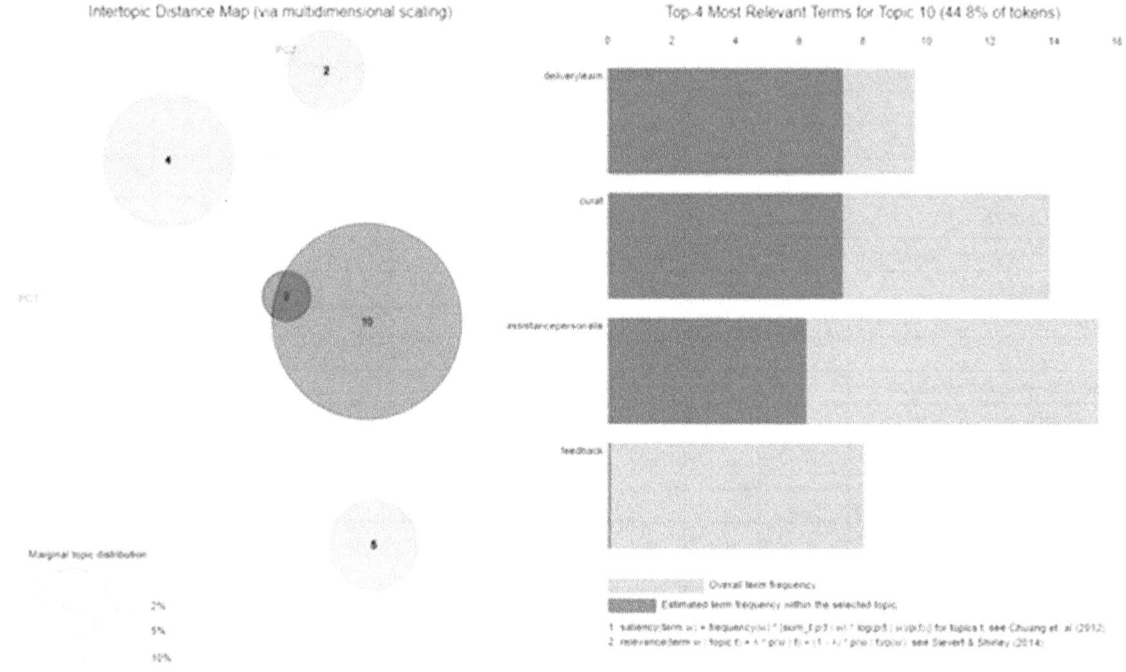

Table 4. Second pass of topic modelling: Latent topic and top keywords

Latent Topic	Percentage of Tokens	Top Keywords
System design and check	*7.5%*	System; Design; Review
Data stewardship and surveillance	*2.9%*	Privacy; Sensitive; Data
Assessment construction and rollout	*44.8%*	Deliver; Curate; Personalize
Assessment administration	*9.6%*	Proctor; Plagiarism; Cheat
Grading and evaluation	*20.7%*	Evaluation; Feedback; Response

- *Physical domain* (or the referent or object in semiotics): This includes the: (i) *device layer* which comprises a logical capability operating system layer, and the physical machinery hardware layer; and the (ii) *network layer* which comprises the logical transmission network protocol layer and physical network transport layer.

  Some relevant applications are author systems, intelligent tutoring shells, AI-integrated learning environments, educational robotics, and AI collaborative tools.
- *Cognitive domain* (or the symbol or science in semiotics): This comprises the *content layer* where data is stored, created, mapped, manipulated, utilized, and shared.

  Some relevant examples are multimodal structured contents of text, and unstructured contents of images, sounds and videos of assessment submissions. This layer also provides the metadata and directory information of users, content tags, location stamps, time stamps, encoding and copyright etc.

Figure 10. Network analyses of corpuses involving AI application areas and related ethical principles

- *Information domain* (or the reference or interpretant in semiotics): This comprises the *service layer* which encompasses the functionality of the application and its interaction with users, underpinned by AI algorithms.
  Some relevant examples are use of knowledge representation for instructions, human factor and interface design, and AI-integrated visualization and graphics for feedbacks.

We extend the triadic ontological framework as described by Ashok et al., (2022) to model and visualize the systematic literature map of this chapter (Fig. 11). We note that, over and above the triadic domains, Ashok et al., (2022) further describes a governance domain, defined by Floridi, (2018) as *"the practice of establishing and implementing policies, procedures, and standards for the proper development, use, and management of the infosphere*." In our opinion, governance is a key consideration across all triadic domains, and hence, the governance domain is not explicitly illustrated in our framework.

The five distinct clusters identified by topic modelling and network analyses in Fig. 9 and Fig. 10 are mapped to the triadic ontological framework in Fig. 11, as follows:

- *AI system design and check for assessment purposes*

This phase extends across the physical, cognitive and information domains, and is involved with the design, implementation and maintenance of the AI system for system interactivity, robustness and security. From a predictive analytics point of view, the model constructed should be appropriate – upholding accuracy, inclusivity, accountability, privacy, trust and human centricity.

At this phase, the overriding ethics considerations are explainability and auditability. The AI system should be created with clear, easy-to-understand and transparent protocols, so that relevant stakeholders and independent third-party auditors can review the processes, perform interventions, mitigate issues, and

Figure 11. Visualization of the systematic literature map of key research themes

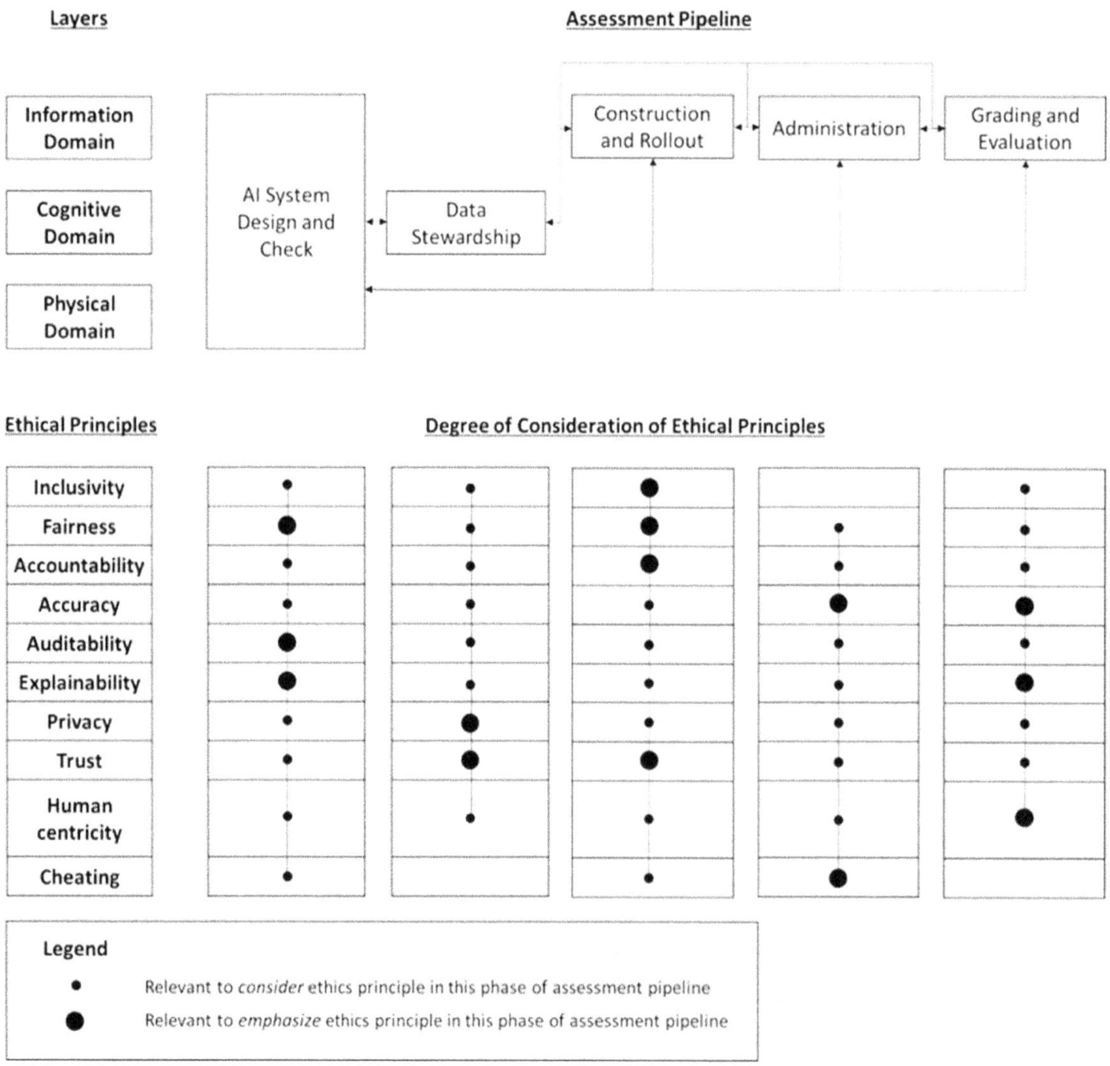

enable redress in an event of negative outcomes that may arise. In addition, fairness is concerned about the treatment of algorithmic bias to ensure diversity, equity, non-prejudice and non-favoritism towards learners' sensitive attributes, so that needs of minority groups are not disadvantaged or underrepresented.

- *Data stewardship and surveillance*

This phase extends across the cognitive and information domains, and is involved with the governance and implementation of good data stewardship, and appropriate surveillance practices (if any).

At this phase, the overriding ethics consideration is privacy. One instance is behavioral surveillance, which may be a violation to human rights to privacy especially when data is used beyond academic purposes, for control and surveillance to modify human behavior. In addition, trust is also an important facet concerned about the preservation of privacy when sensitive data are disclosed.

- *AI-based assessment construction and rollout*

This phase is predominantly situated in the information domain, and is involved with the construction, curation or delivery of assessment, the communication of evaluation and feedback with stakeholders via AI-integrated communication dashboards, and the carrying out of interventions and assistances to improve assessment and evaluation performance. Assessment and evaluation can be in the form of formative (or summative) individual (or group) cognitive (or socio-emotional) assessment. It can also be a form of teaching evaluation.

At this phase, the overriding ethics considerations are inclusivity and fairness, so that appropriate and equitable assessments and evaluations are rolled out, embracing diversity, empathy and sensitivity towards the evaluated stakeholders. Furthermore, accountability is an important ethics consideration, as there should exist a responsible discharge of AI ethical principles and compliance with relevant rules and guidelines, when designing and delivering AI-driven assessments. In addition, there should exist trust and confidence on AI systems to achieve assessment and evaluation objectives.

- *Administration of assessments using AI systems*

This phase is predominantly situated in the information domain, and is involved with the administration of assessment and evaluation, which may comprise authentication and security measures, proctoring and/or plagiarism detection.

At this phase, the overriding ethics considerations are the overcoming of cheating violations, and the application of accuracy to correctly identify assessment candidates and cheating cases.

- *AI-facilitated assessment grading and evaluation*

This phase is predominantly in the information domain, and is involved primarily with the interpretation of textual and/or audio-visual responses collected by AI systems, the evaluation of performance, and the provision of feedbacks. These may be performed by autonomous intelligent agents. From an educator's point of view, this phase may involve the evaluation of teaching effectiveness.

At this phase, the overriding ethics considerations are explainability, so evaluators can understand and adjudge if the grading and/or ranking is accurate and reliable. In addition, there is an element of human centricity. This largely relates to the agency and autonomy of human users, in the presence of AI-generated decisions, and the capacity to intervene for correction and redress.

There is an emphasis that the framework does not draw clear delineations when categorizing AI assessment use cases across triadic domains. For instance, the *Grading and Evaluation* research theme is predominantly arising from the cognitive domain. However, coding and rolling out a moral reasoning AI system for AI-generated decisions, evaluations, responses and feedbacks, a sub-item of this research theme, may straddle across all cognitive, information and physical domains. This said, the framework provides a guide to generalize observed phenomena.

Theoretical Implications

Understanding the ethical dimensions of the application of AI in assessments across the assessment creation pipeline, in a conceptual framework as shown in Fig. 11, are but the first steps toward informing a critical awareness and a more holistic approach in the governance, stewardship and regulation practices of ethics in this subject matter.

To steer this ethical discourse, building upon the framework proposed by Floridi (2018), it is useful to consider what are (i) politically feasible, (ii) culturally sustainable, (iii) socially acceptable, (iv) institutionally preferred, and (v) legally or rule enforceable, before elaborating and enforcing a system of rules to regulate agents' ethical behaviors. This requires a proactive and constructive normative cascade underpinned by theoretical and empirical foundations, rather than a reactive add-on afterthought that arise from societal backlashes, e.g., when stakeholders are negatively affected or when the public rejects legal recommendations.

A significant aspect of the theoretical discourse in this study discusses about hard ethics (i.e., the morally good or bad, or right or wrong duties, behavior, responsibilities, values and rights). This is a fundamentally important discourse as hard ethics helps make and shape regulations. However, there also exists the plane of soft ethics, that embodies normative ground over and above hard ethics, as a "*post-compliance ethics*" (Floridi, 2018). Even if regulations may already exist in the right side of the moral against the immoral divide, regulations do not cover everything, and human agents will need to leverage on ethics evaluation to guide and perform self-regulation of morality, especially if competing interests or values arise that need to be assessed and adjudged. Only then can we achieve good moral citizenry towards a mature infosphere.

Practical Implications

The triadic framework as discussed in this chapter provides a thematic guide to future applied research. In the translation of principles to practice, there may exist ethical risks that should be avoided. Floridi (2021) highlights the following "*ethics gerund*", namely: (i) *ethics shopping*, or the picking and choosing of ethics principles that are justified as a posteriori and retrofitted to pre-existing behaviors, (ii) *ethics bluewashing*, or the implementation of superficial or misleading measures to appear ethical, (iii) *ethics lobbying*, or the use of ethics to avoid or delay good and necessary regulation and enforcement, (iv) *ethics dumping*, or the export or import of unethical activities to a place with less strict regulations, and (v) *ethics shirking*, or the engaging of less ethical works over a period of time to lower the perceived resistance against such works. A misjudgment or misunderstanding can over time, in the lens of Socrates, lead to ethical malpractices.

CONCLUSION

Ethical check and balances should be put in place with the increasingly pervasive use of AI, especially when its growth trajectory appears seemingly aimed towards anthropomorphism, a reality further taking shape by recent advances in generative AI. Possible violations of fundamental human ethics in a societal institution as important as education should be looked upon with scrutiny.

In this study, we looked at how the design and use of AI in education, and in particular, assessments, can conform as closely as possible to basic ethical principles. We systematically investigated the key assessment components and ethical principles highlighted in existing literature, mapped them across the end-to-end assessment pipeline while accounting for different assessment types, and constructed a systematic literature mapping framework highlighting key archetypical research themes. The proposed systematic literature mapping framework allows researchers and practitioners to deep dive into key thematic research areas, facilitating practical implementation of ethics programs and activities in educational institutions.

Research identified five key archetypical research themes, namely (i) AI system design and check for assessment purposes, (ii) data stewardship and surveillance, (iii) AI-based assessment construction and rollout, (iv) administration of assessments using AI systems, and (v) AI-facilitated assessment grading and evaluation. Ten literature-derived ethical principles, namely, accuracy, privacy, human centricity, fairness, inclusivity, trust, explainability, cheating, accountability and auditability, were mapped to these research themes. The study summarizes and rationalizes the impact of each ethical element in each research area, and discusses theoretical and practical implications of the findings.

As highlighted in the limitations section, future work can extend the use of literature databank beyond Scopus, to include e.g., Web of Science, IEEE Xplore or EBSCO Host, in the systematic literature mapping exercise. Furthermore, to account for thematic diversity, the intrinsic value of the diversification of the archetypical research themes can be studied.

While this study is based upon the subject of assessments, the ethical elements of the discourse has relevance beyond assessments, and can be applied to other areas of AIED. Other future works can contribute to the examination on the underpinning theories relating the ontological, semantics, and the epistemological deliberations and practical applications of ethics in this subject matter, across the spheres of philosophy, learning, psychology, sociology and technology. In addition, practical applications of the actionable insights in this chapter, in a form of strategic and operational frameworks or case studies, can be another pragmatic endeavor by practitioners and researchers.

Herwix et al. (2022) highlighted the importance of more serious and systematic engagement with the selection, framing and prioritization of ethical issues. There is an emphasis among the state-of-the-art for the need to be more aware, anticipatory, reflecting and informed about the variety of perspectives and contemporary debates concerning AIED ethics. In particular, the relevancy and idiosyncrasy to assessments in our study can help bring forward distinctive actionable applications in this realm.

REFERENCES

Abdi, S., Khosravi, H., Sadiq, S., & Gasevic, D. (2020, March). Complementing educational recommender systems with open learner models. In *Proceedings of the Tenth International Conference on Learning Analytics & Knowledge* (pp. 360-365). ACM. 10.1145/3375462.3375520

Ahn, J., Nguyen, H., Campos, F., & Young, W. (2021, April). Transforming everyday information into practical analytics with crowdsourced assessment tasks. In *LAK21: 11th International Learning Analytics and Knowledge Conference* (pp. 66-76). ACM. 10.1145/3448139.3448146

Andersson, H., Svensson, A., Frank, C., Rantala, A., Holmberg, M., & Bremer, A. (2022). Ethics education to support ethical competence learning in healthcare: An integrative systematic review. *BMC Medical Ethics*, *23*(1), 29. doi:10.118612910-022-00766-z PMID:35305627

Andrews, D., Leitner, P., Schön, S., & Ebner, M. (2022). Developing a Professional Profile of a Digital Ethics Officer in an Educational Technology Unit in Higher Education. In *International Conference on Human-Computer Interaction* (pp. 157-175). Springer, Cham. 10.1007/978-3-031-05657-4_12

Ashok, M., Madan, R., Joha, A., & Sivarajah, U. (2022). Ethical framework for artificial intelligence and digital technologies. *International Journal of Information Management*, *62*, 102433. doi:10.1016/j.ijinfomgt.2021.102433

Australian Government. (2019). *Australia's Artificial Intelligence Ethics Framework*. Department of Industry, Science and Resources. https://www.industry.gov.au/publications/australias-artificial-intelligence-ethics-framework

Awad, E., Dsouza, S., Kim, R., Schulz, J., Henrich, J., Shariff, A., Bonnefon, J.-F., & Rahwan, I. (2018). The moral machine experiment. *Nature*, *563*(7729), 59–64. doi:10.103841586-018-0637-6 PMID:30356211

Aynaud, T. (2020). Python-louvain. *Louvain algorithm for community detection*. GitHub. https://github.com/taynaud/python-louvain

Bastani, H., Bastani, O., & Kim, C. (2018). Interpreting predictive models for human-in-the-loop analytics. *arXiv preprint arXiv:1705.08504.*

Bessen, J., Impink, S. M., & Seamans, R. (2022, July). The cost of ethical AI development for AI startups. In *Proceedings of the 2022 AAAI/ACM Conference on AI, Ethics, and Society* (pp. 92-106). ACM. 10.1145/3514094.3534195

Bigman, Y. E., & Gray, K. (2018). People are averse to machines making moral decisions. *Cognition*, *181*, 21–34. doi:10.1016/j.cognition.2018.08.003 PMID:30107256

Blanchard, E. G. (2012). On the weird nature of ITS/AIED conferences. In *International Conference on Intelligent Tutoring Systems* (Vol. 7315, pp. 280–285). Springer. 10.1007/978-3-642-30950-2_36

Bommasani, R., Hudson, D. A., Adeli, E., Altman, R., Arora, S., von Arx, S., & Liang, P. (2021). On the opportunities and risks of foundation models. *arXiv preprint arXiv:2108.07258.*

Borenstein, J., & Howard, A. (2021). Emerging challenges in AI and the need for AI ethics education. *AI and Ethics*, *1*(1), 61–65. doi:10.100743681-020-00002-7

Bozkurt, A. (2020). Educational technology research patterns in the realm of the digital knowledge age. *Journal of Interactive Media in Education*, *2020*(1), 18. doi:10.5334/jime.570

Breucker, P., Cointet, J., Hannud Abdo, A., Orsal, G., de Quatrebarbes, C., Duong, T., Martinez, C., Ospina Delgado, J. P., Medina Zuluaga, L. D., Gómez Peña, D. F., Sánchez Castaño, T. A., Marques da Costa, J., Laglil, H., Villard, L., & Barbier, M. (2016). *CorTexT Manager (version v2).* Cortext. https://docs.cortext.net

Campedelli, G. M. (2021). Where are we? Using Scopus to map the literature at the intersection between artificial intelligence and research on crime. *Journal of Computational Social Science*, *4*(2), 503–530. doi:10.100742001-020-00082-9

Casas-Roma, J., & Conesa, J. (2021). A literature review on artificial intelligence and ethics in online learning. *Intelligent Systems and Learning Data Analytics in Online Education*, 111-131. . doi:10.1016/B978-0-12-823410-5.00006-1

Chassang, G., Thomsen, M., Rumeau, P., Sèdes, F., & Delfin, A. (2021). An interdisciplinary conceptual study of Artificial Intelligence (AI) for helping benefit-risk assessment practices. *AI Communications*, *3*(4), 1–26. doi:10.3233/AIC-201523

Chaudhry, M. A., & Kazim, E. (2022). Artificial Intelligence in Education (AIEd): A high-level academic and industry note 2021. *AI and Ethics*, *2*(1), 157–165. doi:10.100743681-021-00074-z PMID:34790953

Chen, X., Xie, H., Zou, D., & Hwang, G. J. (2020). Application and theory gaps during the rise of artificial intelligence in education. *Computers and Education: Artificial Intelligence*, *1*, 100002. doi:10.1016/j.caeai.2020.100002

Chounta, I. A., Bardone, E., Raudsep, A., & Pedaste, M. (2022). Exploring teachers' perceptions of artificial intelligence as a tool to support their practice in Estonian K-12 education. *International Journal of Artificial Intelligence in Education*, *32*(3), 725–755. doi:10.100740593-021-00243-5

Conati, C., Barral, O., Putnam, V., & Rieger, L. (2021). Toward personalized XAI: A case study in intelligent tutoring systems. *Artificial Intelligence*, *298*, 103503. doi:10.1016/j.artint.2021.103503

Costas-Jauregui, V., Oyelere, S. S., Caussin-Torrez, B., Barros-Gavilanes, G., Agbo, F. J., Toivonen, T., Motz, R., & Tenesaca, J. B. (2021, October). Descriptive analytics dashboard for an inclusive learning environment. In 2021 IEEE Frontiers in Education Conference (FIE) (pp. 1-9). IEEE. doi:10.1109/FIE49875.2021.9637388

Deho, O. B., Zhan, C., Li, J., Liu, J., Liu, L., & Duy Le, T. (2022). How do the existing fairness metrics and unfairness mitigation algorithms contribute to ethical learning analytics? *British Journal of Educational Technology*, *53*(4), 822–843. doi:10.1111/bjet.13217

Duignan, P. A. (2020). *Navigating the future of learning: the role of smart technologies. Leading Educational Systems and Schools in Times of Disruption and Exponential Change: A Call for Courage, Commitment and Collaboration.* Emerald Publishing Limited., doi:10.1108/978-1-83909-850-520201012/full/html

Eicher, B., Polepeddi, L., & Goel, A. (2018). Jill Watson doesn't care if you're pregnant: Grounding AI ethics in empirical studies. *Proceedings of the 2018 AAAI/ACM Conference on AI, Ethics, and Society* (pp. 88-94). ACM. 10.1145/3278721.3278760

Elsevier. (2022). How Scopus works, Scopus contents. Elsevier. https://www. elsevier.com/solutions/ scopus/how-scopus-works/content

Elshafey, A. E., Anany, M. R., Mohamed, A. S., Sakr, N., & Aly, S. G. (2021). Dr. Proctor: A multi-modal AI-based platform for remote proctoring in education. In *International Conference on Artificial Intelligence in Education* (pp. 145-150). Springer, Cham. 10.1007/978-3-030-78270-2_26

European Parliament. (2021). Report on artificial intelligence in education, culture and the audiovisual sector (2020/2017(INI)). Committee on Culture and Education. https://www.europarl.europa.eu/ doceo/ document/A-9-2021-0127_EN.html

Fahimnia, B., Sarkis, J., & Davarzani, H. (2015). Green supply chain management: A review and bibliometric analysis. *International Journal of Production Economics*, *162*, 101–114. doi:10.1016/j. ijpe.2015.01.003

Floridi, L. (2018). Soft ethics and the governance of the digital. *Philosophy & Technology*, *31*(1), 1–8. doi:10.100713347-018-0303-9 PMID:30322997

Floridi, L. (2021). Translating principles into practices of digital ethics: Five risks of being unethical. In *Ethics, Governance, and Policies in Artificial Intelligence* (pp. 81–90). Springer. doi:10.1007/978-3-030-81907-1_6

Floridi, L., & Cowls, J. (2019). A unified framework of five principles for AI in society. *Harvard Data Science Review*, *1*(1).

Gedrimiene, E., Silvola, A., Pursiainen, J., Rusanen, J., & Muukkonen, H. (2020). Learning analytics in education: Literature review and case examples from vocational education. *Scandinavian Journal of Educational Research*, *64*(7), 1105–1119. doi:10.1080/00313831.2019.1649718

González-Calatayud, V., Prendes-Espinosa, P., & Roig-Vila, R. (2021). Artificial intelligence for student assessment: A systematic review. *Applied Sciences (Basel, Switzerland)*, *11*(12), 5467. doi:10.3390/ app11125467

Gruber, T. R. (1993). A translation approach to portable ontology specifications. *Knowledge Acquisition*, *5*(2), 199–220. doi:10.1006/knac.1993.1008

Gupta, S., & Chen, Y. (2022). Supporting inclusive learning using chatbots? A chatbot-led interview study. *Journal of Information Systems Education*, *33*(1), 98–108.

Hakami, E., & Hernández Leo, D. (2020). How are learning analytics considering the societal values of fairness, accountability, transparency and human well-being: A literature review. In Martínez-Monés A, Álvarez A, Caeiro-Rodríguez M, Dimitriadis Y (Eds.), Learning Analytics Summer Institute Spain 2020 (pp. 121-41). Aachen: CEUR. Valladolid, Spain.

Hanna, R., & Kazim, E. (2021). Philosophical foundations for digital ethics and AI ethics: A dignitarian approach. *AI and Ethics*, *1*(4), 405–423. doi:10.100743681-021-00040-9 PMID:34790944

Hendrycks, D., Carlini, N., Schulman, J., & Steinhardt, J. (2021). Unsolved problems in ML safety. *arXiv preprint arXiv:2109.13916.*

Heo, J., & Lee, J. (2019, July). CiSA: An inclusive chatbot service for international students and academics. In *International Conference on Human-Computer Interaction* (pp. 153-167). Springer, Cham. 10.1007/978-3-030-30033-3_12

Herwix, A., Haj-Bolouri, A., Rossi, M., Tremblay, M. C., Purao, S., & Gregor, S. (2022). Ethics in information systems and design science research: Five perspectives. *Communications of the Association for Information Systems, 50*(1), 589–616. doi:10.17705/1CAIS.05028

High-Level Expert Group on Artificial Intelligence (AI HLEG). (2019). *Ethics guidelines for Trustworthy AI.* European Commission. https://ec.europa.eu/futurium/en/ai-alliance-consultation.1.html

Hill, P., & Barber, M. (2014). *Preparing for a renaissance in assessment.* Pearson.

Hoekstra, A., & Kaptein, M. (2021). The integrity of integrity programs: Toward a normative framework. *Public Integrity, 23*(2), 129–141. doi:10.1080/10999922.2020.1776077

Hu, Q., & Rangwala, H. (2020). Towards fair educational data mining: A case study on detecting at-risk students. In *Proceedings of the 13th International Conference on Educational Data Mining (EDM 2020)* (pp. 431–437). ERIC.

Hussar, W. J., & Bailey, T. M. (2020). Projections of Education Statistics to 2028 (NCES 2020-024). U.S. Department of Education, Washington, DC: National Center for Education Statistics.

Hwang, G. J., & Chien, S. Y. (2022). Definition, roles, and potential research issues of the metaverse in education: An artificial intelligence perspective. *Computers and Education: Artificial Intelligence*, 100082.

IEEE. (2019). *Ethically aligned design.* IEEE. https://ethicsinaction.ieee.org/

Kabudi, T., Pappas, I., & Olsen, D. H. (2021). AI-enabled adaptive learning systems: A systematic mapping of the literature. *Computers and Education: Artificial Intelligence, 2*, 100017. doi:10.1016/j.caeai.2021.100017

Khairy, D., Alkhalaf, S., Areed, M. F., Amasha, M. A., & Abougalala, R. A. (2022). An algorithm for providing adaptive behavior to humanoid robot in oral assessment. *International Journal of Advanced Computer Science and Applications, 13*(9). doi:10.14569/IJACSA.2022.01309119

Khan, A. A., Badshah, S., Liang, P., Waseem, M., Khan, B., Ahmad, A., & Akbar, M. A. (2022, June). Ethics of AI: A systematic literature review of principles and challenges. In *Proceedings of the International Conference on Evaluation and Assessment in Software Engineering 2022* (pp. 383-392). ACM. 10.1145/3530019.3531329

Khosravi, H., Demartini, G., Sadiq, S., & Gasevic, D. (2021, April). Charting the design and analytics agenda of learnersourcing systems. In *LAK21: 11th International Learning Analytics and Knowledge Conference* (pp. 32-42). ACM. 10.1145/3448139.3448143

Khosravi, H., Sadiq, S., & Gasevic, D. (2020, February). Development and adoption of an adaptive learning system: Reflections and lessons learned. In *Proceedings of the 51st ACM Technical Symposium on Computer Science Education* (pp. 58-64). ACM. 10.1145/3328778.3366900

Khosravi, H., Shum, S. B., Chen, G., Conati, C., Tsai, Y. S., Kay, J., & Gašević, D. (2022). Explainable artificial intelligence in education. *Computers and Education: Artificial Intelligence*, *3*, 100074.

Kiennert, C., De Vos, N., Knockaert, M., & Garcia-Alfaro, J. (2019). The influence of conception paradigms on data protection in e-learning platforms: A case study. *IEEE Access : Practical Innovations, Open Solutions*, *7*, 64110–64119. doi:10.1109/ACCESS.2019.2915275

Kim, J. H., Baek, J., Hwang, C., Bae, C., & Park, J. (2021, June). Condensed discriminative question set for reliable exam score prediction. In *International Conference on Artificial Intelligence in Education* (pp. 446-450). Springer, Cham. 10.1007/978-3-030-78270-2_79

Klinger, J., Mateos-Garcia, J., & Stathoulopoulos, K. (2020). A narrowing of AI research? *arXiv preprint arXiv:2009.10385.*

Kramer, A. D., Guillory, J. E., & Hancock, J. T. (2014). Experimental evidence of massive-scale emotional contagion through social networks. *Proceedings of the National Academy of Sciences of the United States of America*, *111*(24), 8788–8790. doi:10.1073/pnas.1320040111 PMID:24889601

Kumar, V., & Boulanger, D. (2020, October). Explainable automated essay scoring: Deep learning really has pedagogical value. [). Frontiers Media SA.]. *Frontiers in Education*, *5*, 572367. doi:10.3389/feduc.2020.572367

Kung, C., & Yu, R. (2020). Interpretable models do not compromise accuracy or fairness in predicting college success. In *Proceedings of the Seventh ACM Conference on Learning@ Scale* (pp. 413–416). ACM. 10.1145/3386527.3406755

Last, M., & Danon, G. (2020). Automatic question generation. *Wiley Interdisciplinary Reviews. Data Mining and Knowledge Discovery*, *10*(6), e1382. doi:10.1002/widm.1382

Latham, A., & Goltz, S. (2019, June). A survey of the general public's views on the ethics of using AI in education. In *International Conference on Artificial Intelligence in Education* (pp. 194-206). Springer, Cham. 10.1007/978-3-030-23204-7_17

Leslie, D. (2019). Understanding artificial intelligence ethics and safety. *arXiv preprint arXiv:1906.05684.*

Lim, T., Gottipati, S., & Cheong, M. (2022). Authentic Assessments for Digital Education: Learning Technologies Shaping Assessment Practices. *Proceedings of the 30th International Conference on Computers in Education (ICCE 2022)*, Kuala Lumpur, Malaysia.

Litman, D., Zhang, H., Correnti, R., Matsumura, L. C., & Wang, E. (2021, June). A fairness evaluation of automated methods for scoring text evidence usage in writing. In *International Conference on Artificial Intelligence in Education* (pp. 255-267). Springer, Cham. 10.1007/978-3-030-78292-4_21

Luckin, R. (2017). Towards artificial intelligence-based assessment systems. *Nature Human Behaviour, 1*, 0028. . doi:10.1038/s41562-016-0028

Martin Nunez, J. L., & Diaz Lantada, A. (2020). Artificial intelligence aided engineering education: State of the art, potentials and challenges. *International Journal of Engineering Education*, *36*(6), 1740–1751.

Martinez-Maldonado, R., Gaševic, D., Echeverria, V., Fernandez Nieto, G., Swiecki, Z., & Buckingham Shum, S. (2021). What Do You Mean by Collaboration Analytics? A Conceptual Model. *Journal of Learning Analytics*, *8*(1), 126–153. doi:10.18608/jla.2021.7227

Mayfield, E., Madaio, M., Prabhumoye, S., Gerritsen, D., McLaughlin, B., Dixon-Román, E., & Black, A. W. (2019, August). Equity beyond bias in language technologies for education. In *Proceedings of the Fourteenth Workshop on Innovative Use of NLP for Building Educational Applications* (pp. 444-460). Association for Computational Linguistics. 10.18653/v1/W19-4446

Megahed, N. A., Abdel-Kader, R. F., & Soliman, H. Y. (2022). Post-pandemic education strategy: Framework for artificial intelligence-empowered education in engineering (AIEd-Eng) for lifelong learning. In *International Conference on Advanced Machine Learning Technologies and Applications* (pp. 544-556). Springer, Cham. 10.1007/978-3-031-03918-8_45

Merikko, J., Ng, K., Saqr, M., & Ihantola, P. (2022). To opt in or to opt out? Predicting student preference for learning analytics-based formative feedback. *IEEE Access : Practical Innovations, Open Solutions*, *10*, 99195–99204. doi:10.1109/ACCESS.2022.3207274

Moher, D., Liberati, A., Tetzlaff, J., & Altman, D. G.Prisma Group. (2009). Preferred reporting items for systematic reviews and meta-analyses: The PRISMA statement. *PLoS Medicine*, *6*(7), e1000097. doi:10.1371/journal.pmed.1000097 PMID:19621072

Morley, J., Floridi, L., Kinsey, L., & Elhalal, A. (2020). From what to how: An initial review of publicly available AI ethics tools, methods and research to translate principles into practices. *Science and Engineering Ethics*, *26*(4), 2141–2168. doi:10.100711948-019-00165-5 PMID:31828533

Mougiakou, E., Papadimitriou, S., & Virvou, M. (2018, July). Intelligent tutoring systems and transparency: The case of children and adolescents. In *2018 9th International Conference on Information, Intelligence, Systems and Applications (IISA)* (pp. 1-8). IEEE.

Nazaretsky, T., Cukurova, M., & Alexandron, G. (2022). An instrument for measuring teachers' trust in AI-based educational technology. In *LAK22: 12th International Learning Analytics and Knowledge Conference* (pp. 56-66). ACM. 10.1145/3506860.3506866

Nguyen, A., Ngo, H. N., Hong, Y., Dang, B., & Nguyen, B. P. T. (2022). Ethical principles for artificial intelligence in education. *Education and Information Technologies*. Advance online publication. doi:10.100710639-022-11316-w PMID:36254344

Ogden, C. R., & Richards, I. A. (1923). *The Meaning of Meaning: A Study of the Influence of Language upon Thought and of the Science of Symbolism*. Routledge & Kegan Paul.

Papa, R., & Jackson, K. M. (2021). Enduring questions, innovative technologies: Educational theories interface with AI. In *Intelligent Computing* (pp. 725–742). Springer. doi:10.1007/978-3-030-80126-7_51

Peña-Ayala, A. (2018). Learning analytics: A glance of evolution, status, and trends according to a proposed taxonomy. *Wiley Interdisciplinary Reviews. Data Mining and Knowledge Discovery*, *8*(3), e1243. doi:10.1002/widm.1243

Pereira, J. (2016). Leveraging chatbots to improve self-guided learning through conversational quizzes. *Proceedings of the Fourth International Conference on Technological Ecosystems for Enhancing Multiculturality* (pp. 911-918). ACM. 10.1145/3012430.3012625

Petersen, K., & Gencel, C. (2013). Worldviews, research methods, and their relationship to validity in empirical software engineering research. In *2013 Joint Conference of the 23rd International Workshop on Software Measurement and the 8th International Conference on Software Process and Product Measurement* (pp. 81-89). IEEE. 10.1109/IWSM-Mensura.2013.22

Petersen, K., Vakkalanka, S., & Kuzniarz, L. (2015). Guidelines for conducting systematic mapping studies in software engineering: An update. *Information and Software Technology*, *64*, 1–18. doi:10.1016/j.infsof.2015.03.007

Pontual Falcão, T., Lins Rodrigues, R., Cechinel, C., Dermeval, D., Harada Teixeira de Oliveira, E., Gasparini, I., ... Ferreira Mello, R. (2022, March). A Penny for your Thoughts: Students and Instructors' Expectations about Learning Analytics in Brazil. In *LAK22: 12th International Learning Analytics and Knowledge Conference* (pp. 186-196). 10.1145/3506860.3506886

Popper, K. (1979). *Three worlds*. University of Michigan.

Project, P. E., & Peirce, C. S. (1998). *The essential peirce* (Vol. 2). Indiana University Press.

Raji, I. D., Scheuerman, M. K., & Amironesei, R. (2021, March). You can't sit with us: Exclusionary pedagogy in ai ethics education. In *Proceedings of the 2021 ACM Conference on Fairness, Accountability, and Transparency* (pp. 515-525). ACM. 10.1145/3442188.3445914

Rodrigues, S. P., van Eck, N. J., Waltman, L., & Jansen, F. W. (2014). Mapping patient safety: A large-scale literature review using bibliometric visualisation techniques. *BMJ Open*, *4*(3), e004468. doi:10.1136/bmjopen-2013-004468 PMID:24625640

Romero, C., & Ventura, S. (2020). Educational data mining and learning analytics: An updated survey. *Wiley Interdisciplinary Reviews. Data Mining and Knowledge Discovery*, *10*(3), e1355. doi:10.1002/widm.1355

Sadler, D. R. (1989). Formative assessment in the design of instructional systems. *Instructional Science*, *18*(2), 119–144. doi:10.1007/BF00117714

Sánchez-Prieto, J. C., Gamazo, A., Cruz-Benito, J., Therón, R., & García-Peñalvo, F. J. (2020). AI-driven assessment of students: Current uses and research trends. In P. Zaphiris & A. Ioannou (Eds.), *Learning and Collaboration Technologies. Design, Experiences*. Springer Nature. DOI: 10.1007/978-3-030-50513-4_22

Schiff, D. (2021). Out of the laboratory and into the classroom: The future of artificial intelligence in education. *AI & Society*, *36*(1), 331–348. doi:10.100700146-020-01033-8 PMID:32836908

Schneider, B., Dowell, N., & Thompson, K. (2021). Collaboration analytics—Current state and potential futures. *Journal of Learning Analytics*, *8*(1), 1–12. doi:10.18608/jla.2021.7447

Shabaninejad, S., Khosravi, H., Abdi, S., Indulska, M., & Sadiq, S. (2022, June). Incorporating explainable learning analytics to assist educators with identifying students in need of attention. In *Proceedings of the Ninth ACM Conference on Learning@ Scale* (pp. 384-388). ACM. 10.1145/3491140.3528292

Shapiro, J., & Blackman, R. (2020). Four steps for drafting an ethical data practices blueprint. *TechCrunch.* https://techcrunch.com/2020/07/24/four-steps-for-an-ethical-data-practices-blueprint/

Siau, K., & Wang, W. (2020). Artificial intelligence (AI) ethics: Ethics of AI and ethical AI. *Journal of Database Management*, *31*(2), 74–87. doi:10.4018/JDM.2020040105

Sibai, F. N. (2020, June). AI crimes: a classification. In *2020 International Conference on Cyber Security and Protection of Digital Services (Cyber Security)* (pp. 1-8). IEEE.

Sievert, C., & Shirley, K. E. (2014). A method for visualizing and interpreting topics. *Proceedings of the Workshop on Interactive Language Learning, Visualization, and Interfaces* (pp. 63–70). Baltimore, Maryland, USA. 10.3115/v1/W14-3110

Smith, B., & Welty, C. (2001). *Ontology: Towards a new synthesis. Formal Ontology in Information Systems*. ACM Press.

Stahl, B. C., Timmermans, J. O. B., & Mittelstadt, B. D. (2016). The ethics of computing: A survey of the computing-oriented literature. *ACM Computing Surveys*, *48*(4), 1–38. doi:10.1145/2871196

Stark, L., & Hoey, J. (2021). The ethics of emotion in artificial intelligence systems. In *Proceedings of the 2021 ACM Conference on Fairness, Accountability, and Transparency* (pp. 782-793). ACM. 10.1145/3442188.3445939

Stringer, R. (2018). Realist ethical naturalism for ethical non-naturalists. *Philosophical Studies*, *175*(2), 339–362. doi:10.100711098-017-0870-0

The Open University. (2014). *Policy on Ethical use of Student Data for Learning Analytics*. The Open University. https://help.open.ac.uk/documents/policies/ethical-use-of-student-data/files/22/ethical-use-of-student-data-policy.pdf

Tlili, A., Essalmi, F., Jemni, M., & Chen, N. S. (2018). A complete validated learning analytics framework: Designing issues from data preparation perspective. [IJICTE]. *International Journal of Information and Communication Technology Education*, *14*(2), 1–16. doi:10.4018/IJICTE.2018040101

Tlili, A., Essalmi, F., Jemni, M., & Chen, N. S. (2019). A complete validated learning analytics framework: Designing issues from data use perspective. [IJICTE]. *International Journal of Information and Communication Technology Education*, *15*(3), 42–59. doi:10.4018/IJICTE.2019070104

United Nations Educational, Scientific and Cultural Organization (UNESCO). (2021). Recommendation on the ethics of artificial intelligence. UNESDOC Digital Library. https://unesdoc.unesco.org/ark:/48223/pf0000380455

van Otterlo, M. (2017). From algorithmic black boxes to adaptive white boxes: Declarative decision-theoretic ethical programs as codes of ethics. *arXiv preprint arXiv:1711.06035.*

Weitzman, M. L. (1993). What to preserve? An application of diversity theory to crane conservation. *The Quarterly Journal of Economics*, *108*(1), 157–183. doi:10.2307/2118499

White, J. P., Dennis, S., Tomko, M., Bell, J., & Winter, S. (2021). Paths to social licence for tracking-data analytics in university research and services. *PLoS One*, *16*(5), e0251964. doi:10.1371/journal.pone.0251964 PMID:34019592

White, M. C., & Bembenutty, H. (2013). Not all avoidance help seekers are created equal: Individual differences in adaptive and executive help seeking. *SAGE Open*, *3*(2), 2158244013484916. doi:10.1177/2158244013484916

Whittlestone, J., Nyrup, R., Alexandrova, A., Dihal, K., & Cave, S. (2019). *Ethical and societal implications of algorithms, data, and artificial intelligence: A roadmap for research.* Nuffield Foundation.

Williamson, B. (2021). Psychodata: Disassembling the psychological, economic, and statistical infrastructure of 'social-emotional learning.'. *Journal of Education Policy*, *36*(1), 129–154. doi:10.1080/02680939.2019.1672895

KEY TERMS AND DEFINITIONS

Accountability: This ethics principle relates to the responsible discharge of AI ethics when designing and delivering AI systems, depending on the roles and contexts, in a consistent manner.

Accuracy: In the context of educational assessments, this ethics principle relates to the reliability and validity of assessments when an AI system is applied.

Applied Ethics: The study of the practical application of philosophical tools to examine and provide solutions to real world morality issues.

Artificial intelligence in education (AIED): The machine mimicry of human-like consciousness and behavior to achieve educational goals, through the use of technology that allows digital systems to perform tasks commonly associated with intelligent beings.

Auditability: This ethics principle relates to the permitting of independent third-party reviewers to audit, analyze and report findings relating to the usage and design of data and AI algorithms in education.

Cheating: This ethics principle relates to dishonest and deceptive learner behavior to violate educational rules and regulations.

Consequentialism: A type of normative ethics that emphasizes that the outcome of an action defines the morality of an action.

Deontological Ethics: A type of normative ethics that emphasizes on an individual's rights and duties, including the presence of natural, absolute rights (i.e., natural rights theory), the presence of human rationality and inviolable moral laws (i.e., Kantian categorical imperative), and the morality of good actors arising from unbiases behind a veil of ignorance (i.e., contractualism).

Ethics Bluewashing: The implementation of superficial or misleading measures to appear ethical.

Ethics Dumping: The export or import of unethical activities to a place with less strict regulations.

Ethics Lobbying: The use of ethics to avoid or delay good and necessary regulation and enforcement.

Ethics Shirking: The engaging of less ethical works over a period of time to lower the perceived resistance against such works.

Ethics Shopping: The picking and choosing of ethics principles that are justified as a posteriori and retrofitted to pre-existing behaviors.

Explainability: This ethics principle relates to the lowering of opacity relating to data, AI algorithms and AI-driven decisions, the justification of its use, and the communication of details in a non-technical easy-to-understand manner to relevant stakeholders.

Fairness: This ethics principle relates to fair, equitable and appropriate educational practices that should be perpetuated by AI systems.

Human Centricity: This ethics principle relates to the aim towards upholding human agency, dignity and autonomy, minimization of harm (and when necessary, weighed against a greater good), and equitable distribution of benefits.

Inclusivity: This ethics principle relates to inclusive and accessibility considerations applied to AI systems to meet different student needs in a personalized environment at scale.

Metaethics: The study of the nature (i.e., moral ontology), meaning (i.e., moral semantics), and the scope and knowledge to defend or support (i.e., moral epistemology) moral judgments.

Normative Ethics: The study of the moral rules and standards that guide how individuals, institutions and societies should behave in a moral sense.

Privacy: This ethics principle relates to the protection of data subjects against injurious effects from the use of personal information applied in AI systems, without unduly affecting regulatory compliance tied to privacy and restricting AI development.

Trust: This ethics principle relates to the placing of confidence on AI systems and the provision of data to achieve educational objectives.

Virtue Ethics: A type of normative ethics that emphasizes the inherent disposition of an individual, and not specific actions.

Chapter 4
Artificial Intelligence and Literacy Development in K-12 Schools

Damian Maher
University of Technology, Sydney, Australia

Kirsty Young
University of Technology Sydney, Australia

ABSTRACT

The use of artificial intelligence (AI) is becoming widespread in educational settings including schools. It has the potential to support teaching and learning across all subjects. The focus of the chapter is to explore how it can be used to support literacy development. In understanding use by teachers, the TPACK model is investigated. This is then followed by a focus on the teacher's role and the importance of teacher training. The focus then moves to AI and literacies. As part of this section, digital story writing and AI is investigated as well as special and inclusive education. This section concludes with a focus on assessment and feedback. The ethical use of AI is an important consideration and is an area that is currently engaging researchers and educators. This aspect is investigated. To conclude the chapter, areas of future research are discussed.

INTRODUCTION

The use of artificial intelligence (AI) in schools has received significant attention with the advent of ChatGPT, which was launched in late 2022. It has been claimed that the "application of Artificial Intelligence … in the teaching and learning process has the potential to revolutionize education by providing personalized, engaging, and effective learning experiences for students" (Vinay, 2023, p. 1). AI-powered tools, which include adaptive assessments, intelligent tutoring systems, language learning models, virtual and augmented reality, chatbots, and grading and assessment tools, can help teachers support students' learning experiences based on needs, strengths, and challenges.

DOI: 10.4018/979-8-3693-0205-7.ch004

AI is predicted to greatly affect the global workforce. People who have developed expertise in AI technologies will experience an advantage over those who do not have such knowledge. The McKinsey Global Institute estimates that 15 percent of global working hours will be automated by 2030 (Manyika et al., 2017). These trends make it essential for educators and students to engage with AI technologies throughout the school years to ensure graduates are prepared for future employment in AI-driven workplaces.

In this chapter, the focus is on ways that AI can be used to support literacy development for students in the K–12 setting. The text begins with an overview of the TPACK framework, which is presented as a vehicle to explore how technology integration in education is built on three core components: technological knowledge (TK), pedagogical knowledge (PK), and content knowledge (CK). The role of the teacher in facilitating AI technology is examined.

The issue of adequate professional development to allow teachers to develop sufficient TK-, PK- and CK-type knowledge to effectively harness the affordances of AI technologies is explored. The chapter then provides specific examples of AI technologies being incorporated into K–12 education settings, with a focus on AI and literacy. Illustrative examples are provided that focus on digital story writing (DSW) and special education practices. This section concludes with a discussion on the use of AI for assessment and feedback. The chapter concludes with a discussion of ethical issues associated with the use of AI technologies in K–12 settings and future directions for research.

UNDERSTANDING AI USING THE TPACK MODEL

The TPACK framework, developed by Mishra and Koehler (2006), recognizes that successful technology integration in education requires the fusion of the three core components: TK, PK, and CK. TK refers to the understanding of various technologies and their functions and how these can be effectively utilised. PK involves the ability to employ effective teaching strategies and methods to engage students and promote learning. CK represents a teacher's deep knowledge of the subject matter. The TPACK model is widely used to identify "how teachers can incorporate technologies into their pedagogical methods and content knowledge, and conceptualizes their capacity and knowledge that is needed to integrate relevant technologies in AI literacy education" (Ng et al., 2021, p. 6).

In the context of AI integration, teachers play a crucial role as facilitators, guiding students to leverage AI tools for enhanced learning experiences. To effectively fill this role, teachers need to develop a solid foundation in all three components of TPACK. Most importantly, teachers must possess the TK necessary to navigate AI systems, understand their capabilities, and identify appropriate tools and resources. Familiarity with AI technologies empowers teachers to make informed decisions regarding implementation in the classroom.

PK comes into play as teachers explore innovative ways to incorporate AI into their instructional practices. Teachers must determine how to use AI tools to engage students, promote critical thinking, and foster collaboration. Those with strong PK can design activities that harness the power of AI to individualise instruction and cater to diverse learning styles and needs. By understanding their students' strengths and weaknesses, teachers can guide students to use AI effectively and ethically (Celik, 2023).

CK serves as a foundation for integrating AI into subject-specific contexts. Teachers must possess a deep understanding of their respective disciplines and identify opportunities where AI can enhance content delivery, provide real-world examples, or facilitate data analysis. By leveraging AI, teachers can expose students to authentic problem-solving experiences, enabling them to apply theoretical knowledge in practical scenarios.

The Role of the Teacher

With the advent of computer technologies including the Internet, the role of the teacher has changed from being the provider of knowledge to a facilitator of knowledge, where the role is seen as one of transferring skills, facilitating learning, teaching critical thinking, and explaining where to find information (e.g., Guilherme, 2017). This change is likely to continue as AI becomes more firmly embedded in schools. As suggested by Felix (2020), the teacher will "no longer be 'the' repository of knowledge – only a rather decidedly secondary one, at best" (p. 35), and this has implications for teacher–student relationships.

A systematic review by Celik et al. (2022, p. 621) revealed new and varied roles for the teacher as a result of AI technologies (Table 1).

AI is assuming some of the responsibilities of the teacher through intuitive educational packages that include the content material, some level of academic support, monitoring, and evaluation (Koh et al., 2022b). This has alarmed many teachers (Celik et al., 2022), who see this as a first step to reducing the teacher's role to that of a facilitator (Koh et al., 2022a), which could diminish the teacher–student relationship. The benefits of positive teacher–student relationships have been reported across all year levels from early-school-age years (Pianta et al., 1995) and during the transition to middle school (Davis, 2003). Meaningful relationships between students and teachers contribute to the learning process (Brekelmans et al., 2002). The benefits include improved behavioral outcomes and student engagement, which have been found, among other things, to improve reading outcomes (Lee, 2012). Positive teacher–student relationships contribute to teacher well-being through internal validation and give meaning to teachers' work (Split et al., 2011). Positive teacher–student relationships are often cited as a primary reason for teachers remaining in the profession (O'Connor, 2008).

Automating educational experiences using AI technologies has implications for students' learning experience (Shen & Su, 2020). It is important that AI be used in ways that can support the teacher in creating

Table 1. Teachers' roles in educational AI research

Role of the teacher	Description
Being a model for AI training	Teachers acted as sources of data for an effective teaching process or moment.
Feeding AI systems with data on professional development	Teachers participated in research for more accurate prediction of teacher-related variables (e.g., teaching quality and teacher performance and engagement).
Feeding AI algorithms with student information and behaviors	Teachers provided information on students' characteristics for AI implementation (or intervention).
Checking the accuracy of assessments	Teachers graded assignments and essays to test the accuracy of AI grading algorithms.
Determining the assessment criteria	Teachers defined the criteria for AI-based assessment.
Providing pedagogical guidance for the selection of materials	Teachers provided pedagogical guidance for the selection of materials for AI-based implementation (or intervention).
Providing feedback on technical issues	Teachers gave feedback and raised their views on technical issues (e.g., on AI design or usability) in AI-based education.

Note. Adapted from Celik et al. (2022, p. 621).

opportunities for interactions with students and, in doing so, help build the teacher–student relationship. According to the United Nations Educational, Scientific and Cultural Organization (UNESCO, 2022a):

AI tools actually interfere with the teacher–student relationship and can undermine teacher agency. Teachers may, for example, lose key opportunities to learn about their students' formative strategies and capabilities with the use of AI tools to automate formative assessment and grading. (p. 3)

It is essential that education systems, regulators, and teachers themselves carefully consider how AI is being used and take action to minimise activities that diminish the teacher–student relationship.

Training of the Teacher

To ensure educators can successfully integrate AI to support students, the professional learning of teachers, at both the pre-service (university) and in-service (school) level should be supported. Implementing AI in the classroom without adequate professional development can lead to inefficient utilisation or misuse of AI tools. Through training, teachers can learn to identify appropriate AI technologies that align with their pedagogical goals and with student needs. They can also acquire the skills to evaluate and select AI tools based on educational value, reliability, and related ethical considerations. Proper training enables teachers to optimise AI integration, creating a balance between technology and human interaction and maximising the benefits for students.

Achieving the potential of AI technologies to enhance student engagement and improve learning outcomes relies on teachers' ability to effectively integrate AI into their instructional practices. Well-constructed teacher training programs will enable educators to leverage adaptive learning platforms, intelligent tutoring systems, and automated assessment tools to successfully personalise instruction and cater to individual student needs. Adequately trained teachers can develop the capacity to effectively interpret AI-generated data and tailor interventions, thereby enhancing student engagement and promoting deeper learning experiences.

To contextualise the issues raised to this point, the chapter moves to apply concepts to AI and literacy. This incorporates the use of AI technologies in the development of traditional literacy skills (e.g., reading and writing) alongside more contemporary literacies (e.g., digital literacy) and the introduction of new AI literacy relevant to the skills needed by students to effectively and ethically use AI technologies.

AI and Literacies

Traditionally, literacy was understood as the ability to read, write, speak, and listen (McBride, 2015). Over time, the term literacy has been extended to incorporate new forms of literacy, such as media, digital, information, and computer literacy (Kong et al., 2021). In this chapter, the concept of literacy is addressed from a sociocultural perspective where, rather than thinking of literacy as one unified practice, we understand it as literacies. This incorporates Lankshear and Knoble's (2008) perception that forms of literacy vary enormously and are culturally situated. From a sociocultural perspective, learning is viewed "as the appropriation and mastery of communicative (including conceptual) and technical tools that serve as mediational means in social practices" (Säljö, 1996, p. 91) and so, "meaningful digital literacy education should encompass a broad suite of skills reflecting young people's social and cultural engagement in a networked society, their self-expression, identity formation and participation in an online world"

(Connolly & McGuinness, 2018, p. 77). A definition of what constitutes digital literacy also includes "knowing how to act safely and responsibly online" (Australian Government, cited in NSW Education Standards Authority, 2017, p. 7).

More recently, AI literacy has emerged as a new skill set needed for participation in the contemporary era of intelligence. AI literacy is conceptualised in this chapter as forming part of students' overall digital literacies. To combine AI and literacy means having the essential abilities that students need to live, learn, and work in a digital world with the use of AI-driven technologies, and this should be taught at the K–12 levels (Steinbauer et al., 2021). In much of the literature and in this chapter, this is referred to as AI literacy. Ng et al. (2021) have identified four components of AI literacy: (1) understanding basic functions and use of AI technologies, (2) using and applying AI technologies in different scenarios, (3) drawing on higher-order thinking skills to evaluate AI technologies, and (4) ethical and safety considerations.

In relation to the first component, students need to learn the basic function of AI and how to use applications; this is a functional view of literacy. An example of such learning is reported in a project conducted with 420 sixth-grade Chinese students. In that study, "students acquired basic AI knowledge, including the meaning of data, data collection and processing, and the outputs generated, and learned about AI applications, including facial and voice recognition, content recommendation, and machine learning" (Lin et al., 2021, p. 3).

For the second component, in other studies, students have learned to use and apply AI applications in different scenarios. In one such example, 102 children (seven to 12 years old) from four countries (USA, Germany, Denmark, and Sweden) were observed using smart devices and toys of the future (Druga et al., 2019). The results indicated that children from low and medium socioeconomic status (SES) schools were better at collaborating compared to high-SES children but had less experience with coding and interacting with these technologies. Children in high-SES schools initially had trouble collaborating but displayed a stronger understanding of AI concepts.

The third component of AI literacy involves students evaluating AI technologies and creating using AI technologies, both of which draw on higher-order thinking skills, such as evaluation and prediction. In one study examining the development of these skills, students were presented with some scenarios where they were guided to apply theory to practice and to maximise understanding and practice in the field of AI (Han et al., 2018).

The final component of AI literacy relates to ethics, which covers fairness, accountability, and safety, among other considerations. Ethical issues around the use of AI technologies are one of the most prominent concerns discussed in both academic and grey literature and are examined in detail later in this chapter.

To better understand the ways in which AI literacies are applied, we now move to examine specific examples of literacy learning using AI technologies. First, DSW is examined in detail. The application of AI technologies in special and inclusive education contexts is then explored. The section concludes with a consideration of new approaches to assessment and feedback enabled by AI technologies.

Digital Story Writing

DSW can be viewed as an evolution of digital storytelling. The digital storytelling movement commenced in the late 1980s, led by Joe Lambert and Dana Atchley, as co-founders of the Center for Digital Storytelling (Robin, 2008). According to Robin:

At its core, digital storytelling allows computer users to become creative storytellers through the traditional processes of selecting a topic, conducting some research, writing a script, and developing an interesting story. This material is then combined with various types of multimedia, including computer-based graphics, recorded audio, computer-generated text, video clips, and music. (p. 222)

DSW is a combination of technology and pedagogy used to develop students' writing skills and acquire subject knowledge. It can support students to learn new cognitive concepts and combine different semiotic systems (Smyrnaiou et al., 2020) through the integration of narrated audio texts, images, videos, and other multimedia elements to create media artifacts (Boase, 2008). The use of "digital story writing … in the classroom is an effective inquiry-based pedagogical approach to address literacy development by improving language and technological abilities" (Ng et al., 2022, p. 2). It is claimed that twenty-first-century digital skills, including media, information, and technological literacy across disciplines such as computer science and Science, Technology, Engineering, Art, and Mathematics (STEAM) education can be enhanced using DSW (Hill & Grinnell, 2014; Wu et al., 2020).

When producing digital stories, AI technologies offer new possibilities to create content, including characters, dialogue, settings, and plotlines. Through analysis of existing stories and identification of patterns, AI models can suggest unique story concepts and twists or even help to overcome writer's block. AI algorithms can analyse story structures from a wide range of narratives. By leveraging this knowledge, AI can provide suggestions for improving the pacing, coherence, and overall flow of a digital story. However, AI's ability to undertake this process is currently limited due to a lack of semantic cohesiveness, which manifests itself in an inability to grasp some basic literary concepts, such as recurring characters or coherent story arcs (Ghajargar et al., 2022).

To enhance digital stories, AI technologies, such as text-to-image platforms (e.g., DALL-E), can generate custom images to support a specific storyline. To refine and increase the quality of the text, editing tools (such as Grammarly and QuillBot) are able to help with the mechanical features of text, such as grammar (Young and Maher, 2023). AI story generators, such as Sassbook AI, can automatically generate script titles, characters, scenes, and dialogue as references for writers to consider adopting in their writing (e.g., Suh & An, 2022), while tools such as KidPad and StoryJumper (Del-Moral-Pérez et al., 2019) are designed to assist younger students in producing text. It is important to note that while AI can provide valuable support, the creative input and expertise of human writers remain crucial for crafting compelling and meaningful digital stories. AI should be seen as a tool to assist and enhance the writing process, rather than one that replaces human creativity.

AI technologies can also facilitate collaborative writing by allowing multiple authors to work together on a digital story. AI can assist in managing version control, suggesting edits, and maintaining consistency across different sections of a story. Technologies such as Google Slides support collaboration between students in different school locations in providing ideas and recommendations to each other (Maher, 2023). Other collaborative tools that can support co-authoring include Sudowrite and CoAuthor (Lee et al., 2022).

Identifying an audience is a crucial part of the DSW process. AI can assist through analysis of readers' preferences, thus enabling personalised recommendations for story elements, such as character traits, settings, or plotlines, which helps students tailor their stories to specific target audiences, ensuring a more engaging and enjoyable reading experience. This personalisation can be beneficial for students where AI allows for differentiation that is otherwise impossible for teachers who must manage 30 students in each class (Marr, 2018).

Research into the use of AI technologies to support the writing of K–12 students is emerging. Ng et al. (2022) investigated the use of DSW as a pedagogy to develop AI literacy among primary students. They found that in the process of evaluating and creating AI-supported stories, the students were drawing on higher-order thinking skills (the third component of AI literacy outlined earlier). Ng et al. found that while:

AI proved superior at complex calculations and predictions, creativity seems to be the domain which machines can't take over. To reach the level of evaluating and creating AI, students need to achieve the former two levels (i.e., know and understand, use and apply AI). (p. 7)

This indicates that evaluating and creating with AI is a cognitively difficult process, which primary-aged students find challenging. The lack of creativity identified in Ng et al.'s (2022) study could result from AI's inability to capture human complexities and emotions, such as sarcasm, and fail to interpret human contradictions (Lee et al., 2022).

AI technologies, such as those described here to support DSW, are particularly valuable in enabling individualised support and offering efficiencies to support differentiated instruction, both of which are essential in inclusive classroom settings. In addition, AI supports students with disability in unique ways, providing adjustments and improving accessibility to ensure all learners have the opportunity to achieve to their potential.

Special and Inclusive Education

The use of technology to support students with disabilities has a substantial history (Jeffs et al., 2008), and so it is inevitable that new AI technologies, as both assistive devices and instructional tools, will affect the teaching and learning experiences of students with disabilities. Special education teachers are beginning to use AI technologies to support individualised learning in innovative ways to develop students' literacies. This includes the development of both textual literacies (reading, writing, and comprehension skills) and oral literacies (social, expressive, and receptive communication skills).

For students with disabilities enrolled in mainstream classrooms, AI tools support inclusion by offering differentiated instruction. AI can be used to support writing during the production, revision, and presentation stages (Marino et al., 2023; Young & Maher, 2023). AI technologies can also support learning in specific disciplines through tools that support content-specific vocabulary instruction and mastery. One novel approach using AI technologies to support literacy development for high school students experiencing difficulty with reading comprehension includes the use of AI to support personalised learning. In one study, positive outcomes were achieved when school e-books were enriched with AI technologies to provide students with real-time visual and audio feedback (Kapetanaki et al., 2021).

AI technologies are also being used as assistive devices to support students during periods of instruction. For example, wearable AI technologies, such as watches and smartphones, can be used that track student activity to provide auditory or vibrating alarms to aid a child with ADHD who has lost focus with their work (Barua et al., 2022). Eye-gaze AI technologies (such as the Tobii eye tracker system) can be life-changing for students with severe physical disabilities, as cameras pick up eye movements through infrared technology and translate these movements to operate technologies such as Internet searching (Anderson, 2019).

AI technologies are opening opportunities for students to improve their oral literacies by practising asking and answering questions using an AI chatbot (Anderson, 2019). Other ways to support the development of communication skills of students with autism spectrum disorder (ASD) using AI technologies involve software that analyses children's facial expressions and body movements (Barua et al., 2022). AI and social robots have the potential to change the way we teach expressive and receptive communication skills to students with ASD as part of their personal communication program.

In all aspects of literacy education, the use of generative AI to enable personalised tutoring captures performance data to give individualised feedback to students. This is important for students with disabilities to enable them to work at their own pace (Marino et al., 2023). AI tools enabling personalised learning are particularly valuable, as instruction can be targeted toward an individual student's strengths and challenges while enabling repeated learning of concepts that have not been mastered (Tapalova & Zhiyenbayeva, 2022).

While novel approaches to the use of AI to support literacy development are emerging, one area receiving attention is the impact of AI on assessment and feedback. Similar to the use of AI to support development of literacies, AI is being used extensively to differentiate and individualise assessment and feedback for students and make these processes more efficient for teachers.

Assessment and Feedback

Annuš (2023) suggests that "AI-based assessment systems allow teachers to quickly and efficiently evaluate students' work and give them feedback … which allows instructors to better understand the student's strengths and weaknesses and adjust the teaching process accordingly" (p. 2). The essence of AI in both summative and formative contexts is the concept of "machine 'learning'–where the computer is 'taught' how to interpret patterns in data and 'trained' to undertake predetermined actions according to those interpretations" (Gardner et al., 2020, p. 120). Despite these automated processes, the teacher remains critical in facilitating conversations with students around assessment results and providing support and encouragement to ensure students continue to make progress and understand how to use the results and feedback to improve outcomes.

There are specific ways that AI tools are used for assessment and feedback. Tools to create short-answer or multiple-choice questions provide a vehicle for teachers to gather real-time data. For these types of questions, AI tools can immediately analyse data and provide an indication of levels of understanding across a cohort. These immediate data allow the teacher to make adjustments to a lesson based on student understanding. AI can also be used to support longer responses. Automated essay-scoring tools have been in use since the mid-2000s. These tools can identify structural elements of students' writing, including grammar, mechanics (e.g., errors in capitalization, punctuation, and spelling), discourse structure, lexical complexity, sentence variety, source use, and discourse coherence quality (e.g., extent of off-topic writing; Deane, 2013, p. 8).

Peer assessment can also be supported by AI. Teachers can assign students the task of assessing each other's work using AI. Students can review their peers' assignments and engage in a chat conversation with the model, evaluating the quality of the work and providing constructive feedback. This method encourages critical thinking, collaboration, and peer learning. Through using AI to support peer feedback, some of the human bias that can be involved can be reduced (Chattopadhyay, 2018).

The use of AI can stimulate and support discussions or debates on a particular topic. Teachers can assign students roles and have them engage in a conversation with the model, presenting arguments, counterarguments, and supporting evidence. This approach allows teachers to assess students' understanding of a topic and their ability to articulate and defend their viewpoints. AI can also be used to evaluate students' language proficiency, testing their speaking, listening, writing, pronunciation, grammar, vocabulary, and reading (Woo & Choi, 2021). Teachers can design specific tasks or scenarios to assess different language skills, such as describing a process, summarising a text, or engaging in a role-play conversation.

It is important to note that while AI can be a valuable tool for assessment and feedback, it should not replace other traditional methods, nor should it replace teachers. Selwyn (2018) suggests that the cognitive and social connections teachers make with students are critical to learning and that AI cannot replicate this. In using AI to support the teaching and learning process, teachers should consider the limitations of AI and use it in conjunction with other assessment and feedback strategies to gather a comprehensive understanding of students' knowledge and skills.

ETHICAL ISSUES OF AI IN SCHOOLS

Ethical concerns surrounding the use of AI in education date back several decades, where authors such as Aiken and Epstein (2000) identified plagiarism, intellectual property, and honesty as areas where ethics policy guidance specific to K–12 education was lacking but crucial (Adams et al., 2023). It is essential that teachers and students are introduced to the ethical issues surrounding the use of AI applications in K–12 education, alongside measures to respond and navigate these considerations (Akgun & Greenhow, 2021). There is a call for existing ICT digital competency frameworks to be updated to acknowledge new issues surrounding the use of AI technologies in education (UNESCO, 2019).

Tuomi (2018) suggests that "ethical considerations become highly relevant when AI is applied in the society or in educational settings. From a policy perspective, the ethics of AI is a generic challenge, but it has specific relevance for educational policies" (p. 36). In response, guidelines and frameworks are emerging. One is the Ethical Framework for AI in Education produced by the University of Buckingham's Institute for Ethical AI in education (n.d.), which identifies nine key issues (Table 2).

The release of ChatGPT in late 2022 prompted widespread concern about the implications of AI for academic integrity (Waltzer et al., 2023). With its ability to provide specific answers to user questions, AI can be used to complete written assignments and examinations on behalf of students, leading to concerns about AI-assisted cheating (Lo, 2023). Other concerns identified in the literature include incorrect responses and inaccurate citations (Sallam, 2023). As a result of these concerns, many educational institutions have banned the use of AI in school settings. This banning does not mean students may not use platforms such as ChatGPT at home and ignores the fact that many industries value the use of AI generative writing tools. Given this use by students, it remains essential that students are taught how to use AI ethically to support their literacies.

AI systems often collect and analyse vast amounts of data about students, including their personal information, learning progress, and behavior patterns, which has implications for privacy and data security (Regan & Jesse, 2019; Stahl & Wright, 2018). There is a risk of unauthorised access, misuse, or breach of these sensitive data. To address these concerns, AI systems ask for users' consent to access their personal data. Although users provide consent, "many individuals give their consent without knowing or considering the extent of the information (metadata) they are sharing, such as the language spoken, racial identity, biographical data, and location" (Akgun & Greenhow, 2021, p. 435). Schools are

Table 2. Ethical framework for AI in education

Objective	Criteria
Achieving educational goals	AI should be used to achieve well-defined educational goals based on strong societal, educational, or scientific evidence that this is for the benefit of the learners.
Forms of assessment	AI should be used to assess and recognise a broader range of learners' talents.
Administration and workload	AI should increase the capacity of organisations while respecting human relationships.
Equity	AI systems should be used in ways that promote equity between different groups of learners and not in ways that discriminate against any group of learners.
Autonomy	AI systems should be used to increase the level of control that learners have over their learning and development.
Privacy	A balance should be struck between privacy and the legitimate use of data for achieving well-defined and desirable educational goals.
Transparency and accountability	Humans are ultimately responsible for educational outcomes and should therefore have an appropriate level of oversight of how AI systems operate.
Informed participation	Learners, educators, and other relevant practitioners should have a reasonable understanding of AI and its implications.
Ethical design	AI resources should be designed by people who understand the impacts these resources will have.

Note. Adapted from Institute for Ethical AI in Education (n.d.).

environments that are highly regulated to ensure the safety of students. For AI to become accepted in schools, there will need to be structures in place that protect students' privacy. This information should be made available to parents and students, who can provide informed consent. The notion of consent links to transparency. AI algorithms can be complex and opaque, making it difficult for teachers and students to understand how decisions are made. This lack of transparency can lead to distrust and limit the ability to challenge or question the outcomes produced by AI systems and to be accepted by parents.

Another aspect related to ethics is bias and discrimination (Miller et al., 2018). AI algorithms do not exist in a vacuum. Instead, they are shaped by society's ever-evolving historical and institutionalised systemic biases, which ultimately transform into algorithmic bias (O'Neil, 2016). According to Akgun and Greenhow (2021):

The biggest risks of integrating these algorithms in education (particularly in K-12 contexts) are: (a) amplifying societies' existing systemic bias and discrimination, (b) perpetuating privacy, surveillance, and autonomy concerns for students from mostly marginalised and disadvantaged groups, and (c) amplifying exiting gender bias. (p. 432)

AI algorithms can perpetuate biases and discrimination if they are trained on biased or incomplete data. If AI systems are used to make decisions such as on grading, placement, or student evaluations, there is a risk of unfair outcomes based on race, gender, SES, or other factors. For example, AI tools in education may struggle to recognise and respond appropriately to cultural or linguistic diversity. Natural language processing algorithms, for instance, may have difficulty understanding accents or dialects, leading to inaccurate assessments or communication barriers for students from specific linguistic backgrounds. Another form of bias may occur when AI platforms inadvertently reinforce existing achievement gaps and biases. If the AI models primarily rely on historical student data, they can perpetuate biases by offering limited educational opportunities or low expectations for certain students based on their demographic characteristics or past performance.

To address these issues, it is important to ensure diverse and representative datasets, involve educators and students from diverse backgrounds in the design and development process, conduct regular audits of AI systems for bias, and prioritise ethical considerations when implementing AI in educational contexts. Close collaboration between AI developers, educators, policymakers, and communities is necessary to create equitable and inclusive AI-enabled education systems.

In addition, issues around the 'digital divide' may be exacerbated with advancements in AI technologies. AI tools and technologies may not be equally accessible to all students due to availability of resources, Internet connectivity, or socioeconomic disparities. This can exacerbate existing inequalities in education and create a digital divide. As Carter et al. (2020) noted, despite decades of initiatives focused on reducing the digital divide, it has persisted and evolved. Schools can help minimise this ethical problem by having systems in place, such as laptop loans or homework clubs where students can use networked computers linked to AI platforms. At a systemic level, education systems and governments can address equality of resources. Teachers and students need to learn how to use AI technologies judiciously and discriminate between ethical and unethical practices (see Ng et al., 2021). This can be achieved through AI ethics curricula, professional development, and instructional resources that teachers can use to advance K–12 students' understanding of AI and ethics (Akgun & Greenhow, 2021). UNESCO (2022b) recommends their member states should develop, in accordance with their national education programs and traditions, AI ethics curricula for all levels and promote cross-collaboration between AI technical schools' education and humanistic, ethical and social aspects of AI education" (p. 35).

FUTURE RESEARCH

There are countless areas for further exploration in the field of AI and K–12 student literacies. Research is required that measures the effect of existing AI technologies in supporting the development of specific aspects of student literacy, such as grammar, spelling, and text construction, through personalised feedback. Research that examines the impact on learning of using AI technologies to provide real-time feedback and construction of personalised learning experiences would be invaluable in guiding educators on the benefits and limitations of specific AI technologies.

While much of the focus of AI in education tends to be on the role that AI can play in directly supporting teaching, there are other ways that AI can assist educators, such as through the simplification of administrative tasks (Johnson, 2019). One of the ways AI can support administration is through the creation of content and lesson plans. This potential reduction in administrative tasks has important implications, as currently, in many parts of the world, teachers are overburdened with administrative tasks, which is one factor contributing to the loss of early-career teachers.

With the rapid development of AI, the demand for K–12 computer science educators continues to rise (El-Hamamsy et al., 2021). Improved understanding of the role of AI within schools in supporting both student learning and, where possible, contributing to the professional learning of K–12 educators is essential.

Research examining the use of AI technologies to support teacher professional development across a range of pedagogical and content areas is needed. The ways in which AI technologies could provide teachers with personalised feedback on their teaching practices through analysis of video recordings and other sources of rich data could make a significant contribution to both pre- and in-service teacher education.

CONCLUSION

AI, like many preceding technologies, has emerged with the potential for both positive and negative impacts on teaching and learning. With past technologies, many of the predicted negative impacts did not occur, while other unidentified challenges emerged. The transition from oral communication to mass production of texts raised concerns that written text was a poor replacement for true education and it was feared "that writing would lead to forgetfulness and the appearance of wisdom without the reality" (Schiff, 2021, p. 332). Likewise, as suggested by Schiff, alarming predictions have not eventuated in relation to more recent technologies, such as radio (Siepmann, 1941), the Internet (Iseke-Barnes, 1996), and virtual reality (Sunstein, 2018). The use of AI is in its infancy in most K–12 schools and, unsurprisingly, teachers, students, and policymakers are unsure of how to effectively embrace the affordances of AI technologies while avoiding the potential pitfalls. In addition, the technology is advancing at a rapid rate, which makes understanding its potential impacts particularly challenging.

As identified in this chapter, the TPACK framework is a useful model for unpacking the influence of the teacher on AI integration in K–12 schools. The use of AI can allow teachers to undertake focused tasks to support individual students. Through improved AI-enhanced personalisation, teachers can more readily differentiate instruction to meet the needs of a diverse student population. As has been discussed here, for these outcomes to be achieved, it is important that teachers are supported to develop skills in using AI at both the pre- and in-service level. However, with any automation of assessment and feedback come risks to the student–teacher relationship, which is a known factor affecting student engagement and reflection.

Teachers' PK will significantly influence the ways in which they integrate AI tools to support students' literacies. This is challenging, given the rapid rate at which AI tools are developing, alongside concerning ethical issues. However, we are seeing positive outcomes in the use of AI technologies to support students in specific areas such as DSW. Novel approaches to support students with disabilities are also emerging. It is essential that informed discussion takes place among the various stakeholders, with subsequent decisions on the use of specific AI technologies being based on empirical data relevant to school contexts. It is necessary to ensure that AI tools relevant to K–12 education are integrated into classrooms to enhance student learning and, in the longer term, to also prepare young people for workplaces where AI technologies are established.

REFERENCES

Adams, C., Pente, P., Lemermeyer, G., & Rockwell, G. (2023). Ethical principles for artificial intelligence in K-12 education. *Computers and Education: Artificial Intelligence*, *4*, 100131. doi:10.1016/j.caeai.2023.100131

Aiken, R. M., & Epstein, R. G. (2000). Ethical guidelines for AI in education: Starting a conversation. *International Journal of Artificial Intelligence in Education*, *11*(2), 163–176.

Akgun, S., & Greenhow, C. (2021). Artificial intelligence in education: Addressing ethical challenges in K-12 settings. *AI and Ethics, 2*(3), 431–440. doi:10.100743681-021-00096-7 PMID:34790956

Anderson, A. (2019). *Virtual reality, augmented reality and artificial intelligence in special education: A practical guide to supporting students with learning differences*. Routledge. doi:10.4324/9780429399503

Annuš, N. (2023). Weigh the pros and cons of using artificial intelligence in education. *International Journal of Science, Engineering and Technology, 11*(3), 2–5. https://www.ijset.in/wp-content/uploads/IJSET_V11_issue3_385.pdf

Barua, P. D., Vicnesh, J., Gururajan, R., Oh, S. L., Palmer, E., Azizan, M. M., Kadri, N. A., & Acharya, U. R. (2022). Artificial intelligence enabled personalised assistive tools to enhance education of children with neurodevelopmental disorders—A review. *International Journal of Environmental Research and Public Health, 19*(3), 1192. doi:10.3390/ijerph19031192 PMID:35162220

Boase, J. (2008). Personal networks and the personal communication system: Using multiple media to connect. *Information Communication and Society, 11*(4), 490–508. doi:10.1080/13691180801999001

Brekelmans, M., Wubbels, T., & Den Brok, P. (2002). Teacher experience and the teacher–student relationship in the classroom environment. In S. C. Goh & M. S. Khine (Eds.), *Studies in educational learning environments: An international perspective* (pp. 73–99). World Scientific Publishing. doi:10.1142/9789812777133_0004

Carter, L., Liu, D., & Cantrell, C. (2020). Exploring the intersection of the digital divide and artificial intelligence: A hermeneutic literature review. *AIS Transactions on Human-Computer Interaction, 12*(4), 253–275. doi:10.17705/1thci.00138

Celik, I. (2023). Towards Intelligent-TPACK: An empirical study on teachers' professional knowledge to ethically integrate artificial intelligence (AI)-based tools in education. *Computers in Human Behavior, 138*, 107468. doi:10.1016/j.chb.2022.107468

Celik, I., Dindar, M., Muukkonen, H., & Järvelä, S. (2022). The promises and challenges of artificial intelligence for teachers: A systematic review of research. *TechTrends, 66*(4), 616–630. doi:10.100711528-022-00715-y

Chattopadhyay, S., Shankar, S., Gangadhar, R. B., & Kasinathan, K. (2018). Applications of artificial intelligence in assessment for learning in schools. In J. Keengwe (Ed.), *Handbook of research on digital content, mobile learning, and technology integration models in teacher education* (pp. 185–206). IGI Global. doi:10.4018/978-1-5225-2953-8.ch010

Connolly, N., & McGuinness, C. (2018). Towards digital literacy for the active participation and engagement of young people in a digital world. In M. Magkou, R. Schwalbach, & B. Spruyt (Eds.), *Perspectives on youth: Young people in a digitalised world* (Vol. 4, pp. 77–92). Council of Europe. https://book.coe.int/en/perspectives-on-youth/7597-perspectives-on-youth-vol-4-young-people-in-a-digitalised-world.html

Davis, H. A. (2006). Exploring the contexts of relationship quality between middle school students and teachers. *The Elementary School Journal, 106*(3), 193–223. doi:10.1086/501483

Deane, P. (2013). On the relation between automated essay scoring and modern views of the writing construct. *Assessing Writing, 18*(1), 7–24. doi:10.1016/j.asw.2012.10.002

Del-Moral-Pérez, M. E., Villalustre-Martínez, L., & Neira-Piñeiro, M. D. R. (2019). Teachers' perception about the contribution of collaborative creation of digital storytelling to the communicative and digital competence in primary education schoolchildren. *Computer Assisted Language Learning, 32*(4), 342–365. doi:10.1080/09588221.2018.1517094

Druga, S., Vu, S. T., Likhith, E., & Qiu, T. (2019). Inclusive AI literacy for kids around the world. *Proceedings of FabLearn, 2019*, 104–111. doi:10.1145/3311890.3311904

El-Hamamsy, L., Chessel-Lazzarotto, F., Bruno, B., Roy, D., Cahlikova, T., Chevalier, M., Parriaux, G., Pellet, J. P., Lanares, J., Zufferey, J. D., & Mondada, F. (2021). A computer science and robotics integration model for primary school: Evaluation of a large-scale in-service K-4 teacher-training program. *Education and Information Technologies, 26*(3), 2445–2475. doi:10.100710639-020-10355-5 PMID:33162777

Felix, C. V. (2020). The role of the teacher and AI in education. In E. Sengupta, P. Blessinger, & M. S. Makhanya (Eds.), *International perspectives on the role of technology in humanizing higher education* (Vol. 33, pp. 33–48). Emerald Publishing., doi:10.1108/S2055-364120200000033003

Gardner, J., O'Leary, M., & Yuan, L. (2021). Artificial intelligence in educational assessment: 'Breakthrough? Or buncombe and ballyhoo?'. *Journal of Computer Assisted Learning, 37*(5), 1207–1216. doi:10.1111/jcal.12577

Ghajargar, M., Bardzell, J., & Lagerkvist, L. (2022, November). A redhead walks into a bar: Experiences of writing fiction with artificial intelligence. In *Academic Mindtrek 2022: Proceedings of the 25th International Academic Mindtrek Conference* (pp. 230–241). Association for Computing Machinery. 10.1145/3569219.3569418

Guilherme, A. (2017). AI and education: The importance of teacher and student relations. *AI & Society, 34*(1), 47–54. doi:10.100700146-017-0693-8

Han, X., Hu, F., Xiong, G., Liu, X., Gong, X., Niu, X., Shi, W., & Wang, X. (2018, November). Design of AI+ curriculum for primary and secondary schools in Qingdao. In *2018 Chinese Automation Congress (CAC)* (pp. 4135–4140). IEEE. 10.1109/CAC.2018.8623310

Hill, S., & Grinnell, C. (2014). Using digital storytelling with infographics in STEM professional writing pedagogy. In *2014 IEEE International Professional Communication Conference (IPCC)* (pp. 1–7). IEEE. 10.1109/IPCC.2014.7020367

Iseke-Barnes, J. M. (1996). Issues of educational uses of the Internet: Power and criticism in communications and searching. *Journal of Educational Computing Research, 15*(1), 1–23. doi:10.2190/FLYP-YNQC-9T55-MKB5

Jeffs, T., Morrison, W. F., Messenheimer, T., & Rizza, M. G. (2008). A retrospective analysis of technological advancements in special education. *Computers in Schools, 20*(1), 129–152. doi:10.1080/07380560801972961

Johnson, A. (2019). *5 ways AI is changing the education industry*. eLearningIndustry. https://elearningindustry.com/ai-is-changing-the-education-industry-5-ways

Kapetanaki, A., Krouska, A., Troussas, C., & Sgouropoulou, C. (2021). A novel framework incorporating augmented reality and pedagogy for improving reading comprehension in special education. In *Novelties in Intelligent Digital Systems* (pp. 105–110). IOS Press. doi:10.3233/FAIA210081

Koh, J., Cowling, M., Jha, M., & Sim, K. N. (2022a). Collaborating with AIed for better student-teacher reconnection. In *ASCILITE 2022 Conference Proceedings*, Article e22126. ASCILITE. 10.14742/apubs.2022.126

Koh, J., Cowling, M. A., Sim, K. N., & Jha, M. (2022b, June 22). Ways AI will change teaching and learning. *Campus Morning Mail*. https://campusmorningmail.com.au/news/ways-ai-will-change-teaching-and-learning

Kong, S. C., Cheung, W. M. Y., & Zhang, G. (2021). Evaluation of an artificial intelligence literacy course for university students with diverse study backgrounds. *Computers and Education: Artificial Intelligence*, *2*, 100026. doi:10.1016/j.caeai.2021.100026

Lankshear, C., & Knobel, M. (Eds.). (2008). *Digital literacies: Concepts, policies and practices* (*Vol. 30*). Peter Lang. https://www.peterlang.com/document/1104560

Lee, J. S. (2012). The effects of the teacher–student relationship and academic press on student engagement and academic performance. *International Journal of Educational Research*, *53*, 330–340. doi:10.1016/j.ijer.2012.04.006

Lee, M., Liang, P., & Yang, Q. (2022, April). Designing a human-AI collaborative writing dataset for exploring language model capabilities. In *CHI 2022: Conference on Human Factors in Computing Systems* (pp. 1–19). Association for Computing Machinery. 10.1145/3491102.3502030

Lin, P. Y., Chai, C. S., Jong, M. S. Y., Dai, Y., Guo, Y., & Qin, J. (2021). Modeling the structural relationship among primary students' motivation to learn artificial intelligence. *Computers and Education: Artificial Intelligence*, *2*, 100006. doi:10.1016/j.caeai.2020.100006

Lo, C. K. (2023). What is the impact of ChatGPT on education? A rapid review of the literature. *Education Sciences*, *13*(4), 410. doi:10.3390/educsci13040410

Maher, D. (2023). Video conferencing and authentic learning in the primary school classroom. In M. Leask & S. Younie (Eds.), *Teaching and learning with technologies in the primary school* (3rd ed.). Routledge.

Manyika, J., Lund, S., Chui, M., Bughin, J., Woetzel, J., Batra, P., Ko, R., & Sanghvi, S. (2017). *Jobs lost, jobs gained: Workforce transitions in a time of automation*. McKinsey Global Institute. http://hdl.voced.edu.au/10707/444873

Marino, M. T., Vasquez, E., Dieker, L., Basham, J., & Blackorby, J. (2023). The future of artificial intelligence in special education technology. *Journal of Special Education Technology*, *38*(3), 404–416. doi:10.1177/01626434231165977

Marr, B. (2018, July 25). How is AI used in education--Real world examples of today and a peek into the future. *Forbes.* https://www.forbes.com/sites/bernardmarr/2018/07/25/how-is-ai-used-in-education-real-world-examples-of-today-and-a-peek-into-the-future

McBride, C. (2015). *Children's literacy development: A cross-cultural perspective on learning to read and write* (2nd ed.). Routledge. doi:10.4324/9781315849409

Miller, F. A., Katz, J. H., & Gans, R. (2018). AI x I = AI2: The OD imperative to add inclusion to the algorithms of artificial intelligence. *OD Practitioner*, *50*(1), 6–12.

Mishra, P., & Koehler, M. J. (2006). Technological pedagogical content knowledge: A framework for teacher knowledge. *Teachers College Record*, *108*(6), 1017–1054. doi:10.1111/j.1467-9620.2006.00684.x

Ng, D. T. K., Leung, J. K. L., Chu, S. K. W., & Qiao, M. S. (2021). Conceptualizing AI literacy: An exploratory review. *Computers and Education: Artificial Intelligence*, *2*, 100041. doi:10.1016/j.caeai.2021.100041

Ng, D. T. K., Luo, W., Chan, H. M. Y., & Chu, S. K. W. (2022). Using digital story writing as a pedagogy to develop AI literacy among primary students. *Computers and Education: Artificial Intelligence*, *3*, 100054. doi:10.1016/j.caeai.2022.100054

NSW Education Standards Authority. (2017). *Digital literacy skills and learning report.* NSW. https://www.nsw.gov.au/education-and-training/nesa/about/research/reports/digital-literacy-skills-and-learning-report

O'Connor, K. E. (2008). "You choose to care": Teachers, emotions and professional identity. *Teaching and Teacher Education*, *24*(1), 117–126. doi:10.1016/j.tate.2006.11.008

O'Neil, C. (2016). *Weapons of math destruction: How big data increases inequality and threatens democracy.* Penguin Books.

Pianta, R. C., Steinberg, M. S., & Rollins, K. B. (1995). The first two years of school: Teacher–child relationships and deflections in children's classroom adjustment. *Development and Psychopathology*, *7*(2), 295–312. doi:10.1017/S0954579400006519

Regan, P. M., & Jesse, J. (2019). Ethical challenges of edtech, big data and personalized learning: Twenty-first century student sorting and tracking. *Ethics and Information Technology*, *21*(3), 167–179. doi:10.100710676-018-9492-2

Robin, B. R. (2008). Digital storytelling: A powerful technology tool for the 21st century classroom. *Theory into Practice*, *47*(3), 220–228. doi:10.1080/00405840802153916

Säljö, R. (1996). Mental and physical artifacts in cognitive practice. In P. Reimann & H. Spada (Eds.), *Learning in humans and machines: Towards an interdisciplinary learning science* (pp. 83–96). Pergamon.

SallamM. (2023). *The utility of ChatGPT as an example of large language models in healthcare education, research and practice: Systematic review on the future perspectives and potential limitations.* medRxiv. doi:10.1101/2023.02.19.23286155

Schiff, D. (2021). Out of the laboratory and into the classroom: The future of artificial intelligence in education. *AI & Society*, *36*(1), 331–348. doi:10.100700146-020-01033-8 PMID:32836908

Selwyn, N. (2018). *Six reasons AI technology will never take over from human teachers*. Monash University. https://lens.monash.edu/@education/2018/06/15/1352383/ai-technology-will-never-take-over-from-human-teachers

Shen, L., & Su, A. (2020). The changing roles of teachers with AI. In M. K. Habib (Ed.), *Revolutionizing education in the age of AI and machine learning* (pp. 1–25). IGI Global. doi:10.4018/978-1-5225-7793-5.ch001

Siepmann, C. A. (1941). Further thoughts on radio criticism. *Public Opinion Quarterly*, *5*(2), 308–312. doi:10.1086/265500

Smyrnaiou, Z., Georgakopoulou, E., & Sotiriou, S. (2020). Promoting a mixed-design model of scientific creativity through digital storytelling—The CCQ model for creativity. *International Journal of STEM Education*, *7*(1), 1–22. doi:10.118640594-020-00223-6

Spilt, J. L., Koomen, H. M., & Thijs, J. T. (2011). Teacher wellbeing: The importance of teacher–student relationships. *Educational Psychology Review*, *23*(4), 457–477. doi:10.100710648-011-9170-y

Stahl, B. C., & Wright, D. (2018). Ethics and privacy in AI and big data: Implementing responsible research and innovation. *IEEE Security and Privacy*, *16*(3), 26–33. doi:10.1109/MSP.2018.2701164

Steinbauer, G., Kandlhofer, M., Chklovski, T., Heintz, F., & Koenig, S. (2021). A differentiated discussion about AI education K-12. *Kunstliche Intelligenz*, *35*(2), 131–137. doi:10.100713218-021-00724-8 PMID:34007103

Suh, S., & An, P. (2022, March). Leveraging generative conversational AI to develop a creative learning environment for computational thinking. In *27th International Conference on Intelligent User Interfaces* (pp. 73–76). Association for Computing Machinery. 10.1145/3490100.3516473

Sunstein, C. R. (2018). *Republic: Divided democracy in the age of social media*. Princeton University Press.

Tapalova, O., Zhivenbaveva, N., & Gura, D. (2022). Artificial intelligence in education: AIEd for personalised learning pathways. *Electronic Journal of e-Learning*, *20*(5), 639–653. doi:10.34190/ejel.20.5.2597

The Institute for Ethical AI in Education. (n.d.). *The Ethical Framework for AI in Education*. Buckingham. https://www.buckingham.ac.uk/wp-content/uploads/2021/03/The-Institute-for-Ethical-AI-in-Education-The-Ethical-Framework-for-AI-in-Education.pdf

Tuomi, I. (2018). *The impact of artificial intelligence on learning, teaching, and education. Policies for the future. M. Cabrera Giraldez* (R. Vuorikari & Y. Punie, Eds.). Publications Office of the European Union., doi:10.2760/12297

UNESCO. (2019). *Artificial intelligence in education: Challenges and opportunities for sustainable development*. UNESCO. http://repositorio.minedu.gob.pe/bitstream/handle/20.500.12799/6533/Artificial%20intelligence%20in%20education%20challenges%20and%20opportunities%20for%20sustainable%20development.pdf

UNESCO. (2020a). *International forum on AI and education 2022. Steering AI to empower teachers and transform teaching* [Concept note]. UNESCO. https://en.unesco.org/sites/default/files/ai-in-education-forum-2022-cn-en.pdf

UNESCO. (2022b). *Recommendations on the ethics of artificial intelligence*. UNESCO. https://unesdoc.unesco.org/ark:/48223/pf0000381137

Vinay, S. B. (2023). Application of artificial intelligence (AI) in school teaching and learning process - Review and analysis. *International Journal of Information Technology and Management Information Systems*, *14*(1), 1–5. doi:10.17605/OSF.IO/AERNV

Waltzer, T., Cox, R. L., & Heyman, G. D. (2023). Testing the ability of teachers and students to differentiate between essays generated by ChatGPT and high school students. *Human Behavior and Emerging Technologies*, *2023*(1), 1–9. doi:10.1155/2023/1923981

Woo, J. H., & Choi, H. (2021). Systematic review for AI-based language learning tools. *Journal of Digital Contents Society*, *22*(11), 1783–1792. doi:10.9728/dcs.2021.22.11.1783

Wu, F., Lu, C., Zhu, M., Chen, H., Zhu, J., Yu, K., Li, L., Li, M., Chen, Q., Li, X., Cao, X., Wang, Z., Zha, Z., Zhuang, Y., & Pan, Y. (2020). Towards a new generation of artificial intelligence in China. *Nature Machine Intelligence*, *2*(6), 312–316. doi:10.103842256-020-0183-4

Young, K., & Maher, D. (2023). Generative AI technology to support high school students experiencing writing challenges. In R. E. Ferdig, R. Hartshorne, E. Baumgartner, R. Kaplan-Rakowski, & C. Mouza (Eds.), *What PreK-12 teachers should know about educational technology in 2023: A research-to-practice anthology* (pp. 123–132). Association for the Advancement of Computing in Education., http://hdl.handle.net/10453/171654

ADDITIONAL READING

Ayanwale, M. A., Sanusi, I. T., Adelana, O. P., Aruleba, K. D., & Oyelere, S. S. (2022). Teachers' readiness and intention to teach artificial intelligence in schools. *Computers and Education: Artificial Intelligence*, *3*, 100099. doi:10.1016/j.caeai.2022.100099

Chai, C. S., Lin, P. Y., Jong, M. S. Y., Dai, Y., Chiu, T. K., & Huang, B. (2020, August). Factors influencing students' behavioral intention to continue artificial intelligence learning. In *2020 International Symposium on Educational Technology (ISET)* (pp. 147–150). IEEE. 10.1109/ISET49818.2020.00040

Chai, C. S., Lin, P. Y., Jong, M. S. Y., Dai, Y., Chiu, T. K., & Qin, J. (2021). Perceptions of and behavioral intentions towards learning artificial intelligence in primary school students. *Journal of Educational Technology & Society*, *24*(3), 89–101. https://www.jstor.org/stable/27032858

Kangasharju, A., Ilomäki, L., Lakkala, M., & Toom, A. (2022). Lower secondary students' poetry writing with the AI-based Poetry Machine. *Computers and Education: Artificial Intelligence*, *3*, 100048. doi:10.1016/j.caeai.2022.100048

Kong, S. C., Cheung, W. M. Y., & Tsang, O. (2023). Evaluating an artificial intelligence literacy programme for empowering and developing concepts, literacy and ethical awareness in senior secondary students. *Education and Information Technologies*, *28*(4), 4703–4724. doi:10.100710639-022-11408-7

Murphy, R. F. (2019). *Artificial intelligence applications to support K–12 teachers and teaching: A review of promising applications, opportunities, and challenges*. RAND Corporation., doi:10.7249/PE315

Sanusi, I. T., & Olaleye, S. A. (2022, March). An insight into cultural competence and ethics in K-12 artificial intelligence education. In *2022 IEEE Global Engineering Education Conference (EDUCON)* (pp. 790–794). IEEE. 10.1109/EDUCON52537.2022.9766818

Shakhovska, N., Basystiuk, O., & Shakhovska, K. (2019). Development of the speech-to-text chatbot interface based on Google API. In M. Chaki, X. S. Shen, N. Nagabhushan, & G. Chaki (Eds.), *MoMLeT 2019: Proceedings of the 1st International Conference on Machine Learning, Mathematics and Education Technologies* (pp. 212–221). Springer. https://ceur-ws.org/Vol-2386/paper16.pdf

Su, J., Guo, K., Chen, X., & Chu, S. K. W. (2023). Teaching artificial intelligence in K–12 classrooms: A scoping review. *Interactive Learning Environments*, 1–20. Advance online publication. doi:10.1080/10494820.2023.2212706

Su, J., Ng, D. T. K., & Chu, S. K. W. (2023). Artificial intelligence (AI) literacy in early childhood education: The challenges and opportunities. *Computers and Education: Artificial Intelligence*, *4*, 100124. doi:10.1016/j.caeai.2023.100124

Van Brummelen, J., Heng, T., & Tabunshchyk, V. (2021, May). Teaching tech to talk: K-12 conversational artificial intelligence literacy curriculum and development tools. In *Proceedings of the AAAI Conference on Artificial Intelligence* (Vol. 35, No. 11, pp. 15655–15663). AAAI Press. 10.1609/aaai.v35i17.17844

KEY TERMS AND DEFINITIONS

Artificial Intelligence (AI): This aspect of computing is linked to software that is able to engage in human-like thought processes including learning, reasoning, and self-correction.

Literacy: This involves students listening, reading, viewing, speaking, and writing; creating oral, print, visual, and digital texts; and using and modifying language for different purposes in a range of contexts.

Peer Assessment: This is a structured process for students to critique and provide feedback to each other against success criteria related to a learning goal.

TPACK: This framework is used to understand teachers' practice and includes technological knowledge (TK), pedagogical knowledge (PK), and content knowledge (CK).

Chapter 5
Unleashing AI's Potential for Optimal Student Learning in Education:
Ethical Implications

H. Sandhya
CHRIST University (Deemed), India

Bindi Varghese
CHRIST University (Deemed), India

ABSTRACT

The impact of technology and its advancements has proliferated in all the sectors of the economy, including the education sector. The integration of technology into the education sector is very evident from the teaching pedagogy and strategies followed by educational institutions worldwide. The concept of blended learning has gained much attention due to its multifaceted nature; as it includes blending traditional face to face teaching with the use of online and electronic media. As the integration of technology requires huge amounts of student data to be processed, it can also lead to ethical dilemmas and concerns due to its sensitive and confidential nature. This chapter focuses on the various dimensions of technological integration in the education system and its practical implications on enhancing student learning and engagement. In order to provide a road map for future research on developing an education model that can improve learning and teaching experiences, the article also addresses key hurdles, ethical issues, and potential risks of integrating AI for education.

INTRODUCTION

Although the use of artificial intelligence in educational programs is not completely novel, advances in technology are enabling more useful applications. Mathematics and computer sciences are objective and rigid subjects that are ideally suited for computer-based education. They are also apt for classroom

DOI: 10.4018/979-8-3693-0205-7.ch005

or homework assignments where students may have access to a computer due to their affinity with a "drill-and-practice" style (Ahmad et al., 2023). New applications for AI in education will keep developing as the power and diversity of AI expert systems rise and the technology's grasp of natural language processing advances (Müller, 2020).

Organizational adoption of AI has increased by 270 percent over the last four years thanks to the wide range of available AI-enhanced software and service options in the commercial market. It is anticipated that adoption of AI in US education will increase by nearly 48 percent over the next three years (Bonderud, 2019). There are other connections between the uses of AI in education. Despite the fact that many separate programs might be discussed, they can work together and share data (Ansong et al., 2020). The whole capability and strength of these systems, not just individuals, must be taken into account while evaluating the possible advantages and threats of AI (Ahmad et al., 2022).

Two of the main applications of AI in education are intelligent tutoring systems (ITS) and intelligent learning environments (ILE), both of which are being increasingly adopted in a range of institutional learning scenarios (Akgun & Greenhow, 2021). An ITS imitates the function of a human tutor by keeping track of a student's progress, modifying the focus and level of a lesson's content according to the student's aptitude and interest, and offering timely advice (Araújo et al., 2021). Similar to adaptive educational hypermedia systems (AEH), which deliver interactive lessons in many media and in an adaptable manner, intelligent learning environments function by incorporating elements of ITS (Bortoló et al., 2023). Some ILEs, such as microworlds, allow students to approach the provided resources in a constructivist manner and test their ideas through trial and error (Nigam et al., 2021).

These systems continuously create models of learners, including representations of their knowledge, cognition, and metacognition. This learner model is combined with specialized knowledge and teaching skills acquired from the platform's models and external data to provide information to the learner via the user interface (Kay, 2012). The user interface presents the student with a choice of platform- and domain-appropriate learning materials based on the model the system has created for that learner (Bonderud, 2019). The user interface may also provide feedback about the learner model it has produced for all parties involved, including parents and teachers, as well as for student awareness and reflection (Nobre, 2020). Although they have been suggested for inclusion in AI learning platforms, social, environmental, motivational, and emotional, models are still relatively uncommon (Brown et al., 2019).

THE TRANSFORMATIVE OPPORTUNITIES OF AI IN EDUCATION

While it is still important to assist students in acquiring fundamental practical skills, education should also focus on the human development of its pupils as members of local, national, and international society. Education must be perceived as a means of achieving lifelong learning, fulfillment, enjoyment, welfare, opportunities, and the ability to make a positive contribution to humanity (Astle et al., 2019). Therefore, in order to empower all students to make informed decisions and cultivate their passions and distinctive abilities, schools must offer thorough access and in-depth exposure to all subject areas across all years (Chen, 2023).

The use of AI in education has been discussed from a wide variety of perspectives, from non-teaching aspects such as scheduling weekly timetables for classes, allocating resources, tracking student progress, and providing information about students to their parents or guardians in the form of progress reports, to the personalization of teaching and learning, which includes tailored design and marking of assessments, curriculum, and AI apps that support learners, or identifying changes in learner engagement (Oke & Fernandes, 2020). An applications-based view supports the position of AI as an intelligent teacher, tutee, learning tool or partner, or policy-making advisor, as the four major roles of AI in education (Rachha & Seyam, 2023).

Although it has been possible for schools to offer online education for a while and the number of students taking online courses has been rising, it wasn't until the outbreak of the COVID-19 pandemic that this style of delivery became accepted as standard (Ashok et al., 2022; Sun et al., 2020; Zhao, 2020; Sandhya, 2021). Even though there are many strong reasons for schools to revert to what was formerly considered "normal," normalcy may be difficult to attain due to the uncertainty and may not even be preferable (Sandhya & Varghese, 2023; Chennattuserry et al., 2022). According to the United Nations (2020), the shift in teaching pedagogy from being confined to the four walls of a classroom to remote learning and hybrid blended modes of teaching has resulted in a wide range of opportunities for the teachers and the learners. Teachers have been required to engage in remote instruction without being in close contact with the students (Ouyang et al., 2022). Additionally, it has provided many educators with the chance to reconsider how they interact with students and why they educate (Palomares et al., 2021). Furthermore, learning takes place at different times. When learning occurs online and children are not required to attend school or are not required to be there, their learning time is significantly extended beyond the typical school day (UNICEF, 2020). They are always able to learn independently at their own convenience (Pallathadka et al., 2022).

Another crucial point is that they don't have to study at the same time as the teacher or other students. There are numerous options for how schools can offer remote learning (Mhlanga, 2023). The simplest method is to simulate that schools are open using conventional timetables, with the default model having all students attend lessons on monitors at the same time as they do in actual classrooms (Panigrahi, 2020).

Apart from the major teaching assistant roles, AI can also empower teachers by providing the necessary aid in non-teaching activities that are equally important in an educational setting. One of the tasks that classroom aides frequently perform is relieving teachers of time-consuming basic duties like grading (Sandhya & Varghese, 2023). Due to their speedy grading by machines, multiple-choice questions have long been favored; nonetheless, they can be more challenging and time-consuming to create while being less effective for assessing higher-order learning than alternative formats (Sandhya, 2021). AI-powered software has been developed to ease some of this anxiety. The emerging concept of Massive Open Online Courses (MOOCs) has opened opportunities for AI-enabled software and applications to facilitate the grading of the students after each module or course (Sharma et al., 2021). This allows them to proceed to the next section of the course and simultaneously assess their progress.

Since AI facilitates the implementation of a variety of sensors and input devices, this may help lower the barriers between students and educational resources and activities (Celik, 2023). For students with a range of learning difficulties, live captioning with multilingual support and text-to-speech can further boost classroom integration and access to learning materials (Skavronskaya et al., 2023). AI has the potential to revolutionize accessibility in the classroom because it can operate with input and output across a variety of modes and languages. Language Learners' success with both languages and the subject of instruction may increase if they have access to instructional materials in both their native tongue and their second language (Skinner et al., 2019).

The potential ability of teachers to track and assist their students can be improved to a large extent with the help of artificial intelligence (Mhlanga, 2023). These systems are able to identify pupils who exhibit signs of undiagnosed learning, developmental, or mental health difficulties beyond baseline compliance and retention monitoring. Potential uses in surveillance and predictive policing develop as prediction models get better (Uunona & Goosen, 2023). Teachers and administrators could be better able to identify when and how students might require extra support as a result of enhanced monitoring and analysis of educational data (Masters, 2023). Teachers may find it easier to identify at-risk students and help make sure they get the support they need by using predictive analytics delivered by software.

Students perform research, produce products on their own or in small groups, present their findings in interactive discussions, and receive instructions via online resources or virtual meetings. Teachers could make videos of their lectures or find videos made by others to share with students instead of lecturing to the entire class. Additionally, they would meet with specific individuals and small groups for support and guidance. The main argument is that developing more engaging and intricate instructional models will have a greater impact on student engagement than continuous lecturing (Mhlanga, 2023).

Tools for law, medicine, and general business applications have all been developed using Artificial Intelligence. Applications for customer relations, general communication, and the administration of education could be used extensively across sectors (Masters, 2023).

The contact between people and computer applications, and occasionally even the presence of virtual agents like in-home, always-on technology-enabled electronic devices and gadgets, raises legal and ethical concerns, such as what information is gathered, who has access to it, how long the information is held, and where and how it is utilized. While gathering huge amounts of student data, there are chances that a variety of privacy concerns and issues may arise, which may have legal implications across regional boundaries (Kassymova et al., 2023). Depending on the domain in which the agent operates and the degree of exposure of the user group, the nature of these ethical dilemmas changes dramatically.

DIGITAL TECHNOLOGY INTEGRATION IN EDUCATION

Augmented Reality in Smart Classrooms

An additional cutting-edge technology that has the potential to significantly alter traditional education is augmented reality (AR) in the classroom. By adding virtual content to the real-world environment, augmented reality (AR) improves learning by adding engaging, interactive aspects that go along with the real world (Chen et al., 2020). AR may breathe new life into static textbooks and study guides. Students can access extra content like 3D models, films, or interactive quizzes by scanning images or pages with a mobile smartphone or AR-enabled device. AR can imitate scientific experiments or dissections in a secure virtual setting, letting students practice and observe without the use of pricey lab supplies or live animals (Sandhya & Varghese, 2023). By superimposing translations or pronunciations onto actual things, augmented reality can help students learn new languages and form associations (Vincent-Lancrin & Van der Vlies, 2020). Through the use of Augmented Reality (AR), students can experience historical places, natural wonders, or iconic sites from the comfort of their classrooms. It provides experiences that might not otherwise be available because of financial or geographic restrictions (Mhlanga, 2023).

AR can be customized and adjusted to meet the demands of each learner, offering material at varied degrees of difficulty or taking into account different learning preferences. Since students may interact with shared AR content, work on group projects, and solve problems together, AR encourages collaboration and teamwork among students (Uunona & Goosen, 2023). AR can be utilized for skill-based instruction, such as vocational training, where students can put their newly acquired knowledge to use by practicing activities in an enhanced environment.

There are numerous advantages and benefits to integrating AR into a classroom setting, both for the students and the teachers. Using augmented reality (AR) to learn makes the experience more engaging and motivating for students. AR can provide a customized and unique learning experience by taking into account each student's specific educational demands. Students' comprehension of difficult subjects can be increased by having them visualize abstract ideas in 3D (Uunona & Goosen, 2023). AR shows how knowledge is useful in practical contexts, bridging the gap between theory and practice. Interactive AR experiences help students remember and retain knowledge better, and AR may be inclusive and flexible for different learning methods and abilities (Masters, 2023).

Due to the need for more sophisticated technology and software engineering, producing high-quality AR content can take a lot of time and resources (Sandhya & Varghese, 2023). To effectively implement AR into their teaching approaches, educators may need training, and if not used properly, augmented reality (AR) could cause distraction and impair the learning process to a large extent (Kassymova et al., 2023). Despite the difficulties, augmented reality in the classroom has the power to transform education and increase learning's effectiveness. AR is probably going to play a massive role in modern schooling as technology develops and becomes more widely available (Uunona & Goosen, 2023).

Virtual Reality-Based Classrooms and Immersive Learning

Virtual reality education, often known as VR education or virtual learning, is a cutting-edge method of teaching and learning that makes use of virtual reality technology to produce immersive and engaging learning experiences (Gocen & Aydemir, 2021; Sandhya & Varghese, 2023). In VR-based education, students are given access to simulated settings that represent real-world situations or abstract ideas, allowing them to interact more deeply and practically with the material. Important elements of virtual reality-based instruction: Students use virtual reality headsets to fully immerse themselves in the virtual world (Masters, 2023). The movement of their head and eyes is tracked by these headsets, enabling them to look around and engage within the virtual environment (Wolla et al., 2019). VR-based education gives students the chance to investigate and engage with topics that may be challenging or impossible to access in real life. They can explore space, go to historical locations, interact with 3D models, and take part in lifelike simulations (Yan et al., 2023). This is often referred to as immersive learning, as the student is completely immersed in the technology and feels like they are actually seeing, feeling, and experiencing things (Xu et al., 2019). VR-based education is particularly beneficial for skill-based training and skill development. In areas like medical training, aviation, or technical skills, it is particularly helpful since it enables trainees to perform tasks repeatedly in a risk-free setting (Rojas-Sánchez et al.,2023). Virtual reality-based education can be customized to meet the needs and learning preferences of each student (Celik, 2023).

Learning is made more efficient when teachers modify the content or difficulty level to match each student's level of competency. Mutual collaboration, learner engagement, and social learning practices are encouraged by connecting students with other participants in the virtual world (Wolla et al., 2019). Online forums can be used for group projects and debates to improve communication and teamwork. VR delivers a holistic learning environment that improves understanding and memory retention of challenging subjects. VR-based education can be more inclusive by allowing for a variety of learning preferences and giving physically disabled students the opportunity (Masters, 2023). Due to the immersive nature of

VR-based education, student motivation and engagement are elevated. In a secure setting, students can explore and make mistakes without worrying about their future success. Students can use their knowledge in practical situations, which helps them make the transition from academic learning to real-world application (Hwang & Tu, 2021).

Despite the many benefits of VR, it also comes with many shortcomings and challenges. VR technology can be costly, and some educational institutions may find it difficult to adopt it. It might be difficult to incorporate VR-based education into an already-existing curriculum; this calls for support and training for educators (Nguyen et al., 2023). Prolonged use of VR headgear may make some users uncomfortable or queasy, making cautious time management of usage necessary. It takes a lot of time and money to produce high-quality educational VR content. Social interaction with other objects, participants, and across other systems is made possible by VR technology, which makes learning more interactive and participatory (Adiguzel et al., 2023). Within the virtual environment, they can modify items, carry out experiments, and find solutions to issues.

Blended Learning and Smart Classrooms

A method of education known as blended learning amalgamates traditional in-person classroom instruction with online learning activities. In order to provide a more efficient and adaptable learning environment, it aims to take advantage of both the benefits of in-person education and of digital resources (Hwang et al., 2020). Students may participate in a variety of online activities as part of a blended learning paradigm, including watching video lectures, finishing interactive exercises, taking part in online discussions, and accessing educational resources via learning management systems (LMS). The activities that profit from in-person engagement are then carried out during face-to-face time in the classroom, such as group projects, debates, practical experiments, and one-on-one assistance (Tucker, 2020).

Incorporating educational technology to support and enhance the teaching and learning process, a smart classroom is a learning environment that has been digitally advanced. These classrooms frequently include interactive whiteboards or smartboards, as well as audiovisual materials, internet access, and other technological resources (Wang, et al., 2023). The objective is to develop a dynamic and interactive learning environment that promotes student engagement and collaboration. The learning process can be made more dynamic and interactive by utilizing real-time access to digital materials, interactive activities, and multimedia tools in smart classrooms (Xu et al., 2019).

A powerful learning environment that promotes student engagement, personalized learning, and efficient teacher-student communication is produced when blended learning is combined with a smart classroom setup. Students in "smart classrooms" have access to digital resources, enabling them to research online information and interact with educational resources outside of traditional textbooks (Celik, 2023). In order to accommodate various learning styles and supplement in-person courses, teachers can create or curate multimedia resources (Masters, 2023). Teachers can deliver engaging, interactive lessons thanks to smartboards and interactive displays in modern classrooms. Active participation, group problem-solving, and visual concept exploration are all possible for students. Smart classrooms' interactive features can increase student motivation and deepen comprehension (Celik, 2023).

Timely feedback and evaluation are made possible in smart classrooms. Digital tools are used by teachers to monitor student knowledge in class (Wang, et al., 2023). This further helps to pinpoint areas of difficulty and modify their pedagogical approaches if necessary. The combination of blended learning and smart classrooms can enable a smooth transition to remote learning in times of unanticipated disruptions, such as pandemics or natural catastrophes. With the use of internet resources and communication platforms, students can further their education (Kassymova et al., 2023).

Overall, the use of smart classrooms and blended learning can produce a more effective, engaging, and student-centered learning environment that will give students the skills they need to succeed in the digital age without sacrificing the advantages of face-to-face interaction with classmates and teachers (Yan et al., 2023).

Natural Language Processing

By utilizing AI and language understanding capabilities, natural language processing (NLP) has the potential to significantly change education. Artificial intelligence has an area called natural language processing (NLP) that focuses on how computers and human language interact. Numerous applications in the field of education make it possible to comprehend, translate, and produce human language with the help of advanced technologies and software (Vincent-Lancrin & Van der Vlies, 2020). Intelligent tutoring systems with NLP capabilities can offer learners individualized and flexible learning opportunities (Uunona & Goosen, 2023). These systems may examine student replies, gauge their comprehension of the material, and modify the exercises and content accordingly. These tools can help students understand concepts more clearly and advance at their own pace by giving real-time feedback (Masters, 2023).

The NLP models can assess the content, coherence, and grammatical correctness to offer precise assessments. Applications for language learning can be developed using NLP to help students learn new languages. These programs can provide language training, advice on pronunciation, and assistance with translations (Khensous et al., 2023). NLP algorithms can be used to analyze and grade essays and other written assignments automatically. This can free up teachers' time and make it possible to give students consistent, timely feedback (Masters, 2023).

Teachers can assess their students' general levels of involvement and contentment by using NLP approaches to examine their sentiments and emotions. This input can be helpful in revising the course material and teaching strategies. Instances of plagiarism can be detected by NLP algorithms, which can compare student submissions to a huge library of existing texts (Xu et al., 2019). This aids teachers in upholding standards of academic honesty and ensuring the originality of students' work. Based on their preferences, learning history, and competence level, recommendation systems driven by NLP can make pertinent educational content recommendations to students (Kassymova et al., 2023). This aids students in finding fresh sources that complement their unique learning objectives (Wolla et al., 2019). NLP can be used to process and analyze a sizable volume of academic research papers, assisting researchers and educators in keeping up with the most recent developments and trends in their respective fields of study (Celik, 2023; Kooli, 2023).

Machine Learning in Education

Machine learning (ML) has many applications in the realm of education, providing creative means to improve educational outcomes, enrich the learning experience, and assist teachers in their endeavors (Jalil et al.,2019). The use of machine learning (ML) helps forecast students' academic success and spot students who may need extra help. Educators can intervene early and put plans in place to improve student results by reviewing historical data and the numerous factors influencing student success (Kučak et al., 2018). Based on students' interests, prior interactions, and learning goals, ML algorithms can suggest pertinent educational resources, such as books, videos, or online courses. This can help students learn on their own and widen their knowledge base. Based on students' interests, prior interactions, and learning goals, ML algorithms can suggest pertinent educational resources, such as books, videos, or online courses (Xu et al., 2019).

To get insights into learning trends, educational effectiveness, and opportunities for improvement, ML approaches can evaluate large-scale educational data. Policy choices and institutional planning can be made with the help of these insights (Vincent-Lancrin & Van der Vlies, 2020). This can help students learn on their own and widen their knowledge. Overall, the personalization, effectiveness, and efficiency of machine learning have the potential to change education (Alenezi & Faisal, 2020). To make sure that student data is managed ethically and openly, it is crucial to address privacy and ethical issues. In order to develop useful and significant solutions for the learning environment, coordination between educators, technologists, and policymakers is also necessary for successful ML adoption in education (Wang, et al., 2023).

EMERGING CHALLENGES IN AI

Artificial intelligence (AI) is currently a necessary component of everyday life and has an impact on all aspects of our day-to-day lives, including education (Ahmad et al., 2023). Using interdisciplinary learning, collaborative automatic evaluation systems, mobile game-based learning, or interactive chatbots for learning foreign languages reduces a teacher's workload to some extent as a result of using AI technology in the classroom, which also benefits students' learning and academic performance (Bortoló et al., 2023). Fortunately, AI-driven technology cannot, in any case, completely replace teachers' pedagogical work since it lacks the knowledge necessary to determine which instructional techniques are most effective in meeting students' learning goals (Kooli, 2023).

Although there are unquestionable advantages to using AI technology for both students and teachers, there are also some risks and threats related to ethical concerns. These risks should be carefully assessed through conceptual and empirical studies that clearly delineate what the potential threats could be. Privacy, ethical bias and discrimination, student monitoring systems, and governing student autonomy are some of the major concerns (Wolla et al., 2019).

There is an increasing need to address ethical issues including confidentiality of information, algorithmic bias, and full accountability as AI is substantially integrated into education (Limna et al., 2022). It is essential to make sure that AI systems used in education are open, just, and respectful of students' rights and welfare (Skavronskaya et al., 2023). A significant volume of student data, including personal information, learning analytics, and behavioral data, is frequently needed by AI systems in education (Kooli, 2023). To safeguard the confidentiality of the students and avoid illicit access or exploitation of sensitive information, it is crucial to ensure the privacy and security of this data (Vincent-Lancrin & Van der Vlies, 2020). Biases in the data used to train AI algorithms can affect the results, making them biased.

To prevent sustaining and worsening educational gaps, it is essential to overcome algorithmic bias, assure fairness in AI systems, and ensure that learners are not sidelined by existing inequalities like socioeconomic, racial, or gender discrimination (Jalal et al., 2021). To prevent widening the digital divide, it is crucial to ensure that everyone can have access to AI tools and technology (Jalil et al.,2019). This is especially true for disadvantaged students and members of marginalized communities. For accountability and ethical usage, precise descriptions of AI system functioning and decision-making procedures are required. Overuse of AI may compromise students' capacity for autonomous thought and diminish their sense of autonomy in the learning process (Wang et al., 2023).

The dynamics of teacher-student interaction can be significantly impacted by AI systems. It is essential to consider how AI is used in the classroom and how it impacts relationships, trust, and communication between teachers and students (Oke & Fernandes, 2020). AI tools should assist instructors' teaching practices rather than limit or replace their role in the classroom. Instead of replacing human autonomy and decision-making, AI should be developed to augment them. It is crucial to think about the potential effects of AI systems on students' autonomy, critical thinking, and creativity (Pallathadka et al., 2022).

The major ethical concern in AI could pertain to privacy. To ensure that privacy is both built into AI and supported by law, it is the aim of the current legal system to secure sensitive personal data (Kallio & Halverson, 2020). The issue is very much in the limelight and at the forefront as a result of multiple revelations by technology corporations about the extensiveness of data access and breaches. Providing potentially confidential information is necessary for basic access to many internet services. There is an impression that younger people are more willing to give up their privacy because of this, yet there is some research that suggests that younger generations value privacy more than older ones. The deeply interconnected privacy concerns may also be indicators of more profound concerns about bias, monitoring, security, accountability, and transparency (Kengam, 2020).

The multiple legal issues, particularly those involving several bodies of privacy and data protection law, provide another possible risk in the application of artificial intelligence in higher education (Li et al., 2021).Federal student privacy laws are designed to make sure that organizations (1) obtain consent before disclosing personally identifiable information and (2) permit students to access their information and contest any data they believe to be inaccurate (Limna et al., 2022). The first is not that significant if institutions are not disclosing the information to third parties or if they are doing it in accordance with the Family Educational Rights and Privacy Act (FERPA), which means they are not required to obtain students' express approval (Lee et al., 2019).

According to de Saint Laurent (2018), the developers of these AI-enabled applications and those who decide to use them must be held accountable. The potential risk of causing harm or distress to students or educational institutions can cause further damage to the student's cognitive abilities and growth, which often leads them to suffer alone without anyone being able to determine the underlying cause (Lu, 2019). The space of knowledge management with an AI enabled system in place will efficiently examine the significance of running a successful learning curve for students with an efficient management system (B Varghese, YBVL Pratyusha, 2022).

According to Cope & Kalantzis (2019), this ethical principle is crucial for both teachers and students since visualization of data highlights the need for more support from educators and portrays learner behavior. Although AI tools have been steadily employed widely in education to improve teaching and learning practices (Wang & Cheng, 2021), the issue of the transparency of the data created has not yet been resolved. It should be mentioned that transparency pertains to the data's nature, location of collection, content, subsequent handling, and intended use (Digital Curation Center, 2020).

According to recent discussions about ethics, AI systems aim to promote global justice and be equally accessible to everyone (European Commission, 2018). In order for society to really benefit from these technologies, accessibility is essential. Any individual's exclusion constitutes a violation of their human rights. Therefore, it is crucial that accessibility include reasonably priced, user-friendly designs that cater to people from various demographics and cultural backgrounds, especially those with impairments (Malle et al., 2019). The European Commission Report (2021) highlighted that inclusion and equality of access to AI-powered education have basic requirements like the availability of internet connectivity and future-oriented technological infrastructure. The fundamental lack of technology access, such as the lack of personal digital devices for students from socially disadvantaged backgrounds, calls for collaborative discussions with all educational stakeholders on the issues of inclusion in education, such as solving the lack of opportunities, resource sharing initiatives to combat areas that suffer from a lack of learning resources, and eliminating discriminatory structures that cause educational inequities (Kooli, 2023).

There can be concerns with data usage by AI; there might arise many issues, such as data that may be outdated or differ in consistency. This can affect the quality of the analysis and creation of algorithms by the software. Another issue related to data is the comprehensiveness of the data—whether the data is accurate and has complete details about the student. Technology developers and institutions can have different interests from students and institutions occasionally (Mhlanga, 2023).

Technology developers are motivated to create systems that utilize an increasing amount of data in order to produce outcomes that they can claim to be more accurate. This enables them to demonstrate the effectiveness of their systems. This can occasionally lead to a hurry to market or a focus on scale, which may not mean that the best platforms are being used or that the effectiveness of those platforms is being evaluated in any meaningful terms (Mogavi et al., 2023). It's crucial to remember that not all technology developers operate in this manner.

CONCLUSION

Compared to humans, AI systems can collect a considerably greater variety of data at finer scales. And these systems are able to accomplish it instantly. They can also evaluate a large number of students, whether these students are in a class, the student body, or a pool of applicants. Aside from that, AI systems provide high-quality observations and inferences quickly and cheaply. Given the limitations of human understanding, dealing with a diverse group of students and many different elements can be challenging. AI algorithms that are impartial or non-discriminatory are another component of inclusivity. Regardless of their gender, race, religious convictions, sexual orientation, or any other characteristics or situations, all students must be treated equally in order for society to prosper (Palomares et al., 2021).

It takes cross-functional collaboration between educators, legislators, technologists, and ethical philosophers to address these ethical challenges (Chen, 2023). Ethical norms, moral standards, and legal frameworks must be established in order to support ethical AI practices in education while preserving student rights, wellbeing, and educational justice (Gocen & Aydemir, 2021). It is quite challenging to determine if and to what degree technology can be held accountable. Although we are moving further in the direction of human-controlled artificial intelligence, it is nearly impossible to anticipate what robots or artificial intelligence will be capable of in a few decades due to the speed at which technology is advancing.

REFERENCES

Adiguzel, T., Kaya, M. H., & Cansu, F. K. (2023). Revolutionizing education with AI: Exploring the transformative potential of ChatGPT. *Contemporary Educational Technology, 15*(3), 429.

Ahmad, N., Murugesan, S., & Kshetri, N. (2023). Generative Artificial Intelligence and the Education Sector. *Computer, 56*(6), 72–76. doi:10.1109/MC.2023.3263576

Ahmad, S. F., Alam, M. M., Rahmat, M. K., Mubarik, M. S., & Hyder, S. I. (2022). Academic and administrative role of artificial intelligence in education. *Sustainability (Basel), 14*(3), 1101. doi:10.3390u14031101

Akgun, S., & Greenhow, C. (2021). Artificial intelligence in education: Addressing ethical challenges in K-12 settings. *AI and Ethics*, 1–10. doi:10.100743681-021-00096-7 PMID:34790956

Alenezi, H. S., & Faisal, M. H. (2020). Utilizing crowdsourcing and machine learning in education: Literature review. *Education and Information Technologies, 25*(4), 2971–2986. doi:10.100710639-020-10102-w

Ansong, D., Okumu, M., Albritton, T. J., Bahnuk, E. P., & Small, E. (2020). 'The role of social support and psychological well-being in STEM performance trends across gender and locality: Evidence from Ghana'. *Child Indicators Research, 13*(5), 1655–1673. doi:10.100712187-019-09691-x

Araújo, D., Couceiro, M., Seifert, L., Sarmento, H., & Davids, K. (2021). *Artificial Intelligence in Sport Performance Analysis*. Routledge. doi:10.4324/9781003163589

Ashok, M., Madan, R., Joha, A., & Sivarajah, U. (2022). Ethical framework for Artificial Intelligence and Digital technologies. *International Journal of Information Management, 62*, 102433. doi:10.1016/j.ijinfomgt.2021.102433

Astle, D. E., Bathelt, J., & Holmes, J. (2019). 'Remapping the cognitive and neural profiles of children who struggle at school'. *Developmental Science, 22*(1), 22. doi:10.1111/desc.12747 PMID:30171790

Bonderud, D. (2019). *Artificial intelligence, authentic impact: How education AI is making the grade.* EdTech. https://edtechmagazine.com/k12/article/2019/08/artificialintelligence-authentic-impact-how-educational-ai-making-grade-perfcon

Borenstein, J., Mahajan, H. P., Wagner, A. R., & Howard, A. (2020). Trust and pediatric exoskeletons: A comparative study of clinician and parental perspectives. *IEEE Transactions on Technology and Society, 1*(2), 83–88. doi:10.1109/TTS.2020.2974990

Bortoló, G. M., Valdés, J. Á., & Nicolas-Sans, R. (2023). Sustainable, technological, and innovative challenges post Covid-19 in health, economy, and education sectors. *Technological Forecasting and Social Change, 190*, 122424. doi:10.1016/j.techfore.2023.122424 PMID:36811031

Brown, A., Chouldechova, A., Putnam-Hornstein, E., Tobin, A., & Vaithianathan, R. (2019). *Toward algorithmic accountability in public services*. Paper presented at the CHI Conference on Human Factors in Computing Systems, Glasgow, Scotland. https://doi.org/10.1145/3290605.3300271https:// desc.12747

Celik, I. (2023). Towards Intelligent-TPACK: An empirical study on teachers' professional knowledge to ethically integrate artificial intelligence (AI)-based tools into education. *Computers in Human Behavior, 138*, 107468. doi:10.1016/j.chb.2022.107468

Chen, L., Chen, P., & Lin, Z. (2020). Artificial intelligence in education: A review. *IEEE Access : Practical Innovations, Open Solutions, 8*, 75264–75278. doi:10.1109/ACCESS.2020.2988510

Chen, T. J. (2023). ChatGPT and other artificial intelligence applications speed up scientific writing. *Journal of the Chinese Medical Association, 86*(4), 351–353. doi:10.1097/JCMA.0000000000000900 doi:10.1097/JCMA.0000000000000900 PMID:36791246

Chennattuserry, J. C., Varghese, B., Elangovan, N., & Sandhya, H. (2022). Pandemic Recovery Strategies: A Disaster Management Tourism Framework. In *Tourism Through Troubled Times (Tourism Security-Safety and Post Conflict Destinations)* (pp. 133–149). Emerald Publishing Limited. doi:10.1108/978-1-80382-311-920221008

Cope, B., & Kalantzis, M. (2019). Education 2.0: Artificial intelligence and the end of the test. *Beijing International Review of Education, 1*(2-3), 528–543. doi:10.1163/25902539-00102009

De Saint Laurent, C. (2018). In defence of machine learning: Debunking the myths of artificial intelligence. *Europe's Journal of Psychology, 14*(4), 734–747. doi:10.5964/ejop.v14i4.1823 PMID:30555582

Digital Curation Centre Report. (2020). *Global Partnership on Artificial Intelligence*. DCC. https://www.dcc.ac.uk/consultancy/GPAI

European Commission Report. (2018). *Annual Activity Report*. EC. https://commission.europa.eu/publications/annual-activity-reports-2018_en

European Commission Report (2021). The EU in 2021. EC. https://op.europa.eu/webpub/com/general-report-2021/en/

Gocen, A., & Aydemir, F. (2021). Artificial intelligence in education and schools. *Research on Education and Media, 12*(1), 13–21. doi:10.2478/rem-2020-0003

Hwang, G. J., & Tu, Y. F. (2021). Roles and Research Trends of Artificial Intelligence in Mathematics Education: A Bibliometric Mapping Analysis and Systematic Review. *Mathematics, 9*(6), 584. doi:10.3390/math9060584

Hwang, G. J., Xie, H., Wah, B. W., & Gašević, D. (2020). Vision, challenges, roles and research issues of Artificial Intelligence in Education. *Computers and Education: Artificial Intelligence, 1*, 100001. doi:10.1016/j.caeai.2020.100001

Jalal, S., Parker, W., Ferguson, D., & Nicolaou, S. (2021). Exploring the role of artificial intelligence in an emergency and trauma radiology department. *Canadian Association of Radiologists Journal, 72*(1), 167–174. doi:10.1177/0846537120918338 PMID:32309989

Jalil, N. A., Hwang, H. J., & Dawi, N. M. (2019). Machine learning trends, perspectives, and prospects in the education sector. In *Proceedings of the 3rd International Conference on Education and Multimedia Technology* (pp. 201-205). ACM. 10.1145/3345120.3345147

Kallio, J. M., & Halverson, R. (2020). Distributed leadership for personalized learning. *Journal of Research on Technology in Education, 52*(3), 371–390. doi:10.1080/15391523.2020.1734508

Kassymova, G. K., Malinichev, D. M., Lavrinenko, S. V., Panichkina, M. V., Koptyaeva, S. V., & Arpentieva, M. R. (2023). Ethical Problems of Digitalization and Artificial Intelligence in Education: A Global Perspective. *Journal of Pharmaceutical Negative Results*, 2150–2161.

Kengam, J. (2020). Artificial intelligence in education. *Research Gate*, *18*, 1–4.

Khensous, G., Labed, K., & Labed, Z. (2023). Exploring the evolution and applications of natural language processing in education. *Romanian Journal of Information Technology and Automatic Control*, *33*(2), 61–74.

Kooli, C. (2023). Chatbots in education and research: A critical examination of ethical implications and solutions. *Sustainability (Basel)*, *15*(7), 5614. doi:10.3390u15075614

Kučak, D., Juričić, V., & Đambić, G. (2018). Machine Learning In Education-A Survey Of Current Research Trends. *Annals of DAAAM & Proceedings, 29.*

Lee, S. H., Maenner, M. J., & Heilig, C. M. (2019). A comparison of machine learning algorithms for the surveillance of autism spectrum disorder. *PLoS One*, *14*(9), 1–11. doi:10.1371/journal.pone.0222907 PMID:31553774

Li, W., Sun, K., Schaub, F., & Brooks, C. (2021). Disparities in students' propensity to consent to learning analytics. *International Journal of Artificial Intelligence in Education*. doi:10.100740593-021-00254-2

Limna, P., Jakwatanatham, S., Siripipattanakul, S., Kaewpuang, P., & Sriboonruang, P. (2022). A review of artificial intelligence (AI) in education during the digital era. *Advance Knowledge for Executives*, *1*(1), 1–9.

Lu, X. (2019). An empirical study on the artificial intelligence writing evaluation system in China CET. *Big Data*, *7*(2), 121–129. doi:10.1089/big.2018.0151 PMID:31074642

Malle, B. F., Bello, P., & Scheutz, M. (2019). Requirements for an artificial agent with norm competence. In *Proceedings of the 2019 AAAI/ACM Conference on AI, Ethics, and Society*, (pp. 21–27). ACM. 10.1145/3306618.3314252

Masters, K. (2023). Ethical use of artificial intelligence in health professions education: AMEE Guide No. 158. *Medical Teacher*, *45*(6), 574–584. doi:10.1080/0142159X.2023.2186203 PMID:36912253

Mhlanga, D. (2023). Open AI in education, the responsible and ethical use of ChatGPT towards lifelong learning. *Education, the Responsible and Ethical Use of ChatGPT Towards Lifelong Learning*.

Mogavi, R. H., Deng, C., Kim, J. J., Zhou, P., Kwon, Y. D., Metwally, A. H. S., & Hui, P. (2023). Exploring user perspectives on chatgpt: Applications, perceptions, and implications for AI-integrated education. arXiv preprint arXiv:2305.13114.

Müller, V. C. (2020). *Ethics of Artificial Intelligence and Robotics*. Stanford. https://plato.stanford.edu/entries/ ethics-ai/

Nguyen, A., Ngo, H. N., Hong, Y., Dang, B., & Nguyen, B. P. T. (2023). Ethical principles for artificial intelligence in education. *Education and Information Technologies*, *28*(4), 4221–4241. doi:10.100710639-022-11316-w PMID:36254344

Nigam, A., Pasricha, R., Singh, T., & Churi, P. (2021). A systematic review on AI-based proctoring systems: Past, present, and future. *Education and Information Technologies*, *26*(5), 6421–6445. doi:10.100710639-021-10597-x PMID:34177348

Nobre, G. (2020). Artificial Intelligence (AI) in communications: Journalism, public relations, advertising, and propaganda. https://doi.org/doi:10.13140/RG.2.2.33598.31040

Oke, A., & Fernandes, F. A. P. (2020). Innovations in teaching and learning: Exploring the perceptions of the education sector on the 4th industrial revolution (4IR). *Journal of Open Innovation*, *6*(2), 31. doi:10.3390/joitmc6020031

Ouyang, F., Zheng, L., & Jiao, P. (2022). Artificial intelligence in online higher education: A systematic review of empirical research from 2011 to 2020. *Education and Information Technologies*, *27*(6), 1–33. doi:10.100710639-022-10925-9

Pallathadka, H., Sonia, B., Sanchez, D. T., De Vera, J. V., Godinez, J. A. T., & Pepito, M. T. (2022). Investigating the impact of artificial intelligence in education sector by predicting student performance. *Materials Today: Proceedings*, *51*, 2264–2267. doi:10.1016/j.matpr.2021.11.395

Palomares, I., Martínez-Cámara, E., Montes, R., García-Moral, P., Chiachio, M., Chiachio, J., & Herrera, F. (2021). A panoramic view and swot analysis of artificial intelligence for achieving the sustainable development goals by 2030: Progress and prospects. *Applied Intelligence*, *51*(9), 1–31. doi:10.100710489-021-02264-y PMID:34764606

Panigrahi, C. M. A., & Joshi, V. (2020). Use of artificial intelligence in education. *Management Accountant*, *55*(5), 64–67. doi:10.33516/maj.v55i5.64-67p

Rachha, A., & Seyam, M. (2023). Explainable AI In Education: Current Trends, Challenges, And Opportunities. *SoutheastCon*, *2023*, 232–239. doi:10.1109/SoutheastCon51012.2023.10115140

Rojas-Sánchez, M. A., Palos-Sánchez, P. R., & Folgado-Fernández, J. A. (2023). Systematic literature review and bibliometric analysis on virtual reality and education. *Education and Information Technologies*, *28*(1), 155–192. doi:10.100710639-022-11167-5 PMID:35789766

Sandhya, H. (2021). The Survival of Travel and Tourism Industry amidst the Covid 19 Pandemic-Challenges and Opportunities of the Indian Tourism Sector. *Atna Journal of Tourism Studies, 16*(1).

Sandhya, H., & Varghese, B. (2023). The Emerging Role of Innovative Teaching Practices in Tourism Education in the Post-COVID-19 Era. In Innovative Digital Practices and Globalization in Higher Education (pp. 286-299). IGI Global.

Sandhya, H., & Varghese, B. (2023). Big Data and Artificial Intelligence: Creative Tools for Destination Competitiveness. In Multidisciplinary Approaches in AI, Creativity, Innovation, and Green Collaboration (pp. 155-166). IGI Global.

Sharma, U., Tomar, P., Bhardwaj, H., & Sakalle, A. (2021). Artificial intelligence and its implications in education. In Impact of AI Technologies on Teaching, Learning, and Research in Higher Education (pp. 222-235). IGI Global. doi:10.4018/978-1-7998-4763-2.ch014

Skavronskaya, L., Hadinejad, A., & Cotterell, D. (2023). Reversing the threat of artificial intelligence to opportunity: A discussion of ChatGPT in tourism education. *Journal of Teaching in Travel & Tourism*, *23*(2), 253–258. doi:10.1080/15313220.2023.2196658

Skinner, B., Leavey, G., & Rothi, D. (2019). 'Managerialism and teacher professional identity: Impact on well-being among teachers in the UK'. *Educational Review*. doi:10.1080/00131911.2018.1556205

Sun, L., Tang, Y., & Zuo, W. (2020). Coronavirus pushes education online. *Nature Materials*, *19*(6), 687–687. doi:10.103841563-020-0678-8 PMID:32341513

Tucker, C. R. (2020). *Balance With Blended Learning: Partner With Your Students to Reimagine Learning and Reclaim Your Life*. Corwin.

UNICEF. (2020, August 24). Wh*at will a return to school during the COVID-19 pandemic look like?* UNICEF. https://www.unicef.org/coronavirus/what-will-return-school-during-covid-19- pandemic-look

United Nations. (2020, August). *Policy Brief: Education during COVID-19 and beyond*. United Nations. https://www.un.org/development/desa/dspd/wp-content/uploads/sites/22/2020/08/sg_ policy_brief_covid-19_and_education_august_2020.pdf

Uunona, G. N., & Goosen, L. (2023). Leveraging Ethical Standards in Artificial Intelligence Technologies: A Guideline for Responsible Teaching and Learning Applications. In Handbook of Research on Instructional Technologies in Health Education and Allied Disciplines (pp. 310-330). IGI Global. doi:10.4018/978-1-6684-7164-7.ch014

Varghese, B., & Pratyusha, Y. B. V. L. (2022). *Tools and Technologies for the Governance of Knowledge Management*. Understanding, Implementing, and Evaluating Knowledge Management in Business Settings. doi:10.4018/978-1-6684-4431-3.ch008

Vincent-Lancrin, S., & Van der Vlies, R. (2020). *Trustworthy artificial intelligence (AI) in education: Promises and challenges*.

Wang, X., Li, L., Tan, S. C., Yang, L., & Lei, J. (2023). Preparing for AI-enhanced education: Conceptualizing and empirically examining teachers' AI readiness. *Computers in Human Behavior*, *146*, 107798. doi:10.1016/j.chb.2023.107798

Wolla, S., Schug, M. C., & Wood, W. C. (2019). The economics of artificial intelligence and robotics. *Social Education*, *83*(2), 84–88.

Xu, Z., Wijekumar, K., Ramirez, G., Hu, X., & Irey, R. (2019). The effectiveness of intelligent tutoring systems on K-12 students' reading comprehension: A meta-analysis. *British Journal of Educational Technology*, *50*(6), 3119–3137. doi:10.1111/bjet.12758

Yan, L., Sha, L., Zhao, L., Li, Y., Martinez-Maldonado, R., Chen, G., & Gašević, D. (2023). Practical and ethical challenges of large language models in education: A systematic literature review. arXiv preprint arXiv:2303.13379.

Zhao, Y. (2020). Tofu Is Not Cheese: Rethinking Education Amid the COVID-19 Pandemic. *ECNU Review of Education*, *3*(2), 189–203. doi:10.1177/2096531120928082

KEY TERMS AND DEFINITIONS

Artificial Intelligence: The replication of human intelligence functions by machines, particularly computer systems, is known as artificial intelligence.

Augmented Reality: A computer-generated perception of the real world is enhanced through an interactive experience called augmented reality. Augmented reality uses software, apps, and hardware like AR glasses to superimpose digital material over actual settings and objects.

Blended Learning: A learning environment blended with technological applications and software.

Intelligent Tutoring Systems: A computer a computer programme that promises to give students personalized, immediate feedback or instruction, typically without the need for teacher intervention.

Natural Language Processing: The ability of a computer programme to comprehend spoken and written natural language is known as natural language processing (NLP).

Smart Classrooms: Classrooms unlike the traditional conventional chalk and talk method, involving smart technology applications to engage the learners well.

Virtual Reality: The computer-generated three-dimensional image of a virtual environment that can facilitate user interaction with the help of special equipment.

Chapter 6
The Rise of ChatGPT and the Demise of Bloom's Taxonomy of Learning Stages

Robertas Damaševičius
https://orcid.org/0000-0001-9990-1084
Vytautas Magnus University, Lithuania

ABSTRACT

This chapter explores the impact of the development and implementation of the ChatGPT language model on the traditional framework of Bloom's taxonomy of learning stages. Through examination of data and case studies, the study argues that the advanced natural language processing capabilities of ChatGPT have led to a shift away from the linear, hierarchical model of Bloom's taxonomy, towards a more dynamic and fluid approach to knowledge acquisition and application. The results of the study suggest that the incorporation of ChatGPT and similar language models into education and training programs may lead to more effective and efficient learning outcomes.

INTRODUCTION

ChatGPT is a large-scale language model developed by OpenAI. It uses a transformer architecture, which was introduced by Vaswani et al. (2017). The model is trained on a massive dataset of internet text, allowing it to generate human-like text with a high degree of coherence and fluency. One of the key features of ChatGPT is its ability to perform various language understanding tasks such as question answering, machine translation, and text completion. This is achieved through fine-tuning the pre-trained model on a smaller task-specific dataset. This approach is similar to that used in BERT, a transformer-based language model developed by Google, which is trained on a massive dataset of internet text and then fine-tuned for various natural language understanding tasks (Devlin et al., 2018).

ChatGPT has been used in a wide range of applications, including language translation (Liu et al., 2020), dialogue systems (Hosseini-Asl et al., 2020), and text generation (Zellers et al., 2019). It has also

DOI: 10.4018/979-8-3693-0205-7.ch006

been used in the field of education, where it has been employed as a tool for automated essay scoring (Yang et al., 2019) and for generating feedback on student writing (Wang & Hovy, 2020).

Language generation models such as ChatGPT have the potential to revolution-ize the field of education and training by introducing the capabilities of Artificial Intelligence (AI) for 21st century education (Wogu et al., 2019). These models can assist educators in a wide range of tasks, from generating feedback on student writing to creating personalized learning materials (Fernando et al., 2023; Meyer et al., 2023). One of the key advantages of language gen-eration models is their ability to generate high-quality, human-like text (Hsu & Ching, 2023). This can be useful in tasks such as automated essay scoring, where the model can provide detailed and accurate feedback on student writing. For example, a study by Yang et al. (2019) (Yang et al., 2019) used BERT, a language generation model similar to ChatGPT, to evaluate the quality of automated essay scoring. The study found that the model performed comparably to human graders in terms of both accuracy and consistency.

In addition to automated essay scoring, language generation models can also be used to generate personalized learning materials. For example, a study by Wang and Hovy (2020) used a pre-trained language model to generate personalized feedback on student writing. The study found that the feedback generated by the model was effective in helping students improve their writing skills. Language generation models can also be used in conversational agents, such as chatbots, for creating interactive and engaging learning experiences. A study by Hosseini-Asl et al. (2020) (Hosseini-Asl et al., 2020) proposed a few-shot dialogue generation model using pre-trained language models such as GPT-2 and GPT-3 to fine-tune the model for a specific task. The study found that the fine-tuned model generated high-quality and coherent responses in a dialogue setting.

The purpose of this study is to investigate the impact of the development and implementation of the ChatGPT language model on the traditional framework of Bloom's Taxonomy of Learning Stages (Benjamin, 1956). This paper aims to investigate the impact of the development and implementation of the ChatGPT language model on the traditional framework of Bloom's Taxonomy of Learning Stages. The research conducted in this paper will contribute to the field by providing insights into the potential implications of using ChatGPT and similar language models in education and training programs for knowledge acquisition and application. The chapter will also explore the effectiveness and efficiency of using ChatGPT in education and training programs compared to traditional methods, and the potential of ChatGPT to create personalized learning materials and provide automated and personalized feedback to students.

To guide our study, we formulate the following Research Questions:

(a) How does the advanced natural language processing capabilities of ChatGPT affect the traditional linear, hierarchical model of Bloom's Taxonomy?
(b) What are the implications of using ChatGPT and similar language models in education and training programs for knowledge acquisition and application?
(c) How does the incorporation of ChatGPT in education and training programs compare to traditional methods in terms of effectiveness and efficiency?
(d) Can ChatGPT be used to create personalized learning materials and provide automated and personalized feedback to students?
(e) What are the ethical considerations in using language generation models such as ChatGPT in education?

LITERATURE REVIEW

Bloom's Taxonomy of Learning Stages and its Traditional Application in Education

Bloom's Taxonomy of Learning Stages, also known as Bloom's Taxonomy, is a framework for classifying educational goals and objectives into different levels of complexity and specificity. It was first published in 1956 by B. Bloom and his colleagues (Benjamin, 1956) and has since become one of the most widely used frameworks in education. The original taxonomy consisted of three domains: cognitive, affective, and psychomotor. The cognitive domain, which is the most widely used and studied, is further divided into six levels, each representing a different stage of learning:

- **Remembering:** ability to recall previously learned information.
- **Understanding:** ability to comprehend the meaning of learned information.
- **Applying:** ability to use learned information in new situations.
- **Analyzing:** ability to break down learned information into parts and understand their relationships.
- **Evaluating:** ability to make judgments about the value of learned information.
- **Creating:** ability to use learned information to generate new ideas or products.

The original taxonomy has undergone several revisions since its initial publication, with the most recent revision published in 2001 (Anderson, & Krathwohl, 2001). The revised taxonomy made changes to the labels and definitions of the cognitive domain, but the basic structure of the six levels remained unchanged. The traditional application of Bloom's Taxonomy in education is to use the framework as a guide for designing educational goals and objectives. Educators are encouraged to align their instruction and assessments with the different levels of the taxonomy, with the goal of helping students progress through the stages of learning. For example, instruction and assessments at the lower levels (e.g., remembering and understanding) should focus on providing students with basic knowledge and comprehension, while instruction and assessments at the higher levels (e.g. analyzing, evaluating, and creating) should focus on helping students apply, analyze, evaluate, and create with the knowledge they have acquired. One of the key advantages of Bloom's Taxonomy is its ability to provide a clear and measurable framework for educational goals and objectives. By aligning instruction and assessments with the different levels of the taxonomy, educators can more effectively evaluate student learning and provide targeted feedback.

Use of Language Models in Education and Their Potential Effects on the Learning Process

Previous research on the use of language generation models, such as ChatGPT, in education has shown that these models have the potential to revolutionize the field of education and training. Language generation models can assist educators in a wide range of tasks, from generating feedback on student writing to creating personalized learning materials. One of the key advantages of language generation models is their ability to generate high-quality, human-like text. This can be useful in tasks such as automated essay scoring, where the model can provide detailed and accurate feedback on student writing. For example, a study by Yang et al. (2019) (Yang et al., 2019) used BERT, a language generation model similar to

ChatGPT, to evaluate the quality of automated essay scoring. The study found that the model performed comparably to human graders in terms of both accuracy and consistency.

In addition to automated essay scoring, language generation models can help to generate personalized learning materials. A study by Wang and Hovy (2020) used a pre-trained language model to generate personalized feedback on student writing. The study found that feedback generated by the model was effective in helping students improve their writing skills.

Language generation models can also be used in conversational agents, such as chatbots, for creating interactive and engaging learning experiences. A study by Hosseini-Asl et al. (2020) (Hosseini-Asl et al., 2020) proposed a few-shot dialogue generation model using pre-trained language models such as GPT-2 and GPT-3 to fine-tune the model for a specific task. The study found that the fine-tuned model generated high-quality and coherent responses in a dialogue setting.

Generation of education materials is an important capability of language genera-tion models. A study by Li et al. (2021) (Li et al., 2021) used GPT-3 to generate personalized language learning materials, such as flashcards and quizzes, for students learning a foreign language. The study found that the materials generated by the model were effective in helping students improve their language skills. A study by Ramachandran et al. (2021) (Ramachandran et al., 2021) used GPT-3 to generate educational materials such as summaries, questions and answers, and diagrams for science and math education. The study found that the materials generated by the model were effective in helping students improve their understanding of the subject.

However, there are also limitations to the use of language generation models in education (Kasneci et al., 2023; Milano et al., 2023). One limitation is the potential for bias in the model's language generation, which can perpetuate and amplify societal biases (Fuchs, 2023). This can be particularly problematic in tasks such as automated essay scoring, where the model's biases can affect the fairness of the assessment. Additionally, while language gener-ation models can assist in the creation of personalized learning materials (Font de la Vall & Araya, 2023), they can't replace the expertise and guidance of a human teacher.

In summary, previous research on the use of language generation models in education (Alqahtani et al., 2023; Rahman & Watanobe, 2023; Yan et al., 2023) has shown that these models have the potential to revolutionize the field of education and training by providing automated and personalized feedback, generating personalized learning materials, and creating interactive and engaging learning experiences. However, there are also limitations to the use of these models, particularly regarding bias and the potential for these models to replace the expertise and guidance of human teachers.

Limitations of the Traditional Linear Model of Bloom's Taxonomy

The traditional linear model of Bloom's Taxonomy, which presents learning as a progression through a series of stages, has several limitations in light of the capabilities of chatbots such as ChatGPT. One limitation is that the traditional linear model of Bloom's Taxonomy does not fully capture the complexity and dynamic nature of learning (Amer, 2006). Chatbots such as ChatGPT can provide real-time feedback and respond to student's questions and needs, which allows for a more interactive and personalized learning experience. However, the traditional model of Bloom's Taxonomy doesn't consider multiple pathways and non-linear progressions in learning.

Another limitation is that the traditional linear model of Bloom's Taxonomy does not fully leverage the capabilities of chatbots such as ChatGPT in creating personalized and adaptive learning experiences. Chatbots are able to adapt to the needs and abilities of individual students and can provide a personalized learning experience by providing targeted feedback and guidance. However, the traditional linear model of Bloom's Taxonomy does not consider the potential for personalized and adaptive learning.

A third limitation is that the traditional linear model of Bloom's Taxonomy does not fully incorporate the use of technology in education (Alaghbary, 2021). Chatbots such as ChatGPT are able to use natural language processing (NLP) and machine learning to understand and respond to student's questions, providing a more engaging and interactive learning experience. However, the traditional linear model of Bloom's Taxonomy does not fully incorporate the use of technology in education.

Philosophical Roots of the Chatbots' Dialogue-Based Model for Education

The dialogue-based model for education used by chatbots such as ChatGPT has roots in several philosophical perspectives, including constructivism (Fox, 2001) and dialogic learning (Haneda, 2017).

Constructivism, a theory of learning, states that individuals construct their own understanding of the world through their experiences and interactions with it. This theory emphasizes the importance of active and self-directed learning, where learners are encouraged to construct their own understanding of the subject. Chatbots, through their dialogue-based model, provide a platform for interactive and active learning, where learners can engage in a dialogue with the chatbot and construct their own understanding of the subject.

Dialogic learning is a theory that emphasizes the importance of dialogue in learning, which occurs through interaction and communication between individuals. This theory is rooted in the works of Mikhail Bakhtin, who believed that dialogue is essential for meaning making, and that individuals construct their understanding of the world through dialogue with others (Bandlamudi, 2015). Chatbots, through their dialogue-based model, provide a platform for dialogic learning, where learners can engage in a dialogue with the chatbot and construct their understanding of the subject.

Another philosophical root for the dialogue-based model for education used by chatbots is the Socratic method (Ho et al., 2023), which is a method of teaching that emphasizes critical thinking and self-discovery. The Socratic method is based on the belief that the best way to learn is to question and discuss the subject with others. Chatbots, through their dialogue-based model, provide a platform for the Socratic method, where learners can question and discuss the subject with the chatbot (Abdelghani et al., 2023).

Arthur Schopenhauer's philosophical idea of the world as representation (Schopenhauer et al., 2016) posits that the world is perceived differently by individuals and that individuals create their own understanding of the world based on their experiences and perceptions. This idea is related to the style of learning promoted by ChatGPT in that ChatGPT allows individuals to construct their own understanding of the subject through interactive and active learning. ChatGPT, through its dialogue-based model, provides a platform for interactive and active learning, where learners can engage in a dialogue with the chatbot and construct their own understanding of the subject. This is similar to Schopenhauer's idea that individuals construct their own understanding of the world based on their experiences and perceptions. Additionally, ChatGPT provides personalized and adaptive learning, where it adapts to the needs and abilities of individual students, and can provide a personalized learning experience by providing targeted feedback and guidance. This is also in line with Schopenhauer's idea that the world is perceived differently by individuals, and that individuals create their own understanding of the world based on their experiences and perceptions.

Transition to a New Model of E-Learning

The appearance of ChatGPT at a critical time when traditional education models were broken by lockdowns due to the COVID-19 pandemic, has helped spearhead the transition to a new model of e-learning. The pandemic has forced educational institutions to shift to remote and online learning, and chatbots such as ChatGPT have proven to be a valuable tool in this transition. ChatGPT and similar models can provide real-time feedback and respond to student's questions and needs, which allows for a more interactive and personalized learning experience. A study by Chen et al. (2021) (Chen et al., 2021) found that the use of a chatbot in an online course led to improved student engagement and satisfaction. In addition to providing real-time feedback, ChatGPT can also be used to generate personalized learning materials. A study by Wang and Hovy (2020) (Wang & Hovy, 2020) used a pre-trained language model to generate person-alized feedback on student writing. The study found that the feedback generated by the model was effective in helping students improve their writing skills. The use of chatbots such as ChatGPT in e-learning also allows for more flexibility in the learn-ing process. A study by Hosseini-Asl et al. (2020) (Hosseini-Asl et al., 2020) proposed a few-shot dialogue generation model using pre-trained language models such as GPT-2 and GPT-3 to fine-tune the model for a specific task. The study found that the fine-tuned model generated high-quality and coherent responses in a dialogue setting and can be used as a personalized tutor, working according to the student's schedule.

THE DIALOGUE-BASED MODEL OF EDUCATION PROMOTED BY CHATGPT

Ideation as a Learning Stage

Ideation plays a crucial role in the dialogue-based model of education promoted by ChatGPT. Ideation refers to the process of generating and developing new ideas and concepts (McGlashan, 2018). In the context of education, ideation is important because it allows learners to think critically and creatively, and to develop their own understanding of the subject. In the dialogue-based model of education, ChatGPT can help facilitate ideation by providing learners with new information and perspectives, and by encouraging learners to ask questions and generate their own ideas and hypotheses. For example, ChatGPT can be used to generate questions and prompts that encourage learners to think critically and creatively about a topic. These prompts can be used to initiate a dialogue between the learner and the chatbot, where the learner can explore different ideas and concepts related to the topic. Additionally, ChatGPT can provide learners with new information and perspectives that can be used to generate new ideas and hypotheses. Furthermore, ChatGPT can also be used to evaluate and provide feedback on the ideas and concepts generated by learners. This feedback can help learners to refine their ideas and concepts and to develop a deeper understanding of the subject.

Including the Ideation stage into a Revised Bloom's Taxonomy can significantly enhance the learning experience and promote higher-order thinking skills. Ideation, which involves generating creative ideas, solutions, and concepts, adds a crucial dimension to the learning process that goes beyond traditional cognitive levels. Including Ideation can provide support for:

- ***Fostering Creativity***: Ideation encourages learners to think beyond the conventional boundaries and explore innovative solutions. It nurtures creativity, allowing students to come up with original ideas and perspectives.
- ***Real-world Problem Solving***: By incorporating Ideation, learners develop the ability to tackle complex problems by generating novel approaches, leading to practical solutions.
- ***Enhancing Critical Thinking***: Ideation pushes learners to critically evaluate their ideas, identifying strengths and weaknesses. This critical analysis hones their ability to make informed decisions and refine their concepts.
- ***Preparation for Modern Workforce***: In today's dynamic job market, creativity and innovation are highly valued. Including Ideation in education equips learners with skills that are increasingly sought after by employers across industries.
- ***Interdisciplinary Learning***: Many innovative solutions arise at the intersection of different disciplines. Including Ideation can encourage interdisciplinary thinking and collaboration, bridging gaps between subjects.
- ***Lifelong Learning***: Ideation encourages an open mindset and a curiosity-driven approach to learning. These attributes are essential for continuous learning throughout one's life.

Updated Bloom's Taxonomy

By incorporating Ideation into Revised Bloom's Taxonomy not only reflects the evolving educational landscape but also prepares learners to navigate a rapidly changing world. It empowers them to become creative thinkers, problem solvers, and innovators who can contribute meaningfully to their communities and society. Therefore, we present the following Revised Bloom's Taxonomy updated with the concept of Ideation as follows:

1. **Remembering:** recalling information to generate new ideas and concepts.
2. **Understanding:** Interpreting information to generate new ideas and concepts.
3. **Applying:** Using information to generate new ideas and concepts.
4. **Analyzing:** Breaking down information to generate new ideas and concepts.
5. **Evaluating:** Assessing the value of information to generate new ideas and concepts.
6. **Creating:** Putting elements together to form a coherent or new whole.
7. **Ideation:** Generating and developing new ideas and concepts.

The mapping between Updated Bloom's Taxonomy and Dialogue-based Model of Education is presented in Table 1. In this table, the columns represent the concepts of the updated Bloom's Taxonomy and the rows represent the concepts of the Dialogue-based Model of Education Taxonomy. The cells contain a concept-to-concept mapping and discuss the relationship between the corresponding concepts, showing how these concepts are related and how they support each other.

Example of the ChatGPT's Dialogue-Based Learning Model

Here we present an example of instruction in a mathematics course using the dialogue-based learning model generated by ChatGPT.

Table 1. Concept-to-Concept mapping between updated Bloom's taxonomy and dialogue-based model of education

	Remembering	Understanding	Applying	Analyzing	Evaluating	Creating	Ideation
Updated Bloom's taxonomy	Remembering is a necessary step to generate new ideas, by recalling previous information and experiences.	Understanding is a necessary step to generate new ideas, by interpreting and making sense of the information.	Applying is a necessary step to generate new ideas, by using the information to explore different possibilities.	Analyzing is a necessary step to generate new ideas, by breaking down the information to understand its components and relationships.	Evaluating is a necessary step to generate new ideas, by assessing the information and its potential value.	Creating is a necessary step to generate new ideas, by combining different elements of information to form a new whole.	Ideation is the process of generating and developing new ideas and concepts.
Socratic Method	requires students to recall information in order to generate questions and ideas.	requires students to understand the information in order to generate questions and ideas.	encourages students to apply the information in order to generate questions and ideas.	encourages students to analyze the information in order to generate questions and ideas.	encourages students to evaluate the information in order to generate questions and ideas.	encourages students to create new ideas and questions based on the information.	encourages students to generate and develop new ideas and concepts through the asking of questions.
Constructivism	active, hands-on learning, which can help students to recall information and generate new ideas.	understanding information through personal experience, which can help students to generate new ideas.	applying information in order to construct new knowledge, which can help students to generate new ideas.	breaking down information in order to construct new knowledge, which can help students to generate new ideas.	evaluating information in order to construct new knowledge, which can help students to generate new ideas.	creating new knowledge through personal experience, which can help students to generate new ideas.	generating and developing new ideas and concepts through active, hands-on learning and the construction of knowledge through personal experience.
Vygotsky's sociocultural theory of learning	social interaction in recalling and sharing information, which can help students to generate new ideas.	understanding information in the context of culture and society, which can help students to generate new ideas.	applying information within the context of culture and society, which can help students to generate new ideas.	analyzing information within the context of culture and society, which can help students to generate new ideas.	evaluating information within the context of culture and society, which can help students to generate new ideas.	creating new knowledge within the context of culture and society, which can help students to generate new ideas.	generating and developing new ideas and concepts through social interaction and Cultural context.

continued on following page

Table 1. Continued

	Remembering	Understanding	Applying	Analyzing	Evaluating	Creating	Ideation
Schopen-	perceptions	understanding	applying the	analyzing the	evaluating the	creating new	generating and
hauer's	and expe-	the relation-	understanding	relationship	relationship	understanding	developing
"world as	riences in	ship between	of percep-	between per-	between per-	through the	new ideas
representa-	shaping one's	perceptions	tions and	ceptions and	ceptions and	relationship	and concepts
tion"	understanding	and experi-	experiences,	experiences,	experiences,	between per-	through the
	and recall of	ences, which	which can	which can	which can	ceptions and	understanding
	information,	can help	help students	help students	help students	experiences,	of percep-
	which can	students to	to generate	to generate	to generate	which can	tions and
	help students	generate new	new ideas.	new ideas.	new ideas.	help students	experiences.
	to generate	ideas.				to generate	
	new ideas.					new ideas.	

Let us say that a university mathematics professor is teaching a course on Calculus and is discussing the concept of limits with their students.

The professor begins by posing a question to the students:" Can anyone tell me what a limit is in Calculus?"

A student responds by saying," A limit is the value that a function approaches as the input approaches a certain value."

The professor reflects on the student's response and confirms that it is a good start to understanding the concept of limits. The professor then follows up with another question:" Can anyone give me an example of a function that has a limit?"

Another student responds by saying," The function f(x) = 1/x has a limit of zero as x approaches infinity."

The professor reflects on the student's response and confirms that it is correct. The professor then provides further explanation of the concept of limits, using examples and diagrams to help the students understand the concept better.

Then, the professor engages the students in an active learning activity where they work in pairs to identify limits of different functions and provide explanations for their choices. The professor provides feedback and evaluation to the students on their work, correcting any misunderstandings and reinforcing key concepts. The professor summarizes the key concepts covered in the lesson and asks the students to reflect on what they have learned. Finally, the professor closes the session by asking the students to think about how they can apply the concept of limits to real-world problems and encourages them to continue to explore the topic on their own.

The diagram presented in Figure 1 shows the sequence of actions and communication between the professor and the students during the lesson on Calculus. The arrows indicate the flow of communication, with the professor posing questions and providing feedback and the students responding and engaging in active learning activities.

Reinvented Learning Scenario Using ChatGPT

Here, we present a Reinvented learning scenario using ChatGPT that is based on dialogic learning and Updated Bloom's Taxonomy including the Ideation concept.

The professor begins by posing a question to the students:" Can anyone tell me what a limit is in Calculus?"

A student responds by saying," A limit is the value that a function approaches as the input approaches a certain value."

The professor asks ChatGPT to provide additional information on the concept of limits in Calculus.

ChatGPT generates a response that provides a detailed explanation of limits in Calculus, using examples and diagrams to help the students understand the concept better.

The professor reflects on ChatGPT's response and confirms that it is a good addition to the discussion.

The professor follows up with another question: "Can anyone give me an example of a function that has a limit?"

Another student responds by saying," The function f(x) = 1/x has a limit of zero as x approaches infinity."

The professor asks ChatGPT to verify the student's response.

ChatGPT confirms that the student's response is correct and provides additional information on how to find the limit of the function.

The professor reflects on ChatGPT's response and confirms that it is accurate. Then, the professor engages the students in an active learning activity where they work in pairs to identify limits of different functions and provide explanations for their choices. The professor provides feedback and evaluation to the students on their work, correcting any misunderstandings and reinforcing key concepts. The professor summarizes the key concepts covered in the lesson and asks the students to reflect on what they have

Figure 1. Chat GPT

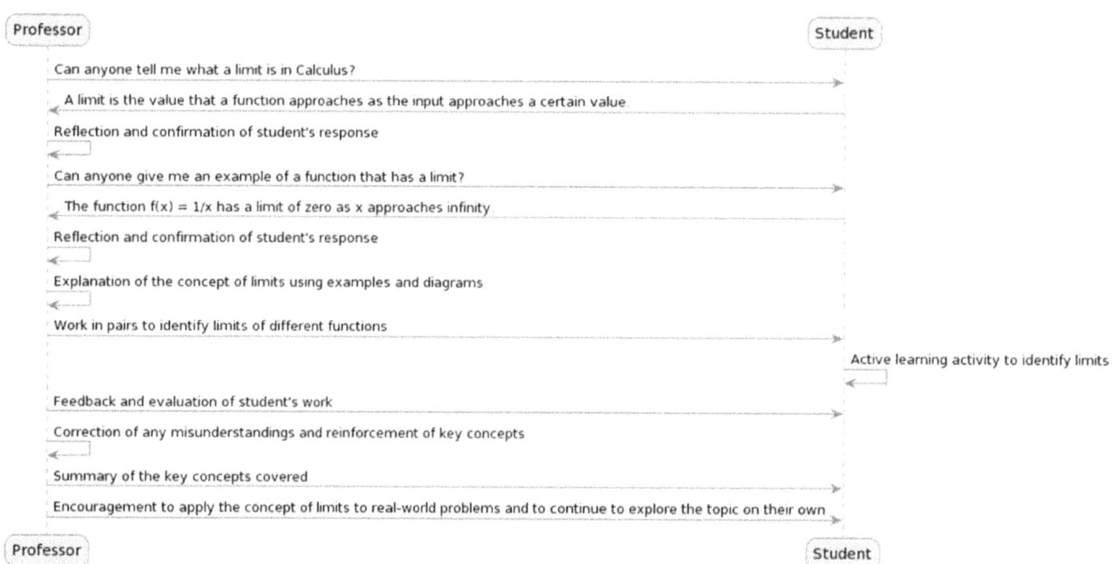

learned. The professor closes the session by asking the students to think about how they can apply the concept of limits to real-world problems and encourages them to continue to explore the topic on their own.

The diagram presented in Figure 2 shows the sequence of actions and communi-cation between the professor, students, and ChatGPT during the lesson on Calculus. The arrows indicate the flow of communication, with the professor posing questions and interacting with ChatGPT, and the students responding and engaging in active learning activities.

This learning scenario incorporates ChatGPT as a part of the learning process to provide additional information and verification of student responses. The use of ChatGPT can enhance the learning experience by providing personalized feedback and support to students. The active learning activity remains unchanged, as it provides an opportunity for students to apply the concepts they have learned. In this example, the dialogue-based learning model promoted by ChatGPT is used to promote active student engagement and to encourage deep learning. The model emphasizes the importance of reflection, feedback, and active learning, which can help students develop a deeper understanding of the subject. By using this model, the professor is able to create a collaborative learning environment where students can share their ideas and learn from each other, while also receiving guidance and feedback from the professor.

Evaluation of Activities

ChatGPT chatbot supported dialogue-based learning involves several main activities, including ChatGPT interaction, reflection, and synthesis. Here's a brief overview of each activity:

- ChatGPT interaction involves the interaction between the student and ChatGPT, where the student asks questions or provides responses, and ChatGPT generates responses based on its NLP capabilities. This interaction allows for a more per-sonalized learning experience, as ChatGPT can provide immediate feedback and support to the student based on their individual needs and preferences.
- Reflection involves the professor or instructor reflecting on ChatGPT's responses and verifying the accuracy of the information provided. This activity is important to ensure that the information provided by ChatGPT is correct and appropriate for the learning objectives.

Figure 2. Sequence diagram of the example dialogue-based learning scenario which included ChatGPT as a participant of the learning process

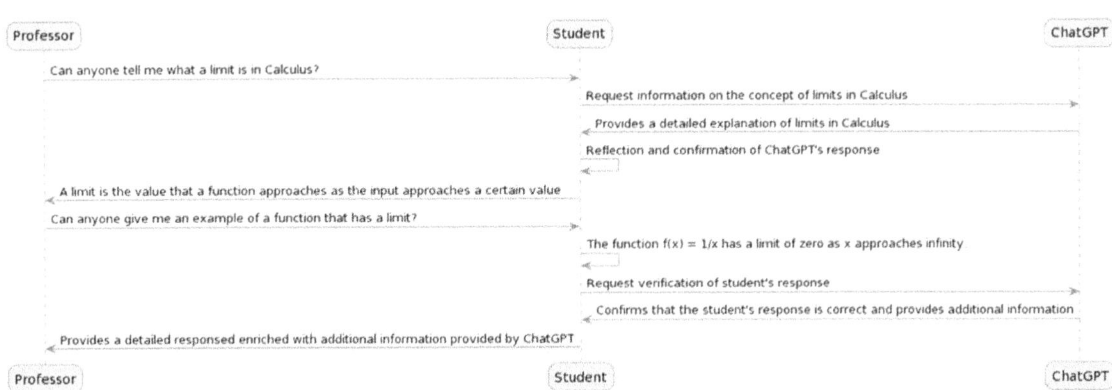

- Synthesis involves summarizing the key concepts covered during the learning session and asking the student to reflect on what they have learned. This activity allows the student to consolidate their understanding of the concepts and apply them to real-world problems.

By incorporating ChatGPT into dialogue-based learning, these activities can help to enhance the learning experience by providing personalized feedback and support to students. ChatGPT interaction allows students to ask questions and receive immediate responses, which can improve the efficiency of the learning process. Reflection and synthesis activities allow for a more flexible and adaptive approach to learning, as the professor or instructor can adjust the content and pace of the lesson based on the student's understanding of the concepts. Overall, ChatGPT chatbot supported dialogue-based learning has the potential to be an effective tool for providing personalized learning experiences and improving learning outcomes.

Limitations of Using ChatGPT's Dialogue-Based Learning Model

While the dialogue-based learning model using ChatGPT has many advantages, there are also some limitations and potential sources of bias to consider. Here are some examples:

- While ChatGPT can provide some level of interaction between the student and the AI, it may not be able to provide the same level of interaction and feedback as a human instructor. This can limit the depth and quality of the learning experience.
- ChatGPT uses NLP to understand and respond to student input. However, NLP can be biased, based on the language data used to train the AI. This can lead to biased responses and feedback that may not be accurate or appropriate.
- ChatGPT may not be able to fully understand the unique needs and learning styles of individual students. This can lead to a one-size-fits-all approach to learning that may not be effective for all students.
- ChatGPT and other AI-based learning tools can be limited by technical issues such as connectivity, server downtime, and software bugs, which can impact the reliability and availability of the tool.

It is important to address these limitations and potential sources of bias by pro-viding additional support and resources for students and by continuously evaluating the effectiveness of the learning tool. Additionally, it is important to consider the ethical implications of using AI in education and to ensure that student data is protected and used appropriately. Overall, while the dialogue-based learning model using ChatGPT has many potential benefits, it is important to use it in a thoughtful and responsible way to ensure that it is effective and inclusive for all learners.

RESULTS

How Does the Advanced NLP Capabilities of ChatGPT Affect the Traditional Linear, Hierarchical Model of Bloom's Taxonomy?

The advanced NLP capabilities of ChatGPT can potentially have an impact on the traditional linear, hierarchical model of Bloom's Taxonomy by allowing for a more personalized and interactive learning experience. ChatGPT's ability to understand and respond to natural language queries can allow for a more conversational and dynamic approach to learning, which may not fit neatly into the linear, hierarchical structure of Bloom's Taxonomy. For example, ChatGPT can use NLP to evaluate student responses and provide feedback that is tailored to the individual student's level of understanding. This can allow for a more flexible and adaptive approach to learning that is not limited by the strict structure of Bloom's Taxonomy. Additionally, ChatGPT can use NLP to generate open-ended questions that encourage higher order thinking and problem-solving, which are key components of Bloom's Taxonomy.

However, while ChatGPT's advanced NLP capabilities can enhance the learning experience, it should not replace the traditional linear, hierarchical model of Bloom's Taxonomy entirely. The model still provides a useful framework for organizing and evaluating learning outcomes, and can be used in conjunction with ChatGPT to ensure that learning is scaffolded and aligned with specific learning objectives. Additionally, there may be some limitations and potential sources of bias in the NLP capabilities of ChatGPT, which should be taken into consideration when using it in an educational setting.

Overall, the advanced NLP capabilities of ChatGPT can potentially have an impact on the traditional linear, hierarchical model of Bloom's Taxonomy by allowing for a more personalized and interactive learning experience. However, it is important to use ChatGPT in conjunction with Bloom's Taxonomy to ensure that learning is scaffolded and aligned with specific learning objectives.

What are the Implications of Using ChatGPT and Similar Language Models in Education and Training Programs for Knowledge Acquisition and Application?

Using ChatGPT and similar language models in education and training programs can have profound implications for knowledge acquisition and application. These AI-powered tools offer learners instant access to vast repositories of information, accelerating the process of acquiring knowledge. Learners can ask questions and receive immediate, tailored responses, leading to quicker comprehension of complex concepts. This personalized approach fosters engagement and enhances knowledge retention by catering to individual learning styles and preferences. An important shift facilitated by language models is the transition from passive learning to active engagement. Learners are encouraged to interact with ChatGPT through queries, discussions, and clarifications. This dynamic exchange stimulates critical thinking and promotes an environment where students take an active role in shaping their learning journey.

Similarly, ChatGPT's assistance extends beyond theoretical understanding, enabling learners to apply acquired knowledge to practical scenarios. Engaging in discussions with the model can lead to insights that aid the application of learned concepts to real-world challenges, fostering problem-solving skills. By using ChatGPT, learners can engage in brainstorming sessions to generate ideas and solutions. The model's responses offer diverse perspectives, pushing learners to think creatively and explore alternative viewpoints. This promotes not only a deeper understanding of the subject but also nurtures essential skills for innovative thinking. As a tool available around the clock, ChatGPT supports continuous learning beyond traditional classroom hours, fostering a culture of lifelong learning and self-directed education. Language models complement educators' roles, offering additional resources and support. This allows educators to focus on higher-order discussions and mentoring, while routine queries can be addressed by ChatGPT. Learners can efficiently gather information for research projects, enabling them to delve deeper into subjects and access a wide array of sources with ease. Moreover, using ChatGPT encourages ethical and critical thinking as learners evaluate the credibility and potential biases of AI-generated content.

How Does the Incorporation of ChatGPT in Education and Training Programs Compare to Traditional Methods in Terms of Effectiveness and Efficiency?

Incorporating ChatGPT in education and training programs can have several potential advantages over traditional methods in terms of effectiveness and efficiency. Here are some examples:

- ChatGPT can provide personalized learning experiences that are tailored to in-dividual learner needs and preferences, which can improve learning outcomes compared to traditional one-size-fits-all approaches.
- ChatGPT can provide learners with immediate feedback and support, which can increase the efficiency of the learning process by allowing learners to correct mistakes and make adjustments quickly.
- ChatGPT can help save time by automating certain tasks, such as grading and assessment, which can free up instructors to focus on other aspects of teaching and training (Chaowicharat & Dejdumrong, 2023).
- ChatGPT has the potential to be a cost-effective solution for education and train-ing, as it can reduce the need for expensive classroom resources and instructors.
- ChatGPT can provide access to education and training to a wider range of learners who may not have access to traditional classroom settings or who may need to learn at their own pace.

However, while ChatGPT can be effective and efficient in some contexts, it may not be suitable for all learners or all types of content. Additionally, ChatGPT is still a relatively new technology, and there is limited research on its effectiveness compared to traditional methods. Therefore, it is important to evaluate the effectiveness and efficiency of ChatGPT in specific contexts and with specific learning objectives in mind. Overall, the incorporation of ChatGPT in education and training programs can potentially be more effective and efficient than traditional methods, but this depends on a range of factors and should be evaluated on a case-by-case basis.

Can ChatGPT Be Used to Create Personalized Learning Materials and Provide Automated and Personalized Feedback to Students?

ChatGPT can be used to create personalized learning materials and provide automated and personalized feedback to students. ChatGPT's can respond to student input in a way that is similar to a human teacher. This means that ChatGPT can be used to create personalized learning materials that are tailored to the needs and preferences of individual students. For example, ChatGPT can use student data, such as learning style preferences and performance history, to generate customized learning materi-als that are optimized for the individual student's learning needs (Okewu et al., 2021). Additionally, ChatGPT can provide automated and personalized feedback to students, which can help them to identify areas where they need to improve and provide guidance on how to improve. For example, ChatGPT can evaluate student responses and provide feedback that is tailored to the individual student's level of understanding. This can allow for a more flexible and adaptive approach to learning that is not limited by the constraints of traditional classroom settings.

Overall, ChatGPT can be an effective tool for creating personalized learning materials and providing automated and personalized feedback to students. However, it is important to use ChatGPT in conjunction with traditional teaching methods and to evaluate its effectiveness on a case-by-case basis. Additionally, there are ethical considerations related to data privacy and algorithmic bias that should be taken into consideration when using ChatGPT in education.

What are the Ethical Considerations in Using Language Generation Models Such as ChatGPT in Education?

The use of language generation models such as ChatGPT in education raises several ethical considerations related to data privacy, algorithmic bias, and the potential for AI to replace human teachers as follows.

- The use of ChatGPT in education requires the collection and storage of student data, which raises concerns about data privacy and security. It is important to ensure that student data is protected and used only for its intended purposes.
- Language generation models such as ChatGPT are trained on large datasets, which can lead to algorithmic bias if the data is not representative of the population. This can result in biased responses and feedback that may not be accurate or appropriate.
- While ChatGPT can provide personalized learning experiences and automate certain tasks, it should not replace human teachers entirely. Human teachers bring unique skills and perspectives to the learning process, including empathy, creativity, and critical thinking, that are not replicable by AI.
- Fairness and accountability: There is a need for transparency and accountability in the development and use of language generation models such as ChatGPT. It is important to ensure that these tools are developed in a way that is fair and ethical, and that they do not perpetuate existing power imbalances or biases.

Overall, the use of language generation models such as ChatGPT in education raises several ethical considerations that should be considered. These tools should be developed and used in a way that is fair, transparent, and respectful of student autonomy. Also, ChatGPT should be used alongside traditional teaching methods to evaluate its effectiveness on a case-by-case basis.

DISCUSSION

ChatGPT is a large-scale transformer-based language model developed by OpenAI, which uses the attention mechanism presented in (Vaswani et al., 2017). It has been fine-tuned for various language understanding tasks and has been applied in various fields such as NLP, computer vision, and education as well. Language generation models such as ChatGPT have the potential to revolutionize the field of education and training by providing automated and personalized feedback, generating personalized learning materials and creating interactive and engaging learning experiences. Studies such as (Hosseini-Asl et al., 2020; Wang & Hovy, 2020; Yang et al., 2019) demonstrate the effectiveness and feasibility of these models in education and training.

The traditional linear model does not fully capture the complexity and dynamic nature of learning, does not fully leverage the capabilities of chatbots in creating personalized and adaptive learning experiences and does not fully incorporate the use of technology in education.

The dialogue-based model for education used by chatbots such as ChatGPT is rooted in several philosophical perspectives, including constructivism, dialogical learning, and the Socratic method. These perspectives emphasize the importance of active, interactive, and dialogic learning, where learners are encouraged to construct their own understanding of the subject through dialogue and communication with others. ChatGPT's style of lerning is related to Schopenhauer's philosophical idea of the world as representation in that it allows individuals to construct their own understanding of the subject through interactive and active learning. It also provides personalized learning that adapts to the needs and abilities of individual students.

Similarly, the dialogue-based model of education promoted by ChatGPT is related to the Vygotsky's sociocultural theory of learning, which emphasizes the role of social interaction and cultural context in cognitive development. This theory posits that cognitive development is mediated by social interaction and that learners actively construct their own understanding of the world with the help of more experienced or knowledgeable others. The dialogue-based model of education promoted by ChatGPT is similar in that it encourages social interaction through dialogue, and it allows learners to construct their own understanding of the world with the help of the chatbot. Ideation plays a crucial role in the dialogue-based model of education promoted by ChatGPT. ChatGPT can facilitate ideation by providing learners with new information and perspectives, generating questions and prompts that encourage critical and creative thinking, and evaluating and providing feedback on the ideas and concepts generated by learners.

The Bloom's Taxonomy, a traditional model of learning stages, could be trans-formed considering the new role of ideation in the dialogue-based model of education promoted by ChatGPT. In the traditional Bloom's Taxonomy, the highest level of cognitive skills is" Creating" which refers to the ability to put elements together to form a coherent or new whole. However, in the dialogue-based model of education promoted by ChatGPT, ideation is an essential component, and it would be necessary to incorporate it into the taxonomy. One way to do this would be to add a new level of cognitive skill called" Ideation" which would sit above" Creating" and would focus specifically on the process of generating and developing new ideas and concepts. This level would include skills such as brainstorming, asking questions, generating hypotheses, and exploring different perspectives.

Another way to incorporate ideation into the taxonomy would be to incorporate it into the existing levels of the taxonomy. For example, the level of" Remembering" could be expanded to include the skill of recalling information to generate new ideas and concepts. The level of" Understanding" could be expanded to include the skill of interpreting information to generate new ideas and concepts. The level of" Applying" could be expanded to include the skill of using information to generate new ideas and concepts.

CONCLUSION

The study explored the implications of integrating ChatGPT and similar language models into education and training programs. These tools offer immediate access to information, enhancing knowledge acquisition. Personalization and tailored re-sponses aid in understanding complex concepts, while active interactions foster crit-ical thinking and engagement. Learners can apply knowledge practically and brain-storm innovative solutions. Continuous availability supports self-directed learning, and educators can focus on higher-level discussions while ChatGPT addresses rou-tine queries. Language models also enhance language proficiency and encourage ethical evaluation of AI-generated content. However, limitations include the lack of human expertise and potential biases. Overall, integrating ChatGPT offers transfor-mative learning experiences, though responsible use and a balanced approach are essential for harnessing their full potential.

The use of ChatGPT and similar language models has the potential to greatly impact future education and training programs:

- ChatGPT and similar models can provide personalized and adaptive learning ex-periences for students by providing targeted feedback and guidance and adapting to the needs and abilities of individual students.
- The use of ChatGPT and similar models can increase interaction and engagement in education and training programs using real-time feedback and dialogue-based interactions.
- ChatGPT and similar models can automate repetitive tasks, such as grading and providing feedback on student work, freeing up educators and trainers to focus on more important tasks such as teaching, mentoring, and providing guidance.
- ChatGPT and similar models can be used to generate educational materials such as summaries, questions, and answers, and diagrams, which can be used to supplement traditional teaching methods.
- ChatGPT and similar models can be used to generate personalized language learn-ing materials, such as flashcards and quizzes, which can be used to supplement traditional teaching methods.
- ChatGPT and similar models can provide access to education for people who are unable to attend traditional in-person classes.
- There are several potential future directions for research in using ChatGPT and similar language models for education and training programs as follows:
- Further refinement of the dialogue-based model by developing new techniques for generating more natural and coherent responses from the chatbot, and for making the interactions more engaging and interactive.
- Developing more advanced techniques for personalization and adaptation, such as using machine learning to tailor the chatbot's responses to the individual learner's needs and abilities.
- Developing techniques for automating assessment and feedback, such as using NLP and machine learning to evaluate student work and provide targeted feedback.
- Addressing ethical and privacy concerns, such as ensuring that student data is protected and used only for educational purposes, and that the chatbot's responses are not biased.
- Integration of ChatGPT and similar models with other technologies, such as virtual and augmented reality, to create more immersive and interactive learning experiences.
- Developing techniques for generating more diverse and high-quality educational materials, such as interactive diagrams, simulations, and videos.
- Understanding the impact of the use of ChatGPT and similar models on different learners, such as students with different backgrounds, abilities, and learning styles.
- Comparing the effectiveness of the use of ChatGPT and similar models in education and training programs with traditional teaching methods.

REFERENCES

Abdelghani, R., Wang, Y.-H., Yuan, X., Wang, T., Lucas, P., Sauzéon, H., & Oudeyer, P.-Y. (2023). Hel'ene' Sauzeon,´ and Pierre-Yves Oudeyer. Gpt-3-driven pedagogical agents to train children's curious question-asking skills. *International Journal of Artificial Intelligence in Education*. doi:10.100740593-023-00340-7

Alaghbary, G. S. (2021). Integrating technology with bloom's revised taxonomy: Web 2.0-enabled learning designs for online learning. *Asian EFL Journal*, *28*(1), 10–37.

Alqahtani, T., Badreldin, H. A., Alrashed, M., & Alshaya, A. I. (2023). The emergent role of artificial intelli-gence, natural learning processing, and large language models in higher education and research. *Research in Social & Administrative Pharmacy*, *19*(8), 1236–1242. doi:10.1016/j.sapharm.2023.05.016 PMID:37321925

Amer, A. (2006). Reflections on bloom's revised taxonomy. *Electronic Journal of Research in Educational Psychology*, *4*(8), 213–230.

Bandlamudi, L. (2015). *Difference, dialogue, and development: A Bakhtinian world*. Academic Press.

Benjamin, S. (1956). *Taxonomy of educational objectives: The classification of educational goals*. Longmans, Green.

Chaowicharat, E., & Dejdumrong, N. (2023). A step toward an automatic handwritten homework grading system for mathematics. *Information Technology and Control*, *52*(1), 169–184. doi:10.5755/j01.itc.52.1.32066

Chen, C., Chen, Y.-M., Hsu, C.-L., & Yu, C.-H. (2021). Effects of a chatbot on student engagement and satisfaction in an online course. *Computers & Education*, *157*, 103951.

Devlin, J., Chang, M.-W., Lee, K., & Toutanova, K. (2018). Bert: Pre-training of deep bidirectional transformers for language understanding. In *Proceedings of the 2018 Conference of the North American Chapter of the Association for Computational Linguistics: Human Language Technologies,* (pp. 4171–4186).

Fernando, A. F. L., David, R. H. T., & Roque, M. M. (2023). Personalized tutoring: Chatgpt as a virtual tutor for personalized learning experiences. *Przestrzen Spoleczna*, *23*(1), 292–312.

Font de la Vall, R. R., & Araya, F´. G´. (2023, January). Exploring the benefits and challenges of AI-language learning tools. *International Journal of Social Sciences and Humanities Invention*, *10*(01), 7569–7576. doi:10.18535/ijsshi/v10i01.02

Fox, R. (2001). Constructivism examined. *Oxford Review of Education*, *27*(1), 23–35. doi:10.1080/03054980125310

Fuchs, K. (2023, May). Exploring the opportunities and challenges of NLP models in higher education: Is chat GPT a blessing or a curse? *Frontiers in Education*, *8*, 8. doi:10.3389/feduc.2023.1166682

Haneda, M. (2017). Dialogic learning and teaching across diverse contexts: Promises and challenges. *Language and Education*, *31*(1), 1–5. doi:10.1080/09500782.2016.1230128

Ho, Y.-R., Chen, B.-Y., & Li, C.-M. (2023). Thinking more wisely: Using the socratic method to develop critical thinking skills amongst healthcare students. *BMC Medical Education*, *23*(1), 173. doi:10.118612909-023-04134-2 PMID:36941597

Hosseini-Asl, E., Chen, X., Bos, J., & Hovy, E. (2020). Few-shot dialogue gen-eration with pre-trained language models. In *Proceedings of the 58th Annual Meeting of the Association for Computational Linguistics*, (pp. 6878–6888). IEEE.

Hsu, Y.-C., & Ching, Y.-H. (2023). Generative artificial intelligence in education, part one: The dynamic frontier. *TechTrends*, *67*(4), 603–607. doi:10.100711528-023-00863-9

Kasneci, E., Sessler, K., K¨uchemann, S., Bannert, M., Dementieva, D., Fischer, F., Gasser, U., Groh, G., G¨unnemann, S., H¨ullermeier, E., Krusche, S., Kutyniok, G., Michaeli, T., Nerdel, C., Pfeffer, J¨., Poquet, O., Sailer, M., Schmidt, A., Seidel, T., & Kasneci, G. (2023). Chatgpt for good? on opportunities and challenges of large language models for education. *Learning and Individual Differences*, *103*, 102274. doi:10.1016/j.lindif.2023.102274

Li, J., Chen, W., Chen, D., & Li, K. (2021). Gpt-3 for personalized language learning. *arXiv preprint arXiv:2103.05874*.

Liu, X., Qiu, X., Chen, W., & Liu, S. (2020). Multilingual pre-training for neu-ral machine translation. In *Proceedings of the 58th Annual Meeting of the Association for Computational Linguistics*, (pp. 6296–6311). IEEE.

Anderson, LKrathwohl, D. (2001). *A taxonomy for learning, teaching, and assessing: A revision of Bloom's taxonomy of educational objectives*. Longman.

McGlashan, A. (2018). A pedagogic approach to enhance creative ideation in classroom practice. *International Journal of Technology and Design Education*, *28*(2), 377–393. doi:10.100710798-017-9404-5

Meyer, J. G., Urbanowicz, R. J., Martin, P. C. N., O'Connor, K., Li, R., Peng, P.-C., Bright, T. J., Tatonetti, N., Won, K. J., Gonzalez-Hernandez, G., & Moore, J. H. (2023). Chatgpt and large language models in academia: Opportunities and challenges. *BioData Mining*, *16*(1), 20. doi:10.118613040-023-00339-9 PMID:37443040

Milano, S., McGrane, J. A., & Leonelli, S. (2023, March). Large language models challenge the future of higher education. *Nature Machine Intelligence*, *5*(4), 333–334. doi:10.103842256-023-00644-2

Okewu, E., Adewole, P., Misra, S., Maskeliunas, R., & Damase-vicius, R. (2021). Artificial neural networks for educational data mining in higher education: A systematic literature review. *Applied Artificial Intelligence*, *35*(13), 983–1021. doi:10.1080/08839514.2021.1922847

Rahman, M. & Watanobe, Y. (2023). Chatgpt for education and research: Opportunities, threats, and strategies. *Applied Sciences (Switzerland)*, *13*(9).

Ramachandran, P., Liu, S., Lasecki, W., & Riedl, M. (2021). Creating educational materials using gpt-3. *arXiv preprint arXiv:2103.05874*, .

Schopenhauer, A., Aquila, R., Carus, D., & Kolak, D. (2016). *Arthur Schopenhauer: The World as Will and Presentation* (Vol. I). Routledge.

Vaswani, A., Shazeer, N., Parmar, N., Uszkoreit, J., Jones, L., & Aidan, N. (2017). Gomez, Lukasz Kaiser, and Illia Polosukhin. Attention is all you need. *Advances in Neural Information Processing Systems*, 5998–6008.

Wang, X., & Hovy, E. (2020). Automatic feedback generation for student writing using pre-trained language models. In *Proceedings of the 58th Annual Meeting of the Association for Computational Linguistics*, (pp. 6835–6846).

Wogu, I. A. P., Misra, S., Assibong, P. A., Olu-Owolabi, E. F., Maskeli¯unas, R., & Damasevicius, R. (2019). Artificial intelligence, smart classrooms, and online education in the 21st century: Implications for human development. *Journal of Cases on Information Technology, 21*(3), 66–79. doi:10.4018/JCIT.2019070105

Yan, L., Sha, L., Zhao, L., Li, Y., Martinez-Maldonado, R., Chen, G., Li, X., Jin, Y., & Gasevic, D. (2023). Practical and ethical challenges of large language models in education: A systematic scoping review. *British Journal of Educational Technology*.

Yang, Z., Dai, Z., Yang, Y., Carbonell, J., & Le, Q. (2019). Evaluating automated essay scoring with bert. *arXiv preprint arXiv:1902.08531*.

Zellers, R., Bau, D., Neelakantan, A., Holtzman, A., Rashkin, H., Yatskar, M., & Farhadi, A. (2019). Defending against neural fake news. *arXiv preprint arXiv:1905.12616*.

Chapter 7
ChatGPT and Other Generative AI Tools in Education:
Transformative Potential and Ethical Considerations

C. V. Suresh Babu
https://orcid.org/0000-0002-8474-2882
Hindustan Institute of Technology and Science, India

S. Adhithya
Hindustan Institute of Technology and Science, India

ABSTRACT

This chapter presents a comprehensive exploration of the transformative influence of generative AI tools in education. It examines the personalized learning experience enabled by AI, the role of AI tools as virtual tutors, content creation aids for educators, and their application in language learning and communication enhancement. Additionally, the chapter delves into the ethical implications associated with AI integration, including data privacy, fairness, and transparency. Practical strategies for responsible AI adoption are proposed, encompassing guidelines for ethical usage and educator training. The chapter concludes by highlighting the vast potential of AI-powered education while underscoring the significance of ethical considerations in its implementation. It encapsulates the evolution of AI in education and foresees a future where learners are empowered through dynamic and personalized educational experiences.

INTRODUCTION

In the landscape of education, where traditional methodologies have long been the cornerstone of knowledge dissemination, a new wave of innovation is reshaping the way we teach and learn. This transformation is being propelled by the rapid advancement of generative artificial intelligence (AI) tools – a category of AI that holds the capacity to generate, mimic, and even enhance human-like creative processes. The

DOI: 10.4018/979-8-3693-0205-7.ch007

emergence of these generative AI tools marks a pivotal moment in education, offering unprecedented opportunities to revolutionize the creation, delivery, and personalization of educational content. Generative AI, powered by complex algorithms and machine learning models, has transcended its role as a mere technological novelty. It has now become an indispensable asset within educational environments, ranging from traditional classrooms to digital learning platforms (Bozkurt, A. et.al, 2023).

By empowering educators and learners with tools that can produce diverse forms of content, such as text, images, and multimedia, generative AI is redefining the boundaries of creativity and pedagogy. This paradigm shift in education is driven by a dual pursuit: to amplify the efficacy of teaching methodologies and to cater to the unique learning proclivities of each individual (Baidoo-Anu, D. et.al, 2023). The ability of generative AI tools to analyze vast datasets, recognize patterns, and generate tailored materials holds immense promise for a more personalized and engaging learning experience. As we stand at the crossroads of technological innovation and pedagogical evolution, it becomes imperative to explore, understand, and navigate the implications, challenges, and transformative potential that generative AI brings to the realm of education. In this discourse, we embark on an exploration of the emergence of generative AI tools in teaching and learning. By delving into real-world applications, benefits, and ethical considerations, we aim to unravel the layers of this technological advancement (Rivas, P. et.al, 2023).

Background: The Emergence of Generative AI Tools in Teaching and Learning

The rapid development of artificial intelligence and the changing dynamics of education have combined to create the rise of generative AI tools in teaching and learning. A group of technologies known as artificial intelligence, and more specifically generative AI, enables machines to imitate and reproduce creative processes that are similar to those of humans ((Suresh Babu C. V., 2022)). These tools can produce information, make judgements, and even engage in creative tasks that were previously only possible for human cognition since they are based on deep learning algorithms, neural networks, and vast data processing capabilities. Due to technology advancements, the old paradigms of teaching and learning have been continuously evolving in the field of education. The boundaries of learning have already been broadened by the incorporation of digital platforms, online resources, and interactive learning environments (Baidoo-Anu, D. et.al, 2023).

Objectives of the Chapter

The goal of this chapter is to give readers a clear understanding of what generative AI tools are and how they differ from other forms of AI. Explain the idea behind generative AI tools. It will delve into the underlying technologies and processes that allow AI systems to produce content in order to advance a fundamental grasp of the topic (Bozkurt, A. et.al, 2023).

- Highlight Current Applications in Education: The chapter aims to present concrete instances of the use of generative AI tools in various educational contexts at the moment. It seeks to highlight the palpable impact these technologies have on the teaching and learning processes through examples of actual implementations (Yu, H, 2023).
- Explore Benefits for Teaching and Learning: This goal entails identifying and describing the benefits of utilising generative AI technologies in the classroom. The chapter will explore how these

tools can promote personalised learning experiences, improve content development, and even address problems with conventional teaching techniques (Baidoo-Anu, D. et.al, 2023).

- Discuss Privacy Implications and Ethical Issues: This chapter will discuss the ethical issues that come up when employing generative AI tools in education. It will look at topics like data privacy, potential biases in content creation, and the ethical application of AI in educational settings (Farrokhnia, M. et.al, 2023).
- Consider Limitations and Challenges: In order to present a complete picture, the chapter will explore the limitations and difficulties of incorporating generative AI technologies into teaching and learning. This includes worries about the possibility of educators losing their jobs and the requirement for a balanced strategy between technology and human direction (Wen, J.; Wang, W, 2023).
- Consider Future Possibilities: This chapter will make some assumptions about the future of generative AI tools in the classroom. It will examine potential future developments of these tools, their potential effects on conventional educational models, and the possibilities for creative educational strategies that make use of AI's capabilities (Bozkurt, A. et.al, 2023).

PERSONALIZED LEARNING WITH GENERATIVE AI TOOLS

Personalized learning has long been an educational ideal, aiming to cater to individual student needs, learning styles, and pace. The integration of generative AI tools into education has opened up exciting new avenues to achieve this aspiration. These tools, powered by advanced algorithms and data analysis, offer the potential to revolutionize personalized learning by tailoring educational content and experiences to the unique characteristics of each learner (Bozkurt, A. et.al, 2023).

Understanding Personalized Education Facilitated by AI

As a way to improve educational outcomes, personalised education, a pedagogical strategy that adapts learning experiences to each student's needs, skills, and preferences, has drawn a lot of attention. By replacing outdated, one-size-fits-all teaching methods with dynamic, adaptable learning experiences, artificial intelligence (AI) has opened up new opportunities for personalised education at scale ((Suresh Babu C. V., 2022)). Fundamentally, personalised education recognises that every student has a distinctive set of learning preferences, speeds, and abilities. Education professionals can now access a wealth of data regarding students' development, performance, and interactions with educational materials thanks to AI technologies, particularly machine learning and data analysis methods. This data-driven methodology makes it possible to design personalised learning experiences that address unique learning profiles (Zhang, C. et.al, 2023).

Analyzing Individual Learning Patterns and Preferences

A key component of personalised education is understanding each student's unique learning styles and preferences, which is made possible by the application of cutting-edge technology like artificial intelligence (AI). In order to gain knowledge about how a learner interacts with educational material, understands concepts, and reacts to various teaching approaches, this process entails gathering, interpreting, and using data. Teachers can modify their approach to produce a more efficient and interesting learning experience by being aware of these trends and preferences (Baidoo-Anu, D. et.al, 2023, Suresh Babu, C. V., and Padma R, 2022).

The key components involved in examining unique learning styles and preferences are broken down as follows:

- Data Collection: Learning platforms equipped with AI tools collect a vast array of data points as students interact with content. This includes factors like time spent on specific topics, responses to quizzes, browsing behavior, and interaction patterns within online modules (Farrokhnia, M. et.al, 2023).
- Data Interpretation: AI algorithms process the collected data to identify trends, correlations, and patterns. This might involve analyzing how quickly a student progresses through modules, which subjects they excel in, and where they tend to struggle (Baidoo-Anu, D. et.al, 2023).
- Identifying Learning Styles: By analyzing data, AI can determine a student's preferred learning style. For instance, some students might learn better through visual aids, while others may prefer textual explanations or interactive simulations (Baidoo-Anu, D. et.al, 2023).
- Pacing and Difficulty: AI tools can gauge the appropriate pace of learning for an individual. If a student consistently grasps concepts quickly, the AI might adjust to provide more challenging material. Conversely, if a student is struggling, the AI can slow down and offer additional resources (Wen, J.; Wang, W, 2023).
- Content Engagement: The AI system can evaluate which types of content and formats (videos, articles, quizzes) a student engages with most effectively. This informs educators about the mediums that resonate with the student (Suresh Babu, C. V. & Rohan, B. (2023)).

Tailored Educational Experiences and Improved Learning Outcomes

Data analysis and technology-driven, personalised learning environments have the potential to greatly enhance student learning results. Teachers can design learning journeys that maximise student engagement, knowledge, and retention by tailoring them to each student's strengths, weaknesses, preferences, and learning speed (Baidoo-Anu, D. et.al, 2023, Suresh Babu, C. V., and Padma R, 2022). Here is a closer examination of how more specialised educational opportunities can result in better learning outcomes:

- Engagement Enhancement: When learning content and activities are tailored to match a student's interests and learning style, they are more likely to stay engaged and motivated. This active participation fosters a deeper connection to the subject matter.
- Personalized Pacing: Every student learns at a different rate. Tailoring educational experiences allows learners to progress at their own pace, preventing frustration from being either rushed or bored due to a uniform curriculum.
- Addressing Learning Gaps: Data analysis can identify specific areas where a student is struggling or excelling. By recognizing and addressing learning gaps promptly, educators can prevent misunderstandings from snowballing into larger knowledge deficits.
- Varied Learning Formats: Tailored experiences can encompass diverse learning formats such as videos, interactive simulations, quizzes, and real-world applications. This variety caters to different learning preferences and helps reinforce concepts through multiple perspectives.

- Immediate Feedback: Personalized learning platforms equipped with AI can offer instant feedback on assignments and assessments. This immediate response aids in understanding and rectifying mistakes in real time (Baidoo-Anu, D. et.al, 2023).

GENERATIVE AI TOOLS AS VIRTUAL TUTORS AND SUPPORT SYSTEMS

The advent of generative AI technologies as adaptive virtual teachers and support systems is transforming the landscape of education (Suresh Babu, C. V., and Padma R, 2022). These AI-driven solutions combine with traditional teaching methods to successfully give students individualised guidance, criticism, and assistance. Utilising state-of-the-art algorithms and data analysis, they do this. In addition to improving educational outcomes, generative AI solutions provide students greater freedom over how they complete their schoolwork and serve as intelligent advisors throughout the learning process (Farrokhnia, M. et.al, 2023).

Instant Feedback and Interactive Learning Experiences

Instant feedback and interactive learning experiences are two essential aspects of contemporary education that technology has greatly improved, especially with the use of AI-driven tools. With the help of these components, traditional passive learning is changed into educational practises that are lively, interesting, and efficient. Let's explore how interactive learning experiences and real-time feedback are advantageous to both students and teachers:

Instant Feedback:

- Instantaneous Correction: AI-driven systems provide immediate feedback on quizzes, assignments, and exams, enabling students to recognise errors and correct them while the concepts are still fresh in their minds.
- Learning from Mistakes: By assisting students in understanding their mistakes and misunderstandings, constructive feedback encourages deeper learning.
- Motivation: Quick feedback helps students feel successful and keeps them motivated by validating their right answers.

Interactive Learning Experiences:

- Engagement: Active engagement is encouraged and distractions are minimised in interactive learning settings, which attract students' attention.
- Hands-On Learning: Interactive exercises, virtual labs, and simulations offer practical learning opportunities that help students better understand difficult ideas.
- Personalization: AI-driven interactivity may adjust to a student's learning pace and manner, ensuring that every learner engages with the subject to the fullest extent possible (Baidoo-Anu, D. et.al, 2023).

Guiding Students Through Complex Concepts

Effective teaching revolves around guiding students through difficult topics, and the incorporation of technology—including tools powered by artificial intelligence—has completely changed how teachers approach this challenge (Wen, J.; Wang, W, 2023). These technologies open up fresh channels for deconstructing complex concepts, encouraging greater comprehension, and encouraging critical thinking (Suresh Babu, C. V., and Padma R, 2022). Let's look at how technology helps teachers lead pupils through difficult concepts:

Visualisations and Simulations:

- Visual Representation: Through the use of interactive visualisations, technology makes it possible to make abstract ideas more understandable. By giving them a clear framework, this aids pupils in understanding complicated concepts.
- Dynamic Exploration: Through the manipulation of variables and the observation of results, simulations give students an experience comprehension of complicated processes that might otherwise be difficult to visualise.

Multimedia Learning:

- Videos and animations: Multimedia materials give step-by-step explanations that accommodate a variety of learning styles while breaking down complicated ideas into small chunks.
- Engagement: Interactive movies and animations hold students' attention while making difficult subjects more relatable and approachable.

Adaptive Learning Platforms:

- Individualised Learning Paths: AI-driven platforms analyse student performance and create learning paths that are specifically tailored to each student's learning gaps before introducing more complicated ideas.
- Progressive Challenges: Adaptive platforms offer progressively harder challenges based on a student's knowledge of fundamental principles, encouraging a smooth transition to complicated concepts.

Scaffolded Learning:

- Concept breakdown: Teachers can utilise technology to break down difficult ideas into smaller, more digestible parts, enabling pupils to gradually develop a thorough comprehension (Suresh Babu, C. V., and Padma R, 2022).
- Guided Exploration: Students are guided through the investigation of intricate ideas by way of questions and prompts, which encourage them to reflect critically and draw connections (Baidoo-Anu, D. et.al, 2023).

Enhancing Engagement and Comprehension

Enhancing engagement and comprehension are two important educational goals, and integrating technology, including tools powered by AI, offers creative methods to accomplish these goals. Teachers can pique students' interest and improve their grasp of the material by using interactive and personalised teaching methods (Kasneci, E et al., 2023, Suresh Babu, C. V., and Padma R, 2022). The following are some ways that technology might improve engagement and comprehension:

- Active Participation: Interactive exercises like quizzes, polls, and conversations that actively involve students and encourage participation, collaboration, and sharing of viewpoints are made possible by technology (Sallam, M., 2023).
- Gamification: Gamified components, such leaderboards and awards, make learning fun and inspire students to participate fully and perform well (Baidoo-Anu, D. et.al, 2023).
- Adaptive Content: AI-driven technologies tailor learning materials to each student's pace, learning preferences, and performance, making sure that the content is both challenging and interesting (Kasneci, E et al., 2023).
- Tailored Feedback: Individualised feedback clarifies each student's misunderstandings and directs learners towards a greater comprehension of the material (Farrokhnia, M. et.al, 2023).
- Infographics and Visual Representations: With the help of technology, complicated concepts may be broken down into more easily understood infographics and diagrams, improving comprehension (Wen, J.; Wang, W, 2023).
- Interactive Visualisations: By letting students control variables and observe cause-and-effect interactions in action, interactive visual models assist students in exploring abstract topics (Hassani, H.et.al. 2023).

AI-GENERATED CONTENT: EASING EDUCATORS' WORKLOAD

AI-generated content is dramatically reducing the burdens of teachers and improving the learning environment, which is having a transformative effect on education. These cutting-edge tools use AI and NLP to generate a variety of educational resources, from lesson planning to evaluations, allowing teachers to concentrate more on individualised instruction and student interactions (Farrokhnia, M. et.al, 2023, Suresh Babu, C. V. & Rohan, B. (2023)).

AI-Driven Content Creation and Curation

The way educational materials are created, arranged, and delivered is changing as a result of AI-driven content production and curation. These innovations use machine learning and artificial intelligence to automate and improve several processes of content creation and selection, providing teachers and students with a variety of advantages (Baidoo-Anu, D. et.al, 2023, Suresh Babu, C. V., and Padma R, 2022)). Here are some ways that education are being impacted by AI-driven content development and curation:

Content Creation:

- Effectiveness: AI can swiftly and repeatedly produce educational content, saving educators a significant amount of time that would otherwise be spent on manual content creation.
- Customization: AI-generated content may be adapted to fit various learning objectives, student levels, and learning styles, making learning experiences more personalised.
- Adaptive Learning: AI-generated information can change based on how well students perform, adding more challenges or explanations as necessary (Yu, H, 2023).

Content Curation:

- Resource Discovery: AI-powered technologies can search through a large amount of internet content to find pertinent resources, saving educators time while looking for good resources .
- Curriculum Alignment: Using curriculum standards and educational objectives as a guide, AI may create content that is specifically matched to the desired learning results.
- Individualised Learning routes: By recommending materials that specifically meet each student's needs, AI-driven content curation can help create personalised learning routes for each student (Kasneci, E et al., 2023).

Empowering Educators for Personalized Teaching and Mentoring

A crucial component of utilising technology, particularly AI, to improve educational quality is empowering teachers for personalised instruction and mentorship (Suresh Babu, C. V., and Padma R, 2022). Technology can empower teachers with the resources and assistance they require to design individualised learning experiences, develop deep relationships with students, and promote academic achievement (Yu, H, 2023). Here's how technology enables teachers to provide individualised instruction and mentorship:

- **Student analytics:** With the use of technology, educators can detect learning patterns, areas that need improvement, and strengths and weaknesses in their students' academic performance.
- **Adaptive Platforms:** Platforms fuelled by AI are able to deliver content that adapts to different learning styles and rates, providing a customised path through the curriculum.
- Tailor-made information: Thanks to technology, instructors may produce or choose information that is appropriate to students' interests and skills, making learning more interesting and interesting.
- **Content Creation:** By automating content creation, technology frees up educators to devote more time to pedagogy and mentoring and less time to administrative duties.
- **Assessment and Grading:** AI-driven systems can help with assignment grading, giving teachers more time for individualised feedback and interaction (Yu, H, 2023).

Optimizing Learning Material and Resources

A key component of modern education is optimising learning resources and materials, and technology, notably AI-driven tools, is heavily influencing this process. Teachers can guarantee that students have access to excellent, pertinent, and engaging materials that improve their learning experiences by using technology to curate, create, and deliver information (Farrokhnia, M. et.al, 2023, Suresh Babu, C. V., and Padma R, 2022). Here are some ways that technology is improving educational tools and content:

- **Visual Learning:** Using visual aids might make it easier for students to understand and retain difficult concepts.
- **Progressive Challenges:** Adaptive platforms present progressively harder challenges as students grasp ideas, offering ongoing challenge and development.
- **Current Information:** Technology makes ensuring that educational materials are current, pertinent, and represent the most recent news and developments.
- **Online collaboration tools:** By giving students a place to collaborate on projects, share materials, and communicate ideas, technology supports collaborative learning.
- **Peer Contributions:** AI tools can assist students in compiling and sharing their own resources, encouraging a sense of ownership and participation in the educational process (Yu, H, 2023).

GENERATIVE AI TOOLS IN LANGUAGE LEARNING AND COMMUNICATION

By providing creative ways to improve language learning, practise, and communication abilities, generative AI technologies are revolutionising the fields of language learning and communication. For personalised, engaging, and successful language learning experiences, these solutions combine artificial intelligence and natural language processing (Baidoo-Anu, D. et.al, 2023).

Facilitating Language Practice and Pronunciation Correction

Using generative AI tools in language acquisition has several advantages, two of which are facilitating language practise and correcting pronunciation. These technologies use artificial intelligence and sophisticated language processing algorithms to build engaging and useful platforms for language learners to improve their proficiency. Here are some examples of how language learning and pronunciation correction are being changed by generative AI tools.

Language Practice:

- **Interactive discussions:** Chatbots and virtual language partners driven by AI engage students in simulated discussions that give them a safe setting to practise speaking, listening, and understanding.
- **Real-world Scenarios:** AI-generated scenarios are modelled after real-world settings, allowing students to use their language abilities in real-world situations.
- **Authentic Materials:** Generative AI technologies can produce books, articles, and conversations that expose students to real-world language usage and cultural nuances.

Pronunciation Correction:

- **Accurate Feedback:** AI technologies assess learners' intonation and pronunciation, providing detailed feedback on specific sounds and patterns. This helps learners develop their spoken language abilities.
- **Practise Sessions:** Using AI-driven practise sessions, students can continually work on difficult sounds and sentences until they improve their accuracy.

- **Phonetic Guides:** AI-generated phonetic guides help students understand how to pronounce sounds correctly by explaining the proper way to enunciate each syllable (Baidoo-Anu, D. et.al, 2023).

Real-Time Translation for Language Acquisition

A potent use of generative AI tools that significantly aids in language learning and acquisition is real-time translation. These tools enable communication between speakers of many languages by utilising cutting-edge machine translation and natural language processing algorithms (Bozkurt, A. et.al, 2023). This allows students to connect with information and other people in languages they are not yet fluent in. Here are some ways that real-time translation aids in language learning:

- **Multilingual information:** Real-time translation enables students to access a variety of information in the languages they are studying, including books, articles, videos, and websites (Zhang, C. et.al, 2023).
- **Reading Complex writings:** Real-time translation aids students in understanding academic writings, technical documents, and other complex texts that may be difficult to understand in a foreign language (Wen, J.; Wang, W, 2023).
- **Conversational Practise:** Real-time translation helps students participate in discussions and practise speaking while chatting with native speakers.
- **Quick Response:** Learners get instant translations for terms or phrases that they don't understand, enabling them to follow discussions in real time (Sallam, M., 2023).
- **Language Exchange:** With the help of real-time translation, learners can interact in language exchange activities with native speakers (Farrokhnia, M. et.al, 2023).

Improving Communication Skills Through AI-Assisted Interactions

A revolutionary method for teaching communication skills is to use AI-assisted interactions to give students important practise, feedback, and direction in a variety of communication-related areas. These AI tools enable customised, immersive experiences that improve written, oral, and nonverbal communication abilities. The following examples show how interactions with AI support communication skill development:

- Language practise: Learners are engaged in dialogues by AI-powered chatbots and virtual language partners, giving them the chance to practise speaking, listening, and understanding in a safe setting.
- Accent reduction: AI systems can identify learners' accent patterns and offer advice on how to weaken strong accents, improving verbal communication clarity and effectiveness.
- Grammar and Style: Platforms powered by AI provide in-the-moment grammar and style recommendations, boosting the calibre of written communication.
- Video Analysis: Using AI, instructors can review video records of their students and give comments on nonverbal signs including body language, facial expressions, and eye contact.
- Presentation Skills: AI-assisted technologies assess how well trainees present while making recommendations to enhance their gestures, tones, and general presence (Hassani, H, et al., 2023).

ETHICAL IMPLICATIONS IN THE INTEGRATION OF AI IN EDUCATION

Although there are many advantages to integrating AI in education, there are also significant ethical issues that educators, governments, and technologists must face. These ethical ramifications cover a wide range of topics, including responsibility, bias, and equitable access (Rivas, P. et.al, 2023).

Data Privacy and Security Concerns

When incorporating AI in education, there are important ethical considerations about data privacy and security. The gathering, storing, and use of student data by AI systems raises crucial issues on how to safeguard people's privacy and sensitive data security (Skavronskaya, L, et al., 2023). The following are some important issues with data security and privacy in the context of AI in education:

- Data Collection: AI systems collect a wide range of data, including behavioural, academic, and personal data. It's crucial to confirm the need for data collection (Skavronskaya, L, et al., 2023).
- Consent procedures: Students and parents should be made aware of the types of information that are gathered, why they are gathered, and how they will be utilised. It is essential to get express, informed consent (Sallam, M., 2023).
- Third-party Access: To avoid data misuse and breaches, sharing student data with third-party AI providers must be carefully considered (Skavronskaya, L, et al., 2023).
- De-identification: Before analysis, anonymizing data helps reduce privacy risks by making sure that specific pupils cannot be readily identified (Sabzalieva, E, et al., 2023).
- Fair data usage: Making sure that AI algorithms don't unfairly affect particular groups based on delicate characteristics like gender, colour, or financial status (Sabzalieva, E, et al., 2023).

Ensuring Fairness and Mitigating Bias in AI Algorithms

Responsible AI integration in education must include fairness assurance and bias mitigation in AI algorithms. Bias in AI systems can produce unfair results and exacerbate already-existing inequities (Zhang, C. et.al, 2023). The following are tactics to encourage equity and lessen bias in AI algorithms used in education:

- Data Pre-processing: Use approaches for data pre-processing to spot and correct biases in training data. Re-sampling, re-weighting, or altering data points may be necessary for this.
- Bias Audits: Perform extensive audits of biases to determine whether AI systems make biassed predictions or suggestions. Any biases found should be addressed and corrected.
- Transparency and Definability: Use AI systems that offer clear justifications for their choices. This clarifies the decision-making process and aids in locating potential bias sources.
- Fair measures: To guarantee that AI systems treat all groups equally, use evaluation measures that take fairness into account, such as disparate impact analysis.
- Assemble varied teams of developers, data scientists, and subject matter experts to ensure that all viewpoints are taken into account throughout the construction and evaluation of algorithms (Suresh Babu, C. V. & Rohan, B. (2023)).

- Bias Testing Frameworks: To assess differences in results, use bias testing frameworks that assess AI models across multiple demographic groupings (Zhang, C. et.al, 2023).

Transparency and Explainability of AI-Generated Content

Responsible AI integration in education must include both transparent and explicable AI-generated content. It's critical to make sure that users, educators, and learners can comprehend how the content is generated and trust the information provided as AI plays a larger role in the creation of educational resources (Bozkurt, A. et.al, 2023). Here are some examples of how explainability and transparency can be accomplished in AI-generated content:

- Clearly State Attribution: State when content was produced by AI. Users can now distinguish material produced by humans from content produced by AI thanks to this (Hassani, H.et.al. 2023).
- Disclosure of Process: Describe the algorithms, data sources, and procedures used in the AI process used to create content (Hassani, H.et.al. 2023).
- User-Friendly Explanations: Educators, students, and parents may easily understand AI ideas and procedures when they are explained in straightforward language (Baidoo-Anu, D. et.al, 2023).
- Visual Explanations: Use pictures to explain the AI content generating process, such as flowcharts, graphs, or infographics (Bozkurt, A. et.al, 2023).
- Interactivity: Develop interactive modules that let consumers discover how content supplied by AI is made and altered (Lo, C.K, 2023).
- Visualising Data Inputs: Make the data inputs that the AI uses to create content visible to aid people in understanding the sources and categories of information taken into account (Farrokhnia, M. et.al, 2023).
- Plain Language: Create explanations of complex AI topics in simple terms that non-technical stakeholders may understand (Wen, J.; Wang, W, 2023).

STRATEGIES FOR RESPONSIBLE AI INTEGRATION IN EDUCATION

A careful and thorough strategy that prioritises ethical considerations, privacy, equity, and educational effectiveness is necessary for the responsible integration of AI in education (Rivas, P. et.al, 2023).

Guidelines for Ethically Using Generative AI Tools

It is essential to use generative AI technologies responsibly in order to maximise their benefits while minimising risks and negative effects (Sabzalieva, E, et al., 2023). The following rules should be adhered to while incorporating generative AI tools ethically:

- Data Privacy and Consent: Ensure that users give their informed consent, especially when using AI tools that need data gathering and processing. Ascertain that user data is safely saved, guarded, and utilised exclusively for the stated educational goals.
- Bias Awareness and Mitigation: Recognise any potential biases in the algorithms and training data. Conduct routine checks for bias in content produced by AI, then take appropriate action.

- Transparency and Explainability: Make it abundantly clear when content is produced by AI, setting it apart from content that was authored by humans. Give users descriptions of the production process for AI-generated material to aid in their understanding.
- Accountability and Oversight: Continue human review of AI-generated information, particularly in educational contexts, to guarantee accuracy and suitability. Create accountability systems in case of mistakes or bad outcomes.
- Equity and Accessibility: Create AI tools that are usable by all users, irrespective of their backgrounds or skill levels. Make sure artificial intelligence-generated content doesn't exacerbate current educational inequalities.
- Human-Centric Design: Give consideration to people's welfare when creating AI products. Think about the wants, needs, and learning objectives of the user.
- Educational Enhancement: Use AI tools to improve educational experiences rather than taking the place of critical thinking or interpersonal communication. Aligning material produced by AI (Sabzalieva, E, et al., 2023).

Training Educators and Stakeholders in AI Ethics

It is essential to use generative AI technologies responsibly in order to maximise their benefits while minimising risks and negative effects Rivas, P. et.al, 2023. The following rules should be adhered to while incorporating generative AI tools ethically:

- Data Privacy and Consent: Ensure that users give their informed consent, especially when using AI tools that need data gathering and processing. Ascertain that user data is safely saved, guarded, and utilised exclusively for the stated educational goals.
- Bias Awareness and Mitigation: Recognise any potential biases in the algorithms and training data. Conduct routine checks for bias in content produced by AI, then take appropriate action.
- Explicitness and Transparency: Distinguishing AI-generated content from human-created content requires a clear indication when it is present. Give users descriptions of the production process for AI-generated material to aid in their understanding.
- Accountability and Oversight: Continue human review of AI-generated information, particularly in educational contexts, to guarantee accuracy and suitability. Create accountability systems in case of mistakes or bad outcomes.
- Equity and Accessibility: Create AI tools that are usable by all users, irrespective of their backgrounds or skill levels. Make sure artificial intelligence-generated content doesn't exacerbate current educational inequalities.
- Human-Centric Design: Give consideration to people's welfare when creating AI products. Think about the wants, needs, and learning objectives of the user.
- Educational Enhancement: Use AI tools to improve educational experiences rather than taking the place of critical thinking or interpersonal communication. Align curriculum standards and instructional objectives with content produced by AI.
- Awareness of AI's Limitations: Know what AI tools are capable of and what they can't do. Do not assume they are perfect or overestimate their capabilities Rivas, P. et.al, 2023.

Implementing Safeguards for Responsible AI Usage

To guarantee that AI technologies are incorporated in ways that prioritise ethics, privacy, equity, and educational effectiveness, it is vital to implement safeguards for responsible AI usage. Consider the following safety measures when using AI to educational settings:

- Ethical Guidelines and rules: Create ethical guidelines and rules that are explicit and describe how to use AI in education in a responsible manner. These documents ought to cover issues like bias, accountability, openness, and data privacy (Yu, H, 2023).
- Data Privacy and Security: To protect student and educator data, put strict data protection measures in place, such as encryption, access controls, and frequent security audits (Suresh Babu, C. V. & Rohan, B. (2023)).
- Strategies to Reduce Bias: Utilise algorithms and data pretreatment methods to identify and minimise bias in material produced by AI. Periodically check AI systems for bias (Zhang, C. et.al, 2023).
- Human Oversight and Review: Continue to conduct human reviews of information produced by AI to make sure it is accurate, appropriate, and in line with educational objectives (Farrokhnia, M. et.al, 2023).
- Equity and Accessibility Assurance: Create AI tools and content that are accessible to all students while taking into account their varied backgrounds and learning styles (Baidoo-Anu, D. et.al, 2023).
- Educator Training: Give educators thorough instruction on the moral implications of AI, how to use it responsibly, and how to successfully incorporate AI tools into their pedagogical strategies (Baidoo-Anu, D. et.al, 2023).
- Ethical Review Boards: Establish interdisciplinary review panels to assess the ethical implications of AI technologies prior to deployment, taking into account their effects on various stakeholders (Sallam, M., 2023).

CONCLUSION

The ethical integration of AI in education necessitates a multidimensional strategy that puts an emphasis on ethics, openness, equity, and privacy. Educational institutions can benefit from AI while preventing biases, ensuring data privacy, and promoting equitable learning environments by following clear ethical guidelines, putting in place strong data protection measures, and encouraging transparency through explicable AI processes Rivas, P. et.al, 2023. The revolutionary promise of AI may be realised in ways that respect moral standards, advance student wellbeing, and improve educational outcomes for all through ongoing monitoring, educator training, and stakeholder engagement (Lo, C.K, 2023).

In conclusion, generative AI tools have a profoundly revolutionary potential in teaching and learning. By analysing user preferences and tailoring content accordingly, guiding students through difficult concepts, giving immediate feedback, and increasing engagement, these platforms provide personalised learning experiences (Bozkurt, A. et.al, 2023). By making it easier to create content, allowing for personalised instruction, and maximising learning resources, they provide educators more authority. Real-time translation and communication practise are beneficial to language acquisition, while ethical considerations, transparency, and prejudice reduction provide responsible AI integration. As AI permeates education, its capacity to transform conventional methods and customise learning to various needs promises a future of enhanced outcomes and enriched educational experiences (Zhang, C. et.al, 2023).

It is crucial to emphasise the significance of ethical issues in AI integration to make sure that technical breakthroughs are in line with our values and obligations. We must acknowledge that AI technologies have ethical ramifications as they progressively influence different facets of our lives, including education (Baidoo-Anu, D. et.al, 2023). We can manage the difficulties of AI integration while guarding against biases, maintaining data security, and upholding human dignity by prioritising openness, justice, privacy, and responsibility. In addition to defending people's rights and wellbeing, ethical considerations also help build dependable, long-lasting AI systems that benefit society. Let's make sure that our actions reflect our dedication to responsible innovation and the improvement of education for all as we use AI to improve learning experiences (Lo, C.K, 2023).

The integration of AI technologies is shaping a dynamic and personalized learning landscape, promising a transformative path forward for education (Lo, C.K, 2023). Through the utilization of AI, learners stand to gain significant advantages over conventional approaches:

Personalized Learning Paths: AI will dynamically adapt the pace, content, and assessments to cater to diverse learning preferences, optimizing retention and engagement.

Inclusive Accessibility: AI-driven tools will democratize education, providing all students access to high-quality learning materials, irrespective of their geographical or financial constraints.

Enhanced Collaboration: AI-supported online learning platforms and collaborative tools will foster cross-cultural communication among students and subject matter experts.

Nurturing Future Talents: AI systems will identify sought-after skills and guide learners in acquiring the competencies essential for the evolving job market.

Lifelong Learning Facilitation: AI will simplify the process of acquiring new skills and adjusting to emerging technologies and industries (Baidoo-Anu, D. et.al, 2023).

This confluence of AI and education holds the potential to redefine learning paradigms, fostering personalized growth, equitable access, and continuous adaptation.

REFERENCES

AlAfnan, M. A., Dishari, S., Jovic, M., & Lomidze, K. (2023). Chatgpt as an educational tool: Opportunities, challenges, and recommendations for communication, business writing, and composition courses. *J. Artif. Intell. Technol.* **2023**, *3*, 60–68. Rahimi, F.; Abadi, A.T.B. ChatGPT and publication ethics. *Archives of Medical Research*, *54*, 272–274.

Baidoo-Anu, D.; Owusu Ansah, L. Education in the era of generative artificial intelligence (AI): Understanding the potential benefits of ChatGPT in promoting teaching and learning. *Soc. Sci. Res. Netw.* **2023**.

Bozkurt, A., Xiao, J., Lambert, S., Pazurek, A., Crompton, H., Koseoglu, S., Farrow, R., Bond, M., Nerantzi, C., & Honeychurch, S. (2023). Speculative Futures on ChatGPT and Generative Artificial Intelligence (AI): A collective reflection from the educational landscape. *Asian J. Distance Educ*, *18*, 50–130.

Farrokhnia, M., Banihashem, S. K., Noroozi, O., & Wals, A. (2023). A SWOT analysis of ChatGPT: Implications for educational practice and research. *Innovations in Education and Teaching International*, •••, 1–15. doi:10.1080/14703297.2023.2195846

Hassani, H., & Silva, E. S. (2023). The role of ChatGPT in data science: How ai-assisted conversational interfaces are revolutionizing the field. *Big Data Cogn. Comput.*, *7*(2), 62. doi:10.3390/bdcc7020062

Kasneci, E., Seßler, K., Küchemann, S., Bannert, M., Dementieva, D., Fischer, F., Gasser, U., Groh, G., Günnemann, S., Hüllermeier, E., Krusche, S., Kutyniok, G., Michaeli, T., Nerdel, C., Pfeffer, J., Poquet, O., Sailer, M., Schmidt, A., Seidel, T., ... Kasneci, G. (2023). ChatGPT for good? On opportunities and challenges of large language models for education. *Learning and Individual Differences*, *103*, 102274. doi:10.1016/j.lindif.2023.102274

Lo, C. K. (2023). What is the impact of ChatGPT on education? A rapid review of the literature. *Education Sciences*, *13*(4), 410. doi:10.3390/educsci13040410

Rivas, P.; Zhao, L. Marketing with chatgpt: Navigating the ethical terrain of gpt-based chatbot technology. *AI* **2023**, *4*, 375–384.

Sabzalieva, E., & Valentini, A. ChatGPT and Artificial Intelligence in Higher Education: Quick Start Guide. 2023. Available online: https://eduq.info/xmlui/handle/11515/38828

Sallam, M. (2023). ChatGPT utility in healthcare education, research, and practice: Systematic review on the promising perspectives and valid concerns. *Health Care*, *11*, 887. PMID:36981544

Skavronskaya, L., Hadinejad, A., & Cotterell, D. (2023). Reversing the threat of artificial intelligence to opportunity: A discussion of ChatGPT in tourism education. *Journal of Teaching in Travel & Tourism*, *23*(2), 253–258. doi:10.1080/15313220.2023.2196658

Suresh Babu, C. V. (2022). *Artificial Intelligence and Expert Systems*. Anniyappa Publications.

Suresh Babu, C. V., & Padma, R. (2022) "Technology Transformation Through Skilled Teachers in Teaching Accountancy." Advancing STEM Education and Innovation in a Time of Distance Learning, edited by Roberto Alonso Gonzâlez-Lezcano, IGI Global, 2023, pp. 211-233. doi:10.4018/978-1-6684-5053-6.ch011

Suresh Babu, C. V., & Rohan, B. (2023). Evaluation and Quality Assurance for Rapid E-Learning and Development of Digital Learning Resources. In M. Santally, Y. Rajabalee, & R. Rajputh (Eds.), *Implementing Rapid E-Learning Through Interactive Materials Development* (pp. 139–170). IGI Global., doi:10.4018/978-1-6684-4940-0.ch008

Wen, J., & Wang, W. (2023). The future of ChatGPT in academic research and publishing: A commentary for clinical and translational medicine. *Clinical and Translational Medicine*, *13*(3), 1207. doi:10.1002/ctm2.1207 PMID:36941774

Yu, H. (2023). Reflection on whether Chat GPT should be banned by academia from the perspective of education and teaching. *Frontiers in Psychology*, *14*, 2156. doi:10.3389/fpsyg.2023.1181712 PMID:37325766

Zhang, C., Zhang, C., Li, C., Qiao, Y., Zheng, S., Dam, S. K., Zhang, M., Kim, J. U., Kim, S. T., & Choi, J. (2023). One small step for generative ai, one giant leap for agi: A complete survey on chatgpt in aigc era. *arXiv*.2304.06488.

KEY TERMS AND DEFINITIONS

AI Ethics: The principles and guidelines that govern the responsible and ethical use of artificial intelligence technologies.

AI Integration: Incorporating AI tools and technologies into educational settings to enhance learning and teaching experiences.

AI-Assisted Interactions: Using AI tools to enhance and improve human-to-human or human-to-machine communication interactions.

Content Generation: The process of using AI to create various types of educational materials, such as quizzes, exercises, study guides, and even entire lesson plans.

Data Privacy: The protection of individuals' personal and sensitive information from unauthorized access, use, or disclosure.

Empowered Learners: Students who are equipped with tools and resources, including AI tools that enable them to take control of their learning journey and achieve better outcomes.

Engagement: The level of interest, participation, and involvement that students have in their learning experiences.

Ethical Implications: Concerns and considerations related to the moral and responsible use of technology, particularly in areas like data privacy, fairness, transparency, and bias mitigation.

Explainability: The ability to provide understandable explanations for the decisions and recommendations generated by AI models.

Fairness: Ensuring that AI systems and their outcomes do not disproportionately favor or discriminate against particular groups of people.

Generative AI Tools: AI tools that are capable of creating new content, responses, or solutions based on patterns and data they've learned from existing examples.

Guidelines: Set of recommendations or rules that provide direction for using AI tools in an ethical and responsible manner.

Language Learning: The process of acquiring skills in a new language, which includes vocabulary, grammar, pronunciation, and communication skills.

Language Practice: Engaging in exercises, conversations, or interactions to improve language skills and fluency.

Mitigating Bias: Taking steps to reduce and eliminate biases that might be present in AI algorithms, ensuring equitable outcomes.

Personalized Learning: An educational approach that tailors instruction, content, and pacing to individual students' learning preferences, strengths, and needs.

Real-time Translation: Instantaneous conversion of spoken or written content from one language to another.

Safeguards: Protective measures or protocols put in place to prevent unintended negative consequences or misuse of AI tools.

Transparency: Making AI algorithms and processes understandable and interpretable, so users can understand how decisions are made.

Virtual Tutors: AI-powered systems that simulate a human tutor's role, providing students with personalized guidance, feedback, and explanations.

Chapter 8
AI Game Activities for Teaching and Learning

Many Wanja Kanja
Pan Africa Christian University, Kenya

Mahona Joseph Paschal
St. Augustine University of Tanzania, Tanzania

ABSTRACT

The role of AI in education is not doubtful. This chapter critically explores the potential benefits, challenges, and implication of integrating AI game activities in educational settings. It underlines how Al algorithms are vital in promoting critical thinking, problem solving skills, and knowledge retention among learners. Moreover, this chapter also discusses the utilization of simulation, virtual reality, and interactive narrative in Al- driven gaming activities to amplify active engagement and foster a deeper understanding of complex concepts. Additionally, the chapter explores how Al games have the capacity to enhance collaborative leaning, foster social interaction, and facilitate the growth of essential skills needed in the of 21st- century. The chapter addresses the crucial topics of ethics concerns, safeguarding data privacy, and promoting inclusivity. Furthermore, it underscores the potential of AI game activities in addressing the evolving requirements of learners in the digital age and equipping them for a technology-driven future.

INTRODUCTION

Student learning in school organizations has been broadly explored, including areas such as critical thinking, student engagement, problem solving skills training, interpersonal communication skills as well as skills development for teamwork (Paschal & Mkulu, 2020 a). However, there is limited training methods for these skills that includes service learning, critical and creative education. These methods have done little to respond the challenges. In a competitive and global workplace, the emergence of artificial intelligence (AI) and game-based learning has been highlighted as a powerful approach of learning and developing comprehensive skills for problem solving (Paschal & Gougou, 2022; Opondo, & Paschal,

DOI: 10.4018/979-8-3693-0205-7.ch008

2023). The combination of AI and game-based learning promote high level of teamwork, motivation to learning, create immersive and captivating personalized experiences.

PERSONALIZED LEARNING EXPERIENCE

The field of AI has been rapidly evolving, permeating various industries, applied sciences, medicine and financial sectors. On the contrary, in the education field, learning institutions have not embraced fully the value of technology (Luckin & Cukurova, 2019). Nonetheless, several studies (Mahona & Pacho, 2021; Makira & Owino, 2021; Owic et al. 2021; Pacho, & Adewoyin, 2022; Paschal & Mkulu, 2020; Paschal; Rahayu et al. 2022) confirm that COVID 19 brought the realization that AI adaptation in the education sector was inevitable. As such it is imperative for learning institutions to adapt and leverage the potential of AI to enhance teaching methods and optimize personalized learning process for learners (Tapalova & Zhiyenbayeva, 2022). Innovations in AI technologies have opened new avenues for transforming traditional educational practices especially on how knowledge is delivered thereby fostering a positive personalized learning experience.

AI advancement has raised awareness of various solutions that offer alternatives for learners and foster the adoption of novel teaching and learning methods (Paschal & Mahama, 2023). Further, the progress in AI has significantly contributed to the development of personalized learning pathways in education (Tapalova & Zhiyenbayeva, 2022). Learning pathways assist in comprehending and interpreting the learner's action as they engage in the process of learning. This is due to distinct knowledge structures based upon their previous experiences and capacities. Moreover, learning paths also unveil the routes of learning as learners navigate through interactive environment Hoatching as cited by (Elshani, & Nuçi, 2021). Such learning trajectory helps learners to acquire knowledge incrementally and empowers them tto take active role of navigating their course of learning.

Learning pathways can also be tailored to facilitate autonomous and self-paced learning encounters. However, it is essential to note that merely personalizing learning experiences does not guarantee the desired learning outcomes (Tetzlaff, et al. 2021). These authors explain that ineffective personalization attempts may arise when adapting to characteristics that are not closely tied to the learning process, such learning styles or relying on static modelling for adaptation. To achieve successful personalized learning, it is crucial to utilize dynamic modelling to assess and adapt to relevant learners' characteristics that will result in positive personalized learning achievement (Tetzlaff, et al. 2021).

Personalized learning is a methodical approach to education that tailors the learning process to match the individual learner's strengths, preferences needs and aspirations (Walkington & Bernacki, 2020). As opposed to fixed learning where learners follow a set of prescribed learning sequences that might not be suitable for every learner's need (Elshani & Nuçi, 2021), personalized learning experience involves tailoring instructions to suits the individual needs of each learner optimizing the pace of learning and the instructional approach accordingly (Leitner et al. 2023). The objective of personalized learning is to facilitate learning success of each learner by first defining the unique needs, interest, and aspirations of each learner, then provide personalized learning experience. This is achieved by providing a conducive personalized learning environment (Ivanović, 2021). This approach allows for flexibility in learning objectives, instructional methods, and content sequencing, all bases in the specific requirements of each individual learner. Also, the learning activities are designed to be meaningful, relevant, and aligned with the learners' interests, often initiated by the learners themselves (Elshani & Nuçi, 2021).

Personalized learning as a methodological approach result in an extensive learning journey, offering a diverse array of subjects and different pathways and skill development opportunities (Tetzlaff, et al., 2021). In the environment of personalized learning, teachers play a vital role in empowering learners to take charge of their learning experience, guiding them to set and achieve educational objectives aligned with their personal interests, requirements, and abilities (Aberbach et al.2021). The implementation of personalized learning systems and approaches fosters learners' motivation and leads to improved academic performance subsequently enhancing positive learning experiences (Zlatarove et al, 2021).

Personalized learning underscores the significance of individual growth and the learning environment. A personalized learning environment encompasses a diverse of learning tools, and application tailored to meet the unique needs of each learner. Utilization of AI adaptive systems aims at developing cost effective training, enhancing user experiences, and creating personalized student profiles Samah et al as cited by (Klašnja-Mili´ & Ivanovi, ´2021). besides it can be tailored to cater to the specific requirements of individual learners, prioritizing specific topics and offering repeated exposure to learning materials that have been effectively mastered (Klašnja-Mili´&Ivanovi, 2021).

AI game activities combine the interactive and engaging elements of games with the intelligence of AI systems, offering personalized and immersive learning experiences. AI algorithms possess the capability to analyse individual learning patterns and adapt content accordingly. Additionally, it assesses a learner's performance in real- time and it identifies strengths and weakness in their understanding of the content. Russell and Norvig (2020) assert that Algorithms can be expressed in various ways including natural language, pseudo code flowcharts, and programming languages. They are also utilized in a wide range of applications, from simple tasks like sorting a list of numbers to complex computations, data analysis, and artificial intelligence. By customizing learning paths, content, and assessments, AI-driven games cater to each student's unique strengths and weaknesses, fostering a more effective and personalized learning experience (Leitner, et al, 2022). Personalized learning according to Shemshack and Spector (2020) is an inherent human capacity that originates from a personal encounters, cognitive understanding, and individual biases, viewpoints, cultural upbringing, and surroundings. A personalized learning process broadens one's knowledge, alters mental perspective and develops practical skills.

AI GAME ACTIVE LEARNING AND IMMEDIATE FEEDBACK

AI game activities create a highly an engaging and motivating learning environment. It not only promotes active learning but also nurtures positive and constructing learning experience for students of all ages and backgrounds. The element of competition or gamification often present in AI games fuels learners' intrinsic motivation to perform better. AI game active learning is defined as "an interactive, computer-based system in which users (i.e., players / learners) engage in artificial activities involving fun, challenge, and/or fantasy, instructional and entertainment. goals are part of the system, and pre-defined rules to guide game play activities to promote active learning by providing interactive challenges and simulations that encourage students to actively participate in the learning process (McLaren & Nguyen, 2023).These interactive games engage students in hands on, immersive personalized experiences that demand critical thinking, problem-solving, and quick decision making (Khan, et al. 2021; Li, et al. 2021; Pandemic, 2021). By integrating AI into educational games, learners are presented with challenging script that require active participation, encouraging them to apply their knowledge and skills in real life situations. This dynamic approach not only enhances understanding but also gives immediate feedback and foster a deeper connection between theoretical concepts and real-world applications, making learning more meaningful and memorable to learners.

Similarly, real-time feedback from AI systems enables students to assess their performance instantly, facilitating a deeper understanding of concepts and allowing for immediate corrective action (Mena-Guaca et al. 2023; Wagan et al .2023). The concept of game based- learning involves associating principles and characteristics of games with educational promotional opportunities. Several studies including (Castellar et al. 2021; Kaimara, et al. 2021; Lei, et al., 2022; Pandemic, 2021 Wang, & Zheng; 2021) acknowledge that the notion of game-based learning involves associating principles and characteristics of games with educational opportunities within a learning community. They purport that by incorporating elements like badged, leader boards, quizzes, and discussion boards game-based foster the learner's engagement and participation in the learning process. The interactive and challenging nature of these games captivates the learners' attention and encourages them to stay actively involved throughout the learning process (McLaren & Nguyen, 2023). Using platforms that encourage faster responses further enhances the appeal of this technology. Teachers can also leverage digital academic rewards, such as granting students extra time to complete final projects or assignments, to incentivize learning in the classroom (McLaren & Nguyen, 2023).

Earlier scholars including (Muhammad, et al., 2022; Li et al., 2021; Pandemic, 2021) established that gamified learning is an active approach to education, designed to enhance leaner intelligence by promoting critical thinking and problem-solving skills. It is classified in two categories: digital games and non-digital games. AI digital games involve interactive personalized experiences on electronic platforms, on the other hand non digital games, such as experiments, offer students hands on personalized learning opportunities (Khan et al., 2021). An early study by Gee (2003) underscored that AI Digital game when used as a learning tool often times immerse learners in a state 'flow' – this is an intense and focused concentration in what the learners are doing in the present moment i.e. merging action and awareness (Abuhamdeh, 2020). This fosters a positive personalized learning experience that elicit a sense of accomplishment. In the early days cognitive science researchers identified certain concepts that are part of games that seem to enhance flow. McLaren and Nguyen (2023) note that

Flow induces focused concentration and total absorption in an activity . . . one feels strong, alert, in effortless control, loses all self-consciousness, and is at the peak of their abilities. Often, the sense of time seems to disappear, and a person in flow experiences a feeling of transcendence.

Another aspect of AI game in active learning is maintaining of a sense of curiosity in the process of learning. Melone as cited by (Wagan et al. 2023) identified curiosity and challenge as a key contributor in promoting intrinsic motivation and facilitate learning through games. Incorporating AI games in a learning process arouses the learners' interest in concept they would not ordinarily be interested. On the same page Kaufman, and Flanagan (2015) posited that incorporating finance games can establish a connection between learners and content that they would not initially engage with due to conflict with their personality. This amplifies learners hidden abilities therefore promoting their self-efficacy. One of the key advantages of AI game activities is the ability to provide immediate feedback to students as they progress through the game (Chen, et al. 2021).

AI games activities have emerged a powerful tool that enhance active learning experience and provide immediate feedback in educational settings. Immediate feedback is a crucial component of teaching and learning process that provide learners with immediate information about their performance and understanding of the subject matter (Mena-Guacas, 2023). It also provides them with an opportunity to identify and correct their misconceptions or mistakes immediately thus improve the learner's performance during learning process.

Similarly, it informs the instructors about the effectiveness of their teaching methods and how to improve these strategies according to the learners personalized needs (Hooda et al. 2022). This timely feedback reinforces correct responses in addition it also aids learners to recognize and address any knowledge gaps this minimizes the learners dropout rates by motivating them, (Attali & Kleij, 2017). At the same time prompt feedback provides valuable information to teachers so that they can improve feedback practices, tasks, skills, and assessment (Hooda et al. 2022).

A study by Honda et al (2022) established that immediate feedback plays a vital role in aiding learners to accomplish their desired learning objectives. Immediate feedback is not only essential for acquiring knowledge and boosting learners' motivation but also it allows the learners to rectify any misconceptions, thus, prevent reinforcement of incorrect information. Moreover, the personalized nature of AI feedback ensure that learners receive tailored guidance, focusing on their specific areas of improvement. Continuous feedback facilitates a more self-directed personalized learning experience that empower learners to take control of the learning process and monitor their own progress (Wagan et al. 2023). However, it is crucial to be cautious with negative feedback, as studies have shown that it can discourage learners' efforts to accomplish their desired achievements, therefore, feedback should be thoughtfully crafted and delivered (Hooda et al. 2023). Incorporating certain principles including timeless, transparency, and meaningfulness can effectively foster the strength of feedback that can benefit both instructor and the learner.

COLLABORATIVE LEARNING AND SOCIAL INTERACTION

AI-driven games are also designed to encourage collaborative learning and social interaction among learners. Multi player scenarios and group activities within AI games foster teamwork, communication, and the exchange of ideas, enhancing a sense of community in the learning environment. AI games represent an innovative approach to learning process that leverage AI technologies to create interactive and engaging learning experience (Wagan, et al 2023). By combining the elements of gamification, collaborative learning and social interactions, collaborative learning, and social interactions, AI games have the potential to transform traditional classroom settings into dynamic and learner- centric environments.

Collaborative learning is an educational approach where students work together in groups to achieve shared learning goals (Leitner et al. 2023; Seo et al. 2021). It differs from the traditional teacher-centric methods by emphasizing active engagement and cooperation among learners. Social interactions, on the hand, refer to interpersonal relationships and communication within the learning environment. Social interactions create a sense of belonging and a support system within the learning community, contributing to maintaining a healthy emotional support (Hernández-Sellés, et al., 2019; Luo et al. 2017). Additionally social interactions shape student perception of community climate and influence their emotional expressions (Wetcho & Na-Songkhla, 2022).

Several studies including (Hu et al 2021; Karthika, and Selvam, 2022; Zhang et al. 2021) agree that positive socio interactions shared by a group of learners increase the possibility that members would become desirable collaborators during the teamwork. Moreover, learners are more likely to feel motivated and encouraged when they have positive social connections with their peers and teachers. AI games offer peer to peer learning opportunities, allowing collaborative exchange of knowledge and support in mastering game challenges. Collaborative problem- solving nurtures a culture of mutual learning and promotes confidence and risk taking in the learning process (Huang, & Lajoie, 2023).

AI games increase learners' engagement by captivating learners' attention and by providing interactive and immersive learning experiences. The use of AI game not only encourages collaborative learning but also presents complex scenarios and challenges that require learners collaboratively to think critically and develop effective problem solving skill encourage critical thinking and problem solving skills (Zhai et al. 2021). Collaborative learning also encourages learners to discuss and analyse problems collectively. Engagement in group discussions exposes learners to diverse perspectives and allows them to critically evaluate and incorporate different viewpoints in their learning process (Karthika, & Selvam, 2022). Through this process learners can develop stronger problem-solving skills by considering multiple solutions to make informed conclusions (Khan et al 2022). Further, the interactive nature of games give room for learners to learn from their mistakes, promoting cognitive growth and resilience in the face of adversities.

AI collaborative learning and social interactions improve learners' communication abilities. In a collaborative learning settings learners actively communicate and articulate their ideas to others. The shared experiences create a positive and inclusive learning community. This practise enhances their verbal and written communication skills, promoting clear and effective expression of thoughts and concepts (Zhang et al. 2022). Improved communication abilities are invaluable not only in academic but also in professional and personal contexts. Collaborative learning fosters active participative learning approaches that lead to better retention and understanding of the subject matter.

Integrating AI collaborative learning is not without challenges. A study by Zilka, (2020) established that some learners experienced challenges citing personal difficulties connecting to the learning community; difficulties related to exposure and sharing with others. Similarly, Leitner et al. (2022) pointed out some of the challenges learners experience in collaborative learning that includes feelings of competition and pressure from exposure and feeling of threat reading the posts written by their peers because of perceived competitiveness. To address these perceived challenges, instructors need to consider the learners concerns regarding their self-efficacy in course achievement and peer pressure while designing collaborative learning and social interaction and try to maximize the benefits of interactions to foster learning and minimize stressors that might occur during competition (Huang, & Lajoie, 2023 ; Leitner et al. 2022). Additionally, Instructors can establish clear expectations for group members, assign specific roles, and provide opportunities for individual reflection and assessment. Effective conflict management methods for instance promotion of open communication and active listening can help manage conflicts and initiate a harmonious learning environment (Celik et al. 2022).

Constructing knowledge through social interaction provide opportunities for learners to share their knowledge and learn from each other's experiences. In collaborative social learning interactions, learners have the opportunity to enhance their advance cognitive abilities by acquiring valuable perspective from their peers and receiving immediate feedback (Huang, & Lajoie, 2023). It also creates a sense of belonging and support within the learning community. Social interactions promote conducive environment where learners collaboratively discuss concepts and collectively construct meaning as such deepen their understanding of the subject matter (Tan et al. 2022). Working in groups requires learners to develop teamwork and positive interpersonal skills. Where they learn to respect each other's opinions, resolve conflict, and contribute positively to the group's dynamics (Hu et al., 2021).

Successful integration of AI games in learning requires reliable technology infrastructure, reliable hardware, and software support to ensure seamless access to games, skilled instructors, and ethical adherence. Also, AI games integration requires an on-going professional development because of the frequent technology change (Celik et al. 2022). Providing teachers with the necessary skills and knowledge inspire their confidence in effectively utilising and implementation of these innovative tools (Moreno-Guerrero et al 2020). Integration of AI games into the curriculum could encounter challenges such as resistance from the learning community including learners and instructors (Leitner et al 2022) However, creating awareness and showcasing the benefits of AI games integration could help lessen such challenges. AI games collect the learners' data. Thus, it is important for institutions to adhere to ethical consideration regarding data privacy and protection.

REALISTIC SIMULATION AND EXPERIENTIAL LEARNING

Simulation-based learning is a form of hand -on learning that afford learners with a real-life situation to develop and practice their expertise and skills but in a simulated setting (Urquidi-Martín, et al., 2019). Simulation-based learning is used for emergency preparedness, complex decision making, negotiation and conflict resolution, technical training (e.g., aviation) (Lateef, 2010) and for teaching abstract concepts that may be difficult for learners to fully grasp (Shaw & Switky, 2018).

Simulation and games offer learners an opportunity to understand real world situations authentically and engagingly within the confident of the classroom (Urquidi-Martín, et al 2019). It provides a safe environment for learners to experiment their hypothesis and witness the consequences of their decisions and actions while at the same time avoiding any real-world repercussions (Lean et al. 2021). For instance, medical science where simulation-based learning has been applied intensively (Castillo-Segura et al 2022). As a result, these tools offer valuable insights into contexts that may be challenging for learners to experience directly in reality, either due to high risks involved, unaffordability of the experiment or the time frame. Dai and Ke (2022) define simulation-based learning as "an active and immersive experience in a virtual learning environment that re-create a realistic and authentic real-life event or a set of learning situations to solve a problem".

BENEFITS OF EXPERIENTIAL LEARNING WITH AI SIMULATION

There are several advantageous of learning with AI simulation. Realistic simulations captivate learners' attention, creating an immerse and engaging learning personalized experience. The interactive nature of these AI game activities encourages active participation and exploration (Lateef, 2010). Experimental learning usually involves some risk aspect or uncertainty. However, AI- driven simulations provide a safe space for learners to: experiment, make mistakes and learn from them without the actual consequences (Dai & Ke. 2022; Lateef, 2010). AI simulations easily adapt to personalized learners needs, offering personalized challenges and content tailored to their levels. This personalized approach enhances learning efficiency and effectiveness (Mena-Guacas et al. 2023). Simulation can seamlessly integrate various subjects fostering a holistic understanding of complex issues. For example, Education, Neuroscience, Psychology, Linguistics, Sociology and Anthropology (Kabudi, et al.2021) Learners can explore connections between different disciplines and gain a broader perspective of real world challenges.

AI simulations enable learners in science education, to conduct experiments virtually, removing the need for expensive equipment and minimizing hazards. Learners can explore different variables and observe the results of their actions (Dai & Ke. 2022).AI simulations enable history to come to life through AI- driven historical simulations allowing learners step into the shoes of key figures or experience historical events from multiple perspectives. This enhances an in-depth understanding of historical events and their implication. Additionally, AI simulation in social science can recreate economic systems, political scenarios, and societal interactions.

Learners can evaluate factors influencing these systems and realize their implications. These will enhance informed decision (Mena-Guacas et al 202) and increases knowledge retention (Levin-Banchik, 2018). AI simulations assist learners to improve non-technical workplace skills, such as effective communication, teamwork, collaboration, decision-making, and problem-solving (Lateef, 2010) and it can also be fun and exciting for learners (Shaw & Switky, 2018). It is important to note that simulation-based learning is not meant to supplant traditional teaching methods rather it functions as a supplement to traditional teaching methods offering an efficacious avenue for experiential learning. It involves immersing learners in recreated real-life scenarios and guiding their reflection, thereby enhancing the educational process (Shaw & Switky, 2018)

CHALLENGES AND FUT URE DIRECTION OF AI SIMULATION

Implementation of AI-driven simulations may require substantial technological infrastructure and expertise which could present challenges for some educational institutions. AI simulation must be developed with ethical considerations in mind. It is critical to ensure inclusivity and cultural sensitivity (Dremliuga, & Koshel, 2018; Fahimirad, 2018). Beides developing reliable assessment strategies to measure learning objectives. This is because AI simulations may be assessed using traditional methods. AI algorithms exclusively depend on data for their performance. If data is unbalanced and contains disproportionately better information on students from general population in comparison to minorities, the algorithms may produce systematic and repeatable errors disadvantaging minorities (Luan et al 2020). Algorithms have revolutionized the learning cultures learning experiences, and classroom dynamics. Therefore, the learners may be in danger of becoming passive recipients or just merely tracked objects (Loftus & Madden 2020).

AI- driven simulations has institutionalized educational realm by enabling experiential learning in a safe and interactive environment. From scientific experiments to historical to events, these simulations offer innovative opportunities for learners to explore real-world scenarios, fostering critical thinking, problem solving, and decision- making skills. As technology continues to advance, educators and policymakers should work collaboratively to overcome challenges and harness the full potential of AI game activities in enhancing education for future generations.

FINAL THOUGHTS

AI games present a promising approach for collaborative learning and social interactions on learning. AI and gamification tools could enhance learners' engagement, personalized learning pathway, and develop critical thinking skills. Additionally, AI games foster teamwork, encourage peer to peer learning, positive social interactions and build a supportive learning community. There is a need for educators, education institutions, policy heads in education to take control of development of AI utilised for education purposes and not delegate such a critical task to technology firms. At the dawn of AI era, millions of people are non-literate. This calls for further investment in schooling infrastructure and capacity building for teachers and learners as opposed to making machines smart.

Following national policy development and regulations, further implementation guidance is required for AI technology development to ensure machines do not take over the role of humans, but rather enhance human capacities and efficiency. As AI is increasingly being used in many aspects of life, it is important to ensure that AI is not prone to biases, errors, discrimination, among others, and that it doesn't replace human beings. Also, focus should be on the ability for AI to helps human beings perform better and efficiently. Ethical guidelines should be deliberately driven by policy makers at national and international levels to ensure ethical considerations at the development and implementation of AI tools. Once the key human and technical AI competencies have been identified, school systems need to ensure that all students are well prepared for a world in which AI is ubiquitous.

There is an urgent need to have AI literacy and management included in school curricula to have students competent in the discipline from an early age. AI literacy also needs to be developed by all young people and citizens through lifelong learning programmes. Early interventions will provide guidance on how students interact and manipulate AI as the primary players and beneficiaries in shaping the learning outcomes. This will play a critical role in the management of potential negative impact and best practices in AI. Regulation of AI is paramount through development of flexible policies and regulatory frameworks that can accommodate and respond to the rapidly ever-changing dynamics of AI. Technology is never ideologically neutral. It exhibits and privileges certain worldviews and reflects unique ways of thinking and knowing. New generative AI models and utilities are no exception.

REFERENCES

Abuhamdeh, S. (2020). Investigating the "Flow" Experience: Key Conceptual and Operational Issues. *Frontiers in Psychology*, *11*, 158. doi:10.3389/fpsyg.2020.00158 PMID:32116954

Castellar, A. A., & Looy, V. J. (2021). Digital Game-Based Learning effectiveness assessment: Reflections on study design. *Computers & Education*, *2021*(167), 104160.

Castillo-Segura, P., Fernández-Panadero, C. Alario-Hoyos,C P.J. Muñoz- Merino, C.PJ., Kloos C.D. (2021). Objective and automated assessment of surgical technical skills with IoT systems: A systematic literature review *Artificial Intelligence in Medicine, 1*, 1-17. . artmed. 2020.102007 10200. doi:10.1016/j

Celik, I., Dindar, M., Muukkonen, H., & Järvelä, S. (2022). The Promises and Challenges of Artificial Intelligence for Teachers: A Systematic Review of Research. *TechTrends*, *66*(4), 616–630. doi:10.100711528-022-00715-y

Chen, J., Chen, Y., Ou, R., Wang, J., & Chen, Q. (2022). How to Use Artificial Intelligence to Improve Entrepreneurial Attitude in Business Simulation Games: Implications From a Quasi-Experiment. *Frontiers in Psychology*, *13*, 856085. doi:10.3389/fpsyg.2022.856085 PMID:36467165

Chen, X., Zou, D., Xie, H., & Cheng, G. (2021). Twenty years of personalized language learning. *Journal of Educational Technology & Society*, *24*, 205–222.

Dai, C., & Ke, F. (2022). Educational applications of artificial intelligence in simulation-based learning: A systematic mapping review. *Computers and Education: Artificial Intelligence, 3*, 100087. doi:10.1016/j.caeai.2022.100087

Dawson, P., Henderson, M., Mahoney, P., Phillips, M., Ryan, T., Boud, D., & Molloy, E. (2019). What makes for effffective feedback: Staffff and student perspectives. *Assessment & Evaluation in Higher Education, 44*(1), 25–36. doi:10.1080/02602938.2018.1467877

Elshani, L., & Nuçi, K. P. (2021). Constructing a personalized learning path using genetic algorithms approach. *ArXiv. /abs/2104.11276*

Faulconer, E., Griffiffiffith, J., & Gruss, A. (2021). the impact of positive feedback on student outcomes and perceptions. *Assessment & Evaluation in Higher Education, 47*(2), 1–10.

Hernández-Sellés, N., Muñoz-Carril, P., & González-Sanmamed, M. (2019). Computer-supported collaborative learning: An analysis of the relationship between interaction, emotional support and online collaborative tools. *Computers & Education, 138*, 1–12. doi:10.1016/j.compedu.2019.04.012

Hooda, M., Rana, C., Dahiya, O., Rizwan, A., & Hossain, M. D. S. (2022). Artificial Intelligence for Assessment and Feedback to Enhance Student Success in Higher Education Mathematical Problems in Engineering. doi:10.1155/2022/5215722

Hu, W., Huang, Y., Jia, Y., & Ma, N. (2021). Exploring the relationship between socio emotional process and collaborative problem solving. *2021 13th International Conference on Education Technology and Computers*. ACM. 10.1145/3498765.3498834

Huang, X., & Lajoie, S. P. (2023). Social emotional interaction in collaborative learning: Why it matters and how can we measure it? *Social Sciences & Humanities Open, 7*(1), 100447. doi:10.1016/j.ssaho.2023.100447

Ivanović, M. (2021). E-learning Personalization Systems and Sustainable Education. *Sustainability (Basel), 13*(12), 6713. doi:10.3390u13126713

Kabudi, T., Pappas, I., & Olsen, D. H. (2021). AI-enabled adaptive learning systems:A systematic mapping of the literature. *Computers and Education: Artificial Intelligence, 100017*, 100017. doi:10.1016/j.caeai.2021.100017

Kaimara, P., Fokides, E., Oikonomou, A., & Deliyannis, I. (2021). Potential Barriers to the Implementation of Digital Game-Based Learning in the Classroom: Pre-service Teachers' Views. *Technol. Knowl. Learn., 26*(4), 825–844. doi:10.100710758-021-09512-7

Karthika, J., & Selvam, V. (2022). Accessible and engaging voices: Teaching English to adult second-language learners with visual impairment using WhatsApp voice notes in India. *British Journal of Visual Impairment*. doi:10.1177/02646196211070929

Kaufman, G., & Flanagan, M. (2015). A psychologically "embedded" approach to designing games for prosocial causes. *Cyberpsychology (Brno), 9*(3). doi:10.5817/CP2015-3-5

Khan, A. A., Wagan, A. A., Laghari, A. A., Gilal, A. R., Aziz, I. A., & Talpur, B. A. (2022). State-of-the-Art Consortium Serverless Network Architecture for Healthcare System Using Blockchain Smart Contracts. *IEEE Access : Practical Innovations, Open Solutions*, *10*, 78887–78898. doi:10.1109/ACCESS.2022.3194195

Khan, N., Muhammad, K., Hussain, T., Nasir, M., Munsif, M., Imran, A. S., & Sajjad, M. (2021). An Adaptive Game-Based Learning Strategy for Children Road Safety Education and Practice in Virtual Space. *Sensors (Basel)*, *21*(11), 3661. doi:10.339021113661 PMID:34070237

Klašnja-Mili´, A., & Ivanovi´, M. (2021). E-Learning Personalization Systems and Sustainable Education. *Sustainability (Basel)*, *13*(12), 6713. doi:10.3390u13126713

Lateef, F. (2010). Simulation-based learning: Just like the real thing. *Journal of Emergencies, Trauma and Shock*, *3*(4), 348–352. doi:10.4103/0974-2700.70743 PMID:21063557

Lean, J., Moizer, J., Derham, C., Strachan, L., & Bhuiyan, Z. (2021). *Real World Learning: Simulation and Gaming*. Applied Pedagogies for Higher Education. doi:10.1007/978-3-030-46951-1_9

Lei, H., Chiu, M. M., Wang, D., Wang, C., & Xie, T. (2022). Effects of Game-Based Learning on Students' Achievement in Science: A Meta-Analysis. *Journal of Educational Computing Research*, *60*(6), 1373–1398. doi:10.1177/07356331211064543

Leitner, M., Greenwald, E., Wang, N., Montgomery, R., & Merchant, C. (2022). Designing Game-Based Learning for High School Artificial Intelligence Education. *International Journal of Artificial Intelligence in Education*. Advance online publication. doi:10.100740593-022-00327-w

Levin-Banchik, L. (2018). Assessing Knowledge Retention, with our without simulations. *Journal of Political Science Education*, *14*(3), 341–359. doi:10.1080/15512169.2017.1405355

Loftus, M., & Madden, M. G. (2020). A pedagogy of data and Artificial intelligence for student subjectification. *Teaching in Higher Education*, *25*(4), 456–475. doi:10.1080/13562517.2020.1748593

Luan, H., Geczy, P., Lai, H., Gobert, J. H., Yang, S. J., Ogata, H., Baltes, J., Guerra, R., Li, P., & Tsai, C. (2020). Challenges and Future Directions of Big Data and Artificial Intelligence in Education. *Frontiers in Psychology*, *11*, 580820. doi:10.3389/fpsyg.2020.580820 PMID:33192896

Luckin, R., & Cukurova, M. (2019). Designing educational technologies in the age of AI: A learning sciences-driven approach. *British Journal of Educational Technology*, *50*(6), 2824–2838. doi:10.1111/bjet.12861

Luckin, R., Holmes, W., Griffiths, M., & Forcier, L. B. (2016). *Intelligence Unleashed: An Argument for AI in Education*. Pearson Education.

Luo, N., Zhang, M., & Qi, D. (2017). Effects of different interactions on students' sense of community in e learning environment. *Computers & Education, 115*, 153-160. https://doi.org/. 006 doi:10.1016/j.compedu.2017.08

Magomadov, V. S. (2020). The application of artificial intelligence and Big Data analytics in personalized learning. *Journal of Physics: Conference Series*, *1691*(1), 012169. doi:10.1088/1742-6596/1691/1/012169

Mahona, P., & Pacho, T. (2021). Reshaping Education in the Post-COVID-19 Pandemic in Africa. *African Research Journal of Education and Social Sciences (ARJESS), 8*(3), 13-26. http://arjess.org/education-research/reshaping-education-in-the-post-covid-19-pandemic-in- africa-.pdf

Makira, J., & Owino, E. (2021). The Use of Technology for Learning during the Covid-19 Pandemic Season: A Case of Rural Schools in Kenya. *International Journal of Innovative Science and Research Technology*, *6*.https://ijisrt.com/assets/upload/files/IJISRT21JAN172.pdf

McLaren, B. M., & Nguyen, H. A. (2023). Chapter 20: Digital learning games in artificial intelligence in education (AIED): a review. In Handbook of Artificial Intelligence in Education. Cheltenham, UK: Edward Elgar Publishing. doi:10.4337/9781800375413.00032

Mena-Guacas, A. F., Urueña Rodríguez, J. A., Santana Trujillo, D. M., Gómez-Galán, J., & López-Meneses, E. (2023). Collaborative learning and skill development for educational growth of artificial intelligence: A systematic review. *Contemporary Educational Technology*, *15*(3), ep428. doi:10.30935/cedtech/13123

Muhammad, K. N. K., Hussain, T., Nasir, M., Munsif, M., Imran, A., & Sajjad, M. (2021). An Adaptive Game-Based Learning Strategy for Children Road Safety Education and Practice in Virtual Space. *Sensors (Basel)*, *21*(11), 3661. doi:10.339021113661 PMID:34070237

Ochieng, V. O., & Ngware, M. W. (2022). Adoption of Education Technologies for Learning During COVID-19 Pandemic: The Experiences of Marginalized and Vulnerable Learner Populations in Kenya. *International Journal of Educational Reform*, *10567879221076081*. doi:10.1177/10567879221076081

Opondo, J. O., & Paschal, M. J. (2023). Blended Learning: An Emerging Pedagogy for Learning in Higher Education. In O. S. Ambili & M. Omanaseelan (Eds.), *Metamorphosis in Education* (pp. 47–59). Taran Publication.

Owoc, M. L., Weichbroth, P., & Sawicka, A. (2021). Artificial Intelligence Technologies in Education: Benefifits, Challenges and Strategies of Implementation. Artificial Intelligence for Knowledge Management (pp.37-58). doi:10.1007/978-3-030-85001-2_4

Pandemic, E. L. (2021). Induced remote learning increases need for mobile game-based learning to engage learners. *Educational Technology Research and Development*, *69*(1), 185–188. doi:10.100711423-020-09861-7

Paschal, M. J., & Gougou, S. A.-M. (2022). Promoting 21st Century Skills in English Language Teaching: A Pedagogical Transformation in Ivory Coast. *Global Journal of Educational Studies*, *8*(2), 50–74. doi:10.5296/gjes.v8i2.20333

Paschal, M. J., & Mahama, M. (2023). Performance-Based Assessments: Redefining Teacher-Trainees Evaluation. In O. S. Ambili & M. Omanaseelan (Eds.), *Metamorphosis in Education* (pp. 23–46). Taran Publication.

Paschal, M. J., & Mkulu, D. G. (2020). Online Classes during COVID-19 Pandemic in Higher Learning Institutions in Africa. *Global Research in Higher Education*, *3*(3), 1–21. doi:10.22158/grhe.v3n3p1

Paschal, M. J., & Mkulu, D. G. (2020a). Teacher- Students' Relationship and Students 'Academic Performance in Public Secondary Schools in Magu District, Tanzania. *Journal of Research in Education and Society*, *11*(1), 20–23. http://www.icidr.org/jresv11no1-content.php

Paschal, M. J., Pacho, O. T., & Adewoyin, O. (2022). Teaching methods applied in higher education during COVID-19 pandemic in Africa. *International Journal of Educational Policy Research and Review.*, *9*(1). Advance online publication. doi:10.15739/IJEPRR.22.003

Rahayu, S., Rahmadani, E., Syafitri, E., Prasetyoningsih, L. S. A., Ubaidillah, M. F., & Tavakoli, M. (2022). Teaching with Technology during COVID-19 Pandemic: An Interview Study with Teachers in Indonesia. *Education Research International*, *2022*, 1–9. doi:10.1155/2022/7853310

Russell & Norvig. (2023). Mission AI, Research for Policy. Springer. https://doi.org/ doi:10.1007/978-3-031-21448-6_215-39

Seo, K., Tang, J., Roll, I., Fels, S., & Yoon, D. (2021). The impact of artificial intelligence on learner–instructor interaction in online learning. *International Journal of Educational Technology in Higher Education*, *18*(1), 1–23. doi:10.118641239-021-00292-9 PMID:34778540

Shaw, C., & Switky, B. (2018). Designing and Using Simulations in the International Relations Classroom. *Journal of Political Science Education*, *14*(4), 523–534. doi:10.1080/15512169.2018.1433543

Shemshack, A., & Spector, J. M. (2020). A systematic literature review of personalized learning terms. *Smart Learning Environments*, *7*(1), 1–20. doi:10.118640561-020-00140-9

Tan, S. C., Lee, A. V. Y., & Lee, M. (2022). A systematic review of artificial intelligence techniques for collaborative learning over the past two decades. *Computers and Education. Artificial Intelligence*, *3*, 100097. doi:10.1016/j.caeai.2022.100097

Tapalova, O., & Zhiyenbayeva, N. (2022). Artificial Intelligence in Education: AIEd for Personalised Learning Pathways. *The Electronic Journal of e-Learning*, *20*(5). www.ejel.org

Tetzlaff, L., Schmiedek, F., & Brod, G. (2021). Developing personalized education: A dynamic framework. *Educational Psychology Review*, *33*(3), 863–882. doi:10.100710648-020-09570-w

Urquidi-Martín, A. C., Tamarit-Aznar, C., & Sánchez-García, J. (2019). Determinants of the Effectiveness of Using Renewable Resource Management-Based Simulations in the Development of Critical Thinking: An Application of the Experiential Learning Theory. *Sustainability (Basel)*, *11*(19), 5469. doi:10.3390u11195469

Wagan, A. A., Khan, A. A., Chen, Y., Yee, P. L., Yang, J., & Laghari, A. A. (2023). Artificial Intelligence-Enabled Game-Based Learning and Quality of Experience: A Novel and Secure Framework (B-AIQoE). *Sustainability (Basel)*, *15*(6), 5362. doi:10.3390u15065362

Wang, M., & Zheng, X. (2021). Using Game-Based Learning to Support Learning Science: A Study with Middle School Students. *The Asia-Pacific Education Researcher*, *30*(2), 167–17. doi:10.100740299-020-00523-z

Wetcho, S., & Na-Songkhla, J. (2022). An investigation of pre-service teachers using mobile and wearable devices for emotion recognition and social sharing of emotion to support emotion regulation in mCSCL environments. *Contemporary Educational Technology*, *14*(2), ep359. doi:10.30935/cedtech/11668

Zhai, X., Chu, X., Chai, C. S., Jong, M. S. Y., Istenic, A., Spector, M., Liu, J. B., Yuan, J., & Li, Y. (2021). A Review of Artificial Intelligence (AI) in Education from 2010 to 2020. Complexity. doi:10.1155/2021/8812542

Zhang, Q., Lin S., Liu, J & Jin, Y. (2022). A game perspective on collaborative learning among students in higher education. *Cogent Education.* doi:. 2022.2115617 doi:10.1080/2331186X

Zhang, S., Chen, J., Wen, Y., Chen, H., Gao, Q., & Wang, Q. (2021). Capturing regulatory patterns in online collaborative learning: A network analytic approach. *International Journal of Computer-Supported Collaborative Learning*, *16*(1), 37–66. doi:10.100711412-021-09339-5

KEY TERMS AND DEFINITIONS

AI Algorithms: involves the concrete application and execution of computation procedures designed to enable artificial intelligence systems to process data, learn from it, and make informed decisions or predictions.

AI Game Active Learning: encompasses the practical implementation and execution of educational activities that integrate artificial intelligence and gaming elements, encouraging hands-on participation problem- solving and dynamic engagement to facilitate effective personalized learning experiences for learners.

AI-Driven Gaming Activities: Pertains to the practical application and execution of gaming experiences that are guided and enhanced by artificial intelligence algorithms enabling dynamic interactions, personalized challenged and adaptive gameplay based on players' actions and preference.

AI Technology: Artificial intelligence is the catalyst for transformation that focuses on meeting the unique personalized learning requirement and demand of the learner

Collaborative Learning: entails the practical realization and application of an educational approach where learners engage in shared activities, discussions, and group tasks to collectively enhance their understanding, skills, and knowledge.

Intrinsic Motivation: is the extent to which an individual voluntarily engages in an activity sorely for the internal pleasure, satisfaction, or inherent interest derived from the activity itself, without external rewards or pressures influencing their participation. It is measured by the individual's willingness to persist in the activity even when external incentives are absent, the expression of enthusiasm and curiosity during the activity, and sense of personal accomplishment experienced upon completion.

Learning Pathways: refers to the implementing or putting into practice the concept of structured routed that learners follow to achieve specific personalized learning gaols or outcomes.

Personalized Learning: Refers to a wide variety of educational programs, academic strategies, learning experiences, and systematic pedagogical approaches designed to address learners 's specific learning needs, aspirations, and interests on an individual basis.

Simulation-Based Learning: refers to the practical implementation and execution of a teaching approach that utilizes simulations to provide learners with environment closely resembling dream-world situations. This enables them to actively build and refine their knowledge and skills within a controlled and simulated context.

Social Interactions: is defined as observable and measurable behaviours involving communication, engagement, or exchange of information between two or more individuals within a given context. This interaction encompass verbal and non-verbal communication, such as conversations, gestures, expressions, and shared activities. They are assessed based on the frequency, duration, and quality of the observed behaviours, with particular attention to the mutual influence and responses between participants.

Chapter 9

ChatGPT and Other Generative Artificial Intelligence (AI) Tools in Teaching and Learning as Integrative Pathways to Contemporary University Education

Oluwabunmi Dorcas Bakare
https://orcid.org/0000-0002-4665-3969
Lead City University, Nigeria

Taofeek Oladokun
https://orcid.org/0000-0001-7015-9496
Lead City University, Nigeria

Ganiyu Oluwaseyi Quadri
University of Ibadan, Nigeria

Temitope Oluwatofunmi Idowu-Davies
Emmanuel Alayande University of Education, Nigeria

ABSTRACT

The emergence of artificial intelligence such as ChatGPT and other generative AI tools is redefining the educational landscape. This chapter discusses how ChatGPT and other generative AI tools are used for teaching and learning globally, with a focus on the difference between developing and developed countries. Varied responses between educators and institutions in Africa compared to the developed world and highlights of the skill gaps to be filled to ensure effective and ethical use of generative AI tools by both learners and educators in the developing world were discussed. The chapter concludes by highlighting the implication of poor handling of the current epoch on the future of education and the overall development of the African continent. The study was significant to practice, society, and policy based on a developing country's perspectives.

DOI: 10.4018/979-8-3693-0205-7.ch009

INTRODUCTION

Technological advancement has trailed human history which has made the innovation of the latter era surpass that of the former, thus leading to technological development that speaks to the dictates of each epoch. The 21st century is not an exception which is witnessing technological advancement in emerging trends such as Artificial Intelligence which according to Bakare (2023) is ushered in by the Fourth Industrial Revolution (4thIR). Bozkurt (2023) averred this technology as a phenomenon that is influencing the human domain in the 21st century at an unprecedented rate and at the same time redefining all aspects of human endeavour of which the educational ecosystem hinged on teaching and learning is core.

Artificial Intelligence (AI) among digital technologies seems to disrupt global space in medicine, science, health, aviation, and education in contemporary times. This technology which is sometimes called machine intelligence is not natural as it involves developing computer programs to complete tasks that would otherwise require human intelligence. Chaudhry and Kazim (2022, p. 157) defined AI as "a computer system that can achieve a particular task through certain capabilities (like speech or vision) and intelligent behaviour that was once considered unique to humans". This is leading to a paradigm shift in which there is expected to be a synergy between technology and humans as the former cannot do without the latter, though there might be changes in practices as well as delivery on the part of humans.

According to Mander (1978) as cited in Quadri (2022) who asserted that technology more often than not disrupts traditional practices, requiring people to adapt and consider the potential benefits and drawbacks of new technologies. This disruption has also been a source of concern to educators who felt their roles would be displaced (Selwyn, 2019). Howbeit, Bakare (2023) have recommended that these technologies should be seen as enablers and not a displacer as the place of human cannot be overemphasized in the technological ecosystem; but what needs to be adjusted is "the human mindset" to embrace this innovation. This is in tandem with the affirmation of Bozkurt et al., (2023) who argued that any technology is an extension of man's capabilities and AI is an addendum as well as the exhibition of human intelligence.

The advent of AI into the education domain is a watershed, that is changing the education landscape in terms of teaching and learning; instructional technology; archival and library; assessment, and many more. Artificial Intelligence (AI) seems to be able to improve and change the whole educational system worldwide which higher institutions of learning in the Global North are keying into but the same cannot be said of these institutions in the Global South like Nigeria. The tendency of its application to be adopted by lecturers to complement their efforts in higher education institutions is also high as its advantages cannot be overlooked. In addition, AI seems to have demonstrated the capacity to assist learners in receiving more personalized support and providing a student-centric approach to teaching and learning due to the ubiquity of the technology.

Artificial intelligence has been a part of education for a while before the recent phenomena arrival of ChatGPT which has also drawn attention to other similar but (probably) less effective tools. Both teachers and learners were already familiar with tools such as Grammarly, Quillbot, Google Lens, ProWriter, Article Rewriter, and other writing and creative assistants (OSU, 2023; Sánchez-Prieto et al., 2020). Nonetheless, the arrival of ChatGPT in November 2022 ushered in an unprecedented interactive model with seemingly unparalleled natural language processing ability that captured the imagination of the world, specifically the academic world. More reason Baidoo-Anu and Owusu Ansah (2023) affirmed ChatGPT and other generative AI as extending educational frontiers that are setting the pace for remodelling and remodification of the educational ecosystem. Thus, beckoning both tutors and students into a phase of learning, unlearning, re-learning, and upskilling to be able to navigate this technological space seamlessly.

ChatGPT and other similar tools such as Google Bard by Google and Bing by Microsoft are Generative Artificial Intelligence (G-AI). According to Lim et al., (2023), G-AI can be defined as a technology with a multitude of capabilities such as the ability to leverage deep learning models which enable it to generate human-like content in various formats in response to complex and varied prompts. According to UNESCO (2023), ChatGPT is described as a language model that allows individuals to interact with computer technology conversationally or naturally. In an actual sense, GPT implies a Generative Pre-trained Transformer generally for a family of natural or conversational language models specifically invented by Open Artificial Intelligence (AI), which also refers to a form of AI generative tool owing to its capability of producing original outcomes or results.

Generative AI (G-AI) tools such as ChatGPT can generate various forms of content such as music scores, computer codes, food recipes, and academic papers capable of passing the scrutiny of the strictest reviewers. Trained on a tremendous amount of information and data up to the year 2021, ChatGPT can hold human-like interaction on a wide range of topics and explain complex concepts clearly and concisely (Farrokhnia et al, 2023). It is also capable of synthesizing literature to create 'original' well-written documents on virtually all subjects. This has endeared it to students who now make use of it to write assignments, pursue self-directed studies, and understand concepts that hitherto seemed too complex. Despite its numerous advantages in all spheres of human endeavour, its influx into the educational domain is generating heated discourse of two sides to a coin that cannot be overlooked if the educational ecosystem does not want to be left behind in this innovative wagon. It is based on this premise that this chapter will navigate the world of ChatGPT and Other Generative AI (G-AI) Tools in Teaching and Learning, and take into perspective its implication for practice, society, and educational policies most especially in a developing country like Nigeria.

GENERATIVE AI IN TEACHING AND LEARNING

The place of generative AI in recent times cannot be neglected as educators across the world have also found these tools to be highly useful in generating lesson plans, conducting assessments, and grading students. Others have also used the tools to generate examination questions and designed interactive tutorials for their students and to conduct basic research. However, only lecturers in developed countries seem to have publicly embraced the use of Chat GPT and openly used it in their official duties (Baidoo-Anu and Owusu Ansah, 2023). Educators in Africa are mostly uncertain about the use of generative AI in education believing that it promotes intellectual laziness and encourages cheating. This could be due to the misconception that is making them see this technology as taking over their jobs and displacing their significance in society (Bakare, 2023). As a result, it is rare to have any official viewpoint on the use of generative AI by educators and learners alike.

On the contrary, Western educators are taking a direct and practical approach to address the disruptions created by the emergence of generative AI. While some states in the United States of America (USA) recently placed a ban on the use of generative AI tools in its school districts (NBC, 2023), virtually every tertiary institution in the United Kingdom (UK) and USA has acknowledged the pervasiveness of generative AI and are therefore developing coping strategies which should have been the attitude of educators most especially within the Nigerian educational space. Many lecturers have started using generative AI to help in their research while others have integrated it into their teaching activities. Some educators have also understood that they must properly understand how generative AI tools work so that they can point out their strengths and weaknesses to students who have begun to see the tools as the ultimate arbiter of knowledge (Cooper, 2023; Mhlanga, 2023).

In addition to this, some institutions have also developed programmes for both students and educators by providing them with the requisite skills and competencies for the effective use of generative AI. This includes developing a skill set in the usage of AI content detectors such as Originality.ai, GPTZero, Sapling, Copyleaks, OpenAI Text Classifier, CrossPlag AI, AISEO, etc. developed to show the authenticity and originality of digital content. This is expected to furnish both parties with the capabilities of staying ahead of the technological curve, or when that is not possible, to keep pace with development in this critical and pertinent area. Most of these trainings are domiciled in the university libraries and have now formed a part of the digital literacy training usually offered to the students (Teal, 2023). Bakare (2023) averred this as the provision of sustainable library services which is not inhibited by time, means, or location due to the ubiquitous nature of this technology.

Many tertiary institutions have also come up with policies such as mandating students and educators to make full disclosure of any content generated through AI tools to instill a sense of accountability in addition to guiding against ethical issues in the usage of these technologies. In addition, some universities have also created caveat statements that educators must share with their students to warn them about the shortcomings of G-AI tools (Boston University, 2023). This is supposed to be the outlook of educators in the Global South knowing fully well that these technologies are game changers which when infused into the nitty-gritty of academic activities helps in facilitating pedagogical participation in addition to strengthening existing traditional system (Bakare and Okuonghae, 2023)

High-ranking universities, such as those in the USA have admitted that they have not fully decided on the place of G-AI tools, thus they are proceeding to err on the side of caution by leaving a bulk of the decision in the hands of teachers who must ensure that they share the caveat of the university and ensure that the students make effective and ethical use of the tools. One issue that is widely discussed is the ethics of using G-AI tools (Boston University, 2023) while Bozkurt (2023) outlined the challenges of quality control, reliability of knowledge sources, downplaying human agency in educational knowledge chain, technical complexity, the possibility of teacher replacement, dependence on technology, a lack of creativity and critical thinking, etc. These are topical issues of concern in the Use of Generative AI among Educators and Learners.

THE POTENTIAL OF CHATGPT INTEGRATION IN THE NIGERIAN EDUCATIONAL SYSTEM

The ChatGPT is a very recent technological development that has been applied to the educational industry in developed countries, especially in higher education but the reverse is the case within the Nigerian educational landscape. The area where the ChatGPT can be used in education is not but limited to teaching, learning, research, administration, library service delivery, and community engagement. Owing to its capability to generate and assess information at an unprecedented rate, ChatGPT is capable of performing some functions relating to teaching, learning, and research processes with the assistance of other forms of AI, it is imperative to note that ChatGPT could enhance both the process as well as experience of learning particularly for students (UNESCO, 2023). Given this, ChatGPT could be utilized as an independent tool or could be integrated into some other platforms or systems employed by higher education institutions, particularly in Nigeria.

The application of technology is always seen as a positive vibe for education. The advent of ChatGPT and other generative AI tools, therefore, holds great potential for both teachers and learners in Nigeria if it can be embraced positively with open hands and a broad mind. Indeed, it holds greater potential for the entire educational system in the nation knowing fully well the significant role as the giant of Africa in the continent. This is viewed from the perspective of rising demand for education among the teeming youths in an environment of limited access to education and emerging technologies that make students stand the test of time as well as able to compete favourably with their peers on the global landscape. On the other hand, many public tertiary institutions in Nigeria are battling with the steam of increased student enrollment and fewer infrastructural facilities in addition to a lack of recent educational technological equipment to meet the demands. Private universities that were at the forefront of academic continuity amid the Covid-19 pandemic which redefined the phase of online learning within the Nigerian space (Bakare and Ademakinwa, 2020) are not keeping up with the pace in the usage of G-AI in recent times which could have been a morale booster for the public institutions. More reason, the recent shift towards online learning by both private and public educational institutions would benefit from the strategic use of G-AI tools within the Nigerian educational space.

In addition, distance education systems such as the Open University and various programs run by other universities in Nigeria can benefit from these tools. Students who have to engage in self-directed study now have a tool that can break down complex concepts and make them better understand the course content. In addition, they would also be empowered to make their contribution to the learning process thereby enriching the course content and becoming more empowered to acquire deeper knowledge and gain the necessary skills (Domenech, 2023).

As academic curriculum evolves in response to market demand, G-AI also has the potential to help both teachers and learners incorporate the latest knowledge into the existing course content so that learners do not continue to gain knowledge that would be obsolete even before their graduation. This will go a long way in inculcating recent skills into students that fit into the dictates of contemporary times and be able to navigate the labor market curve seamlessly. What G-AI offers is the opportunity to infuse dynamism and creativity into the curriculum to prepare students for the rapid evolution of knowledge and ideas in the modern world (Malinka et al., 2023) which will put them on a better pedestal globally.

Most importantly, G-AI tools allow students to have a globalized education even in their local environment. Generative AI tools (especially internet-enabled tools) synthesize their responses to each prompt based on information from a wider range of sources that students may not ordinarily have access to or skills to obtain by themselves. Reading these contents, therefore, empowers Nigerian learners to participate in the global scholarship arena without any iota of constraint. Of course, this depends on the ability to leverage information from these tools to conduct deeper searches and wider studies on each subject. The stimulation provided by these platforms cannot be discounted.

The potential for educators is also considerable which will inform the sustainability of the Nigerian educational system. Educators can use ChatGPT and G-AI tools for administrative tasks such as setting up class schedules, communicating with students, and developing test questions, marking guides, and worksheets among others (Domenech, 2023). There are also reports of ChatGPT being used to develop a language learning tool to facilitate effective second language acquisition (Topsakal and Topsakal, 2022). If this is being done in other countries, it can also be done in Nigeria where lecturers' workload is so enormous that each lecturer needs significant assistance to cope. However, the use of ChatGPT and G-AI tools has not become institutionalized or widespread in Nigeria due to various factors. It is important to echo that ChatGPT can perform several simple or technical functions (UNESCO, 2023) for example conducting basic research, calculations as well and proofreading. To grasp further how ChatGPT can be applied or incorporated into teaching and learning, the below table displays these as noted by (UNESCO, 2023).

Apart from the above submission, the possible benefits of ChatGPT and other related generative AI in facilitating teaching and learning in higher education institutions are highlighted by Baidoo-Anu and Ansah (2023). This was situated within the Nigerian educational landscape and is presented below:

Personalized Tutoring: Nigerian educators can harness ChatGPT to offer personalized tutoring as well as feedback to students based on learning needs and progress. This is supported by Chen, Chen, and Heffernan (2020) who reported that ChatGPT is capable of providing personalized mathematics tutoring to students, which will in turn enhance learning outcomes.

Automated Essay Grading: Nigerian educators can use ChatGPT to grade and assess student essays which affords teachers ample time to focus on other aspects of teaching. The study by Kim, Park, and Lee (2019) revealed that ChatGPT is instructed and trained on how to use datasets to grade human essays, Essays written by students, especially high school pupils could be graded accurately without errors.

Language Translation: Nigerian educators can use ChatGPT to translate course materials into several languages making them accessible to students irrespective of the languages they speak knowing fully well that there are diverse languages in Nigeria. The above statement was affirmed in a study conducted by Johnson et al. (2016) and revealed that ChatGPT is trained on a dataset of bilingual sentence pairs

Table 1. Ways ChatGPT can be applied or incorporated into teaching and learning

Descriptions of AI in Teaching and Learning	Examples of Areas of Application in Teaching and Learning
AI creates alternative ways of uttering an idea	Students generate queries in ChatGPT and use the regenerated answers to examine alternative responses.
AI as an alternative to developmental tools for augmenting teaching and learning	Students enter information into ChatGPT depending on the structure of a debate. Students can ask to use ChatGPT for discussions
AI assists groups of people to research and solve problems collectively	Teamwork helps students in using ChatGPT to locate information required to complete specific tasks or assignments.
AI performs as a guide in navigating both physical and conceptual spaces	Teachers use ChatGPT to generate course content for classes and advise students on how to sustain learning specific ideas.
AI teaches students and gets instant feedback	ChatGPT offers a feedback mechanism to students based on the provided information by tutors e.g. exam scores.
AI helps during the design process	Teachers ask ChatGPT ideas relating to curriculum designing to focus on goals and objectives.
AI offers tools to play with and for data	Teachers offer information to students who write different questions in ChatGPT to find additional information. ChatGPT could be used in supporting language learning.
AI assists the student to reflect on learning material	Students describe their level of understanding of ChatGPT and inquire about ways to assist them in mastering the learning material. ChatGPT can also be utilized to perform other functions such as job interviews.
AI provides games and problems to extend learning	Both the teachers and students could ask ChatGPT for ideas about how to extend students' learning after providing a summary of the current level of knowledge for example through quizzes and exercises.
AI offers teachers a profile of individual students' current knowledge states	Students interact with ChatGPT in a tutorial-type dialogue and ask ChatGPT to produce a summary of their current knowledge state to share with their teacher for assessment.

which could accurately translate between languages on several translation benchmarks. This ensures that no Nigerian student is left out within the educational ecosystem.

Interactive Learning: Nigerian educators can use ChatGPT to create an interactive learning environment especially where the students can interact with a teacher virtually in a discussion manner. Kim, Park, and Lee (2019) noted that ChatGPT model-based discussion or conversation agent can support students effectively in learning English as a second language which in turn improves English proficiency. This will ensure that all Nigerian students are vast in the usage of the English language since it is the official language of the nation.

Adaptive Learning: Educators in Nigeria can use ChatGPT when creating adaptive learning systems that adjust teachers' teaching methodologies to students' progress reports and performance. This was supported by Chen, Chen, and Heffernan (2020) who showed that ChatGPT as an adaptive learning system could offer more effective support for students learning programming which is expected to improve performance on programming assessments.

In summary, ChatGPT can be an influential tool capable of improving teaching and learning through personalized tutoring, systems essay grading, and language translation as well as interactive and adaptive learning within the Nigerian educational ecosystem.

ISSUES IN THE USE OF GENERATIVE AI TOOLS

It is important to note that despite the rave reviews that have trailed the emergence of AI tools, there are specific issues that may undermine the idea behind its development in the African educational system. As pointed out by Arakpogun et al., (2021), Africa is about a decade late to the AI race which means that its specific needs may not be properly catered for by existing AI tools. Available literature has raised issues such as training data bias in ChatGPT and other tools (Borenstein and Howard, 2021; Akgun and Greenhow, 2021; Vargo and Hopp, 2023). This means that the tools designed by mostly American and European developers may have been trained to 'see' issues from the Western perspective which has always been the bane of technological development in each era. Scholars such as Gondwe (2023) observed that existing G-AI tools are light on African corpus and may not be properly trained on cultural sensibilities peculiar and indigenous to Africans. However, there is also the recognition of the fact that the tools can also learn from the inputs of various people from all over the world, including Africans.

Of major concern, however, are other issues such as the technological capacity of African countries such as Nigeria to support an AI-driven educational process. Many tertiary institutions in Nigeria are still lacking the critical infrastructure necessary for digital learning. This may make it difficult for technology enthusiasts to effectively push the agenda of integrated use of G-AI in education in Nigeria. For instance, tertiary institutions in the Global North have developed or acquired technology to detect unethical use of generative AI in the academic world while there is a dearth of reports of the existence of these tools in Nigeria.

In addition to the inadequate infrastructure, there is also the challenge of skilled personnel necessary to properly onboard students and lecturers in the use of G-AI. As pointed out by Celik et al., (2022), it is important to have educators with adequate pedagogical knowledge combined with technology skills for effective integration of AI into education. Another major issue in the adoption of ChatGPT in Nigeria is the lack of clear policy guidelines on its use or non-use. Due to its sudden emergence and continuous evolution, there has been no official directive from the Nigerian Universities Commission (NUC) regarding the response to the emergence of these tools. This probably accounts for why no university in Nigeria has also articulated a response to its adoption and usage as against their counterparts in developed countries. The consequence is that critical issues are not discussed thereby leaving several grey areas for many lecturers.

The lack of a robust conversation on the use of AI tools is probably responsible for some negative attitudes towards it among some Nigerian educators who view the use of ChatGPT as unethical and a way of watering down the quality of academic outputs. There is a commonly expressed opinion that scholars who rely on AI tools would become lazy and unable to pay attention to the details of their academic work. ChatGPT was also seen by some as a tool that might facilitate cheating and other forms of academic fraud, as students see it as a veritable opportunity to copy and paste one another's works (Morocco-Clarke, Sodangi, and Momodu, 2023).

Existing literature has also shown that, while academic institutions are seeking means of mastering the use of AI tools for effective teaching and learning, educators and institutions in Africa have not demonstrated that they are aware of the existence of these tools not to talk of devising strategies to ensure their effective use and making them useful in teaching and learning. This has grave implications for the future of the educational space in Africa. Gondwe (2023) observed that this crop of boundary-spanning educators is not readily available in countries such as Nigeria which may hinder the effective use of AI tools. Other issues noted by Baidoo-Anu and Ansah (2023) are as follows:

Lack of human interaction: ChatGPT and other AI cannot offer the same level of real human interaction as a teacher, lecturer, or tutor. The implication of this is that educators have the instinctive ability to decide if there is any error or glitch in the teacher-student interaction which is alien to a technology like ChatGPT.

Limited understanding: ChatGPT does not understand the true concepts that student is trying to learn because they are trained on a pattern in which it could function. This implies that educators are professionally trained to factor in the environmental condition during the learning process which the ChatGPT might not be aware of unless it is part of the code used to develop it.

Bias in training data: ChatGPT and other G-AI are only good in the data they are trained on and then if there are biases in the training received, there will also be bias in the model. This implies that there is a limitation to the knowledge that ChatGPT can provide in answering a query as extant literature has shown that it can only provide data up to the year 2021. This is in contradiction to the intelligent nature of man who has a sense of history and can also use present information to make predictions for the future.

Lack of creativity: ChatGPT can only generate and create responses based on the pattern of data they received during training; this can reduce the originality of responses received from the data. This is unlike the educators who can infer and make meaning from different datasets in solving an identified societal issue

Dependency on data: ChatGPT is trained on a large amount of data, if the data is not enough or relevant, the model may malfunction. Educators have been trained to work with data in addition to using their intuition to make meaningful decisions

Lack of contextual understanding: ChatGPT cannot understand the context which could lead to poor responses. Educators can consider environmental factors in making informed decisions and read learners' moods to decipher what could be causing emotional instability that is causing mental imbalance.

Limited ability to personalize instruction: ChatGPT can only offer or provide overall information about a phenomenon but may not be able to personalize instruction that can meet the student's particular needs. Contemporary education has transcended to embracing student-centrism which is fostering lecturer-student interactions.

IMPACT OF THE STUDY

Practice: Educators within the African space and Nigeria are aware of the significant role that the ChatGPT and other G-AI tools are playing, and there is a need to change their perspective as well as remove any misconception about the adoption and usage of these technologies so that they can fit into the contemporary standards in the discharge of their duties. Students' horizons have also been broadened in the various ethical issues involved in the usage of these technologies despite their myriad of advantages.

Society: Nigerian society will be better informed when ChatGPT is well-harnessed ethically.

Policy: Stakeholders in the educational landscape most especially the Nigerian Universities Commission (NUC) should promote the adoption and usage of ChatGPT and G-AI in addition to putting up a policy framework as well as strategies to ensure the smooth sale of these technologies within the Nigerian educational ecosystem.

CONCLUSION

Like previous innovations, ChatGPT and G-AI tools have become an integral part of education just as it has permeated other areas of human endeavour. These technologies are currently perceived as disruptive by some while others see it as a paradigm shift laced with innovations and creativity. The most tenable position is that ChatGPT and G-AI tools offer great opportunities for education in Nigeria if positively harnessed. When integrated strategically and efficiently, it can help bridge the digital divide between Nigeria and other advanced countries. This will showcase the nation as the giant of Africa and take the proper place in technologically advancing the course of the African continent. It also has the potential to revolutionize teaching and learning in Nigeria with new methods and insight into teaching courses that focus on contemporary societal needs and dictates. The current apathy toward generative AI tools among educational stakeholders, therefore, needs to be urgently addressed.

RECOMMENDATIONS

There is an urgent need for a policy document on the use of generative AI tools, particularly ChatGPT in African tertiary institutions and also within the Nigerian educational clime. The Association of African Universities (AAU) should handshake stakeholders in the formulation of policies that should spell out what constitutes fair use and what should be considered academic fraud in line with global standards within the knowledge economy.

There is also the need for training and skill development for educators in Nigeria regarding the workings and effective use of ChatGPT and G-AI tools. This is necessary to obtain their full support for the integration of G-AI tools in teaching and learning and to ensure that they are empowered to guide their students in the ethical use of these tools.

Professionals such as librarians should step up awareness creation, advocacy, and capacity development programs to enlighten and empower both tutors and learners in Nigeria on the adoption and use of ChatGPT and G-AI tools. This will go a long way in showcasing the significant roles of the library in solving any identified societal issues. In the long run, it will ensure that Nigeria is strategically positioned to take advantage of the opportunities inherent in the use of generative AI and other modern tools.

REFERENCES

Akgun, S., & Greenhow, C. (2021). Artificial intelligence in education: Addressing ethical challenges in K-12 settings. *AI and Ethics*, 1–10. PMID:34790956

Arakpogun, E. O., Elsahn, Z., Olan, F., & Elsahn, F. (2021). Artificial intelligence in Africa: Challenges and opportunities. *The fourth industrial revolution: Implementation of artificial intelligence for growing business success,* 375-388.

Baidoo-AnuD.Owusu AnsahL. (2023). Education in the era of generative artificial intelligence (AI): Understanding the potential benefits of ChatGPT in promoting teaching and learning. SSRN 4337484. doi:10.2139/ssrn.4337484

Bakare, O. D. (2023). Emerging Technologies as a Panacea for Sustainable Provision of Library Services in Nigeria. In *Global Perspectives on Sustainable Library Practices* (pp. 1–21). IGI Global.

Bakare, O. D., & Ademakinwa, M. A. (2021). The Impact of COVID-19 on Mentorship of Graduate Students in Nigerian Universities. *Journal of the Nigerian Pastoral Counselling Association*, *1*(1), 15–19.

Bakare, O. D., & Okuonghae, N. (2023). Digital Technologies and Resources for Learning Under Lockdown. In Impact of Disruptive Technologies on the Socio-Economic Development of Emerging Countries (pp. 87-103). IGI Global. doi:10.4018/978-1-6684-6873-9.ch006

Borenstein, J., & Howard, A. (2021). Emerging challenges in AI and the need for AI ethics education. *AI and Ethics*, *1*(1), 61–65. doi:10.100743681-020-00002-7

Bozkurt, A. (2023). Generative artificial intelligence (AI) powered conversational educational agents: The inevitable paradigm shift. *Asian Journal of Distance Education*, *18*(1).

Bozkurt, A., Xiao, J., Lambert, S., Pazurek, A., Crompton, H., Koseoglu, S., & Jandrić, P. (2023). Speculative futures on ChatGPT and generative artificial intelligence (AI): A collective reflection from the educational landscape. *Asian Journal of Distance Education*, *18*(1).

Celik, I., Dindar, M., Muukkonen, H., & Järvelä, S. (2022). The promises and challenges of artificial intelligence for teachers: A systematic review of research. *TechTrends*, *66*(4), 616–630. doi:10.100711528-022-00715-y

ChatGPT and generative AI in the classroom. (n.d.). University of Toronto. https://www.viceprovostundergrad.utoronto.ca/strategic-priorities/digital-learning/special-initiative-artificial-intelligence/

ChatGPT and other AI tools: Challenges, opportunities, and strategies for teaching. (2023, February 14). Boston University. https://www.bu.edu/dli/2023/02/14/chat-gpt-and-other-ai-tools-challenges-opportunities-and-strategies-for-teaching/

Chaudhry, M. A., & Kazim, E. (2022). Artificial Intelligence in Education (AIEd): A high-level academic and industry note 2021. *AI and Ethics*, *2*(1), 1–9. doi:10.100743681-021-00074-z PMID:34790953

Chen, Y., Chen, Y., & Heffernan, N. (2020). Personalized math tutoring with a conversational agent. arXiv preprint arXiv:2012.12121.

Cooper, G. (2023). Examining science education in ChatGPT: An exploratory study of generative artificial intelligence. *Journal of Science Education and Technology*, *32*(3), 1–9. doi:10.100710956-023-10039-y

Domenech, J. (2023). ChatGPT in the Classroom: Friend or Foe? *9th International Conference on Higher Education Advances (HEAd'23)*. IEEE. 10.4995/HEAd23.2023.16179

Farrokhnia, M., Banihashem, S. K., Noroozi, O., & Wals, A. (2023). A SWOT analysis of ChatGPT: Implications for educational practice and research. *Innovations in Education and Teaching International*, 1–15. doi:10.1080/14703297.2023.2195846

García-Peñalvo, F. J. (2023). The perception of Artificial Intelligence in educational contexts after the launch of ChatGPT: Disruption or Panic? .

Gondwe, G. (2023). *CHATGPT and the Global South: How are journalists in sub-Saharan Africa engaging with generative AI?* Online Media and Global Communication.

Johnson, M., Schuster, M., Le, Q., Krikun, M., Wu, Y., Chen, Z., & Chen, Y. (2016). Google's neural machine translation system: Bridging the gap between human and machine translation. *arXiv pre*.

Kim, S., Park, J., & Lee, H. (2019). Automated essay scoring using a deep learning model. *Journal of Educational Technology Development and Exchange*, *2*(1), 1–17.

Lim, W. M., Gunasekara, A., Pallant, J. L., Pallant, J. I., & Pechenkina, E. (2023). Generative AI and the future of education: Ragnarök or reformation? A paradoxical perspective from management educators. *International Journal of Management Education*, *21*(2), 100790. doi:10.1016/j.ijme.2023.100790

Malinka, K., Peresíni, M., Firc, A., Hujnák, O., & Janus, F. (2023, June). On the educational impact of ChatGPT: Is Artificial Intelligence ready to obtain a university degree? In *Proceedings of the 2023 Conference on Innovation and Technology in Computer Science Education* V. 1 (pp. 47-53). IEEE. 10.1145/3587102.3588827

Mhlanga, D. (2023). Open AI in education, the responsible and ethical use of ChatGPT towards lifelong learning. *Education, the Responsible and Ethical Use of ChatGPT Towards Lifelong Learning*.

Morocco-Clarke, A., Sodangi, F. A., & Momodu, F. (2023). The implications and effects of ChatGPT on academic scholarship and authorship: A death knell for original academic publications? *Information & Communications Technology Law*, 1–21. doi:10.1080/13600834.2023.2239623

NBC. (2023, January 5). *ChatGPT banned from New York City public schools' devices and networks*. NBC News. https://www.nbcnews.com/tech/tech-news/new-york-city-public-schools-ban-chatgpt-devices-networks-rcna64446

Oregon State University. (2023, March 22). *ChatGPT and other AI tools: Implications for teaching and learning*. Center for Teaching and Learning. https://ctl.oregonstate.edu/chatgpt-and-other-ai-tools-implications-teaching-and-learning

Rudra, S. (2023, March 30). *ChatGPT in education: The pros, cons and unknowns of generative AI*. Technology Solutions That Drive Education. https://edtechmagazine.com/k12/article/2023/03/chatgpt-in-education-generative-ai-perfcon

Sánchez-Prieto, J. C., Cruz-Benito, J., Therón Sánchez, R., & García Peñalvo, F. J. (2020). Assessed by machines: Development of a TAM-based tool to measure ai-based assessment acceptance among students. *International Journal of Interactive Multimedia and Artificial Intelligence*, *6*(4), 80–86. doi:10.9781/ijimai.2020.11.009

Teal, M. (2023, April 18). *The ethics of college students using ChatGPT*. Ethics and Policy. https://ethicspolicy.unc.edu/news/2023/04/17/the-ethics-of-college-students-using-chatgpt/

Topsakal, O., & Topsakal, E. (2022). Framework for A Foreign Language Teaching Software for Children Utilizing AR, Voicebots and ChatGPT (Large Language Models). *The Journal of Cognitive Systems*.

UNESCO. (2023). *ChatGPT and Artificial Intelligence in higher education: quick start guide*. United Nations Education, Scientific and Cultural Organisation.

Vargo, C., & Hopp, T. (2023). *Incivility on Popular Politics and News Subreddits: An Analysis of In-groups*. Community Guidelines and Relationships with Social Media Engagement.

KEY TERMS AND DEFINITIONS

AI Content Detectors: These are AI-driven tools that ensure that digital content shows human intellectual prowess rather than machine input to promote authenticity and originality.

Artificial Intelligence (AI): This is a computer system that can achieve a particular task through certain capabilities (like speech or vision) and intelligent behaviour that was once considered unique to humans.

ChatGPT: This is a language model that allows individuals to interact with computer technology conversationally or naturally.

Fourth Industrial Revolution (4thIR): This is opined as the 21st-century era of technological advancement driven by emerging technologies like AI.

Generative Artificial Intelligence (G-AI): These are technologies with a multitude of capabilities such as the ability to leverage deep learning models which enable it to generate human-like content in various formats in response to complex and varied prompts.

Global North: These are developed countries that have embraced the use of ChatGPT and other Generative AI tools in the mainstream of teaching and learning.

Global South: These are developing countries that are faced with myriads of challenges in embracing and infusing AI technologies into the educational ecosystem.

GPT: This is a Generative Pre-trained Transformer generally for a family of natural or conversational language models specifically invented by Open Artificial Intelligence (AI).

UNESCO: The United Nations Educational, Scientific and Cultural Organization.

Chapter 10
ChatGPT and the Education System:
Challenges and Risks in Teaching Learning Systems

Kiran Lokesh Maney
https://orcid.org/0000-0002-6624-4396
CMS, Jain University (Deemed), India

ABSTRACT

ChatGPT is an AI chatbot gaining popularity in education. Educators have concerns about its impact. Chatbots are emerging in various sectors, including education and STEM. However, their use as a pedagogical tool is unclear. ChatGPT provides direct answers to difficult questions, raising concerns about essays and research production in universities. Pedagogical changes will be needed to adapt to ChatGPT. This chapter reviews ChatGPT's applications in higher education, highlighting challenges, risks, and ethical considerations. The chapter emphasizes the need for further investigation and suggests using ChatGPT as a memory tool for creative learning.

INTRODUCTION

The utilization of technological applications has consistently expedited the teaching-learning process within educational environments. Advancements in technology have been instrumental in reshaping the dissemination and acquisition of knowledge, ultimately elevating the educational journey for educators and students alike. Over the years, advancements in technology have transformed how knowledge is imparted and acquired, enhancing the overall educational experience for both teachers and students. Artificial intelligence (AI) has evolved and improved over the recent past, finding its applications in all the fields. AI's integration into the education system has gained momentum, offering a multitude of avenues to augment the teaching-learning process in recent times. AI's increasing involvement in edu-

DOI: 10.4018/979-8-3693-0205-7.ch010

cation, has contributed to innovative enhancements that facilitate learning and instruction. AI has been predominantly used in professional learning for hybrid and remote learning modes (Educause, 2022).

One of the primary way technologies accelerates the teaching-learning process is through the facilitation of information access. The internet and digital resources provide vast amounts of educational content and research materials, making it easier for students to explore and engage with a wide range of subjects. Moreover, teachers can access a plethora of educational tools, multimedia resources, and online platforms to enrich their teaching methods.

Technology also enables personalized learning experiences. With the aid of educational software, learning management systems, and adaptive learning platforms, educators can tailor lessons and assignments to meet individual students' needs and learning styles. This personalized approach fosters better comprehension and engagement, allowing students to progress at their own pace.

Collaborative learning has also been significantly amplified by technology. Virtual classrooms, video conferencing tools, and online discussion forums enable seamless communication and interaction among students and educators, irrespective of geographical barriers. Collaborative projects and group activities become more accessible and effective, promoting teamwork and peer learning.

Assessment and feedback constitute integral components of the teaching-learning process, and technology has streamlined these aspects effectively. Online quizzes, interactive assessments, and automated grading systems save time and provide instant feedback to students, helping them identify their strong areas and areas of improvement promptly.

Additionally, immersive technologies like virtual reality (VR) and augmented reality (AR) have revolutionized the learning experience. These technologies offer interactive and engaging simulations, making complex subjects more comprehensible and enhancing experiential learning. The integration of technology in education has expedited the sharing of knowledge, improved instructional strategies, and diversified learning experiences. As technology continues to evolve, educators and institutions need to stay abreast of new advancements to harness their full potential in optimizing the teaching-learning process for the benefit of all learners.

Technology is often learned quicker by students when compared to teachers and academic staff, they adopt to the new technology real time through social media. The introduction of the trending technology ChatGPT is not unfamiliar to the education system; however, its rapid dissemination within the market has exceeded expectations. ChatGPT, an AI-powered chatbot, had been released to the public on November 30, 2022, by a company called OpenAI. A chatbot is a computer program intended to reproduce discussion with human clients, particularly over the Web (Lord, 2022). ChatGPT has found its way into students' learning process and has become a staple in students' search requirements within the classroom. It belongs to the family of language models known as GPT (Generative Pre-trained Transformer). A generative model is a kind of model that creates new information, rather than just characterizing or foreseeing in light of data information (Pavlik, 2023).

ChatGPT is specifically designed to generate human-like text based on the input it receives. This text generation capability allows it to engage in natural language conversations, answering questions, providing explanations, and generating coherent responses. What sets ChatGPT apart is its ability to understand context and produce contextually relevant text, making it particularly useful for various applications in communication, content creation, customer support, and more. It has been trained on a vast amount of text data, which enables it to produce coherent and contextually appropriate responses across a wide range of topics and prompts.

This chapter brings to the forefront several critical domains that educational institutions must give paramount attention to. With its potential to streamline the evaluation process and curate bespoke assignments tailored to individual students, ChatGPT emerges as a game-changer. However, it's crucial to acknowledge that despite its capacity to swiftly generate text, the accuracy of ChatGPT's output is not always guaranteed. The convenience of generating substantial amounts of text with a mere click often comes at the cost of reliability. There exists a notable discrepancy between the ease of text production and the assurance of correctness. In several instances, ChatGPT's responses, though expedient, can be incorrect, raising concerns about its accuracy in delivering correct information.

REVIEW OF LITERATURE

Open computer-based intelligence created ChatGPT, a computer-based intelligence chatbot auto-age framework, for online client service (Pocock, 2023). It utilizes regular language handling Natural Language Processing and is a pre-prepared generative discussion. It draws on data from books, sites, and various articles to make a model for the language it will use to answer human collaboration. GPT-3 chatbots are man-made reasoning projects that can be designed to cooperate in a manner that is regular and human-like. Through artificial intelligence, this chatbot framework offers data and responses to questions. The GPT-3 model of the GPT is the most broadly utilized kind. Because of improvement utilizing motors, for this situation OpenAI's GPT-3, which empowers preparing in both composed and communicated in human language, they can offer remarkable commitment and handiness.

The latest improvement in OpenAI's iterative arrangement of protected and useful computer-based intelligence frameworks is ChatGPT. ChatGPT can answer follow-up questions, recognize failures, disprove unwarranted suppositions, and reject ill-advised demands as a result of the exchange style. The twin model of InstructGPT (Gilson et al., 2023), prepared to adhere to directions in prompts and convey careful reactions, is ChatGPT. Clients are asked to impart their insights on tricky model results and misleading up-sides or negatives from the outside happy channel, which is additionally important for the point of interaction, utilizing the User Interface (UI). The security alleviations set up for this delivery have been educated by a number regarding illustrations gained from the organization of earlier models like GPT-3 and Codex, especially the huge decreases in unsafe and untruthful results acquired by the use of support gaining from human feedback (Transforming Human Interactions With AI via Reinforcement Learning With Human Feedback (RLHF), 2023).

OpenAI's ChatGPT, (Leiter et al., 2023) when made available on internet, ChatGPT attracted a lot of interest and traffic and generated a lot of discussion on various internet forums. For applications involving natural language processing, such as text production and language translation, OpenAI created the ChatGPT large language model. The GPT-3.5 (Generative Pretrained Transformer 3.5) model, one of the biggest and most sophisticated language models currently available, serves as its foundation. An example of a neural network with numerous layers of connected nodes is the GPT-3 architecture. The network's nodes are each built to handle a particular component of the incoming text, such as the general meaning, the structural construction, or the related data.

ChatGPT has been prepared on an enormous corpus of text information (ChatGPT Pro, 2023). The specific measure of information used to prepare the model isn't freely accessible, however being in that frame of mind of many billions of words is accepted.

The immense measure of information used to prepare ChatGPT is the crucial motivations behind why the model can create human-like text reactions to prompts. By presenting the model to an extensive variety of message information, the scientists at OpenAI had the option to prepare the model to grasp the subtleties and nuances of normal language. This permits the model to produce reactions that are intelligent, syntactically right, and exceptionally applicable to the brief. GPT-3 can generate personalized dialogue containing diverse persona (Lee et al., CCGPK 2022).

The study "Fine-Tuning GPT-3 for Text Classification" on fused the GPT-3 model (including ChatGPT) for text-based dialogue generation and compared its performance with other state-of-the-art models, (Maria Kustikova et al., 2021). This research described a study that fine-tuned the GPT-3 model for text classification and evaluates its performance on several benchmark datasets. "Exploring the Limits of Transfer Learning with a Unified Text-to-Text Transformer" (Thomas Wolf et al., 2019) - This research described the creation of the OpenAI GPT language model, including the original version of ChatGPT, and its evaluation on various NLP tasks.

ChatGPT is a Huge Language Model

ChatGPT is a vast language model, representing a significant advancement in artificial intelligence. With its immense capacity for generating human-like text, ChatGPT demonstrates the potential of AI to comprehend and produce coherent language. Its size and capabilities mark a significant milestone in natural language processing, paving the way for innovative applications across communication, content creation, and beyond.

Educators have valid concerns about the potential drawbacks of using technology in education. While technological tools can enhance the teaching-learning process, they also bring challenges that need to be addressed. Individuals will find out in what way the text they need to modify. However, many educators believe that AI does not have to be an academic catastrophe. ChatGPT can offer feedback on writing style and assist students in improving their writing. According to academicians the universities should create new examinations and valuations systems for adopting the artificial intelligence as a teaching tool. The educational system is generally obsessed with testing, which often comes at the expense of learning. Many schools implemented online proctoring tools that were essentially spyware. The only meaningful solution is to change schools' approaches in response to changing contexts and technology.

The AI company OpenAI's ChatGPT, a potent chatbot (Stern, 2022) surpassed 1 million users. Amazingly human-like prose and frequently amusing drivel are served up by ChatGPT. It received extensive conversational text training. Although it performs a great job of following directions, it is not particularly imaginative.

Almost every response from ChatGPT serves as a gentle reminder that it is not a human and has no thoughts, feelings, or emotions. The creators of the bot admit that it "may occasionally generate inaccurate information." ChatGPT declines to offer political commentary or directions for aggressive or unlawful action.

The Generative Pretrained Transformer 3 the OpenAI's GPT-3 (Hughes, 2023) can produce and reproduce human-like text and has a varied variety of applications, as well as language transformation, language modelling, and text generating using chatbots. The model is language-specific. It cannot generate video, sound, or images, but it has a thorough understanding of the spoken and written word. After 2021, the software has only a limited understanding of the world. It is unaware of world leaders who have assumed power since 2021. Because the system was largely trained using words from the internet, it can detect biases, stereotypes, and general opinions.

ChatGPT-3 works by pre-preparing a thoughtful neural network on an enormous text dataset and afterward calibrating it for explicit undertakings like responding to questions or producing text (Wampler, 2023). The organization is made out of a progression of interconnected layers called "transformer blocks," which process the info text and produce a result forecast. ChatGPT-3 isn't associated with the web and hence can't get to outside information. All things being equal, it produces reactions in light of the information it has been prepared on. This informational index contains a large number of texts from different sources, like books, articles, and sites. One likely issue with ChatGPT is that the innovation might deliver hostile or wrong reactions. Moreover, OpenAI has expressed that it means to charge for ChatGPT in coming days.

CHALLENGES IN INTEGRATING CHATGPT IN EDUCATION

The chapter includes various studies for understanding the usage of AI tools with specific mention of ChatGPT by students and academicians' challenges. Research articles, newspaper articles, journal articles, blogs, and internet data are encompassed in the secondary data. The views, published articles related to ChatGPT during the period 2022 December to 2023 March was included to concept and how it has impacted the Education System in India. An overview of the challenges the academicians and education systems facing to deal with students' exposure and adoption of ChatGPT in completing their assignments and assessments was studied.

This chapter outlines issues and suggestions in dealing with this emerging technology: Human involvement, Investing in OpenAI, Embrace benefits of AI, and Widening the debate.

- **Human Involvement - Improving Student Performance**

Students using ChatGPT risk being misinformed by incorrect or partial information, and may lead to wrong conclusions. Misinterpretation of information may also lead to erroneous conceptual understanding. The chatbot reproduces text without citations of the original sources or authors, researchers using it are at risk of not giving credit to earlier work. Chatbots can understand only the relationship between the words as it is trained statistical relationships from the trained data set, rather than understanding the meaning of the words. It is able to reminiscence and produce what researchers have already done and not display human characteristics during the innovation process like applying creativity and conceptualization. The relationship between human and technology working together as "intelligent partnerships" humans have outperformed the intellectual ability (Salomon, Perkins & Globerson., 1991). These "intelligent partnerships" should to beat the past level while speeding up both the partner's scholarly capacity and intellectual ability of origination and imagination.

Academicians can use this tool to their own advantage by making use of it to build interactive quizzes, games, and other engaging activities to enhance their regular teaching approaches (Archibald & Clark, 2023).

Decision making is often influenced by a combination of factors such as instincts, intuition, risk assessment, and emotions (Gutnik et al., 2006). These factors can play a significant role in guiding individuals to make certain choices. While rational thinking and logical analysis are also important aspects of decision making, emotions and instincts can sometimes override them and lead to decisions based on gut feelings or personal preferences. Ultimately, the best approach to decision making is to consider all relevant factors, weigh the pros and cons, and make a choice that aligns with one's values and goals.

Students' creativity and originality, education, training and productive communications for career building will probably remain essential for adopting the technology in positive way. Educational institutions can invest in tools that envisage the probability that the content is developed using AI – ChatGPT or by humans. Integrating AI technology like ChatGPT in the teaching learning process is more beneficial rather than competing against the technology. Adopting innovative ways of integrating technology in a transparent way might involve exploring new approaches for understanding concepts, developing user-friendly platforms for sharing information, or adopting emerging technologies to ensure effective teaching learning process.

- **Investing in open AI by education institutions**

Educational institutes should consider investing in open AI as it has the potential to revolutionize the traditional way of teaching learning process. Open AI offers a variety of tools and resources (He et al., 2019) that can help instructors to personalize learning experiences for individual students, track progress, and provide timely feedback. With the help of open AI, teachers can analyze large amounts of data to identify patterns and insights that can inform their instructional practices. Furthermore, open AI can assist teachers in creating and delivering engaging and interactive learning content that meets the needs of diverse learners. By investing in open AI, teachers can stay updated with the newest technological advancements related to education and prepare their students for the future.

- **Embrace benefits of AI**

The worldwide market of academic applications and robotic trainings has observed the development of innovative start-ups with vast capital funding (Osetskyi et al., 2020).

Across the world the adoption of educational robots in educational institutions has seen arise. There are several innovative initiatives around the world aimed at promoting the use of educational robots in educational institutions, particularly in the fields of STEM – science, technology, engineering, and mathematics education. Here are some examples:

Robotics Education and Competition Foundation (REC): This non-profit organization aims to inspire and educate young people about STEM by providing access to robotics education programs and competitions. They organize the VEX Robotics Competition, which is the largest middle and high school robotics competition in the world.

FIRST (For Inspiration and Recognition of Science and Technology): This international organization aims to inspire young people to become future innovators by engaging them in exciting and challenging STEM programs. They organize several robotics competitions, including the FIRST Robotics Competition, FIRST Tech Challenge, and FIRST Lego League.

Robot Education Initiative: This initiative, launched by the Korean government in 2009 (Gang-Hoon et al., 2014), aims to promote the use of educational robots in schools throughout the country. The initiative provides funding and support for schools to purchase and use robots in their classrooms.

European Robotics League: This initiative aims to promote robotics research and innovation in Europe by organizing competitions and challenges for robotics researchers and students (Johansen & Schanke, 2013).

RoboCup: This international initiative aims to advance the state of the art in robotics and artificial intelligence by organizing competitions in which autonomous robots compete in soccer matches.

Worldwide investment in artificial intelligence-based Learning organizations in 2018. (Bhatia, 2019). 2018 saw the greatest financing rounds of all, netting USD$ 529.52 million, 20% not exactly the joined portion of arrangement volume throughout recent years 2014-2017, where the all out venture was USD $661 million (Bhatia, 2019).

All the high-development organizations that pulled in expensive subsidizing man-made intelligence as a center item or are applying man-made intelligence, Machine Learning technologies to verticals like medical services, finance, production network and energy.

- **Relationship between AI and Education**

The field of education system is undergoing a revolutionised change due to artificial intelligence in multiple ways. From personalized learning to automated grading, AI can enhance the educational experience for both students and teachers.

Individual or personalised learning is most skillful applications of AI compared to other applications in education sector. The student data can be analysed with AI algorithms for understanding their learning patterns, styles, strengths, and weaknesses. This information can then be used to create personalized learning experiences that cater to the needs of each individual student. This not only improves student engagement and motivation but also leads to better learning outcomes.

AI can also be used to automate certain tasks that teachers typically spend a lot of time on, such as grading. By using AI-powered grading tools, teachers can save time and focus on more meaningful tasks such as providing feedback and support to students.

AI can also adopt intellectual teaching systems to enhance the teaching learning process in the education system. These systems use AI algorithms to provide students with individualized guidance and support. Intelligent tutoring systems can help students to identify areas where they are struggling and provide them with targeted resources to improve their understanding. AI can also play a role in the development of educational materials. By using natural language processing and machine learning algorithms, educational content can be created and customized to meet the needs of different learners.

Though AI has its own advantages it is important to understand that amalgamation and adoption of artificial intelligence in academic system invites new challenges such as confidentiality concerns, unfairness, and ethical deliberations. Hence the adoption of AI in education should be done with utmost care and attention.

Overall, AI has the potential to greatly improve the field of education by providing personalized learning experiences, automating certain tasks, and enhancing the development of educational materials.

A portion of the world's greatest scholarly research journals have prohibited or controlled their creators from utilizing the high level chatbot, ChatGPT (Vincent, 2023). Since the bot utilizes data from the web to create profoundly discernible solutions to questions, the journals are concerned that inaccurate or copied research work could enter the pages of scholarly writing. A few specialists have proactively recorded the chatbot as a co-creator on scholastic investigations.

RISKS OF CHATGPT IN EDUCATION

The use of ChatGPT in the education system offers several benefits, but it also comes with potential risks that need to be carefully addressed. Some of the major risks associated with its implementation are as follows:

- Lack of Human Interaction: One significant risk is the potential reduction in human interaction. As ChatGPT takes over certain aspects of teaching and learning, there is a risk of diminishing the crucial teacher-student relationship, which plays a vital role in students' emotional and social development. The human touch and emotional support provided by educators are essential for students' well-being and learning experiences. Striking a balance between AI integration and human involvement is essential.
- Over reliance on AI: Over depending on ChatGPT for various educational tasks may hinder critical thinking and problem-solving skills among students. Relying solely on AI-generated answers can deter students from exploring different perspectives and seeking creative solutions to challenges. Students may sort out assistance from ChatGPT even for simple tasks. This may lead to overdependency and lack of interest in learning and understanding the concepts. Completing assignments and work would take priority over understanding the concepts and understanding its applications.
- Ethical Concerns: The use of AI raises ethical questions, especially in an educational context. There could be concerns about privacy and data security when students interact with the AI model. Additionally, there may be ethical dilemmas about AI-generated content being presented as original work or plagiarism issues. Students may ignore the importance of giving credit to the author of the original content developer. Integrating AI in education raises questions about accountability and responsibility. Determining who is responsible for the actions or decisions made by AI systems can be complex. Ensuring clear lines of accountability and understanding the limitations of AI technology is crucial.
- Bias in Responses: ChatGPT operates based on the data it is trained on, which might inadvertently introduce biases in its responses. Biased responses could perpetuate stereotypes, leading to an uneven and inaccurate educational experience for students. Students may not evaluate the information provided by AI systems and seek diverse sources to gain a comprehensive understanding of the subject matter.
- Impact on Teacher Roles: The integration of ChatGPT might raise concerns about the role of human teachers. There may be apprehensions among educators about job security or the perception that their expertise is replaceable by AI. While AI can assist in various educational tasks, it lacks emotional intelligence and empathy. Therefore, teachers remain indispensable in providing emotional support and nurturing students' socio-emotional development. AI-generated content can support traditional teaching materials, but teachers remain essential for fostering creativity and critical thinking in students. They can design stimulating learning experiences that encourage curiosity and exploration.
- Technological Barriers: Not all students and educational institutions have equal access to technology. Uneven access to AI tools like ChatGPT could widen the digital divide, creating disparities in educational opportunities and outcomes. Students from economically disadvantaged backgrounds or remote areas may lack access to devices like computers or smartphones, hindering their ability

to benefit from AI-powered educational tools. This digital divide can exacerbate educational inequalities. Some educational institutions may face constraints in implementing AI technology due to insufficient technological infrastructure. Inadequate network bandwidth or outdated systems may result in slow processing speeds or restricted access to AI-powered applications. Lack of proper training and familiarity with AI technology may hinder teachers' ability to leverage its full potential, limiting its impact on student learning. The integration of AI involves the collection and analysis of student data. Ensuring data privacy and security is paramount to safeguard sensitive information and comply with relevant regulations.

- Misinterpretation of Information: ChatGPT might generate answers that seem accurate but could be based on incorrect or outdated information. Students might unknowingly accept such responses as reliable, leading to misconceptions and misinformation. While AI can provide quick and vast amounts of information, there is a possibility that the generated responses may be misunderstood or misinterpreted by students. AI language models like ChatGPT operate based on patterns and associations learned from large datasets. As a result, they might produce responses that seem accurate but are based on incorrect or outdated information present in their training data. Students who rely solely on AI-generated content for their assignments and research might unknowingly accept these responses as reliable, leading to potential misconceptions and misinformation. Misinterpretation of information can hinder students' learning and critical thinking, as they might not verify the accuracy or validity of the responses they receive from AI.
- Limited Emotional Intelligence: AI models like ChatGPT lack emotional intelligence, making it challenging for them to understand and respond to students' emotions, empathy, or complex social cues, which are essential in the learning process. Though AI can be a valuable tool for certain educational tasks, it cannot replace the unique abilities of human educators in recognizing and responding to the emotional aspects of the learning process. It is crucial to strike a balance between leveraging AI technology for its strengths while recognizing the irreplaceable role of human teachers in providing emotional support and fostering a positive and enriching educational experience for students.
- Decreased Cognitive Effort: If students excessively rely on ChatGPT for their assignments and assessments, it may lead to decreased cognitive effort, reducing the development of critical research and analytical skills.

CONCLUSION

As an AI language model, ChatGPT is not a threat to academicians, publishers, and researchers, but rather a valuable tool that can aid in their work (Sunilkumar, 2023). ChatGPT can help researchers find relevant articles and papers, generate new ideas and hypotheses, and even assist in writing and editing academic papers.

Publishers can also benefit from ChatGPT by using it to automate the peer-review process, which can save time and resources. Additionally, ChatGPT can be used to suggest potential reviewers for papers, based on their area of expertise.

Academicians can also leverage ChatGPT to assist in teaching and learning. For instance, ChatGPT can be used to create personalized learning materials and quizzes for students. It can also be used to answer

Figure 1.

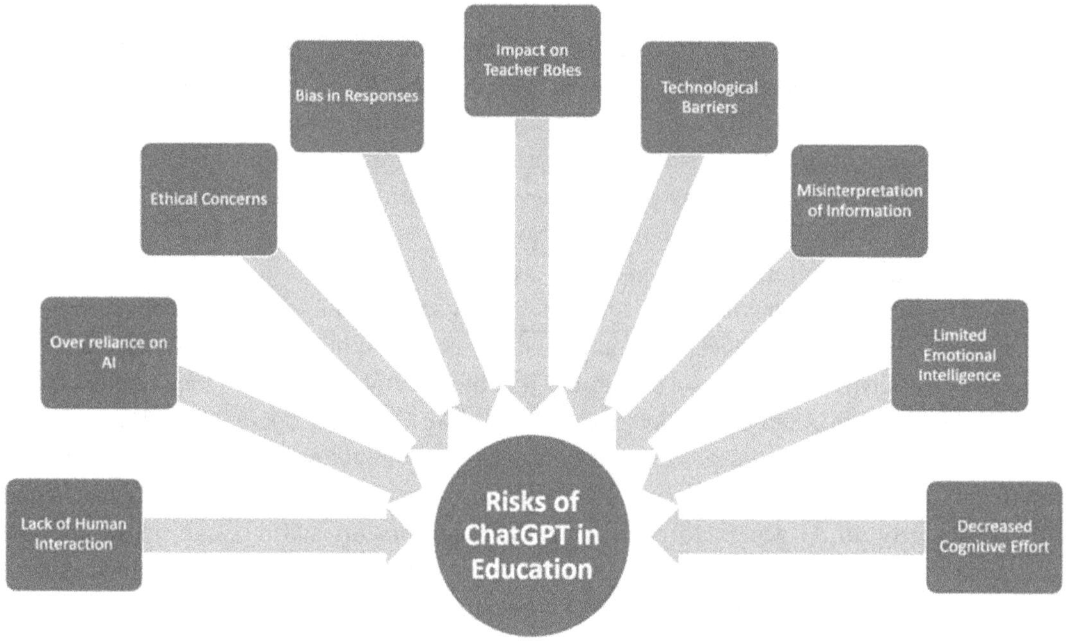

student questions and provide feedback on their assignments. ChatGPT should not be seen as a threat to academicians, publishers, and researchers, but rather as a valuable tool that can aid in their work, saving time and resources and enhancing the quality of research, teaching, and publishing. It can be adopted in the teaching learning process in multiple ways such as in curriculum development and lesson planning.

Curriculum Development

ChatGPT can be a valuable resource for teachers looking to create curriculum content. As a large language model, ChatGPT has the ability to generate natural language responses to a wide range of questions and topics.

Research: Teachers can ask ChatGPT to research a specific topic or concept related to their curriculum. ChatGPT can provide relevant information, statistics, and examples to help teachers develop lesson plans.

Brainstorming: Teachers can use ChatGPT to generate ideas for activities, projects, and assignments related to their curriculum. ChatGPT can provide creative prompts and suggest different approaches to teaching a particular topic.

Feedback: Teachers can ask ChatGPT to review and provide feedback on their lesson plans and curriculum content. ChatGPT can provide suggestions on how to improve the clarity and effectiveness of the content.

Personalization: Teachers can use ChatGPT to personalize the curriculum content for individual students. ChatGPT can suggest different teaching strategies and materials based on a student's learning style and needs.

Accessibility: Teachers can use ChatGPT to create curriculum content that is accessible to students with disabilities. ChatGPT can provide guidance on how to create content that is inclusive and meets accessibility standards.

ChatGPT can be a helpful tool for teachers looking to create curriculum content. It can provide research, brainstorming ideas, feedback, personalization, and accessibility guidance to support the development of effective and inclusive curriculum content.

Lesson Plans

ChatGPT can be a useful tool for teachers who want to create lesson plans. A lesson plan is a written guide that outlines the objectives, content, teaching strategies, and assessments for a particular lesson or series of lessons. It serves as a roadmap for teachers to follow during the delivery of instruction to students. A well-crafted lesson plan should include the following components: Learning objectives, Introduction, Content, Activities, Assessment, and Closure.

ChatGPT can help generate ideas for lesson plans by providing examples and suggestions for different topics and activities. It can help in the research process by providing relevant and reliable information about the topic being covered in the lesson. ChatGPT can provide feedback on the lesson plan, offering suggestions on how to improve the plan to better meet the learning goals of the lesson. ChatGPT can suggest resources, such as videos, articles, or online tools, to enhance the lesson plan and provide students with additional learning opportunities. A well-designed lesson plan can help teachers deliver effective instruction and improve student learning outcomes.

Assignments for Students

As an AI language model, ChatGPT can create a variety of assignments for students across different subjects and grade levels. ChatGPT can generate assignments for a wide range of subjects and grade levels, from basic math to advanced literature analysis. ChatGPT can generate assignments of varying length, complexity, and format. ChatGPT can be a valuable tool for creating assignments that are tailored to for courses specific needs and requirements. By providing clear prompts and parameters, teachers can leverage the power of AI to generate high-quality assignments that engage and challenge.

Rubrics and Checklists to Document Student's Progress

ChatGPT can be a useful tool for creating rubrics and checklists to document student progress. Rubrics are scoring guides that outline the criteria for evaluating student work, while checklists are lists of tasks or items that students must complete. ChatGPT can provide examples of effective rubrics and checklists, helping teachers understand how to structure and design them. Teachers can provide ChatGPT with specific criteria or tasks that they want to include in the rubric or checklist. ChatGPT can then generate a rubric or checklist based on those inputs. ChatGPT can provide feedback on the rubric or checklist, suggesting ways to improve it to better align with the learning objectives or standards being assessed. ChatGPT can help ensure that the rubric or checklist is aligned with the learning objectives or standards being assessed, helping to maintain consistency in grading. ChatGPT can assist in revising rubrics or checklists over time, based on changes in curriculum, feedback from colleagues, or new research.

ChatGPT can assist in creating templates for teacher reports and correspondence, such as progress reports, parent-teacher conference notes, or emails to parents or colleagues. It can suggest a basic structure for the report or correspondence, including key sections such as introduction, body, and conclusion. ChatGPT can assist in personalizing the report or correspondence by including specific details about the student or situation. Teachers can save time and ensure that they are using a consistent and professional format. However, it is important to note that these templates should be customized and personalized for each student or situation, and that direct communication and personal interactions with parents and colleagues are still important for building relationships and addressing specific needs.

Questions and Answer Keys

ChatGPT can be a helpful tool for creating questions and answer keys for various purposes, such as quizzes, exams, or assignments. ChatGPT can help generate ideas for questions based on a particular topic or learning objective. Teachers can provide ChatGPT with specific parameters or keywords to guide the question generation process. Teachers can provide ChatGPT with specific parameters or criteria for the questions and answer keys, such as the level of difficulty, type of question, or specific content to be covered. ChatGPT can assist in researching the content area to ensure that the questions and answers are accurate, up-to-date, and aligned with the learning objectives. ChatGPT can provide feedback on the questions and answer keys, suggesting ways to improve them to better align with the learning objectives or standards being assessed. ChatGPT can assist in revising the questions and answer keys over time, based on changes in curriculum, feedback from colleagues, or new research.

Discussions With Parents

ChatGPT can be a useful tool to assist teachers in responding to discussions with parents. ChatGPT can assist in translating messages into different languages, which can be helpful when communicating with parents who may not speak the same language as the teacher. It can assist in researching specific topics that parents may be asking about, to ensure that the information provided is accurate and up-to-date. ChatGPT can assist in clarifying any misunderstandings or confusion that parents may have about a particular issue or policy. Teachers can provide ChatGPT with the specific questions or concerns that parents have raised, and ChatGPT can generate appropriate responses based on the context. It can provide information on specific topics that parents may be asking about, such as curriculum, teaching methods, or assessment practices.

Book Summaries

Teachers can provide ChatGPT with a book that students are reading. ChatGPT can generate a summary that highlights the key themes, plot points, and character developments. This can be helpful in providing a quick overview of the book and ensuring that students are comprehending the main ideas.

REFERENCES

Archibald, M. M., & Clark, A. M. (2023). ChatGTP: What is it and how can nursing and health science education use it? *Journal of Advanced Nursing*, jan.15643. Advance online publication. doi:10.1111/jan.15643 PMID:36942780

Bhatia, R. (2019). Indian AI Startup Funding 2018: Total Global Investment In India Touched USD$ 529.52 Million. *Analytics India Magazine*. https://analyticsindiamag.com/indian-ai-startup-funding-total-global-investment-in-india-touched-usd-529-52-million/

Gang-Hoon, K., Trimi, S., & Ji-Hyong, C. (2014). Big-data applications in the government sector. *Communications of the ACM*, *57*(3), 78–85. doi:10.1145/2500873

Germain, T. (2023, January 20). The CEO behind ChatGPT says schools need to get over their cheating fears. Some experts agree. *Gizmodo*. https://gizmodo.com/chatgpt-openai-ceo-sam-altman-schools-cheating-1850011314

Gilson, A., Safranek, C. W., Huang, T., Socrates, V., Chi, L., Taylor, A., & Chartash, D. (2023). How does ChatGPT perform on the United States medical Licensing examination? The implications of large language Models for Medical Education and knowledge Assessment. *JMIR Medical Education*, *9*, e45312. doi:10.2196/45312 PMID:36753318

Göçen, A., & Aydemir, F. (2020). Artificial intelligence in education and schools. *Research on Education and Media*, *12*(1), 13–21. doi:10.2478/rem-2020-0003

GPTChat. (2023, July 12). *ChatGPT: The Most Advanced AI Chatbot By OpenAI* [Video]. ChatGPT Pro. https://chatgpt.pro/

Gutnik, L., Hakimzada, A. F., Yoskowitz, N. A., & Patel, V. L. (2006). The role of emotion in decision-making: A cognitive neuroeconomic approach towards understanding sexual risk behavior. *Journal of Biomedical Informatics*, *39*(6), 720–736. doi:10.1016/j.jbi.2006.03.002 PMID:16759915

He, J., Baxter, S. L., Xu, J., Xu, J., Zhou, X., & Zhang, K. (2019). The practical implementation of artificial intelligence technologies in medicine. *Nature Medicine*, *25*(1), 30–36. doi:10.103841591-018-0307-0 PMID:30617336

Hughes, A. (n.d.). *ChatGPT: Everything you need to know about OpenAI's GPT-4 tool*. Science Focus. https://www.sciencefocus.com/future-technology/gpt-3/

Jeong, S., Lee, I. Y., Jun, B. O., Ryu, Y., Sohn, J. W., Kim, S., Woo, C., Koo, J. W., Cho, I., Oh, U., Kim, K., & Suh, P. (2019). Korea Brain Initiative: Emerging Issues and Institutionalization of Neuroethics. *Neuron*, *101*(3), 390–393. doi:10.1016/j.neuron.2019.01.042 PMID:30731064

Johansen, V., & Schanke, T. (2013). Entrepreneurship Education in secondary education and training. *Scandinavian Journal of Educational Research*, *57*(4), 357–368. doi:10.1080/00313831.2012.656280

K, M., K, M., & K, M. (2022). What is ChatGPT? Best use cases for ChatGPT. *Aalpha*. https://www.aalpha.net/blog/what-is-chatgpt-best-use-cases-for-chatgpt/

Lee, Y.-J., Lim, C.-G., Choi, Y., Lm, J.-H., & Choi, H.-J. 2022. PERSONACHATGEN: Generating Personalized Dialogues using GPT-3. In *Proceedings of the 1st Workshop on Customized Chat Grounding Persona and Knowledge*, pages 29–48, Gyeongju, Republic of Korea. Association for Computational Linguistics.

Leiter, C., Zhang, R., Chen, Y., Belouadi, J., Larionov, D. Y., Fresen, V., & Eger, S. (2023). ChatGPT: A Meta-Analysis after 2.5 Months. *arXiv (Cornell University)*. https://doi.org//arxiv.2302.13795 doi:10.48550

Lucey, B. (n.d.). *ChatGPT: our study shows AI can produce academic papers good enough for journals – just as some ban it*. The Conversation. https://theconversation.com/chatgpt-our-study-shows-ai-can-produce-academic-papers-good-enough-for-journals-just-as-some-ban-it-197762

Lund, B., & Wang, T. (2023). Chatting about ChatGPT: How may AI and GPT impact academia and libraries? *Library Hi Tech News*, *40*(3), 26–29. doi:10.1108/LHTN-01-2023-0009

Mok, A. (2023, January 19). CEO of ChatGPT maker responds to schools' plagiarism concerns: 'We adapted to calculators and changed what we. *Business Insider*. https://www.businessinsider.in/tech/news/ceo-of-chatgpt-maker-responds-to-schools-plagiarism-concerns-we-adapted-to-calculators-and-changed-what-we-tested-in-math-class/articleshow/97147698.cms

Mollick, E. (2022, December 14). *ChatGPT is a tipping point for AI*. Harvard Business Review. https://hbr.org/2022/12/chatgpt-is-a-tipping-point-for-ai

Pocock, K. (2023). What is ChatGPT and how can you use it? *PC Guide*. https://www.pcguide.com/apps/what-is-chat-gpt/

Salomon, G., Perkins, D. N., & Globerson, T. (1991). Partners in Cognition: Extending Human Intelligence with Intelligent Technologies. *Educational Researcher*, *20*(3), 2–9. doi:10.3102/0013189X020003002

Stern, J. (2022, December 16). Five chats to help you understand ChatGPT. *The Atlantic*. https://www.theatlantic.com/technology/archive/2022/12/openai-chatgpt-chatbot-messages/672411/

Sunilkumar, S. R. (2023, January 21). ChatGPT co-authors research papers; Is it even ethical, academia debates. *Hindustan Times*. https://www.hindustantimes.com/technology/chatgpt-co-authors-research-papers-is-it-even-ethical-academia-debates-101674303574136.html

Today, I. (2023, February 8). ChatGPT and its impact on education sector. *India Today*. https://www.indiatoday.in/education-today/featurephilia/story/chatgpt-and-its-impact-on-education-sector-2331895-2023-02-08

Vincent, J. (2023, January 5). ChatGPT and AI language tools banned by AI conference for writing papers. *The Verge*. https://www.theverge.com/2023/1/5/23540291/chatgpt-ai-writing-tool-banned-writing-academic-icml-paper

Wampler, M. (2023, January 5). The technology behind Chat GPT-3. *ClearCOGS*. https://www.clearcogs.com/post/the-technology-behind-chat-gpt-3

Zawacki-Richter, O., Marín, V. I., Bond, M., & Gouverneur, F. (2019). Systematic review of research on artificial intelligence applications in higher education – where are the educators? *International Journal of Educational Technology in Higher Education*, *16*(1), 39. Advance online publication. doi:10.118641239-019-0171-0

KEY TERMS AND DEFINITIONS

Artificial Intelligence: Creation of algorithms and technologies that enable machines to perform tasks that typically require human intelligence, such as learning from experience, making decisions, understanding natural language, recognizing patterns, and solving complex problems.

Assessment: A systematic process of evaluating and measuring an individual's knowledge, skills, abilities, or performance in a specific area or subject.

Augmented Reality: Integration of digital information with the user's surroundings in real time.

Curriculum: The curriculum encompasses various components, including textbooks, lesson plans, assessments, and resources, all organized in a coherent and sequential manner.

Emotional Intelligence: The ability to recognize, understand, manage, and effectively navigate one's own emotions and the emotions of others.

Feedback: The information, opinions, or responses provided by individuals, often in response to a particular action, process, or output.

Lesson Plan: A detailed outline or guide that teachers use to organize and structure their instructional activities for a specific class or lesson.

Natural Language Processing (NLP): NLP is a branch of artificial intelligence that focuses on enabling computers to understand, interpret, and interact with human language in a way that is both meaningful and valuable.

Rubrics: Rubrics are structured guidelines or scoring criteria used to evaluate and assess the quality of performance, work, or assignments.

Spyware: Software or programs that are designed to secretly gather information from a user's computer or device without their knowledge or consent.

User Interface (UI): UI refers to the point of interaction between a person and a digital device or system.

Virtual Reality: Virtual reality involves a computer-generated simulation of a three-dimensional image or environment that individuals can engage with in a manner that appears real or physical.

Chapter 11
AI and Ethics in Education:
Implications and Strategies for Responsible Implementation

Beatrice Akoth Owino
United States International University – Africa, Kenya

Mahona Joseph Paschal
St. Augustine University of Tanzania, Tanzania

ABSTRACT

AI is rapidly changing the world and has been increasingly used in a variety of fields (e.g., industry, finance, and education) to promote innovation and increase work efficiency. AI ethics has sparked ample debate about the principles and values that should guide its development and use. This chapter gives a general overview of the ethical concerns raised using artificial intelligence in general and in the education sector while highlighting important goals for responsible deployment. It examines the challenges associated with AI and ethics across different sectors. It offers a brief overview of some of the technologies and ethical dilemmas that exist today. Additionally, it proposes a model with strategies for various stakeholders involved in the ethical use of AI in education, including educational institutions, policymakers, teachers, students, and AI developers. The study is based on the socio-technical theory.

INTRODUCTION

Computers in education have had mixed results for decades. Computers sometimes work differently than advertised (McFarlane, 2019). Students and teachers can use Artificial Intelligence (AI) powered apps inside and outside classrooms. There is widespread agreement that using AI in classrooms is among the century's most significant advances (Becker et al., 2018; Seldon & Abidoye, 2018). More understanding is needed must about what ethical principles should drive the design, development, and deployment of trustworthy AI in education despite the rising popularity of AI for education (AIED). With the shift to remote learning due to school closures and social distancing measures during the COVID 19 pandemic, AI has played a crucial role in facilitating virtual classrooms (Shah & Sarker, 2020).

DOI: 10.4018/979-8-3693-0205-7.ch011

AI-powered platforms and tools enable teachers to deliver online lessons, interact with students, and manage coursework. These platforms often incorporate features like video conferencing, chatbots, and content management systems, providing a more seamless virtual learning experience. AI-driven adaptive learning platforms have become even more relevant during the pandemic. These platforms use AI algorithms to assess students' knowledge and skills, identify learning gaps, and provide personalized learning paths. As students navigate remote learning environments, adaptive learning systems can adapt to their needs, ensuring targeted support and a tailored learning experience (Lepori et al., 2020; UNESCO, 2020).

AI has been leveraged to automate remote learning scenarios' assessment and feedback processes. Through natural language processing and machine learning techniques, AI algorithms can analyze students' written responses, provide instant feedback, and generate automated grading. This allows for timely assessment, immediate feedback, and tracking of student progress, even in virtual classrooms (Coniam, 2020). AI-powered virtual tutors and mentoring systems have gained popularity during the pandemic. These systems provide individualized student support by simulating one-on-one interactions with tutors or mentors. Through AI chatbots or virtual assistants, students can receive guidance, ask questions, and access resources anytime, helping to bridge the gap caused by the lack of in-person support (Vandewaetere et al., 2020).

The pandemic has generated vast amounts of data related to remote learning. AI-based data analytics tools enable educational institutions to analyze this data to gain insights into student engagement, performance, and overall well-being (Ifenthaler, 2020). These insights can help identify areas for improvement, track student progress, and inform decision-making to enhance remote learning strategies. AI-powered tools have been developed to provide social and emotional support to students during the pandemic. Chatbots and virtual assistants with sentiment analysis capabilities can detect and respond to students' emotional states (Clarke, 2019). These tools offer resources, coping strategies, and referrals to mental health professionals, helping to address the dynamic challenges students may face during remote learning (Rambe, 2020).

In the United States, Intelligent teaching systems that cater to each student's needs are being developed with the help of AIe. These systems adapt to individual students' needs and provide targeted instruction, feedback, and support. Additionally, AI is employed for automated grading and feedback in assignments and assessments, saving teachers' time and providing timely feedback to students (Heikkila & Kankaanranta, 2020). China has been at the forefront of AI adoption in education. Intelligent tutoring systems powered by AI deliver students personalized instruction and adaptive learning experiences. AI chatbots are employed to answer student queries and provide 24/7 support. Facial recognition technology is also utilized in some schools to monitor students' engagement and behavior in the classroom (Liu & Hu, 2020; Australian Government, 2020). In Finland, AI is utilized to develop virtual learning assistants to support students' independent learning. These assistants provide guidance, answer questions, and recommend personalized learning resources based on students' needs and learning styles. AI also analyzes large amounts of educational data to gain insights into student performance and inform educational policy decisions (Taylor, 2019).

The UK utilizes AI-powered learning platforms that leverage natural language processing and machine learning to support language learning. These platforms provide interactive language practice, speech recognition, and personalized feedback to enhance language acquisition. AI is also employed for data analysis to identify students at risk of falling behind academically and provide targeted interventions. AI is utilized in Australia to develop adaptive learning platforms that tailor instruction to individual students' strengths, weaknesses, and learning preferences. These platforms employ AI algorithms to analyze student performance data and adjust the curriculum and resources accordingly. AI is also used for automated essay grading and feedback to assist teachers in managing large class sizes (National Science & Technology Council, 2016). The collection and storage of student data by AI systems raise concerns about privacy and security. They protect sensitive information and ensure compliance with data protection regulations (Selwyn, 2019). AI algorithms can perpetuate biases present in the training data, leading to unfair treatment or discrimination against certain groups of students. Addressing algorithmic biases is crucial for ensuring equitable educational outcomes (Bolukbasi, 2016).

The capacity of AI algorithms poses challenges in understanding how decisions are made, leading to a need for more transparency and explainability. Ensuring transparency and explaining AI-generated outcomes is crucial for building trust and accountability (UNESCO, 2021). The ethical use of student data involves obtaining informed consent, protecting data privacy, and ensuring that data is used solely for educational purposes. Responsible data governance practices are necessary to safeguard student information (Voigt, Von dem Bussche & Even, 2019). The digital divide and unequal access to AI technologies can deepen educational inequalities. Ensuring equitable access to AI tools and addressing socioeconomic disparities are critical for promoting inclusive education. The introduction of AI in classrooms can impact teacher-student relationships. Balancing AI as a supportive tool while maintaining the human connection and personalized guidance teachers provide is essential (Sonmez, 2021).

Baker et al. (2019) showed that educational technology that achieved influence at scale and changed school systems beyond a limited number of schools is rarer than expected. Positively, Baker et al. (2019) evaluated nine cases of technology benefiting large numbers of learners, three in Italy, three in Europe, and three worldwide. The Lemann Foundation and Khan Academy's relationship in Brazil has attracted millions of students since 2012. Most Brazilian schools only educate four hours daily in one of three sessions. This alliance improved mathematics achievement relative to controls (Fundaçao Lemann, 2018).

According to the National Strategy for AI, the most excellent way to prevent ethical issues in schools is to provide enough training for educators and pupils. The goals are improved knowledge and the "reasoned use" of AI. The French educational system has established many initiatives and collaborations, such as P2IA (Partnership for Innovation and Artificial Intelligence). This has prompted the creation of math education programs like Mathia and Adaptativ'Math, aimed at pupils in grades one through three. Some maths classes are actively experimenting using this program in their lessons. Other projects, such as AI4T (artificial intelligence for and by teachers), are also being carried out with other European countries.

Moodle is utilized as early as secondary school, but because of a relationship between the Ministry of Education and the company, there are several AI-based solutions for higher education. Sciences Po, ESSEC, and HEC are just a few universities that use this LMS (Learning Management System) to design and deliver individualized courses and MOOCs (Massive et al.). Let us add that AI researchers and programmers are among the first to face moral questions about integrating AI into classrooms. The European Commission's "Ethics guidelines for trustworthy AI" stress the importance of corporations showing greater transparency with data processing to show that they adhere to ethical principles in AI research. Groups and businesses, such as those in the Partnership on AI and the European AI Alliance, are working together to implement and create trustworthy AI. Several apps and AI tools, like Beegup, have received funding thanks to the Edu'Up program, which the French Ministry of National Education and Youth backs. High school students can use the stage to practice speaking in their target language.

TRANSPARENCY

Transparency is a fundamental ethical guideline that plays a critical role in the responsible and ethical use of artificial intelligence (AI) in education. It involves open and transparent communication regarding AI systems' presence, purpose, and functioning. Transparency in AI implementation builds trust among stakeholders, including students, educators, parents, and administrators. By providing clear information about the presence and purpose of AI systems, educational institutions establish an environment of openness and understanding. Research indicates trust is essential for successfully adopting and accepting AI technologies in educational settings (Bulger et al., 2019). Transparent communication enables individuals to make informed decisions, participate actively, and engage meaningfully with AI tools and technologies. Transparency is vital in addressing biases that may arise from AI algorithms. AI systems learn from data, and if that data contains biases or discriminatory patterns, the algorithms can perpetuate and amplify those biases. Transparent AI systems allow stakeholders to examine and challenge these biases. By understanding how AI algorithms are trained, what data is used, and how decisions are made, stakeholders can identify and rectify biases, ensuring that AI technologies do not perpetuate discrimination or unfair treatment (Holstein et al., 2019). Transparency is closely linked to accountability in the use of AI in education.

Educational institutions, developers, and providers of AI systems should be accountable for the design, implementation, and impact of these systems. Transparent communication about the functioning of AI systems helps establish clear lines of accountability, ensuring that responsibility is assigned to the appropriate parties. Regular auditing and monitoring of AI systems, along with transparent reporting on their performance and impact, contribute to accountability and provide an opportunity for continuous improvement (European Commission, 2021). Transparency respects the rights and privacy of students and educators. Transparent AI systems provide precise data collection, storage, and usage information. This transparency allows individuals to understand what personal information is being collected, for what purposes, and how it is protected. With this knowledge, stakeholders can make informed consent decisions, understand their rights regarding data privacy, and have confidence in the security measures put in place (Lepri et al., 2018).

According to Larsson and Heintz's (2020) analysis of data ethics in the context of educational AI, this emphasis on openness is warranted. Although artificial intelligence (AI) tools have been increasingly used in schools to improve teaching and learning, privacy and security concerns about the resulting data have yet to be resolved (Wang & Cheng, 2021). Data visualization shows learner behavior and highlights further support teachers can provide, so Cope Kalantzis (2019) emphasized the importance of this ethical principle for both teachers and students. What the data is, where it comes from, what it reveals, what happens to it, and how it is used all contribute to its apparent openness (Digital Curation Centre, 2020). Once data ownership, accessibility, and explainability are maintained, these questions may be answered.

Understanding who owns and has the legal right to access students' information is central to data ownership, which is inherently an issue of openness and fairness (Remain, 2019). Whether or not data usage invades students' privacy has been a hotly debated issue for a long time, even though Data collectors may obtain consent from subjects frequently. There is a solid case to be made for students to retain ownership of their data due to concerns about the reliability of the research's stated purpose. Students have the right to ownership and control over their data and how it is used for educational purposes (Holmes et al., 2021). Since institutions systematically document learners' interactions and performance, the notion that they have the right to access and utilize this data is plausible.

Transparency in AI systems is emphasized by several international organizations and policy documents, including the European Commission's ethics guidelines for trustworthy AI, the European Parliament (2021), UNESCO Education & AI (Miao et al., 2021), the Beijing Consensus of UNESCO (2019), and the OECD's Principles for responsible stewardship of trustworthy AI (2021). However, the definition and description of transparency are only sometimes consistent throughout different reports and standards. In contrast to the European Commission's (2019) definition, which states that it is "closely linked with the principle of explicability and encompasses transparency of elements relevant to an AI system: the data, the system, and the business model," the UNESCO 2020 Draft describes it as being "associated to adequate responsibility and accountability measure" (AHEG, 2020). Transparency in data and algorithms should be treated as equally important in regulations for the use of AI in educational settings. Regulation By the Transparency Principle, establishing, carrying out, monitoring, and controlling artificial intelligence regulations in education should be open and clear about who is responsible for what and how it will be done. Related to the suitability discussed above, the ethical principle of regulatory responsibility is fundamental to regulating AI in the classroom.

ACCOUNTABILITY

Accountability is a crucial ethical guideline in using artificial intelligence (AI) in education. It entails the responsibility and answerability of educational institutions, developers, and stakeholders for designing, implementing, and impacting AI systems. Accountability ensures that AI is used that aligns with ethical principles, safeguards against potential harm, and upholds the well-being and interests of students and educators. Accountability in AI implementation requires establishing clear lines of responsibility. Educational institutions should define roles and responsibilities for individuals overseeing AI systems, including administrators, educators, and AI developers. Each stakeholder should be responsible for ensuring that AI technologies are implemented ethically and responsibly. This clarity ensures that AI systems' decision-making processes are transparent and that individuals can be held accountable for their actions (OECD, 2019).

While AI can provide valuable insights and automate various tasks, it should only partially replace human oversight and intervention. Accountability in using AI in education necessitates maintaining human agency and judgment. Educational institutions should ensure that there is human oversight to review and validate the decisions made by AI systems. This oversight allows for critical thinking, contextual understanding, and intervention when necessary, ensuring that the use of AI aligns with educational goals and values (Bulger et al., 2019).

Regular auditing and evaluation of AI systems contribute to accountability. Educational institutions should conduct systematic assessments to monitor AI technologies' performance, impact, and ethical implications. Auditing helps identify potential biases, errors, or unintended consequences that may arise from using AI. It enables institutions to take corrective measures, address issues, and ensure ongoing compliance with ethical standards. Auditing and evaluation also provide an opportunity for continuous improvement and refinement of AI systems (European Commission, 2021).

Accountability extends to the developers and providers of AI systems in education. They are responsible for ensuring that their AI technologies are designed and implemented ethically, adhering to legal and regulatory requirements. Developers should be transparent about the functioning of their AI algorithms, including the data used, the training process, and potential biases. They should also provide clear documentation and support for educational institutions to understand and address ethical concerns about using their AI systems (Bulger et al., 2019). Accountability in AI implementation involves transparent reporting on the use and impact of AI systems. Educational institutions should communicate with stakeholders, including students, parents, and educators, about the presence and purpose of AI technologies. Transparent reporting helps build trust, enables scrutiny, and ensures that stakeholders can understand how AI systems operate and how decisions are made. It also allows for external evaluation and validation, reinforcing accountability and promoting the responsible use of AI in education (European Commission, 2021).

In this context, "responsible AI" refers to the ethical practice of designing, developing, and deploying AI to empower key stakeholders and society fairly; this is central to the concept of "accountable AI" in the context of educational AI. Despite the rise in popularity of the term "responsible AI," neither "accountability" nor "responsibility" are typically defined (Jobin et al., 2019). However, it is widely understood to mean behaving honestly and forthrightly while also considering any and all relevant risks. The accountability of AI has been called into question, with some arguing that it should never be expected to be held to the same standards as humans and that humans should always be the sole actors responsible for AI. Along with human-centered AI in education, which promotes human oversight of AI, we argued that those with a vested interest in education should always be the ones to assume responsibility for AI in the classroom. According to specific laws, AI regulation in education should consider the accountability of individuals and institutions, sustainability, and proportionality (AHEG, 2020).

PRIVACY

Respecting privacy in AI implementation involves protecting the personal information of students and educators. Educational institutions must establish strict data protection policies and practices that comply with applicable laws and regulations. AI systems should only collect and store necessary data, ensuring that personal information remains secure and confidential. Data anonymization techniques should be employed to minimize the risk of re-identification. Furthermore, consent should be obtained from students, parents, or guardians regarding using their data in AI applications (Lepri et al., 2018). Privacy as an ethical guideline emphasizes the importance of obtaining informed consent from individuals whose data is collected and used by AI systems. Educational institutions should provide clear information about the purposes for which data is collected, its types, and how it will be used. Individuals should have the right to opt in or out of data collection and usage, empowering them to make informed decisions regarding their privacy. Informed consent ensures that individuals can control their personal information and exercise autonomy (Bulger et al., 2019). Privacy in AI implementation requires educational institutions to ensure the secure storage and usage of data. Adequate measures should be in place to protect against unauthorized access, use, or sharing of personal data. Encryption, access controls, and other security protocols should be implemented to safeguard the confidentiality and integrity of data. Educational institutions should also have clear policies regarding data retention and deletion to ensure that personal information is retained only when necessary (European Commission, 2021).

Privacy as an ethical guideline emphasizes the minimization of data collection. Educational institutions should only collect the data necessary to function and improve AI systems. Collecting excessive or unnecessary data increases the risk of privacy breaches and potential misuse of personal information. By adopting a data minimization approach, educational institutions can limit the collection and storage of personal data, reducing privacy risks (OECD, 2019). Privacy in AI implementation requires accountability and transparency regarding data handling practices. Educational institutions should be accountable for adequately managing and protecting personal information. Transparent communication should be maintained, informing individuals how their data is collected, used, and protected. Any changes in data handling practices should be communicated to individuals, allowing them to make informed decisions regarding their privacy (European Commission, 2021).

Teachers' and students' opinions should be considered when deciding how artificial intelligence (AI) should be implemented in the classroom in order for students to interact with more intelligent machines and computer agents during the learning process (Miao et al., 2021). Using actual time gesture recognition technology is one example of forecasting students' emotional state or attendance without their knowledge or agreement, raising ethical concerns (Pattnaik & Mohanty, 2020). Educators and developers should make AI aware of potential dangers to students' academic, professional, and social lives and discuss these risks with pupils. The goal is to help students feel safe sharing information online and give them the tools to transfer their knowledge from one setting to another without giving up control of their personal information (Jobin et al., 2019). Many artificial intelligences (AIs) interact with humans on multiple levels, unlike learning analytics, which are governed by data ethics (Bryson & Theodorou, 2019; Manoharan, 2019; O'Sullivan et al., 2019). This brings up an enormous number of technical safety worries about the employment of AI throughout its lifetime, particularly in extreme environments or where other agents (both human and artificial) can potentially cause malfunctions.

EQUITY

Equity is a fundamental ethical guideline in using artificial intelligence (AI) in education. It refers to all individuals' fair and just treatment, ensuring equal access to opportunities, resources, and outcomes. Equity as an ethical guideline highlights the importance of leveraging AI to bridge educational gaps, promote inclusivity, and eliminate biases and discrimination. Equity in AI implementation involves addressing biases and discrimination that may arise from AI algorithms. AI systems learn from data, and if the data used is biased or reflects discriminatory patterns, the algorithms can perpetuate and amplify those biases. Educational institutions should strive to mitigate bias by incorporating diverse datasets and perspectives into AI training. They should also regularly assess and monitor AI systems to identify and rectify emerging biases.

By actively working to reduce bias and discrimination, AI can contribute to a more equitable educational experience (Holstein et al., 2019). Equity as an ethical guideline emphasizes inclusive design in developing and implementing AI systems in education. Educational institutions should ensure that AI technologies are accessible and usable by all students, regardless of their abilities, socioeconomic backgrounds, or geographical locations. The inclusive design considers learners' diverse needs and circumstances, aiming to create AI systems that accommodate different learning styles, languages, and accessibility requirements. By prioritizing inclusivity, educational institutions can foster equitable access to educational opportunities (Bulger et al., 2019).

Equity in AI implementation aims to reduce educational disparities and promote equal opportunities. AI can be used to identify and address disparities in access to quality education, resources, and support systems. By leveraging AI analytics and data-driven insights, educational institutions can better understand the factors contributing to disparities and design targeted interventions. For example, AI-powered personalized learning platforms can help identify and address individual learning gaps, ensuring that all students receive the necessary support to succeed (European Commission, 2021). Equity as an ethical guideline requires the fair allocation of resources in AI implementation. AI technologies should not perpetuate or exacerbate existing resource inequalities. Educational institutions should ensure that AI systems are accessible to all students, regardless of their socioeconomic backgrounds or geographical locations. Efforts should be made to provide equal access to AI-powered educational tools, resources, and technologies. By promoting the equitable distribution of resources, AI can help level the playing field and provide equal opportunities for all learners (OECD, 2019). Equity in AI implementation entails promoting diversity and representation in AI systems. AI algorithms should be designed to recognize and account for the diversity of students, including different ethnicities, genders, cultures, and abilities. Educational institutions should actively seek diverse perspectives and ensure that the development and training of AI systems involve a wide range of voices. By embracing diversity and representation, AI can avoid reinforcing existing inequalities and foster an inclusive and equitable learning environment (Bulger et al., 2019).

This chapter adapted constructivist theory to discuss the ethical guidelines for using AI in education. Moreover, this chapter intends to discuss the methods and approaches that could be used to ensure the effective and efficient use of AI in the education sector. The chapter was based on a case study design, and researchers used an ethnography as a qualitative research approach to get insights from the participants on their perceptions and views on diversity, inclusion, and equity in the use of AI in education. In light of the results, it is apparent that protecting personal data and limiting its possible leakages is one of the issues posed by the widespread usage of data. Data governance management is crucial because more or proper governance can lead to information loss. Indeed, "data governance" is predicated on principles like data quality management, data localization, and the identification of actors who can take such measures on such data in such a scenario and using such a manner.

However, the indicated countries can retrieve all data flowing through their jurisdiction thanks to the US Cloud Act and China's Global Data Security Initiative. Therefore, data governance is a severe concern for Europeans, who have every reason to want to keep their data within the European Union (EU), where it can be better protected and safeguarded from unauthorized use. There is a need to validate AI systems to assure their trustworthiness and address data concerns. Because AI in education has the potential to profoundly impact some of the most impressionable people in society—children—safety measures must be taken. The goal of validating an AI system is to consider many concepts, such as the system's resilience, transparency, and explainability of its methods. These ideas are intertwined with the quest to rid AI of the prejudice that has long plagued its operations. Algorithmic validation of AI provides users with confidence in the system's accuracy. It gives them insight into how the system operates, which is essential for building trust in AI. Furthermore, since 2015, new school curricula in France have included teaching algorithms from the fourth grade onward, reflecting the country's recognition of the significance of these technical breakthroughs and the societal difficulties they present.

THEMATIC ANALYSIS

Artificial intelligence of education, for example, incorporating an illustration of how (AIED) can be used to enable Artificial neural networks, machine learning, and CALL (Computer-Assisted Language Learning) to be used in formal, non-formal, and informal learning settings thanks to new paradigms of instruction, technological advancement, and breakthroughs in educational research. As stated by Akgun and Greenhow (2021), it encourages using automated evaluation, facial recognition technologies, and predictive analytics while lowering the cost of personally customized education. This is why there is mounting proof that AIED can "foster a transformation of knowledge, cognition, and culture" (Hwang et al., 2020). However, there have been many roadblocks to implementing AIED due to ethical and legal concerns. Despite recent efforts to formulate such guidelines, the issue of a global agreement and standards for AIED still needs to be addressed. As regulation and ethical consensus of these technologies are required for exploiting their various possibilities in education, this study aims to present an integrative overview of ethical principles for AIED.

AIED has the potential to change the face of education altogether. However, Kay & Kummerfeld (2019) note that this "highly technology-dependent and cross-disciplinary field" (Hwang et al., 2020) creates several challenges for anyone studying or implementing associated systems or procedures. Developing quality and inclusive data systems, making research on AIED significant, ensuring ethics and transparency in data collection, use, and dissemination, and preparing teachers for AI-powered education are the six challenges facing artificial intelligence in education (AIED) identified by UNESCO (2019) for achieving sustainable development of AIED on a global scale. There are significant societal consequences, such as systemic prejudice, discrimination, unfairness for marginalized student groups, and xenophobia, as well as complex ethical challenges connected to privacy and bias in gathering and analyzing information (Holmes et al., 2021; Hwang et al., 2020) are just two examples of the difficulties individuals face. The commercialization of education and the growing gap between homeschoolers and students in traditional schools are just two examples of the adverse effects that some fear may result from the broad adoption of AIED (Reiss, 2021). The effects of the current COVID-19 pandemic could exacerbate the issue, which could become pervasive AI in every sense, where those involved may be exposed to threats without being aware of them (Borenstein & Howard, 2021). Because of these challenges, educating educators and students on the ethical considerations inherent in AI education is more important than ever.

In addition, Russell and Norvig (2002) and Holmes et al. (2021) note that there are ethical implications and privacy hazards associated with the use of artificial intelligence in education and that it is, therefore, essential to distinguish between doing ethical things and doing things ethically when utilizing AI in this context. Indeed, a wealth of research has shown the emergence of competing ethical themes relating to general AI and artificial intelligence in education, most of which are associated with the liability of data across settings like higher education (Zawacki-Richter et al., 2019; Holstein et al., 2019), schools (Luckin, 2017), and subjects (Hwang & Tu, 2021). These included problems like unfairness, lack of responsibility, statistical apophenia, and more common ones such as a lack of informed consent or a breach of privacy. User confidentiality, integrity, and inclusivity (Deshpande et al., 2017); learner privacy (Sacharidis et al., 2020); identity configuration (Sacharidis et al., 2020); surveillance and consent (Sacharidis et al., 2020), and other AI-related topics have also been called into question. The ethics of data collected for teaching and learning analytics has also been a concern. Among these are the power dynamics between stakeholders, including students, teachers, and educational goals; the nuances of data interpretation and administration; and the range of viewpoints on how data is used. Problems with data collection, limited availability of data sources, bias and representation, data ownership and control, data autonomy, the artificial intelligence of education systems, and human agency are also a concern when it comes to the ethics of AI in education (Akgun & Greenhow, 2021; Miao et al., 2021). In order to make ethical and accountability-driven judgments in education, it is essential to have a firm grasp of these guiding principles.

Recent efforts to build distinct ethical frameworks for general AI use (Ashok et al., 2022) may not apply to education because of the suggested contextualization of ethical and privacy issues (Ifenthaler & Schumacher, 2016). Concerns about ethics and privacy in the educational setting may be best addressed by taking a contextual approach to the design and use of AI in education. According to previous studies, the sociotechnical framework set by educational technology and pedagogical practices is crucial to ethical issues (Kitto & Knight, 2019). Ethical and trustworthy artificial intelligence for education could be developed and adopted if people had a deeper grasp of ethics and privacy from various perspectives. In addition, we broadened Ashok et al.'s (2022) ethical perspective by considering the policies and standards put forward by international organizations like UNESCO, the OECD, and the European Union. An all-encompassing and coordinated set of recommendations for implementing AI in education might be derived from a consensual evaluation of relevant policies and principles. This helps lay the groundwork for expanding the use of AI in education and implementing its benefits moving forward.

More effort is needed to enforce ethical guidelines for AI systems to better align with societal values, and there have been repeated calls for comprehensive ethical guidelines and open communications with beneficiaries (Berendt et al., 2020; Nigam et al., 2021; Hagendorff, 2020). There must be safeguards and human control for these AI systems as they are developed, used, and improved. Dhanrajani (2018) argues that developers of AI would be intrinsically motivated by behavioral science knowledge, emphasizing self-awareness and empathy. This paper aimed to employ inductive analysis, modeled after Braun and Clarke's (2012) thematic analysis process, to extract and expand upon a core set of themes. The analysis begins with a basic understanding of the relevant ethical standards and relevant reports. This required rereading the reports and recording commonalities such as terminology, topics covered, and definitions used. After that, we use an open coding method to assign unique codes to each group of related concepts and definitions. The result was 39 unique codes. After that, we looked at the more significant meaning patterns among the codes and extracted seven overarching themes (principles). A researcher-researcher corroboration technique was also in place to ensure the authenticity and trustworthiness of the proposed principles and code mapping during the iterative coding and theme-generating process (Patton, 2015).

Because of the novel ways in which AI use influences human thinking, interaction, and decision-making and affects education, human, social, and natural sciences, culture, communication, and information, we must acknowledge the profound and dynamic positive and negative effects of AI on societies, environments, ecosystems, and human lives, including the human mind. While artificial intelligence (AI) has the potential to improve life on Earth and in all countries, it also raises ethical concerns, such as the need for transparency and understanding of algorithmic workings; the threat to cultural, social, and biological diversity and social or economic divides; and the embedding and exacerbation of biases.

Justice, trust, and fairness must be upheld so that no country and no one is left behind, either by having fair access to AI technologies and enjoying their benefits or by protecting against their harmful effects while taking into account the unique circumstances of each country and the legitimate concerns of those who do not want to see their way of life compromised by artificial intelligence. The risks of misinformation, disinformation, hate speech, and personal data misuse will only increase with the development of AI technology; therefore, data, media, information literacy, and access to independent, pluralistic, credible sources of information are necessary. Although many positive outcomes can result from the development of AI technologies, the process of implementing them can amplify tensions related to innovation, asymmetric access to knowledge and technologies (such as the public's digital and civic literacy deficit, which hinders their ability to engage in AI topics), information barriers and capacity gaps, as well as human and institutional capacities, technological innovation barriers, and inadequate physical infrastructure.

Using information requires respect for international law and national authority. This means that States can, by international law, regulate the data created on or transiting their territories and take steps toward effective regulation of data, including data protection, based on respect for the right to privacy and other human rights norms and standards. For inclusive approaches to AI governance, where the benefits can be shared by all and sustainable development is furthered, stakeholder participation across the whole life cycle of an AI system is required. Governments, NGOs, academics, activists, journalists, policy wonks, business leaders, civil rights groups, equality advocates, anti-discrimination watchdogs, youth organizations, and children's advocacy groups are all examples of stakeholders. Open standards and interoperability should be implemented to make teamwork easier. In the case of Indigenous Peoples, appropriate steps should be taken to respect their right to self-governance of their data and to ensure that marginalized groups, communities, and individuals can participate meaningfully in the decision-making process.

Following are specific policy areas where the values and principles outlined in this recommendation can be put into effect. Governments should take the lead in implementing effective measures, such as policy frameworks or mechanisms, and ensuring that other stakeholders, including businesses, universities, and civil society, adhere to them. This can be done partly by encouraging all stakeholders to develop human rights, the rule of law, democracy, ethical impact assessment, and due diligence tools aligning with these principles. All relevant parties should be consulted during the policy or mechanism development process, and each Government's unique situation and priorities should be considered. When working with countries, UNESCO may assist with creating and evaluating policy processes.

UNESCO recognizes that states may differ in their levels of preparedness to effectively implement this Recommendation, considering various factors such as scientific, technological, economic, educational, legal, regulatory, infrastructure, sociological, cultural, and other relevant elements. It is important to emphasize that "readiness" is a subjective condition within this particular context. Consequently, UNESCO intends to undertake two key initiatives. Firstly, it aims to create a methodology for readiness assessment, which will assist Member States in determining their level of preparedness for implementing the Recommendation above. This methodology will encompass various dimensions and enable governments to identify their position along a continuum. Secondly, UNESCO will support interested governments by aiding in developing an Ethical Impact Assessment (EIA) methodology designed explicitly for AI technologies.

Additionally, UNESCO will facilitate the exchange of best practices and explore alternative avenues of assistance. It is recommended that governments adopt risk prevention, mitigation, and monitoring strategies alongside ethical impact assessment frameworks in order to identify and assess the advantages, concerns, and risks associated with artificial intelligence systems. In alignment with the values and principles delineated in this Recommendation, impact assessments must examine the effects on human rights and fundamental freedoms. This includes, but is not restricted to, the rights of marginalized and vulnerable individuals or those in precarious circumstances, labor rights, the environment, and ecosystems, as well as ethical and social ramifications.

To better forecast outcomes, reduce risks, prevent unintended consequences, encourage citizen engagement, and address societal concerns, governments should create a legislative framework that lays out a mechanism, especially for public authorities, to conduct ethical impact evaluations on AI systems. Algorithms, data, and design processes may all be evaluated with the help of this evaluation, and the external review of AI systems should also be established as part of this process. Ethical impact assessments must be conducted in an open and public manner. Multicultural, pluralistic, inclusive, and interdisciplinary approaches are encouraged in these evaluations. Authorities at all levels of Government should be obligated to keep an eye on the artificial intelligence systems they develop and use.

Governments should guarantee that AI governance processes are open and accessible to all interested parties, as well as being transparent, multidisciplinary, multilateral (allowing for cross-border harm mitigation and reparation), and include multiple stakeholders. In particular, governance must cover foresight, efficient protection, impact monitoring, enforcement, and reparation. To guarantee that human rights, fundamental freedoms, and the rule of law are respected in both the digital and physical spheres, governments should investigate and redress harms caused through AI systems by enacting robust enforcement mechanisms and remedial actions. Remediation options offered by private and public companies should be included in such procedures and actions. This can be achieved by encouraging auditability and traceability in AI systems. Governments should also work with researchers and other stakeholders to detect, prevent, and mitigate any malicious applications of AI systems, and they should develop their institutional capacities to deliver on this pledge. Governments are urged to develop national and regional AI strategies and consider forms of soft governance, such as a certification mechanism for AI systems and the mutual recognition of their certification, considering the sensitivity of the application domain and expected impact on human rights, the environment and ecosystems, and other ethical considerations outlined in this Recommendation.

Ethical considerations could be factored into the design of this mechanism, which could involve multiple tiers of auditing of systems, data and adherence to ethical principles and procedural requirements. However, this method should not burden small and medium-sized businesses, start-ups, the civil sector, or scientific and academic institutions. To ensure robustness, continuous integrity, and adherence to ethical principles across the AI system's entire life cycle, these methods should also contain a component for regular monitoring, with recertification required if necessary. It is essential to remember that the context of artificial intelligence in education and its influences on constructivist theory is the only place to make sense of the theoretical account of constructivist theory and its growth (Tuitt et al., 2018). This research confirms the assertion made by Claxton (2015) that "the fact we are fundamentally doers means we are also inveterate makers." Since bias presents itself in the AIED system with biased training data, data quality is critical in evaluating whether AIED might produce accurate and impartial conclusions (Borgesius, 2018; Digital Curation Centre, 2020)—multiple sources of skewed information, including sexual orientation, race, ethnicity, and special education requirements. West-Smith et al. (2018) provide a helpful example in the field of language education technology in which input data in the form of rubric writing and scoring systems may impose limitations on student task selection and writing preferences. Ethical rules for applying artificial intelligence in education require, therefore, unbiased data to prevent the development of biased algorithms.

CONCLUSION

The use of AI in education holds immense potential, but robust ethical guidelines must accompany it. Transparency, accountability, privacy, and equity are the pillars upon which these guidelines should be built. Ongoing training and awareness programs should be provided to educators and stakeholders to ensure they understand AI's ethical considerations and implications in education. Additionally, regular audits and evaluations should be conducted to assess the impact and effectiveness of AI systems, identify and address biases or unintended consequences, and make necessary improvements. Feedback from students, educators, and other stakeholders should be actively sought and incorporated into designing and implementing AI technologies in education.

International cooperation and information sharing among countries and organizations can contribute to developing comprehensive and globally accepted ethical guidelines. This collaboration can help address the challenges posed by the rapid advancements in AI technology and ensure that AI is utilized in education for the benefit of all learners. Educational institutions, policymakers, developers, and stakeholders must collaborate to develop and enforce ethical standards that ensure AI systems enhance the educational experience without compromising student well-being, privacy, or social equality. By adhering to these ethical guidelines, we can harness the transformative power of AI to create a more inclusive and equitable educational landscape.

AI systems in education should uphold strong privacy and data protection principles to safeguard the personal information of students and educators. This includes obtaining informed consent, anonymizing data when possible, and implementing robust security measures. Institutions must adhere to relevant laws such as the General Data Protection Regulation (GDPR) in the European Union (GDPR, 2019). AI algorithms used in education should be transparent and explainable to ensure that decisions made by these systems can be understood and justified. It is essential to avoid using "black box" algorithms that make decisions without providing clear explanations, as this can undermine trust and accountability (Floridi et al., 2018). AI should be developed and deployed in education to promote equity and fairness. This involves avoiding biases in data collection, algorithm design, and implementation that could perpetuate or exacerbate existing social inequalities.

Regular audits and ongoing monitoring are necessary to ensure that AI systems do not discriminate against any group (Crawford et al., 2019). AI technologies should be designed to be inclusive and accessible, accommodating diverse learners with varying abilities and needs. This includes providing appropriate support for learners with disabilities and ensuring that AI systems do not create educational barriers or reinforce existing biases (Darling-Hammond et al., 2017). Student data collected through AI systems should be used solely for educational purposes and not be exploited for commercial gain or any other unauthorized purposes. Institutions must establish clear policies regarding collecting, storing, and using student data, focusing on maintaining confidentiality and respecting individual rights. (OECD, 2019).

AI systems used in education should be subject to ongoing evaluation to assess their effectiveness, identify potential biases, and address unintended consequences. Regular feedback from students, educators, and other stakeholders should be sought to improve the design and functionality of AI technologies in education (Floridi et al., 2018). Given the prevailing linguistic, social, and cultural disparities, various stakeholders such as governments, intergovernmental organizations, civil society, academia, the media, community leaders, and the private sector must collaborate in order to enhance public awareness and comprehension of artificial intelligence (AI) technologies and the significance of data. This can be achieved through the implementation of inclusive and easily accessible educational initiatives, active civic participation, the provision of digital skills and AI ethics training, as well as media and information literacy programs.

REFERENCES

Australian Government. (2020). *Artificial Intelligence (AI) Ethics Framework*. Australian Government. https://www.aiia.com.au/Documents/ethics_framework.pdf

Becker, M., Lepori, B., & Kedziora, D. (2018). Intelligent Tutoring Systems: A Review of the Ethical Issues. In *Proceedings of the 26th International Conference on Computers in Education* (pp. 493-502).

Bolukbasi, T., Chang, K. W., Zou, J. Y., Saligrama, V., & Kalai, A. T. (2016). *Man is to Computer Programmer as Woman is to Homemaker?* Debiasing Word Embeddings. In Advances in Neural Information Processing Systems.

Bulger, M., Ciancio, A., Faulkner, D., Stobart, G., & Deterding, S. (2019). *Ethical AI in Education*. Nesta.

Clarke, S. (2019). Ethical Considerations for AI in Education. In *Proceedings of the 25th International Conference on Computers in Education* (pp. 38–43). IEEE.

Coniam, D. (2020). Ethical Issues in Using AI for Language Learning: A Perspective from CALL. *Computer Assisted Language Learning*, *33*(1-2), 53–71.

Crawford, K., Dobbe, R., Fried, G., Joon, M., Lewis, D., & West, S. M. (2019). The AI Now Report 2018. AI Now Institute. Retrieved from https://ainowinstitute.org/AI_Now_2018_Report.pdf

Darling-Hammond, L. (2017). *AI in Education: Automatic Teaching?* Stanford University. https://edpolicy.stanford.edu/sites/default/files/publications/ai-in-education-report.pdf

European Commission. (2021). *Ethics Guidelines for Trustworthy AI*. European Commission. https://ec.europa.eu/digital-single-market/en/news/ethics-guidelines-trustworthy-ai

Floridi, L., Cowls, J., Beltrametti, M., Chatila, R., Chazerand, P., Dignum, V., & Luetge, C. (2018). AI4People—An Ethical Framework for a Good AI Society: Opportunities, Risks, Principles, and Recommendations. *Minds and Machines*, *28*(4), 689–707. doi:10.100711023-018-9482-5 PMID:30930541

General Data Protection Regulation (GDPR). (2019). *Home*. GDPR. https://gdpr-info.eu/

Heikkilä, A., & Kankaanranta, M. (2020). Ethical Perspectives on Learning Analytics: A Systematic Review. *Educational Technology Research and Development*, *68*(2), 461–494.

Holstein, K., Wortman Vaughan, J., Daumé, H. III, Dudík, M., Wallach, H., & Heller, S. (2019). Improving fairness in machine learning systems: What do industry practitioners need? In *Proceedings of the 2019 CHI Conference on Human Factors in Computing Systems* (p. 666). ACM. 10.1145/3290605.3300830

Ifenthaler, D. (2020). Ethical Considerations for AI in Education. Technology. *Knowledge and Learning*, *25*(3), 333–336.

Lepori, B., Becker, M., & Cattaneo, A. (2020). Ethical Challenges of Artificial Intelligence and Big Data in Education. In Ethical Technology and Digital Competence (pp. 227-247). Springer.

Lepri, B., Oliver, N., Letouzé, E., Pentland, A., Vinck, P., & de Montjoye, Y. A. (2018). Fair, transparent, and accountable algorithmic decision-making processes. *Philosophy & Technology*, *31*(4), 611–627. doi:10.100713347-017-0279-x

Liu, M., & Hu, X. (2020). Ethical Issues of AI in Education: An Empirical Study. *International Journal of Emerging Technologies in Learning*, *15*(23), 39–54.

National Science and Technology Council. (2016). *Preparing for the Future of Artificial Intelligence*. The White House. https://obamawhitehouse.archives.gov/sites/default/files/whitehouse_files/microsites/ostp/NSTC/preparing_for_the_future_of_ai.pdf

OECD. (2019). *AI in Education: Tertiary Education, Skills, and Lifelong Learning*. OECD Publishing.

OECD. (2019). *AI in Education: Tertiary Education, Skills, and Lifelong Learning*. OECD Publishing.

Rambe, P. (2020). A Framework for Ethical Integration of AI in Education: Core Components and Approaches. In Artificial Intelligence in Education (pp. 295-299). Springer.

Seldon, A., & Abidoye, T. R. (2018). The Ethics of AI in Education: A Research Agenda. *Journal of Learning Analytics*, *5*(3), 169–183.

Selwyn, N. (2019). Should We Be Worried About... Artificial Intelligence in Education? *Learning, Media and Technology*, *44*(1), 1–4.

Shah, M., & Sarker, M. H. (2020). Ethical Considerations of Artificial Intelligence and Intelligent Tutoring Systems in Education. In *Proceedings of the 2020 IEEE Technology and Engineering Education Conference (ITEEA)* (pp. 1-10). IEEE.

Sönmez, V. (2021). Ethical Issues in AI-Based Educational Technologies: A Systematic Literature Review. *Journal of Educational Computing Research*, *59*(7), 1144–1175.

Taylor, K. (2019). Ethical Principles for AI and Education. In *Proceedings of the 9th International Conference on Learning Analytics & Knowledge* (pp. 479-480). IEEE.

UNESCO. (2020). *Artificial Intelligence in Education: Challenges and Opportunities for Sustainable Development*. UNESCO. https://unesdoc.unesco.org/ark:/48223/pf0000374845

UNESCO. (2021). AI *in Education: Ethics Guidelines for UNESCO Member States*. UNESCO. https://en.unesco.org/ai-edu-ethics

Vandewaetere, M., Cornillie, F., & Desmet, P. (2020). Ethical Guidelines for Using Artificial Intelligence in Education: Teachers' Perspectives. *International Journal of Artificial Intelligence in Education*, *30*(4), 526–561.

Voigt, R., Von dem Bussche, A., & Even, M. (2019). Artificial Intelligence in Education: A Critical Look Beyond the Hype. *Journal of Educational Technology*, *16*(2), 41–52.

KEY TERMS AND DEFINITIONS

Artificial Intelligence: To create and use computer systems or machines that can carry out tasks that generally need human intelligence is known as "artificial intelligence" (AI). It includes various approaches and methods to give computers the capacity for perception, reasoning, learning, and decision-making. AI aims to simulate human cognitive processes, such as problem-solving, pattern recognition, natural language understanding, and decision-making, to perform tasks autonomously or with minimal human intervention.

Education: The acquisition of information and understanding using formal instruction, study, or observation. It is a never-ending procedure that helps people grow in all aspects of themselves: mentally, emotionally, socially, and physically. Education is crucial in personal growth, fostering critical thinking, promoting socialization, and preparing individuals for societal roles.

Ethical Guidelines: Rules or principles for making moral judgments and behavior in a particular context or domain. They serve as a moral compass, guiding individuals or organizations to act by ethical standards and values. Ethical guidelines help ensure responsible and ethical conduct by establishing standards of behavior, promoting fairness, protecting rights, and minimizing harm.

Technology: Use scientific information, apparatus, and techniques to produce usable items, services, or systems. It incorporates an extensive choice of tools, machines, devices, and techniques developed and utilized to solve problems, enhance productivity, and improve the quality of life. Technology is crucial in various domains, including communication, transportation, healthcare, manufacturing, and education.

Chapter 12
The Potential Impact of Chatbots on Student Engagement and Learning Outcomes

Oluwabunmi D. Bakare
https://orcid.org/0000-0002-4665-3969
Lead City University, Nigeria

Omeiza Victor Jatto
https://orcid.org/0000-0002-8586-6289
Lead City University, Nigeria

ABSTRACT

Emerging technologies such as Chatbots are redefining communication, engagement, and outcomes in the digital space in contemporary times. Academic institutions are now left behind as the majority of students who are Gen Z feel comfortable in this space, thus leaving the institutions of higher learning with no choice but to embrace these technologies to improve students' engagement and lead to a better learning outcome. However, despite its myriads of potentials, there are also consequences. It is based on this premise that this chapter will examine the usage of chatbots on students' engagement and learning outcomes by taking into perspective its potentials and consequences. Vygostsky's sociocultural theory and the Ranganathan law of library science will underpin this chapter. The chapter is expected to contribute to practice, society, policy, and theory based on the conceptual model that would be developed.

INTRODUCTION

To the academicians and librarians as information specialists, chatbot which as a sub-set of Artificial intelligence (AI) is a tool or a means to an end not an end itself. Therefore, it is necessary to understudy or talk about how it can be used to ensure and achieve efficiency as well as effectiveness in student's

DOI: 10.4018/979-8-3693-0205-7.ch012

engagement with the aim of disseminating knowledge on time and in an appropriate manner. Technology has completely changed how humans connect and interact with the world around them in the current age and time. The chatbot, an AI-driven tool that can mimic human communication, is one such innovation that has gained prominence in recent years.

Chatbots have completely changed how business organizations communicate with their customers, but their potential as a teaching and knowledge disseminating tool is only now being investigated. Finding fresh, creative approaches to engage students and make learning enjoyable and engaging is crucial for teachers as well as academicians among which are librarians. An interesting chance to achieve that is provided by chatbots. Chatbots have the potential to create, foster and mastermind a dynamic and interesting learning environment that can keep students motivated and interested thanks to their capacity to deliver immediate feedback, individualized responses, and a conversational interface. In addition to assisting students with their schoolwork and responding to their inquiries, chatbots can also give interactive courses and quizzes. By imitating real-life settings and offering feedback on appropriate behavior, they can also be used to teach social skills and emotional intelligence skills.

CHATBOTS

A chatbot is an AI-powered computer software or app that can mimic human interaction and carry on conversations with users in a conversational, textual style. Its major function is to carry on natural, conversational exchanges with users, during which it provides information, responds to questions, and offers assistance with a variety of tasks. Users can interact with chatbots in the same way they would with a real person by incorporating them into messaging platforms, websites, mobile apps, and other digital interfaces.

About Chatbots

Use of Natural Language Processing (NLP): In order to comprehend and react to user input, chatbots use cutting-edge NLP methods. The chatbot can now understand subtleties in human language such as phrasing, slang, context, and intent thanks to NLP.

User Interaction: Chatbots communicate with users in real time, carrying on natural dialogues in response to user messages and questions. They take the information provided to them and employ pre-programmed conversational patterns, algorithms, and AI models to come up with a suitable response.

Types of Chatbots

Rule-Based Chatbots: These chatbots follow a predefined set of rules and patterns to determine their responses. They are typically more limited in their capabilities and are suitable for handling simple tasks and queries.

AI-Powered Chatbots: These chatbots leverage machine learning and AI techniques, often incorporating large language models like GPT (Generative Pre-trained Transformer), to generate more dynamic and contextually relevant responses. They can learn and adapt over time, improving their conversation quality based on user interactions and feedback.

Used For:

Customer Support: Chatbots are commonly used for providing customer support by addressing frequently asked questions, troubleshooting issues, and guiding users through processes.

E-commerce: They can assist users in finding products, making purchase decisions, and completing transactions.

Information Retrieval: Chatbots can retrieve specific information from databases, websites, or knowledge bases.

Appointment Booking: Chatbots can help users schedule appointments, set reminders, and manage their calendars.

Language Learning: They can provide language practice and lessons, engaging users in interactive language exercises.

Entertainment: Chatbots can offer entertainment through jokes, riddles, storytelling, and interactive games.

Integration and Platforms: It is possible to incorporate chatbots into a variety of platforms, such as websites, social networking platforms, messaging applications (such as Facebook Messenger, WhatsApp, and Slack), mobile apps, and voice assistants (such as Amazon Alexa and Google Assistant).

THE CONCEPT OF STUDENT ENGAGEMENT

Student engagement is a vital component of effective teaching and learning. It is the degree of interest, attention, and participation that students demonstrate in their educational experiences. it is assumed to be the responsibility of the teacher to command students' attention and carry them along purely to make sure that learning takes place. A robust student engagement theory helps educators understand how to create a learning environment that promotes active learning, critical thinking which in turn results in academic success. Student engagement encompasses various dimensions that contribute to a student's involvement and investment in the learning process.

Theory of Students' Engagement

Vygotsky's Theory of Cognitive Development

Several theories have been proposed in respect to learning, social interaction and teachers to learners relationship. The sociocultural theory, which emphasizes the relevance of social interactions and cultural factors in cognitive development, is the foundation of Vygotsky's idea of classroom involvement. This hypothesis, put out by the Russian psychologist Lev Vygotsky, contends that learning is a social activity that takes place through meaningful interactions with others, especially those who have more experience (Erbil, 2020).

Vygotsky asserts that active involvement in class activities, interest, and the integration of new knowledge with prior understanding go beyond simple participation in activities. The Zone of Proximal growth (ZPD), which is the distance between a learner's present level of growth and their prospective level of development with the help of a More Knowledgeable Person (MKO), was emphasized by Vygotsky.

This means that the instructor, teacher or the librarian who serves as the main MKO in the classroom, is extremely important. Collaboration between the teacher and students as well as between the students themselves was stressed by Vygotsky. The teacher can scaffold students' learning experiences and lead them through the ZPD so they can gain new information and skills by developing a socially engaging learning environment. This engaging leaning environment in the digital age includes chatbots.

Furthermore, the idea of scaffolding which is an important component of Vygotsky's theory posited that the support given by a teacher to help students comprehend and solve problems is referred to as scaffolding. Depending on the demands of the pupils, the teacher modifies their degree of support, gradually lowering it as the students advance in skill. The teacher helps students close the knowledge gap between what they already know and what they are capable of learning by scaffolding.

To interest students in the classroom and library users in the library, Vygotsky also emphasized the value of cultural tools and artifacts. Language, symbols, and other types of mediational aids that influence and improve the learning process are among them. Particularly when it comes to communication, cognition, and self-control, language plays a vital influence. The teacher/librarian stimulates active engagement and higher comprehension by encouraging students to share their ideas through meaningful conversation and dialogue.

Vygotsky also emphasized the importance of play for student involvement in the classroom. He thought that through play, kids can experiment with and practice new ideas and abilities in a fun and secure environment. student can develop their creativity, social skills, and problem-solving ability through play. To encourage engagement and enhance learning, the teacher might include play-based activities and games into the classroom (Nicolopoulou, 1993). This in library parlance could be regarded as gamification of library services (Adeyemi, Esan, Aleem, 2021). Teachers as well as librarians can assist students' cognitive growth and foster meaningful involvement by fostering a collaborative and encouraging learning environment, which will improve learning results.

RANGANATHAN'S FIVE LAWS OF LIBRARY

The Five Laws of Library Science by S. R. Ranganathan serve as a guide for efficiently setting up and running libraries (Ranganathan, 1931). Through the usage of chatbots, these laws can be tied in numerous ways to the idea of student participation.

Information Resources Are for Use

This law underlines that a library's fundamental goal is to make its materials accessible to its patrons. Similar to this, chatbots can increase student engagement by making information more accessible. Chatbots can act as virtual librarians for students, helping them find the right sources, proposing books, articles, or internet resources, and aiding them as they conduct their study. Chatbots promote active engagement with the resources in the library by assisting students in finding the information they require.

Every Reader His/Her Information Resources

This law emphasizes how crucial it is to cater library services to the preferences and needs of specific consumers. By providing individualized recommendations based on the student's preferences, academic standing, and field of study, chatbots can improve the student experience. Students can interact with chatbots to receive personalized reading lists, study tips, and recommendations for resources that fit their unique learning objectives, increasing their engagement with the library's resources.

Every Information Resources its Reader/User

According to this law, libraries must work to match the appropriate book with the appropriate reader because every book has a reader. Chatbots can help with this process by encouraging peer-to-peer book recommendations and reviews, holding virtual book discussions, suggesting pertinent books based on a student's reading preferences, and more. Chatbots can improve students' engagement with the library's collection by fostering a feeling of community and facilitating book-related interactions.

Save the Time of the Reader, Students/Library User

The fourth law of Ranganathan highlights the need to reduce obstacles and inefficiencies in using library resources. By giving short answers to frequently asked inquiries, assisting with simple research requests, and guiding them through the library's catalog and online resources, chatbots can help students save time. Chatbots help to a smooth and hassle-free experience by providing prompt and effective support, hence raising student interest in the library's services.

The Library is a Growing Organism

The developing character of libraries and their ongoing attempts to adjust to shifting user needs and technology developments are highlighted by this law. By giving real-time updates about new acquisitions, future events, seminars, and other library-related activities, chatbots can help maintain the library's services current and useful. Students can take an active role in the expansion and improvement of the library by remaining engaged and informed through chatbot conversations. Incorporating chatbots into library services can increase student engagement by offering tailored support, quick access to resources, chances for social interaction, and real-time updates. Libraries may create a more dynamic and engaging environment for their users by combining Ranganathan's Five Laws with chatbot capabilities, thereby promoting a deeper connection between students and the library's resources (Safii, 2019).

Conceptual Model

From both Vygotsky's theory of sociocultural leaning and Ranganathan five laws of library and seeing the librarian as an inevitable factor in students engagement both in the library and in the academic context where librarianship as a result of the cataclysmic change caused by Information and Communication Technology has evolved from sitting in the library to being blended into the academic system whether as a subject specialist, information resources person with the sole aim of providing, suggesting and dishing out viable information in relation to what the students have learnt thereby complementing the effort of the academicians like lecturers in creating an enabling environment for leaning. A conceptual model made up of both Vygotsky's theory of sociocultural learning and Ranganathan's five laws of library is developed.

As stated earlier, Vygotsky's sociocultural theory emphasizes the importance of social interaction and cultural context in the learning process. According to Vygotsky, learning is facilitated through interactions with more knowledgeable individuals, such as teachers and peers. The zone of proximal development (ZPD) is a central concept, representing the range of tasks a learner can accomplish with the guidance of a more capable person.

Figure 1. Synthesized classroom engagement model (SCEM)

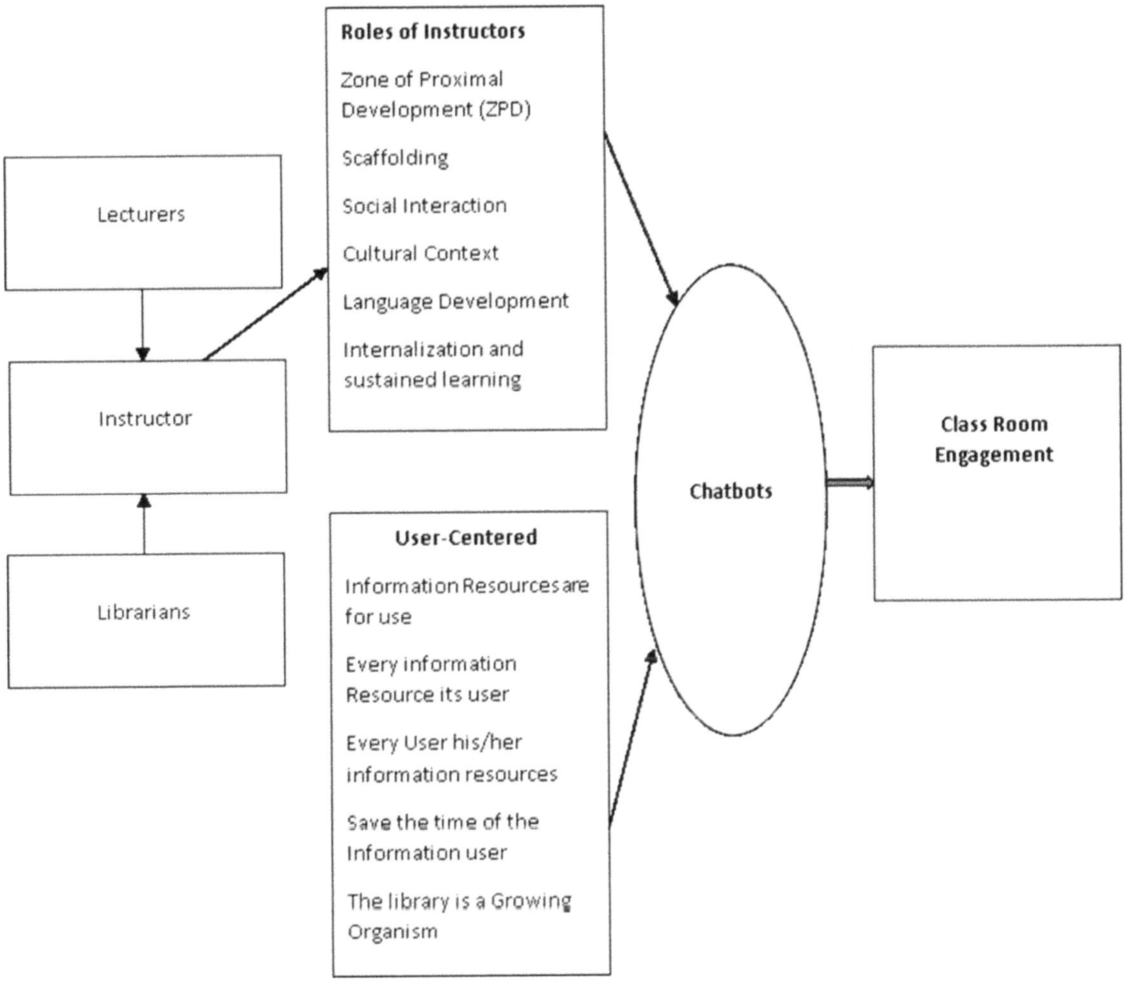

On the other hand, S.R. Ranganathan's Five Laws of Library Science provide principles for effective library management and user engagement which includes Books Are for Use: Books and resources in a library should be accessible and usable by patrons. Every Reader His/Her Book: Libraries should cater to the diverse needs and interests of users. Every Book Its Reader: Every book should find its appropriate user. Save the Time of the Reader: Libraries should be organized to facilitate easy access and efficient use of resources and the library is a Growing Organism: Libraries should constantly evolve and adapt to changing needs and technologies. Books in modern concept is everything that carries information otherwise regarded in library parlance as information resources.

Synthesis and Application

Combining Vygotsky's theory and Ranganathan's laws, we can design a well-engaged classroom environment using chatbots, where librarians and lecturers collaborate to enhance learning experiences: Chatbots can imitate a "more knowledgeable other" in the Zone of Proximal Development. Helping students face difficult activities and develop higher-order thinking is facilitated by their ability to provide quick feedback, scaffolded instruction, and individualized support.

Librarians and chatbots can collaborate to create a collection of materials that are accessible to students of varying backgrounds, interests, and skill levels. Based on a user's interests and desired outcomes, a chatbot might suggest more resources to further their education.

Chatbots can correlate with Ranganathan's "Every Book Its Reader" idea by matching learners with materials based on an analysis of students' profiles, interests, and learning progress.

Chatbots can help students get the information they need at the library quickly and easily, adhering to Ranganathan's time-saving principle as they do so.

Adaptive learning and development, the system can learn from students' preferences as they interact with chatbots, refining their recommendations over time. This is consistent with Ranganathan's concept of a living organism.

In this synthesized approach, librarians and lecturers collaborate to design a dynamic and engaging learning environment. Librarians contribute their expertise in resource curation and organization, while chatbots facilitate personalized learning experiences and foster interaction within the ZPD. This combination ensures that the classroom environment is well-engaged, diverse in content, efficient in resource utilization, and adaptable to individual learning journeys.

Chatbot and Classroom Engagement

This can be achieved by the adoption of AI tools like chatbot. As earlier said, Chatbot is a programmed interaction platform with program answers provided based on the foreknowledge of the teacher about the students. Chatbots serve as intermediate between the learner and the teacher. This means that the teacher/librarian based on community analysis, experience and a closer study must have had a clearer understanding of the students which will enables him or her to provide program veritable and accurate answers to students' questions and queries.

Component of Student Engagement

The behavioral engagement component entails acts and participation that are clearly apparent, such as consistent attendance in class, finishing assignments, and actively participating in discussions and group activities. The degree of commitment and involvement a student has with their academic obligations is reflected in their behavioral engagement.

Cognitive Engagement: Mental effort and intellectual involvement are related to cognitive engagement in learning. It entails processes like deep information processing, critical thinking, and problem solving. Students that are intellectually engaged exhibit higher-order thinking abilities and a sincere interest in the material.

Emotional involvement: Students' motivation, interest, and delight in learning are all reflected in students' emotional involvement. It includes the emotional bond that students have with their academic environment, instructors, classmates, and subject matter. Students are more likely to persevere despite difficulties and have a positive attitude about learning when they are emotionally involved.

Chatbots in Nigeria

Nigerian being an African country is at the forefront of technological adoption. Off the field of academic, a study revealed that a total of 10 out of the 22 commercial banks in Nigeria have implemented chatbots as part of their current or previous strategies for product and service delivery. The categorization of these chatbots is determined by their gender presentation, which is classified according to three distinct traits.

Out of the 10 chatbots under consideration, it can be observed that, based on their given names, the gender assigned to them using pronouns or descriptions on the banks' social media or official website, as well as the visual representation of their avatars, seven of the chatbots are categorised as having a female gender.

These chabots are associated with Zenith Bank, United Bank for Africa, Sterling Bank, First City Monument Bank, Fidclity Bank, Ecobank, and Access Bank. In contrast, the chatbot of Heritage Bank, which was seamlessly included into its Octopus application, did not exhibit any gendered characteristics, and was simply displayed as a functionality within the mobile app. On the other hand, Keystone Bank's Oxygen chatbot was visually represented by either a robotic arm or a stylized depiction of "O2". Leo, the chatbot developed by United Bank for Africa, was the sole chatbot on the list that was assigned a male gender.

The analysis of the chatbots presented provides insights into their characteristics within the 10 banks. The table displays the names, assigned gender, and avatars of the chatbots. It is evident that a significant proportion of the chatbots are assigned a female gender and are designed with attributes that align with stereotypical female traits, as indicated by their names or avatars, or both. However, it is worth noting that this pattern is not observed in three of the banks. These banks include Keystone Bank, which utilises a robot as its avatar and possesses a neutral name, as well as Heritage Bank.

Chatbots, both with and without educational goals, are currently being employed within the field of education for a multitude of purposes. Chatbots designed with an educational focus can serve multiple purposes, such as facilitating interactive quizzes, functioning as virtual tutors, offering exercise and practise programmes, conducting assessments, responding to inquiries, and delivering recorded lectures. These chatbots are developed based on socio-constructivist approaches to learning.

Chatbots that are designed using behaviourist and cognitivist learning approaches are utilised for a range of tasks that are not primarily educational in nature. These tasks include responding to frequently asked questions about courses, addressing repetitive inquiries from students regarding project guidelines, deliverables, deadlines, grades, and so on. The utilisation of chatbots in the field of education remains a subject that has received limited attention, necessitating greater investigation into the adoption of chatbots by education stakeholders, as well as their integration and efficacy within educational settings (Lakshmi, Vijaya and Ishfaq, 2022).

Prospects

Chatbots are referred to by various terms, including talkbots, chatterbots, conversational AI bots, AI chatbots, AI assistants, intelligent virtual assistants, virtual customer assistants, digital assistants, conversational agents, virtual agents, and conversational interfaces, among others. Chatbots exhibit a range of intelligence levels, with increasing degrees of intelligence corresponding to an increased capacity to provide satisfactory responses. Like any other AI, Chatbots has numerous prospects. For instance, in a study conducted by Ritu and Hayley (2020), a significant majority of higher education stakeholders in the United States, reaching as high as 99.4 percent, hold the belief that artificial intelligence (AI) will play a crucial role in enhancing the competitiveness of educational institutions within the next three years. Furthermore, 15 percent of these stakeholders referred to AI as a "game-changer." Additionally, a minimum of 54 percent of higher education institutions in the United States have initiated AI experimentation, while 38 percent have fully integrated AI into their core business strategy.

The field of Artificial Intelligence has witnessed significant advancements over the years.

At the present time, certain chatbots possess capabilities such as recognition and oral expression, as well as the ability to identify emotional states. These qualities enable chatbots to effectively connect with individuals or other chatbots, thereby creating an illusion of interacting with a genuine human being (Gracia, Fuertes, & Molas, 2018). Chatbots are increasingly being recognised as a novel interface that has the potential to substitute or supplement traditional apps and website visits. These chatbots are designed to facilitate user interaction by allowing them to engage in conversations. (Knill, et. al. 2004). One advantage of incorporating chatbots into educational settings is their ability to operate continuously, 24 hours a day, 7 days a week. Furthermore, these chatbots possess desirable attributes such as tenacity, honesty, reactivity, and friendliness, as highlighted by Zoroayka (2018) and Tsvetkova et al. (2017). According to Artificial Solutions (2020), the predicted compound annual growth rate of the Chatbot Market is expected to experience a 34.75 percent increase from 2019 to 2025.

Chatbots can also prove to be valuable assets in hybrid courses, which combine traditional in-person classroom instruction with online platforms for student self-directed learning. AI-based chatbot solutions in educational settings have the capability to do various administrative tasks, including attendance management. Certain educational institutions have started implementing artificial intelligence (AI) systems for the purpose of grading examinations and evaluating selected student assignments (Artificial Intelligence and Chatbots in Higher Education, 2020).

The utilisation of chatbots in the educational context can serve as a form of programmed instructional content, guiding students towards relevant learning resources based on their individual abilities.

Chatbots can also prove to be valuable assets in hybrid courses, which combine traditional in-person classroom instruction with online platforms for student self-directed learning. AI-based chatbot solutions in educational settings have the capability to do various administrative tasks, including attendance management. Certain educational institutions have started implementing artificial intelligence (AI) systems for the purpose of grading examinations and evaluating selected student assignments (Artificial Intelligence and Chatbots in Higher Education, 2020).

The utilisation of chatbots in the educational context can serve as a form of programmed instructional content, guiding students towards relevant learning resources based on their individual abilities.

In their study, Ndukwe, Daniel, and Amadi (2019) examined the potential of utilising Chatbots for automated assessment and student engagement. The researchers reported that a significant level of agreement was seen between the automated grading system and human graders. According to Han (2017), chatbots have the potential to do many jobs such as delivering reminders, introducing novel concepts, addressing frequently asked questions, and providing training to newly hired personnel. Chatbots have the potential to serve as a tool for offering virtual language practise to pupils at any given time. Chatbots have the potential to actively involve students in classroom activities through the provision of interactive quizzes. Students may also utilise chatbots to seek assistance in accessing information that may be challenging to locate inside a Learning Management System (LMS) setting, regardless of their location and time constraints (Clark (2018).

According to recent research conducted by Clarizia et al. (2018), it has been emphasised that chatbots have the potential to tackle the issue of inadequate interaction between students and instructors. Within the context of higher education institutions in Nigeria, where there is a high instructor-student ratio (Essel et al., 2019; Tsyhaniuk & Akenten, 2021), the use of a chatbot can offer students prompt and automated solutions to their inquiries, akin to engaging in a conversation with a course instructor. As a result, there is a decrease in the instructor's workload and an increase in the students' engagement with the learning process.

In a study conducted by Kamita et al. (2019), the use of chatbots and web courses to boost students' mental well-being was examined. The findings indicated a heightened likelihood of effectiveness when chatbots were employed to facilitate self-directed learning, foster increased motivation, and alleviate stress. The implementation of a chatbot dubbed 'Jill Watson' was developed by the University of Georgia for integration into a computer science course. According to Lipko (2016), the students who took part in the study shown a higher level of responsiveness and expressed a desire to utilise the chatbot in various instructional contexts. The capacity of students to engage in dialogue with their instructors, through the act of posing inquiries, is a fundamental aspect of the learning process that has the potential to positively impact academic achievement.

According to scholarly sources such as Göschlberger and Brandstetter (2019), Jomah et al. (2016), and Smith and Evans (2018), a chatbot has the capability to imitate human-like dialogue-based interactive communications. This functionality can be utilised to support students in reviewing learning resources. Additionally, research conducted by Chang et al. (2021) suggests that the use of chatbots can contribute to improved learning outcomes and increased self-efficacy among students. Furthermore, Fadhil and Villafiorita (2017) argue that chatbots can also enhance adaptive learning.

In addition, the utilisation of chatbots can help mitigate this challenge by proactively engaging in dialogue tailored to the specific circumstances of the student, thereby creating a sense of personalised interaction (Hien et al., 2018; Howlett, 2017). According to Wang et al. (2021), a chatbot has the potential to serve as a mediator between students and instructors, enabling students to independently manage their learning and progress at their own preferred speed, without imposing limitations. Additionally, it has been observed that chatbots have the potential to elicit inquiries from students who may feel hesitant to participate in a traditional educational setting (Verleger & Pembridge, 2018).

Clark and Clark, asserted that the implementation of a chatbot can alleviate the administrative burden placed on teachers by effectively addressing inquiries related to logistical details such as location, timing, and methodology, provided that the chatbot is appropriately educated.

- Student Engagement: Students are prompted to adhere to deadlines and actively participate in discussions.
- In the field of education, the utilisation of Artificial Intelligent bots has been observed to facilitate self-directed learning by providing learners with answers, guidance, and advice that simulates a real-person dialogue.
- Additionally, chatbots have the potential to function as audio converters, enabling the conversion of text into speech and vice versa.
- Feedback: Throughout the course, chatbots have the capability to gather feedback from students as a consequence of various assessments and are inclined to rectify errors through repeated resolution of common issues.

- Anonymity: Students should feel unrestricted in posing any inquiries, alleviating concerns about their personal identity being revealed.
- Evaluation of knowledge delivery: The bot appears to be more adept at addressing problem-solving and enhancing critical thinking skills rather than serving as a teaching tool for students to acquire knowledge.
- Promotion of critical thinking: Bots developed using Artificial Intelligence and Machine Learning technologies are anticipated to function as genuine tutors, actively seeking evidence of students' critical thinking abilities in their responses, and fostering such skills through error correction and prompts.
- Versatile instructor: Unlike humans, bots have the potential to possess extensive expertise in multiple domains and can also perform administrative functions.

AI powered chatbots and recommendation systems can help librarians provide more personalized and efficient assistance to users. Chatbots can handle common queries and direct users to relevant resources, while recommendation systems can help librarians suggest resources based on users' interests and needs. AI can also be used to improve search functionality, making it easier for librarians to find the resources they need. For instance, AI-powered natural language processing (NLP) can help librarians find resources that match specific keywords or phrases, even if those resources are not catalogued using those exact terms (Kane, 2020).

Chatbots Use in Nigeria

Like other Artificial Intelligence, Chatbots are becoming increasingly popular in Nigeria, with banks and other business organizations using them to provide services and improve customer experience. Some of the services chatbots can provide include processing basic banking tasks such as inquiries about balances, account details, and loans, airtime top-up, account enquiry, and more. Chatbots can also be used to increase customer engagement, monitor customer data and gain insights, better lead generation, and cost savings. There are several chatbots that are growing in Nigeria, including Leo, an AI-powered Facebook Messenger bot that allows users to perform banking transactions. Other chatbots include:

Kudi.ai: A chatbot that allows users to pay bills, buy airtime, and transfer money.

MyPadi: A chatbot that helps students find accommodation and roommates.

Doctoora: A chatbot that helps users find and book medical appointments.

Aella Credit: A chatbot that provides loans to users.

Zoto: A chatbot that allows users to recharge their mobile phones.

There are also several companies in Nigeria that specialize in chatbot development, including Intelia, Techinnover Analytics Limited, and Zummit Africa. Overall, chatbots are becoming an increasingly important part of the Nigerian business landscape, providing a range of services to customers and improving customer experience (Mogaji, 2021; Borokini, Wakunuma, & Akintoye, 2023; Awosanya, 2018).

Chatbots Used in Nigeria Libraries

While there is limited information specifically about chatbots used in Nigerian libraries, there is a general recommendation for academic libraries in Nigeria to embrace artificial intelligence, including chatbots, for contemporary library services. Academic libraries in Nigeria are encouraged to fully implement artificial intelligence technologies, including chatbots, barcodes, RFIDs, and robots. Chatbots can assist with technical and reader services in libraries, such as answering basic reference inquiries, navigating the library website, assisting with research, cataloguing, classification, and collection development. Chatbots can provide benefits such as increased customer engagement, monitoring customer data and gaining insights, better lead generation, and cost savings. However, it is important to note that chatbots should be seen as a complementary technology rather than a replacement for human librarians, due to the risk of inaccurate query responses, misuse, limited comprehension, input limitation, and technological reliance (Oyetola, Oladokun, Maxwell, & Obotu Akor, 2023; Olusegun, Oladokun, Maxwell, & Akor, 2023; Borokini, Wakunuma, & Akintoye, 2023; Adetayo, 2023).

It is evident that chatbots like other AI has potential, prospects and advantages to the librarian, library user, and the academic world. However, it comes with its own challenges that potential users must be able to understand and guard against. Some challenges are Nigeria specific while some are global. Examples include:

Accuracy of query responses: Chatbots rely on pre-programmed responses and may struggle with understanding complex or nuanced queries. This can lead to inaccurate or incomplete responses, which may impact the user experience.

Misuse and limitations: Chatbots may be prone to misuse or exploitation by users who intentionally try to manipulate or confuse the system. Additionally, chatbots have limitations in terms of their comprehension abilities and may struggle with understanding certain types of queries or context.

Limited comprehension: Chatbots may have difficulty understanding natural language, slang, or regional dialects, which can hinder effective communication with library users. This can be particularly challenging in a diverse country like Nigeria with multiple languages and dialects.

Technological reliance: Implementing chatbots requires a robust technological infrastructure, including reliable internet connectivity and appropriate hardware and software. In some areas of Nigeria, infrastructure limitations may pose challenges to the successful implementation and maintenance of chatbot systems.

User acceptance and trust: Some library users may prefer human interaction and may be hesitant to trust or rely on chatbots for their information needs. Building user trust and acceptance of chatbot technology may require effective communication and education about the benefits and limitations of chatbots.

CHALLENGES OF CHATBOTS

The design, development, and utilisation of chatbots in the field of education are now in their early stages of development. Nevertheless, the creation of chatbots, regardless of whether they are rule-based or machine learning-based, necessitates extensive effort and a profound understanding of the subject matter and individuals involved. Chatbots constructed using a rule-based method may lack efficiency in responding to inquiries that do not conform to the predefined rules upon which the chatbot is trained.

Similarly, the Chatbots that have been developed using a machine learning approach aim to provide responses by considering both keywords and human language. As a result, these Chatbots exhibit superior performance compared to those developed using a rule-based approach. However, it is worth noting that the development process for machine learning-based Chatbots is more challenging in comparison to rule-based Chatbots (Shridhar, 2017; Kharchenko, 2017). According to Skerrett (2017), the effectiveness of a chatbot's response is contingent upon the variables incorporated during its creation, rendering some of them unhelpful.

It is important to acknowledge that the development of chatbots incurs costs, thus necessitating careful consideration before implementing them. According to Molnar and Szüts (2018), chatbots have limited utility in many educational domains, as they are mostly suitable for providing additional information rather than addressing or enhancing content-related challenges.

Additionally, it is argued that inadequate design of chatbots might exacerbate user irritation resulting from poor dialogue. Gracia, Fuertes, and Molas (2018) assert that there is a need for additional exploration regarding the adoption of chatbots by education stakeholders and the chatbot's capacity to adapt to diverse circumstances.

CONCLUSION

The utilization of AI chatbots holds the capacity to greatly augment the services rendered by libraries and librarians. In the library context, AI chatbots have the capacity to meet a range of inevitable demands. The availability of AI chatbots is continuous, operating 24 hours a day and 7 days a week. This enables library customers to receive assistance and access resources at any given time, including periods when physical library facilities are not accessible. The utilization of chatbots enables customers to promptly access information pertaining to library hours, geographical location, the availability of resources, and the range of services offered. This has the potential to optimize time management for both patrons and library staff. In the context of libraries, this allows for the efficient handling of regular reference questions and commonly asked questions. This, in turn, enables librarians to allocate their time and efforts towards addressing more intricate inquiries and engaging in challenging duties.

Resource Recommendations: Chatbots possess the capability to provide users with pertinent book recommendations, scholarly papers, and various other materials that align with their individual interests and specific requirements. This feature has the potential to assist users in uncovering resources that they may not have otherwise encountered.

Libraries frequently cater to a wide range of demographics. Artificial intelligence chatbots have the capability to be built with the ability to converse in several languages, hence facilitating access to support for users from diverse backgrounds.

Personalized Support: Through the examination of user behaviors and preferences, AI chatbots have the capability to provide tailored recommendations and support, hence augmenting the overall user experience.

Educational Assistance: Chatbots possess the capability to aid users in effectively navigating internet databases, research tools, and citation guidelines, thereby providing valuable support to students and researchers in their scholarly pursuits. Virtual tours can be utilized in digital libraries or as a preliminary activity before physical visits. AI chatbots have the capability to provide these virtual tours, effectively assisting users in navigating through the library's various resources and services. The utilization of chatbots in event promotion can effectively enhance user engagement and involvement by providing users with timely information regarding forthcoming library events, workshops, and lectures.

Data Analysis: Artificial intelligence chatbots have the capability to gather data pertaining to user enquiries and interactions, so furnishing librarians with valuable information regarding user requirements and preferences. The data has the potential to provide valuable insights for making informed decisions regarding the allocation of resources and the enhancement of services. AI chatbots have the capability to provide accessibility features such as text-to-speech and vice versa, hence enhancing the usability of the library's resources for individuals with impairments.

Continuous Learning: Artificial intelligence chatbots have the capability to acquire knowledge from every encounter, resulting in enhanced accuracy and refinement as time progresses. The chatbot's performance is enhanced through its flexibility, which is evidenced by its ability to develop as it acquires further experience. The utilization of AI chatbots can effectively alleviate the strain of librarians by managing mundane activities and enquiries, so enabling them to dedicate their attention to more specialized and value-added services.

Community engagement can be enhanced with chatbots, which could promote various forms of interaction such as discussions and book clubs. By using this technology, libraries can create a feeling of community among their users, promoting a more engaging and participatory experience.

Feedback and work: AI chatbots have the capability to collect user feedback and perform sentiment analysis, thereby assisting libraries in identifying areas that require work and enhancing the quality of their services.

RECOMMENDATIONS

Although AI chatbots can provide a multitude of advantages, they cannot serve as a substitute for human librarians. AI systems should be regarded as valuable resources that enhance the efforts of librarians by managing repetitive chores and offering prompt support, thus enabling librarians to dedicate their time and expertise to more intricate and sophisticated interactions with library patrons. Further, the advancement and execution of AI chatbots must adhere to ethical principles, encompassing the protection of privacy, data security, and the provision of human supervision when necessary.

REFERENCES

Adetayo, A. J. (2023). Artificial intelligence chatbots in academic libraries: The rise of ChatGPT. *Library Hi Tech News*, *40*(3), 18–21. doi:10.1108/LHTN-01-2023-0007

Adeyemi, I. O., Esan, A. O., & Aleem, A. (2021). Application of gamification to library services: Awareness, perception, and readiness of academic librarians in Nigeria. *The Electronic Library*, *39*(5), 767–781. doi:10.1108/EL-05-2021-0096

Oracle. (2020). *Artificial Intelligence and Chatbots in Higher Education.* Oracle. http://www.oracle.com/us/ industries/education-and-research/he-artificial-intelligencer-5180773.pdf

Awosanya, Y. (2018). How Nigerian brands and startups are creatively using Chatbots to improve customer experience. *Tech Point.* https://techpoint.africa/2018/02/21/chatbots-in-nigeria/

Borokini, F., Wakunuma, K., & Akintoye, S. (2023). The Use of Gendered Chatbots in Nigeria: Critical Perspectives. In *Responsible AI in Africa: Challenges and Opportunities* (pp. 119–139). Springer International Publishing. doi:10.1007/978-3-031-08215-3_6

Clarizia, F., Colace, F., Lombardi, M., Pascale, F., & Santaniello, D. (2018). Chatbot: An education support system for students. In *the International Symposium on Cyberspace Safety and Security* (pp. 291–302). Springer.

Clark, D. (2018). *The Fallacy of "Robot" Teachers*. Donald Clark Plan B. https://donaldclarkplanb.blogspot.com/search?q=10+uses+for+Chatbots+in+learni ng+(with+examples)

Dan, A. (2020, March 4). Unleashing the power of AI for education. Microsoft. Retrieved from https://www. technologyreview.com/2020/03/04/905535/unleashing-thepower-of-ai-for-education/

Erbil, D. G. (2020). A review of flipped classroom and cooperative learning method within the context of Vygotsky theory. *Frontiers in Psychology, 11*, 1157. doi:10.3389/fpsyg.2020.01157 PMID:32655437

Essel, H. B., Butakor, P. K., & Nortey, S. (2019). Summative e-examination for high stake assessment in higher education: A case of undergraduate students at the Kwame Nkrumah University of Science and Technology. *Global Journal of Human-Social Science: Arts & Humanities-Psychology, 19*, 03.

Fadhil, A., & Villafiorita, A. (2017). An Adaptive Learning with Gamification & Conversational UIs: The Rise of CiboPoliBot. In *25th Conference on User Modeling, Adaptation and Personalization* (pp. 408–412). 10.1145/3099023.3099112

Fleming, M. (2018). Streamlining student course requests using chatbots. [Conference Session]. *29th Australasian Association for Engineering Education Conference 2018 (AAEE 2018)*. Engineers Australia. https://search.informit.org/doi/epdf/10.3316/ informit.166919861347542

Garcia Brustenga, G., Fuertes-Alpiste, M., Molas-Castells, N. (2018). *Briefing paper: chatbots in education*. Barcelona: eLearn Center. Universitat Oberta de Catalunya., doi:10.7238/elc.chatbots.2018

Göschlberger, B., & Brandstetter, C. (2019, December). Conversational AI for corporate e-learning. In *Proceedings of the 21st International Conference on Information Integration and Web-based Applications & Services* (pp. 674-678). IEEE.

Han, V. (2017). Are Chatbots the Future of Training? *TD: Talent Development, 71*(9), 42-46. https://www.td.org/magazines/td-magazine/are-chatbots-the-futureof-training

Hephzibah, T. (2020). Critical Literature Review on Chatbots in Education. [ijtsrd]. *International Journal of Trend in Scientific Research and Development*, *4*(6), 786–788. https://tinyurl.com/2wpc3jv8

Hien, H. T., Cuong, P. N., Nam, L. N. H., Nhung, H. L. T. K., & Thang, L. D. (2018, December). Intelligent assistants in higher-education environments: The FIT-EBot, a chatbot for administrative and learning support. In *Proceedings of the Ninth International Symposium on Information and Communication Technology* (pp. 69–76). IEEE. 10.1145/3287921.3287937

Howlett, N. (2017). How machine learning is developing to get more insight from complex voice-of-customer data. *Applied Marketing Analytics*, *3*(3), 250–254.

Hwang, G. J., & Chang, C. Y. (2021). A review of opportunities and challenges of chatbots in education. *Interactive Learning Environments*, 1–14. doi:10.1080/10494820.2021.1952615

Jomah, O., Masoud, A. K., Kishore, X. P., & Aurelia, S. (2016). Micro learning: A modernized education system. *BRAIN. Broad Research in Artificial Intelligence and Neuroscience*, *7*(1), 103–110.

Kamita, T., Ito, T., Matsumoto, A., Munakata, T., & Inoue, T. (2019). A chatbot system for mental healthcare based on SAT counseling method. *Mobile Information Systems*, *2019*, 2019. doi:10.1155/2019/9517321

Kane, D. (2020). *Analyzing an interactive chatbot and its impact on academic reference service.* Association and college research libraries conference, Cleveland, OH2019.

Lakshmi, Y. (2022). Chatbots in Education System. *University News: A Weekly Journal of Higher Education, 60*(8), 15-18. https://ssrn.com/abstract=4039535

Lipko, H. (2016). Meet Jill Watson: Georgia Tech's first AI teaching assistant. GA Tech. https://pe.gatech.edu/blog/meet-jill-watson-georgia-techs-first-ai-teaching-assistant

Mogaji, E. (2020). More Nigerian banks are using chatbots to serve customers, but with mixed results. *The Conversation.*

Molnár, G., & Szüts, Z. (2018, September). The role of chatbots in formal education. In *2018 IEEE 16th International Symposium on Intelligent Systems and Informatics (SISY)* (pp. 000197-000202). IEEE. 10.1109/SISY.2018.8524609

Ndukwe, I. G., Daniel, B. K., & Amadi, C. E. (2019). A Machine Learning Grading System Using Chatbots. In S. Isotani, E. Millán, A. Ogan, P. Hastings, B. McLaren, & R. Luckin (Eds.), Lecture Notes in Computer Science: Vol. 11626. *Artificial Intelligence in Education. AIED 2019.* Springer. doi:10.1007/978-3-030-23207-8_67

Nicolopoulou, A. (1993). Play, cognitive development, and the social world: Piaget, Vygotsky, and beyond. *Human Development*, *36*(1), 1–23. doi:10.1159/000277285

Olusegun, S., Oladokun, B. D., Maxwell, C. E., & Akor, S. O. (2023). *Artificial intelligence in the library: Potential implications to library and information services in the 21st Century Nigeria.*

Olusegun Oyetola, S., Oladokun, B. D., Ezinne Maxwell, C., & Obotu Akor, S. (2023). Artificial intelligence in the library: Gauging the potential application and implications for contemporary library services in Nigeria. *Data & Metadata*, *2*, 36. doi:10.56294/dm202336

Ranganathan, S. R. (1931). *The five laws of library science. Madras Library Association (Madras, India) and Edward Goldston.* Assessing U.S. Higher Education Sector's AI Adoption and Capabilities. https://edudownloads.azureedge.net/msdownloads/FutureReadyBusiness_HigherEducation_AI_US_Design_v2.pdf?azure-portal=true

Ranganathan, S. R. (1931). The five laws of library science. Madras Library Association (Madras, India) and Edward Goldston (London, UK).

Rogoff, B. (1998). Cognition as a Collaborative Process. In D. Kuhn & R. S. Siegler (Eds.), Handbook of Child Psychology: Vol. 2. *Cognition, Perception, and Language* (5th ed., pp. 679–744). Wiley.

Safii, M. (2019, February). Redefining the five laws of library science in the digital age. In *2nd Internasional Conference on Culture and Language in Southeast Asia (ICCLAS 2018)* (pp. 24-27). Atlantis Press. 10.2991/icclas-18.2019.7

Sandoval, Z. V. (2018). Design and implementation of a chatbot in online higher education settings. *Issues in Information Systems, 19*(4).

Sandoval, Z. V. (2018). Design and implementation of a chatbot in online higher education settings. *Issues in Information Systems, 19*(4), 4452. https:// tinyurl.com/78jvtk1v

Shridhar, K. (2017). *How Close Are Chatbots to Passing the Turing Test?* Chatbots Magazine.

Skerrett, D. (2017). Seven reasons why most chatbots launched in 2017 are dead on arrival. *EContent (Wilton, Conn.), 40*(4), 14–15.

Smith, M. T., & Evans, J. J. (2018). Storytelling as transdisciplinarity: An experiment in first-year composition and communication. In B. Hokanson, G. Clinton, & K. Kaminski (Eds.), Educational technology and narrative: Story and instructional design (pp. 103–112). Springer International Publishing.

Solutions, A. (2020). Chatbots Statistics. *Artificial Solutions.* https://www.artificial-solutions.com/chatbots#12

Stachowicz-Stanusch, A., & Amann, W. (2018). *Artificial intelligence at universities in Poland.* Organizacja i Zarządzanie: kwartalnik naukowy.

Tharp, R. G., & Gallimore, R. (1988). *Rousing Minds to Life: Teaching, Learning, and Schooling in Social Context.* Cambridge University Press.

Tsyhaniuk, D., & Akenten, W. N. (2021). Examining budgeting and fund allocation in higher education. *Financial Markets, Institutions and Risks.* https://doi.org/ doi:10.21272/fmir.5(4).128-138.202

Verleger, M., & Pembridge, J. (2018, October). A pilot study integrating an AI-driven chatbot in an introductory programming course. In IEEE frontiers in Education Conference (FIE), (pp. 1–4). IEEE Publications.

Wertsch, J. V. (1991). *Voices of the Mind: A Sociocultural Approach to Mediated Action.* Harvard University Press.

KEY TERMS AND DEFINITIONS

Chatbots: A software application or web interface that mimics human conversation through text or voice interactions.

Classroom: A virtual setting where students and lecturers, librarians for knowledge transmission.

Instructor: The librarian and the lecturer who via their understanding of the students instruct the chatbots on what to do. The instructor whose voice the chatbot is built or programmed to mimic or represent.

Prospects: possibility and likelihood of chatbots enhancing classroom engagement.

Student engagement: the degree of interest, attention, and participation that students demonstrate in their educational experiences.

Synthesized Classroom Engagement Model (SCEM): A model that explains the place of librarians as lecturers in using Artificial intelligence like chatbots in classroom engagement.

Chapter 13
Ethical Guidelines on the Use of AI in Education

Mahona Joseph Paschal
St. Augustine University of Tanzania, Tanzania

Isaiah K. Melly
Kisii University, Kenya

ABSTRACT

This chapter seeks to conduct a critical analysis and synthesis of relevant literature on the ethical guidelines on the use of artificial intelligence (AI) in education. Moreover, this chapter intended to discuss the approaches that could be used to ensure effective and efficient use of AI in education. The chapter also sheds light on the implication of AI in education which might be the directives to educational stakeholders such as policy makers, educators, students, researchers, and school leaders. This chapter calls for institutions to establish clear policies and frameworks that align with these guidelines and incorporate them into their decision-making processes. The chapter suggests that ongoing training should be provided to educators and stakeholders to ensure they understand the ethical considerations and implications of AI in education sector. Additionally, regular audits and evaluations should be conducted to identify bias, potential impact, and address any unintended consequences and make necessary improvements.

INTRODUCTION

Computers in education have had mixed results for decades. Computers sometimes work differently than advertised (McFarlane, 2019). We use AI systems daily. Evaluating their impact on society is crucial as they evolve and data use grows, particularly in education and training. Students and teachers can use AI-powered apps inside and outside classrooms. There is widespread agreement that using AI in classrooms is among the century's most significant advances (Becker et al., 2018; Seldon & Abidoye, 2018). More must be known about what ethical principles should drive the design, development, and deployment of trustworthy AI in education despite the rising popularity of AI for education (AIED) and the increased need under COVID-19. The COVID-19 pandemic accelerated technology adoption in the

DOI: 10.4018/979-8-3693-0205-7.ch013

education sector, including Artificial Intelligence (AI). With the shift to remote learning due to school closures and social distancing measures, AI has played a crucial role in facilitating virtual classrooms (Shah & Sarker, 2020).

AI-powered platforms and tools enable teachers to deliver online lessons, interact with students, and manage coursework. These platforms often incorporate features like video conferencing, chatbots, and content management systems, providing a more seamless virtual learning experience. AI-driven adaptive learning platforms have become even more relevant during the pandemic. These platforms use AI algorithms to assess students' knowledge and skills, identify learning gaps, and provide personalized learning paths. As students navigate remote learning environments, adaptive learning systems can adapt to their needs, ensuring targeted support and a tailored learning experience (Lepori et al., 2020; UNESCO, 2020). Google Classroom helps teach and learn. Students receive real-time feedback on their progress as they complete tasks. Visual explanations and films can help struggling students. Since time limits prevent real-time tutoring, teachers cannot execute these activities. AI automation allows for this type of problem resolution.

AI has been leveraged to automate remote learning scenarios' assessment and feedback processes. Through natural language processing and machine learning techniques, AI algorithms can analyze students' written responses, provide instant feedback, and generate automated grading. This allows for timely assessment, immediate feedback, and tracking of student progress, even in virtual classrooms (Coniam, 2020). AI-powered virtual tutors and mentoring systems have gained popularity during the pandemic. These systems provide individualized student support by simulating one-on-one interactions with tutors or mentors. Through AI chatbots or virtual assistants, students can receive guidance, ask questions, and access resources anytime, helping to bridge the gap caused by the lack of in-person support (Vandewaetere et al., 2020). The pandemic has generated vast amounts of data related to remote learning. AI-based data analytics tools enable educational institutions to analyze this data to gain insights into student engagement, performance, and overall well-being (Ifenthaler, 2020). These insights can help identify areas for improvement, track student progress, and inform decision-making to enhance remote learning strategies. AI-powered tools have been developed to provide social and emotional support to students during the pandemic. Chatbots and virtual assistants with sentiment analysis capabilities can detect and respond to students' emotional states (Clarke, 2019). These tools offer resources, coping strategies, and referrals to mental health professionals, helping to address the dynamic challenges students may face during remote learning (Rambe, 2020).

In the United States, Intelligent teaching systems that cater to each student's needs are being developed with the help of artificial intelligence. These systems adapt to individual students' needs and provide targeted instruction, feedback, and support. Additionally, AI is employed for automated grading and feedback in assignments and assessments, saving teachers' time and providing timely feedback to students (Heikkila & Kankaanranta, 2020). China has been at the forefront of AI adoption in education. Intelligent tutoring systems powered by AI deliver students personalized instruction and adaptive learning experiences. AI chatbots are employed to answer student queries and provide 24/7 support. Facial recognition technology is also utilized in some schools to monitor students' engagement and behavior in the classroom (Liu & Hu, 2020; Australian Government, 2020). In Finland, AI is utilized to develop virtual learning assistants to support students' independent learning. These assistants provide guidance, answer questions, and recommend personalized learning resources based on students' needs and learning styles. AI also analyzes large amounts of educational data to gain insights into student performance and inform educational policy decisions (Taylor, 2019).

The UK utilizes AI-powered learning platforms that leverage natural language processing and machine learning to support language learning. These platforms provide interactive language practice, speech recognition, and personalized feedback to enhance language acquisition. AI is also employed for data analysis to identify students at risk of falling behind academically and provide targeted interventions. AI is utilized in Australia to develop adaptive learning platforms that tailor instruction to individual students' strengths, weaknesses, and learning preferences. These platforms employ AI algorithms to analyze student performance data and adjust the curriculum and resources accordingly. AI is also used for automated essay grading and feedback to assist teachers in managing large class sizes (National Science & Technology Council, 2016). The collection and storage of student data by AI systems raise concerns about privacy and security. They protect sensitive information and ensure compliance with data protection regulations (Selwyn, 2019). AI algorithms can perpetuate biases present in the training data, leading to unfair treatment or discrimination against certain groups of students. Addressing algorithmic biases is crucial for ensuring equitable educational outcomes (Bolukbasi, 2016).

The capacity of AI algorithms poses challenges in understanding how decisions are made, leading to a need for more transparency and explainability. Ensuring transparency and explaining AI-generated outcomes is crucial for building trust and accountability (UNESCO, 2021). The ethical use of student data involves obtaining informed consent, protecting data privacy, and ensuring that data is used solely for educational purposes. Responsible data governance practices are necessary to safeguard student information (Voigt, Von dem Bussche & Even, 2019). The digital divide and unequal access to AI technologies can deepen educational inequalities. Ensuring equitable access to AI tools and addressing socioeconomic disparities are critical for promoting inclusive education. The introduction of AI in classrooms can impact teacher-student relationships. Balancing AI as a supportive tool while maintaining the human connection and personalized guidance teachers provide is essential (Sonmez, 2021).

Baker et al. (2019) showed that educational technology that achieved influence at scale and changed school systems beyond a limited number of schools is rarer than expected. Positively, Baker et al. (2019) evaluated nine cases of technology benefiting large numbers of learners, three in Italy, three in Europe, and three worldwide. The Lemann Foundation and Khan Academy's relationship in Brazil has attracted millions of students since 2012. Most Brazilian schools only educate four hours daily in one of three sessions. This alliance improved mathematics achievement relative to controls (Fundaçao Lemann, 2018).

According to the National Strategy for AI, the most excellent way to prevent ethical issues in schools is to provide enough training for educators and pupils. The goals are improved knowledge and the "reasoned use" of AI. The French educational system has established many initiatives and collaborations, such as P2IA (Partnership for Innovation and Artificial Intelligence). For example, this has prompted the creation of math education programs like Mathia and Adaptativ'Math, aimed at pupils in grades one through three. Some maths classes are actively experimenting with using this program in their lessons. Other projects, such as AI4T (artificial intelligence for and by teachers), are also being carried out with other European countries.

Moodle is utilized as early as secondary school, but because of a relationship between the Ministry of Education and the company, there are several AI-based solutions for higher education. Sciences Po, ESSEC, and HEC are just a few universities that use this LMS (Learning Management System) to design and deliver individualized courses and MOOCs (Massive et al.). Let us add that AI researchers and programmers are among the first to face moral questions about integrating AI into classrooms. The European Commission's "Ethics guidelines for trustworthy AI" stress the importance of corporations showing greater transparency with data processing to show that they adhere to ethical principles in AI research. More and more groups and businesses, such as those in the Partnership on AI and the European AI Alliance, are working together to implement and create trustworthy AI. Several apps and AI tools, like Beegup, have received funding thanks to the Edu'Up program, which the French Ministry of National Education and Youth backs. High school students can use the stage to practice speaking in their target language.

TRANSPARENCY

Transparency is a fundamental ethical guideline that plays a critical role in the responsible and ethical use of artificial intelligence (AI) in education. It involves open and transparent communication regarding AI systems' presence, purpose, and functioning. Transparency in AI implementation builds trust among stakeholders, including students, educators, parents, and administrators. By providing clear information about the presence and purpose of AI systems, educational institutions establish an environment of openness and understanding. Research indicates trust is essential for successfully adopting and accepting AI technologies in educational settings (Bulger et al., 2019). Transparent communication enables individuals to make informed decisions, participate actively, and engage meaningfully with AI tools and technologies. Transparency is vital in addressing biases that may arise from AI algorithms. AI systems learn from data, and if that data contains biases or discriminatory patterns, the algorithms can perpetuate and amplify those biases. Transparent AI systems allow stakeholders to examine and challenge these biases. By understanding how AI algorithms are trained, what data is used, and how decisions are made, stakeholders can identify and rectify biases, ensuring that AI technologies do not perpetuate discrimination or unfair treatment (Holstein et al., 2019). Transparency is closely linked to accountability in the use of AI in education.

Educational institutions, developers, and providers of AI systems should be accountable for the design, implementation, and impact of these systems. Transparent communication about the functioning of AI systems helps establish clear lines of accountability, ensuring that responsibility is assigned to the appropriate parties. Regular auditing and monitoring of AI systems, along with transparent reporting on their performance and impact, contribute to accountability and provide an opportunity for continuous improvement (European Commission, 2021). Transparency respects the rights and privacy of students and educators. Transparent AI systems provide precise data collection, storage, and usage information. This transparency allows individuals to understand what personal information is being collected, for what purposes, and how it is protected. With this knowledge, stakeholders can make informed consent decisions, understand their rights regarding data privacy, and have confidence in the security measures put in place (Lepri et al., 2018).

According to Larsson and Heintz's (2020) analysis of data ethics in the context of educational AI, this emphasis on openness is warranted. Although artificial intelligence (AI) tools have been increasingly used in schools to improve teaching and learning, privacy and security concerns about the resulting data have yet to be resolved (Wang & Cheng, 2021). Data visualization shows learner behavior and highlights further support teachers can provide, so Cope Kalantzis (2019) emphasized the importance of this ethical principle for both teachers and students. What the data is, where it comes from, what it reveals, what happens to it, and how it is used all contribute to its apparent openness (Digital Curation Centre, 2020). Once data ownership, accessibility, and explainability are maintained, these questions may be answered.

Understanding who owns and has the legal right to access students' information is central to data ownership, which is inherently an issue of openness and fairness (Remain, 2019). Whether or not data usage invades students' privacy has been a hotly debated issue for a long time, even though Data collectors may obtain consent from subjects frequently. There is a solid case to be made for students to retain ownership of their data due to concerns about the reliability of the research's stated purpose. Students have the right to ownership and control over their data and how it is used for educational purposes (Holmes et al., 2021). Since institutions systematically document learners' interactions and performance, the notion that they have the right to access and utilize this data is plausible.

Transparency in AI systems is emphasized by several international organizations and policy documents, including the European Commission's ethics guidelines for trustworthy AI, the European Parliament (2021), UNESCO Education & AI (Miao et al., 2021), the Beijing Consensus of UNESCO (2019), and the OECD's Principles for responsible stewardship of trustworthy AI (2021). However, the definition and description of transparency are only sometimes consistent throughout different reports and standards. In contrast to the European Commission's (2019) definition, which states that it is "closely linked with the principle of explicability and encompasses transparency of elements relevant to an AI system: the data, the system, and the business model," the UNESCO 2020 Draft describes it as being "associated to adequate responsibility and accountability measure" (AHEG, 2020). Transparency in data and algorithms should be treated as equally important in regulations for the use of AI in educational settings. Regulation By the Transparency Principle, establishing, carrying out, monitoring, and controlling artificial intelligence regulations in education should be open and clear about who is responsible for what and how it will be done. Related to the suitability discussed above, the ethical principle of regulatory responsibility is fundamental to regulating AI in the classroom.

ACCOUNTABILITY

Accountability is a crucial ethical guideline in using artificial intelligence (AI) in education. It entails the responsibility and answerability of educational institutions, developers, and stakeholders for designing, implementing, and impacting AI systems. Accountability ensures that AI is used that aligns with ethical principles, safeguards against potential harm, and upholds the well-being and interests of students and educators. Accountability in AI implementation requires establishing clear lines of responsibility. Educational institutions should define roles and responsibilities for individuals overseeing AI systems, including administrators, educators, and AI developers. Each stakeholder should be responsible for ensuring that AI technologies are implemented ethically and responsibly. This clarity ensures that AI systems' decision-making processes are transparent and that individuals can be held accountable for their actions (OECD, 2019).

While AI can provide valuable insights and automate various tasks, it should only partially replace human oversight and intervention. Accountability in using AI in education necessitates maintaining human agency and judgment. Educational institutions should ensure that there is human oversight to review and validate the decisions made by AI systems. This oversight allows for critical thinking, contextual understanding, and intervention when necessary, ensuring that the use of AI aligns with educational goals and values (Bulger et al., 2019).

Regular auditing and evaluation of AI systems contribute to accountability. Educational institutions should conduct systematic assessments to monitor AI technologies' performance, impact, and ethical implications. Auditing helps identify potential biases, errors, or unintended consequences that may arise from using AI. It enables institutions to take corrective measures, address issues, and ensure ongoing compliance with ethical standards. Auditing and evaluation also provide an opportunity for continuous improvement and refinement of AI systems (European Commission, 2021).

Accountability extends to the developers and providers of AI systems in education. They are responsible for ensuring that their AI technologies are designed and implemented ethically, adhering to legal and regulatory requirements. Developers should be transparent about the functioning of their AI algorithms, including the data used, the training process, and potential biases. They should also provide clear documentation and support for educational institutions to understand and address ethical concerns about using their AI systems (Bulger et al., 2019). Accountability in AI implementation involves transparent reporting on the use and impact of AI systems. Educational institutions should communicate with stakeholders, including students, parents, and educators, about the presence and purpose of AI technologies. Transparent reporting helps build trust, enables scrutiny, and ensures that stakeholders can understand how AI systems operate and how decisions are made. It also allows for external evaluation and validation, reinforcing accountability and promoting the responsible use of AI in education (European Commission, 2021).

In this context, "responsible AI" refers to the ethical practice of designing, developing, and deploying AI to empower key stakeholders and society fairly; this is central to the concept of "accountable AI" in the context of educational AI. Despite the rise in popularity of the term "responsible AI," neither "accountability" nor "responsibility" are typically defined (Jobin et al., 2019). However, it is widely understood to mean behaving honestly and forthrightly while also considering any and all relevant risks. The accountability of AI has been called into question, with some arguing that it should never be expected to be held to the same standards as humans and that humans should always be the sole actors responsible for AI. Along with human-centered AI in education, which promotes human oversight of AI, we argued that those with a vested interest in education should always be the ones to assume responsibility for AI in the classroom. According to specific laws, AI regulation in education should consider the accountability of individuals and institutions, sustainability, and proportionality (AHEG, 2020).

PRIVACY

Respecting privacy in AI implementation involves protecting the personal information of students and educators. Educational institutions must establish strict data protection policies and practices that comply with applicable laws and regulations. AI systems should only collect and store necessary data, ensuring that personal information remains secure and confidential. Data anonymization techniques should be employed to minimize the risk of re-identification. Furthermore, consent should be obtained from students, parents, or guardians regarding using their data in AI applications (Lepri et al., 2018). Privacy as an ethical guideline emphasizes the importance of obtaining informed consent from individuals whose data is collected and used by AI systems. Educational institutions should provide clear information about the purposes for which data is collected, its types, and how it will be used. Individuals should have the right to opt in or out of data collection and usage, empowering them to make informed decisions regarding their privacy. Informed consent ensures that individuals can control their personal information and exercise autonomy (Bulger et al., 2019). Privacy in AI implementation requires educational institutions to ensure the secure storage and usage of data. Adequate measures should be in place to protect against unauthorized access, use, or sharing of personal data. Encryption, access controls, and other security protocols should be implemented to safeguard the confidentiality and integrity of data. Educational institutions should also have clear policies regarding data retention and deletion to ensure that personal information is retained only when necessary (European Commission, 2021).

Privacy as an ethical guideline emphasizes the minimization of data collection. Educational institutions should only collect the data necessary to function and improve AI systems. Collecting excessive or unnecessary data increases the risk of privacy breaches and potential misuse of personal information. By adopting a data minimization approach, educational institutions can limit the collection and storage of personal data, reducing privacy risks (OECD, 2019). Privacy in AI implementation requires accountability and transparency regarding data handling practices. Educational institutions should be accountable for adequately managing and protecting personal information. Transparent communication should be maintained, informing individuals how their data is collected, used, and protected. Any changes in data handling practices should be communicated to individuals, allowing them to make informed decisions regarding their privacy (European Commission, 2021).

Teachers' and students' opinions should be considered when deciding how artificial intelligence (AI) should be implemented in the classroom in order for students to interact with more intelligent machines and computer agents during the learning process (Miao et al., 2021). Using actual time gesture recognition technology is one example of forecasting students' emotional state or attendance without their knowledge or agreement, raising ethical concerns (Pattnaik & Mohanty, 2020). Educators and developers should make AI aware of potential dangers to students' academic, professional, and social lives and discuss these risks with pupils. The goal is to help students feel safe sharing information online and give them the tools to transfer their knowledge from one setting to another without giving up control of their personal information (Jobin et al., 2019). Many artificial intelligences (AIs) interact with humans on multiple levels, unlike learning analytics, which are governed by data ethics (Bryson & Theodorou, 2019; Manoharan, 2019; O'Sullivan et al., 2019). This brings up an enormous number of technical safety worries about the employment of AI throughout its lifetime, particularly in extreme environments or where other agents (both human and artificial) can potentially cause malfunctions.

EQUITY

Equity is a fundamental ethical guideline in using artificial intelligence (AI) in education. It refers to all individuals' fair and just treatment, ensuring equal access to opportunities, resources, and outcomes. Equity as an ethical guideline highlights the importance of leveraging AI to bridge educational gaps, promote inclusivity, and eliminate biases and discrimination. Equity in AI implementation involves addressing biases and discrimination that may arise from AI algorithms. AI systems learn from data, and if the data used is biased or reflects discriminatory patterns, the algorithms can perpetuate and amplify those biases. Educational institutions should strive to mitigate bias by incorporating diverse datasets and perspectives into AI training. They should also regularly assess and monitor AI systems to identify and rectify emerging biases. By actively working to reduce bias and discrimination, AI can contribute to a more equitable educational experience (Holstein et al., 2019). Equity as an ethical guideline emphasizes inclusive design in developing and implementing AI systems in education. Educational institutions should ensure that AI technologies are accessible and usable by all students, regardless of their abilities, socioeconomic backgrounds, or geographical locations. The inclusive design considers learners' diverse needs and circumstances, aiming to create AI systems that accommodate different learning styles, languages, and accessibility requirements. By prioritizing inclusivity, educational institutions can foster equitable access to educational opportunities (Bulger et al., 2019).

Equity in AI implementation aims to reduce educational disparities and promote equal opportunities. AI can be used to identify and address disparities in access to quality education, resources, and support systems. By leveraging AI analytics and data-driven insights, educational institutions can better understand the factors contributing to disparities and design targeted interventions. For example, AI-powered personalized learning platforms can help identify and address individual learning gaps, ensuring that all students receive the necessary support to succeed (European Commission, 2021). Equity as an ethical guideline requires the fair allocation of resources in AI implementation. AI technologies should not perpetuate or exacerbate existing resource inequalities. Educational institutions should ensure that AI systems are accessible to all students, regardless of their socioeconomic backgrounds or geographical locations. Efforts should be made to provide equal access to AI-powered educational tools, resources, and technologies. By promoting the equitable distribution of resources, AI can help level the playing field and provide equal opportunities for all learners (OECD, 2019). Equity in AI implementation entails promoting diversity and representation in AI systems. AI algorithms should be designed to recognize and account for the diversity of students, including different ethnicities, genders, cultures, and abilities. Educational institutions should actively seek diverse perspectives and ensure that the development and training of AI systems involve a wide range of voices. By embracing diversity and representation, AI can avoid reinforcing existing inequalities and foster an inclusive and equitable learning environment (Bulger et al., 2019).

This chapter adapted constructivist theory to discuss the ethical guidelines for using AI in education. Moreover, this chapter intends to discuss the methods and approaches that could be used to ensure the effective and efficient use of AI in the education sector. The chapter was based on a case study design, and researchers used an ethnography as a qualitative research approach to get insights from the participants on their perceptions and views on diversity, inclusion, and equity in the use of AI in education. In light of the results, it is apparent that protecting personal data and limiting its possible leakages is one of the issues posed by the widespread usage of data. Data governance management is crucial because more or proper governance can lead to information loss. Indeed, "data governance" is predicated on principles like data quality management, data localization, and the identification of actors who can take such measures on such data in such a scenario and using such a manner.

However, the indicated countries can retrieve all data flowing through their jurisdiction thanks to the US Cloud Act and China's Global Data Security Initiative. Therefore, data governance is a severe concern for Europeans, who have every reason to want to keep their data within the European Union (EU), where it can be better protected and safeguarded from unauthorized use. There is a need to validate AI systems to assure their trustworthiness and address data concerns. Because AI in education has the potential to profoundly impact some of the most impressionable people in society—children—safety measures must be taken. The goal of validating an AI system is to consider many concepts, such as the system's resilience, transparency, and explainability of its methods. These ideas are intertwined with the quest to rid AI of the prejudice that has long plagued its operations. Algorithmic validation of AI provides users with confidence in the system's accuracy. It gives them insight into how the system operates, which is essential for building trust in AI. Furthermore, since 2015, new school curricula in France have included teaching algorithms from the fourth grade onward, reflecting the country's recognition of the significance of these technical breakthroughs and the societal difficulties they present.

THEMATIC ANALYSIS

Artificial intelligence of education, for example, incorporating an illustration of how (AIED) can be used to enable Artificial neural networks, machine learning, and CALL (Computer-Assisted Language Learning) to be used in formal, non-formal, and informal learning settings thanks to new paradigms of instruction, technological advancement, and breakthroughs in educational research. As stated by Akgun and Greenhow (2021), it encourages using automated evaluation, facial recognition technologies, and predictive analytics while lowering the cost of personally customized education. This is why there is mounting proof that AIED can "foster a transformation of knowledge, cognition, and culture" (Hwang et al., 2020). However, there have been many roadblocks to implementing AIED due to ethical and legal concerns. Despite recent efforts to formulate such guidelines, the issue of a global agreement and standards for AIED still needs to be addressed. As regulation and ethical consensus of these technologies are required for exploiting their various possibilities in education, this study aims to present an integrative overview of ethical principles for AIED.

AIED has the potential to change the face of education altogether. However, Kay & Kummerfeld (2019) note that this "highly technology-dependent and cross-disciplinary field" (Hwang et al., 2020) creates several challenges for anyone studying or implementing associated systems or procedures. Developing quality and inclusive data systems, making research on AIED significant, ensuring ethics and transparency in data collection, use, and dissemination, and preparing teachers for AI-powered education are the six challenges facing artificial intelligence in education (AIED) identified by UNESCO (2019) for achieving sustainable development of AIED on a global scale. There are significant societal consequences, such as systemic prejudice, discrimination, unfairness for marginalized student groups, and xenophobia, as well as complex ethical challenges connected to privacy and bias in gathering and analyzing information (Holmes et al., 2021; Hwang et al., 2020) are just two examples of the difficulties individuals face. The commercialization of education and the growing gap between homeschoolers and students in traditional schools are just two examples of the adverse effects that some fear may result from the broad adoption of AIED (Reiss, 2021). The effects of the current COVID-19 pandemic could exacerbate the issue, which could become pervasive AI in every sense, where those involved may be exposed to threats without being aware of them (Borenstein & Howard, 2021). Because of these challenges, educating educators and students on the ethical considerations inherent in AI education is more important than ever.

In addition, Russell and Norvig (2002) and Holmes et al. (2021) note that there are ethical implications and privacy hazards associated with the use of artificial intelligence in education and that it is, therefore, essential to distinguish between doing ethical things and doing things ethically when utilizing AI in this context. Indeed, a wealth of research has shown the emergence of competing ethical themes relating to general AI and artificial intelligence in education, most of which are associated with the liability of data across settings like higher education (Zawacki-Richter et al., 2019; Holstein et al., 2019), schools (Luckin, 2017), and subjects (Hwang & Tu, 2021). These included problems like unfairness, lack of responsibility, statistical apophenia, and more common ones such as a lack of informed consent or a breach of privacy. User confidentiality, integrity, and inclusivity (Deshpande et al., 2017); learner privacy (Sacharidis et al., 2020); identity configuration (Sacharidis et al., 2020); surveillance and consent (Sacharidis et al., 2020), and other AI-related topics have also been called into question. The ethics of data collected for teaching and learning analytics has also been a concern. Among these are the power dynamics between stakeholders, including students, teachers, and educational goals; the nuances of data interpretation and administration; and the range of viewpoints on how data is used. Problems with data collection, limited availability of data sources, bias and representation, data ownership and control, data autonomy, the artificial intelligence of education systems, and human agency are also a concern when it comes to the ethics of AI in education (Akgun & Greenhow, 2021; Miao et al., 2021). In order to make ethical and accountability-driven judgments in education, it is essential to have a firm grasp of these guiding principles.

Recent efforts to build distinct ethical frameworks for general AI use (Ashok et al., 2022) may not apply to education because of the suggested contextualization of ethical and privacy issues (Ifenthaler & Schumacher, 2016). Concerns about ethics and privacy in the educational setting may be best addressed by taking a contextual approach to the design and use of AI in education. According to previous studies, the sociotechnical framework set by educational technology and pedagogical practices is crucial to ethical issues (Kitto & Knight, 2019). Ethical and trustworthy artificial intelligence for education could be developed and adopted if people had a deeper grasp of ethics and privacy from various perspectives. In addition, we broadened Ashok et al.'s (2022) ethical perspective by considering the policies and standards put forward by international organizations like UNESCO, the OECD, and the European Union. An all-encompassing and coordinated set of recommendations for implementing AI in education might be derived from a consensual evaluation of relevant policies and principles. This helps lay the groundwork for expanding the use of AI in education and implementing its benefits moving forward.

More effort is needed to enforce ethical guidelines for AI systems to better align with societal values, and there have been repeated calls for comprehensive ethical guidelines and open communications with beneficiaries (Berendt et al., 2020; Nigam et al., 2021; Hagendorff, 2020). There must be safeguards and human control for these AI systems as they are developed, used, and improved. Dhanrajani (2018) argues that developers of AI would be intrinsically motivated by behavioral science knowledge, emphasizing self-awareness and empathy. This paper aimed to employ inductive analysis, modeled after Braun and Clarke's (2012) thematic analysis process, to extract and expand upon a core set of themes. The analysis begins with a basic understanding of the relevant ethical standards and relevant reports. This required rereading the reports and recording commonalities such as terminology, topics covered, and definitions used. After that, we use an open coding method to assign unique codes to each group of related concepts and definitions. The result was 39 unique codes. After that, we looked at the more significant meaning patterns among the codes and extracted seven overarching themes (principles). A researcher-researcher corroboration technique was also in place to ensure the authenticity and trustworthiness of the proposed principles and code mapping during the iterative coding and theme-generating process (Patton, 2015).

Because of the novel ways in which AI use influences human thinking, interaction, and decision-making and affects education, human, social, and natural sciences, culture, communication, and information, we must acknowledge the profound and dynamic positive and negative effects of AI on societies, environments, ecosystems, and human lives, including the human mind. While artificial intelligence (AI) has the potential to improve life on Earth and in all countries, it also raises ethical concerns, such as the need for transparency and understanding of algorithmic workings; the threat to cultural, social, and biological diversity and social or economic divides; and the embedding and exacerbation of biases.

Justice, trust, and fairness must be upheld so that no country and no one is left behind, either by having fair access to AI technologies and enjoying their benefits or by protecting against their harmful effects while taking into account the unique circumstances of each country and the legitimate concerns of those who do not want to see their way of life compromised by artificial intelligence. The risks of misinformation, disinformation, hate speech, and personal data misuse will only increase with the development of AI technology; therefore, data, media, information literacy, and access to independent, pluralistic, credible sources of information are necessary. Although many positive outcomes can result from the development of AI technologies, the process of implementing them can amplify tensions related to innovation, asymmetric access to knowledge and technologies (such as the public's digital and civic literacy deficit, which hinders their ability to engage in AI topics), information barriers and capacity gaps, as well as human and institutional capacities, technological innovation barriers, and inadequate physical infrastructure.

Using information requires respect for international law and national authority. This means that States can, by international law, regulate the data created on or transiting their territories and take steps toward effective regulation of data, including data protection, based on respect for the right to privacy and other human rights norms and standards. For inclusive approaches to AI governance, where the benefits can be shared by all and sustainable development is furthered, stakeholder participation across the whole life cycle of an AI system is required. Governments, NGOs, academics, activists, journalists, policy wonks, business leaders, civil rights groups, equality advocates, anti-discrimination watchdogs, youth organizations, and children's advocacy groups are all examples of stakeholders. Open standards and interoperability should be implemented to make teamwork easier. In the case of Indigenous Peoples, appropriate steps should be taken to respect their right to self-governance of their data and to ensure that marginalized groups, communities, and individuals can participate meaningfully in the decision-making process.

Following are specific policy areas where the values and principles outlined in this Recommendation can be put into effect. Governments should take the lead in implementing effective measures, such as policy frameworks or mechanisms, and ensuring that other stakeholders, including businesses, universities, and civil society, adhere to them. This can be done partly by encouraging all stakeholders to develop human rights, the rule of law, democracy, ethical impact assessment, and due diligence tools aligning with these principles. All relevant parties should be consulted during the policy or mechanism development process, and each Government's unique situation and priorities should be considered. When working with countries, UNESCO may assist with creating and evaluating policy processes.

UNESCO recognizes that states may differ in their levels of preparedness to effectively implement this Recommendation, considering various factors such as scientific, technological, economic, educational, legal, regulatory, infrastructure, sociological, cultural, and other relevant elements. It is important to emphasize that "readiness" is a subjective condition within this particular context. Consequently, UNESCO intends to undertake two key initiatives. Firstly, it aims to create a methodology for readiness assessment, which will assist Member States in determining their level of preparedness for implementing the Recommendation above. This methodology will encompass various dimensions and enable governments to identify their position along a continuum. Secondly, UNESCO will support interested governments by aiding in developing an Ethical Impact Assessment (EIA) methodology designed explicitly for AI technologies.

Additionally, UNESCO will facilitate the exchange of best practices and explore alternative avenues of assistance. It is recommended that governments adopt risk prevention, mitigation, and monitoring strategies alongside ethical impact assessment frameworks in order to identify and assess the advantages, concerns, and risks associated with artificial intelligence systems. In alignment with the values and principles delineated in this Recommendation, impact assessments must examine the effects on human rights and fundamental freedoms. This includes, but is not restricted to, the rights of marginalized and vulnerable individuals or those in precarious circumstances, labor rights, the environment, and ecosystems, as well as ethical and social ramifications.

To better forecast outcomes, reduce risks, prevent unintended consequences, encourage citizen engagement, and address societal concerns, governments should create a legislative framework that lays out a mechanism, especially for public authorities, to conduct ethical impact evaluations on AI systems. Algorithms, data, and design processes may all be evaluated with the help of this evaluation, and the external review of AI systems should also be established as part of this process. Ethical impact assessments must be conducted in an open and public manner. Multicultural, pluralistic, inclusive, and interdisciplinary approaches are encouraged in these evaluations. Authorities at all levels of Government should be obligated to keep an eye on the artificial intelligence systems they develop and use.

Governments should guarantee that AI governance processes are open and accessible to all interested parties, as well as being transparent, multidisciplinary, multilateral (allowing for cross-border harm mitigation and reparation), and include multiple stakeholders. In particular, governance must cover foresight, efficient protection, impact monitoring, enforcement, and reparation. To guarantee that human rights, fundamental freedoms, and the rule of law are respected in both the digital and physical spheres, governments should investigate and redress harms caused through AI systems by enacting robust enforcement mechanisms and remedial actions. Remediation options offered by private and public companies should be included in such procedures and actions. This can be achieved by encouraging auditability and traceability in AI systems. Governments should also work with researchers and other stakeholders to detect, prevent, and mitigate any malicious applications of AI systems, and they should develop their institutional capacities to deliver on this pledge. Governments are urged to develop national and regional AI strategies and consider forms of soft governance, such as a certification mechanism for AI systems and the mutual recognition of their certification, considering the sensitivity of the application domain and expected impact on human rights, the environment and ecosystems, and other ethical considerations outlined in this Recommendation.

Ethical considerations could be factored into the design of this mechanism, which could involve multiple tiers of auditing of systems, data and adherence to ethical principles and procedural requirements. However, this method should not burden small and medium-sized businesses, start-ups, the civil sector, or scientific and academic institutions. To ensure robustness, continuous integrity, and adherence to ethical principles across the AI system's entire life cycle, these methods should also contain a component for regular monitoring, with recertification required if necessary. It is essential to remember that the context of artificial intelligence in education and its influences on constructivist theory is the only place to make sense of the theoretical account of constructivist theory and its growth (Tuitt et al., 2018). This research confirms the assertion made by Claxton (2015) that "the fact we are fundamentally doers means we are also inveterate makers." Since bias presents itself in the AIED system with biased training data, data quality is critical in evaluating whether AIED might produce accurate and impartial conclusions (Borgesius, 2018; Digital Curation Centre, 2020)—multiple sources of skewed information, including sexual orientation, race, ethnicity, and special education requirements. West-Smith et al. (2018) provide a helpful example in the field of language education technology in which input data in the form of rubric writing and scoring systems may impose limitations on student task selection and writing preferences. Ethical rules for applying artificial intelligence in education require, therefore, unbiased data to prevent the development of biased algorithms.

CONCLUSION

The use of AI in education holds immense potential, but robust ethical guidelines must accompany it. Transparency, accountability, privacy, and equity are the pillars upon which these guidelines should be built. Ongoing training and awareness programs should be provided to educators and stakeholders to ensure they understand AI's ethical considerations and implications in education. Additionally, regular audits and evaluations should be conducted to assess the impact and effectiveness of AI systems, identify and address biases or unintended consequences, and make necessary improvements. Feedback from students, educators, and other stakeholders should be actively sought and incorporated into designing and implementing AI technologies in education.

International cooperation and information sharing among countries and organizations can contribute to developing comprehensive and globally accepted ethical guidelines. This collaboration can help address the challenges posed by the rapid advancements in AI technology and ensure that AI is utilized in education for the benefit of all learners. Educational institutions, policymakers, developers, and stakeholders must collaborate to develop and enforce ethical standards that ensure AI systems enhance the educational experience without compromising student well-being, privacy, or social equality. By adhering to these ethical guidelines, we can harness the transformative power of AI to create a more inclusive and equitable educational landscape.

AI systems in education should uphold strong privacy and data protection principles to safeguard the personal information of students and educators. This includes obtaining informed consent, anonymizing data when possible, and implementing robust security measures. Institutions must adhere to relevant laws such as the General Data Protection Regulation (GDPR) in the European Union (GDPR, 2019). AI algorithms used in education should be transparent and explainable to ensure that decisions made by these systems can be understood and justified. It is essential to avoid using "black box" algorithms that make decisions without providing clear explanations, as this can undermine trust and accountability (Floridi et al., 2018). AI should be developed and deployed in education to promote equity and fairness. This involves avoiding biases in data collection, algorithm design, and implementation that could perpetuate or exacerbate existing social inequalities.

Regular audits and ongoing monitoring are necessary to ensure that AI systems do not discriminate against any particular group (Crawford et al., 2019). AI technologies should be designed to be inclusive and accessible, accommodating diverse learners with varying abilities and needs. This includes providing appropriate support for learners with disabilities and ensuring that AI systems do not create educational barriers or reinforce existing biases (Darling-Hammond et al., 2017). Student data collected through AI systems should be used solely for educational purposes and not be exploited for commercial gain or any other unauthorized purposes. Institutions must establish clear policies regarding collecting, storing, and using student data, focusing on maintaining confidentiality and respecting individual rights. (OECD, 2019).

AI systems used in education should be subject to ongoing evaluation to assess their effectiveness, identify potential biases, and address unintended consequences. Regular feedback from students, educators, and other stakeholders should be sought to improve the design and functionality of AI technologies in education (Floridi et al., 2018). Given the prevailing linguistic, social, and cultural disparities, various stakeholders such as governments, intergovernmental organizations, civil society, academia, the media, community leaders, and the private sector must collaborate in order to enhance public awareness and comprehension of artificial intelligence (AI) technologies and the significance of data. This can be achieved through the implementation of inclusive and easily accessible educational initiatives, active civic participation, the provision of digital skills and AI ethics training, as well as media and information literacy programs.

REFERENCES

Australian Government. (2020). *Artificial Intelligence (AI) Ethics Framework*. Australian Government. https://www.aiia.com.au/Documents/ethics_framework.pdf

Becker, M., Lepori, B., & Kedziora, D. (2018). Intelligent Tutoring Systems: A Review of the Ethical Issues. In *Proceedings of the 26th International Conference on Computers in Education* (pp. 493-502). IEEE.

Bolukbasi, T., Chang, K. W., Zou, J. Y., Saligrama, V., & Kalai, A. T. (2016). *Man is to Computer Programmer as Woman is to Homemaker?* Debiasing Word Embeddings. In Advances in Neural Information Processing Systems.

Bulger, M., Ciancio, A., Faulkner, D., Stobart, G., & Deterding, S. (2019). *Ethical AI in Education*. Nesta.

Clarke, S. (2019). Ethical Considerations for AI in Education. In *Proceedings of the 25th International Conference on Computers in Education* (pp. 38–43). IEEE.

Coniam, D. (2020). Ethical Issues in Using AI for Language Learning: A Perspective from CALL. *Computer Assisted Language Learning*, *33*(1-2), 53–71.

Crawford, K., Dobbe, R., Fried, G., Joon, M., Lewis, D., & West, S. M. (2019). The AI Now Report 2018. AI Now Institute. Retrieved from https://ainowinstitute.org/AI_Now_2018_Report.pdf

Darling-Hammond, L. (2017). *AI in Education: Automatic Teaching?* Stanford University. Retrieved from https://edpolicy.stanford.edu/sites/default/files/publications/ai-in-education-report.pdf

European Commission. (2021). *Ethics Guidelines for Trustworthy AI*. EC. https://ec.europa.eu/digital-single-market/en/news/ethics-guidelines-trustworthy-ai

Floridi, L., Cowls, J., Beltrametti, M., Chatila, R., Chazerand, P., Dignum, V., ... Luetge, C. (2018). AI4People—An Ethical Framework for a Good AI Society: Opportunities, Risks, Principles, and Recommendations. *Minds and Machines*, *28*(4), 689–707. doi:10.100711023-018-9482-5 PMID:30930541

Heikkilä, A., & Kankaanranta, M. (2020). Ethical Perspectives on Learning Analytics: A Systematic Review. *Educational Technology Research and Development*, *68*(2), 461–494.

Holstein, K., Wortman Vaughan, J., Daumé, H. III, Dudík, M., Wallach, H., & Heller, S. (2019). Improving fairness in machine learning systems: What do industry practitioners need? In *Proceedings of the 2019 CHI Conference on Human Factors in Computing Systems* (p. 666). ACM. 10.1145/3290605.3300830

Ifenthaler, D. (2020). Ethical Considerations for AI in Education. Technology. *Knowledge and Learning*, *25*(3), 333–336.

Lepori, B., Becker, M., & Cattaneo, A. (2020). Ethical Challenges of Artificial Intelligence and Big Data in Education. In Ethical Technology and Digital Competence (pp. 227-247). Springer.

Lepri, B., Oliver, N., Letouzé, E., Pentland, A., Vinck, P., & de Montjoye, Y. A. (2018). Fair, transparent, and accountable algorithmic decision-making processes. *Philosophy & Technology*, *31*(4), 611–627. doi:10.100713347-017-0279-x

Liu, M., & Hu, X. (2020). Ethical Issues of AI in Education: An Empirical Study. *International Journal of Emerging Technologies in Learning*, *15*(23), 39–54.

National Science and Technology Council. (2016). *Preparing for the Future of Artificial Intelligence*. White House. https://obamawhitehouse.archives.gov/sites/default/files/whitehouse_files/microsites/ostp/NSTC/preparing_for_the_future_of_ai.pdf

OECD. (2019). *AI in Education: Tertiary Education, Skills, and Lifelong Learning*. OECD Publishing.

OECD. (2019). *AI in Education: Tertiary Education, Skills, and Lifelong Learning*. OECD Publishing.

Rambe, P. (2020). A Framework for Ethical Integration of AI in Education: Core Components and Approaches. In Artificial Intelligence in Education (pp. 295-299). Springer.

Seldon, A., & Abidoye, T. R. (2018). The Ethics of AI in Education: A Research Agenda. *Journal of Learning Analytics*, *5*(3), 169–183.

Selwyn, N. (2019). Should We Be Worried About... Artificial Intelligence in Education? *Learning, Media and Technology*, *44*(1), 1–4.

Shah, M., & Sarker, M. H. (2020). Ethical Considerations of Artificial Intelligence and Intelligent Tutoring Systems in Education. In *Proceedings of the 2020 IEEE Technology and Engineering Education Conference (ITEEA)* (pp. 1-10). IEEE.

Sönmez, V. (2021). Ethical Issues in AI-Based Educational Technologies: A Systematic Literature Review. *Journal of Educational Computing Research*, *59*(7), 1144–1175.

Taylor, K. (2019). Ethical Principles for AI and Education. In *Proceedings of the 9th International Conference on Learning Analytics & Knowledge* (pp. 479-480). IEEE.

UNESCO. (2020). Artificial Intelligence in Education: Challenges and Opportunities for Sustainable Development. Retrieved from https://unesdoc.unesco.org/ark:/48223/pf0000374845

UNESCO. (2021). *AI in Education: Ethics Guidelines for UNESCO Member States*. UNESCO. https://en.unesco.org/ai-edu-ethics

Vandewaetere, M., Cornillie, F., & Desmet, P. (2020). Ethical Guidelines for Using Artificial Intelligence in Education: Teachers' Perspectives. *International Journal of Artificial Intelligence in Education*, *30*(4), 526–561.

Voigt, R., Von dem Bussche, A., & Even, M. (2019). Artificial Intelligence in Education: A Critical Look Beyond the Hype. *Journal of Educational Technology*, *16*(2), 41–52.

KEY TERMS AND DEFINITIONS

Artificial Intelligence: To create and use computer systems or machines that can carry out tasks that generally need human intelligence is known as "artificial intelligence" (AI). It includes various approaches and methods to give computers the capacity for perception, reasoning, learning, and decision-making. AI aims to simulate human cognitive processes, such as problem-solving, pattern recognition, natural language understanding, and decision-making, to perform tasks autonomously or with minimal human intervention.

Education: is the acquisition of information and understanding using formal instruction, study, or observation. It is a never-ending procedure that helps people grow in all aspects of themselves: mentally, emotionally, socially, and physically. Education is crucial in personal growth, fostering critical thinking, promoting socialization, and preparing individuals for societal roles.

Ethical Guidelines: are rules or principles for making moral judgments and behavior in a particular context or domain. They serve as a moral compass, guiding individuals or organizations to act by ethical standards and values. Ethical guidelines help ensure responsible and ethical conduct by establishing standards of behavior, promoting fairness, protecting rights, and minimizing harm.

Technology: Use scientific information, apparatus, and techniques to produce usable items, services, or systems. It incorporates an extensive choice of tools, machines, devices, and techniques developed and utilized to solve problems, enhance productivity, and improve the quality of life. Technology is crucial in various domains, including communication, transportation, healthcare, manufacturing, and education.

Compilation of References

Abdelghani, R., Wang, Y.-H., Yuan, X., Wang, T., Lucas, P., Sauzéon, H., & Oudeyer, P.-Y. (2023). Hel'ene' Sauzeon,´ and Pierre-Yves Oudeyer. Gpt-3-driven pedagogical agents to train children's curious question-asking skills. *International Journal of Artificial Intelligence in Education.* doi:10.100740593-023-00340-7

Abdi, S., Khosravi, H., Sadiq, S., & Gasevic, D. (2020, March). Complementing educational recommender systems with open learner models. In *Proceedings of the Tenth International Conference on Learning Analytics & Knowledge* (pp. 360-365). ACM. 10.1145/3375462.3375520

Abdous, M. (2023, March 21). How AI is shaping the future of higher ed. *Inside Higher Ed.* https://www.insidehighered.com/views/2023/03/22/how-ai-shaping-future-higher-ed-opinion

Abuhamdeh, S. (2020). Investigating the "Flow" Experience: Key Conceptual and Operational Issues. *Frontiers in Psychology, 11*, 158. doi:10.3389/fpsyg.2020.00158 PMID:32116954

Adams, C., Pente, P., Lemermeyer, G., & Rockwell, G. (2023). Ethical principles for artificial intelligence in K-12 education. *Computers and Education: Artificial Intelligence, 4*, 100131. doi:10.1016/j.caeai.2023.100131

Adetayo, A. J. (2023). Artificial intelligence chatbots in academic libraries: The rise of ChatGPT. *Library Hi Tech News, 40*(3), 18–21. doi:10.1108/LHTN-01-2023-0007

Adeyemi, I. O., Esan, A. O., & Aleem, A. (2021). Application of gamification to library services: Awareness, perception, and readiness of academic librarians in Nigeria. *The Electronic Library, 39*(5), 767–781. doi:10.1108/EL-05-2021-0096

Adiguzel, T., Kaya, M. H., & Cansu, F. K. (2023). Revolutionizing education with AI: Exploring the transformative potential of ChatGPT. *Contemporary Educational Technology, 15*(3), 429.

Agata Stachowicz-Stanusch. (2019). *Management and Business Education in the Time of Artificial Intelligence: The Need to Rethink, Retrain, and Redesign.* Information Age Publishing.

Ahmad, N., Murugesan, S., & Kshetri, N. (2023). Generative Artificial Intelligence and the Education Sector. *Computer, 56*(6), 72–76. doi:10.1109/MC.2023.3263576

Ahmad, S. F., Alam, M. M., Rahmat, M. K., Mubarik, M. S., & Hyder, S. I. (2022). Academic and administrative role of artificial intelligence in education. *Sustainability (Basel), 14*(3), 1101. doi:10.3390u14031101

Ahn, J., Nguyen, H., Campos, F., & Young, W. (2021, April). Transforming everyday information into practical analytics with crowdsourced assessment tasks. In *LAK21: 11th International Learning Analytics and Knowledge Conference* (pp. 66-76). ACM. 10.1145/3448139.3448146

Aiken, R. M., & Epstein, R. G. (2000). Ethical guidelines for AI in education: Starting a conversation. *International Journal of Artificial Intelligence in Education, 11*(2), 163–176.

Akgun, S., & Greenhow, C. (2021). Artificial intelligence in education: Addressing ethical challenges in K-12 settings. *AI and Ethics, 2*(3), 431–440. doi:10.100743681-021-00096-7 PMID:34790956

AlAfnan, M. A., Dishari, S., Jovic, M., & Lomidze, K. (2023). Chatgpt as an educational tool: Opportunities, challenges, and recommendations for communication, business writing, and composition courses. *J. Artif. Intell. Technol.* **2023**, *3*, 60–68. Rahimi, F.; Abadi, A.T.B. ChatGPT and publication ethics. *Archives of Medical Research, 54*, 272–274.

Alaghbary, G. S. (2021). Integrating technology with bloom's revised taxonomy: Web 2.0-enabled learning designs for online learning. *Asian EFL Journal, 28*(1), 10–37.

Alenezi, H. S., & Faisal, M. H. (2020). Utilizing crowdsourcing and machine learning in education: Literature review. *Education and Information Technologies, 25*(4), 2971–2986. doi:10.100710639-020-10102-w

Alqahtani, T., Badreldin, H. A., Alrashed, M., & Alshaya, A. I. (2023). The emergent role of artificial intelli-gence, natural learning processing, and large language models in higher education and research. *Research in Social & Administrative Pharmacy, 19*(8), 1236–1242. doi:10.1016/j.sapharm.2023.05.016 PMID:37321925

Alter, S. (2022). Understanding artificial intelligence in the context of usage: Contributions and smartness of algorithmic capabilities in work systems. *International Journal of Information Management, 67*, 102392. doi:10.1016/j.ijinfomgt.2021.102392

Alvero, R. (2023). ChatGPT: Rumors of human providers' demise have been greatly exaggerated. *Fertility and Sterility, 119*(6), 930–931. doi:10.1016/j.fertnstert.2023.03.010 PMID:36921837

Amer, A. (2006). Reflections on bloom's revised taxonomy. *Electronic Journal of Research in Educational Psychology, 4*(8), 213–230.

Amoroso, D., & Tamburrini, G. (2020). Autonomous weapons systems and meaningful human control: Ethical and legal issues. *Current Robotics Reports, 1*(4), 187–194. doi:10.100743154-020-00024-3

Anderson, LKrathwohl, D. (2001). *A taxonomy for learning, teaching, and assessing: A revision of Bloom's taxonomy of educational objectives*. Longman.

Anderson, A. (2019). *Virtual reality, augmented reality and artificial intelligence in special education: A practical guide to supporting students with learning differences*. Routledge. doi:10.4324/9780429399503

Andersson, H., Svensson, A., Frank, C., Rantala, A., Holmberg, M., & Bremer, A. (2022). Ethics education to support ethical competence learning in healthcare: An integrative systematic review. *BMC Medical Ethics, 23*(1), 29. doi:10.118612910-022-00766-z PMID:35305627

Andreas Schleicher - Director for the Directorate of Education and Skills. (n.d.). OECD. https://www.oecd.org/education/andreas-schleicher.htm

Andrews, D., Leitner, P., Schön, S., & Ebner, M. (2022). Developing a Professional Profile of a Digital Ethics Officer in an Educational Technology Unit in Higher Education. In *International Conference on Human-Computer Interaction* (pp. 157-175). Springer, Cham. 10.1007/978-3-031-05657-4_12

Angelo, T. A., & Cross, K. P. (2012). *Classroom assessment techniques*. Jossey Bass Wiley.

Annuš, N. (2023). Weigh the pros and cons of using artificial intelligence in education. *International Journal of Science, Engineering and Technology, 11*(3), 2–5. https://www.ijset.in/wp-content/uploads/IJSET_V11_issue3_385.pdf

Ansong, D., Okumu, M., Albritton, T. J., Bahnuk, E. P., & Small, E. (2020). 'The role of social support and psychological well-being in STEM performance trends across gender and locality: Evidence from Ghana'. *Child Indicators Research, 13*(5), 1655–1673. doi:10.100712187-019-09691-x

Arakpogun, E. O., Elsahn, Z., Olan, F., & Elsahn, F. (2021). Artificial intelligence in Africa: Challenges and opportunities. *The fourth industrial revolution: Implementation of artificial intelligence for growing business success,* 375-388.

Araújo, D., Couceiro, M., Seifert, L., Sarmento, H., & Davids, K. (2021). *Artificial Intelligence in Sport Performance Analysis*. Routledge. doi:10.4324/9781003163589

Araujo, T., Helberger, N., Kruikemeier, S., & De Vreese, C. H. (2020). In AI we trust? Perceptions about automated decision-making by artificial intelligence. *AI & Society, 35*(3), 611–623. doi:10.100700146-019-00931-w

Archibald, M. M., & Clark, A. M. (2023). ChatGTP: What is it and how can nursing and health science education use it? *Journal of Advanced Nursing*, jan.15643. Advance online publication. doi:10.1111/jan.15643 PMID:36942780

Armstrong, S., Bostrom, N., & Shulman, C. (2016). Racing to the precipice: A model of artificial intelligence development. *AI & Society, 31*(2), 201–206. doi:10.100700146-015-0590-y

Ashok, M., Madan, R., Joha, A., & Sivarajah, U. (2022). Ethical framework for artificial intelligence and digital technologies. *International Journal of Information Management, 62*, 102433. doi:10.1016/j.ijinfomgt.2021.102433

Astle, D. E., Bathelt, J., & Holmes, J. (2019). 'Remapping the cognitive and neural profiles of children who struggle at school'. *Developmental Science, 22*(1), 22. doi:10.1111/desc.12747 PMID:30171790

Australian Government. (2019). *Australia's Artificial Intelligence Ethics Framework.* Department of Industry, Science and Resources. https://www.industry.gov.au/publications/australias-artificial-intelligence-ethics-framework

Australian Government. (2020). *Artificial Intelligence (AI) Ethics Framework.* Australian Government. https://www.aiia.com.au/Documents/ethics_framework.pdf

Avnoon, N., Kotliar, D. M., & Rivnai-Bahir, S. (2023). Contextualizing the ethics of algorithms: A socio-professional approach. *New Media & Society*, 14614448221145728. doi:10.1177/14614448221145728

Awad, E., Dsouza, S., Kim, R., Schulz, J., Henrich, J., Shariff, A., Bonnefon, J.-F., & Rahwan, I. (2018). The moral machine experiment. *Nature, 563*(7729), 59–64. doi:10.103841586-018-0637-6 PMID:30356211

Awosanya, Y. (2018). How Nigerian brands and startups are creatively using Chatbots to improve customer experience. *Tech Point.* https://techpoint.africa/2018/02/21/chatbots-in-nigeria/

Aynaud, T. (2020). Python-louvain. *Louvain algorithm for community detection.* GitHub. https://github.com/taynaud/python-louvain

Baidoo-Anu, D.; Owusu Ansah, L. Education in the era of generative artificial intelligence (AI): Understanding the potential benefits of ChatGPT in promoting teaching and learning. *Soc. Sci. Res. Netw.* **2023**.

Baidoo-AnuD.Owusu AnsahL. (2023). Education in the era of generative artificial intelligence (AI): Understanding the potential benefits of ChatGPT in promoting teaching and learning. SSRN 4337484. doi:10.2139/ssrn.4337484

Bakare, O. D., & Okuonghae, N. (2023). Digital Technologies and Resources for Learning Under Lockdown. In Impact of Disruptive Technologies on the Socio-Economic Development of Emerging Countries (pp. 87-103). IGI Global. doi:10.4018/978-1-6684-6873-9.ch006

Bakare, O. D. (2023). Emerging Technologies as a Panacea for Sustainable Provision of Library Services in Nigeria. In *Global Perspectives on Sustainable Library Practices* (pp. 1–21). IGI Global.

Bakare, O. D., & Ademakinwa, M. A. (2021). The Impact of COVID-19 on Mentorship of Graduate Students in Nigerian Universities. *Journal of the Nigerian Pastoral Counselling Association*, *1*(1), 15–19.

Bandlamudi, L. (2015). *Difference, dialogue, and development: A Bakhtinian world.* Academic Press.

Bareis, J., & Katzenbach, C. (2022). Talking AI into being: The narratives and imaginaries of national AI strategies and their performative politics. *Science, Technology & Human Values*, *47*(5), 855–881. doi:10.1177/01622439211030007

Barnett, S. (2023, January 30). ChatGPT is making universities rethink plagiarism. *Wired.* https://www.wired.com/story/chatgpt-college-university-plagiarism/

Barret, M., Branson, L., Carter, S., DeLeon, F., Ellis, J., Gundlach, C., & Lee, D. (2019). Using artificial intelligence to enhance educational opportunities and student services in higher education. *Inquiry*, *22*(1), 1–11.

Barua, P. D., Vicnesh, J., Gururajan, R., Oh, S. L., Palmer, E., Azizan, M. M., Kadri, N. A., & Acharya, U. R. (2022). Artificial intelligence enabled personalised assistive tools to enhance education of children with neurodevelopmental disorders—A review. *International Journal of Environmental Research and Public Health*, *19*(3), 1192. doi:10.3390/ijerph19031192 PMID:35162220

Bastani, H., Bastani, O., & Kim, C. (2018). Interpreting predictive models for human-in-the-loop analytics. *arXiv preprint arXiv:1705.08504.*

Becker, M., Lepori, B., & Kedziora, D. (2018). Intelligent Tutoring Systems: A Review of the Ethical Issues. In *Proceedings of the 26th International Conference on Computers in Education* (pp. 493-502).

Benbya, H., Davenport, T. H., & Pachidi, S. (2020). Artificial intelligence in organizations: Current state and future opportunities. *MIS Quarterly Executive*, *19*(4).

Benjamin, S. (1956). *Taxonomy of educational objectives: The classification of educational goals.* Longmans, Green.

Bessen, J., Impink, S. M., & Seamans, R. (2022, July). The cost of ethical AI development for AI startups. In *Proceedings of the 2022 AAAI/ACM Conference on AI, Ethics, and Society* (pp. 92-106). ACM. 10.1145/3514094.3534195

Bhatia, R. (2019). Indian AI Startup Funding 2018: Total Global Investment In India Touched USD$ 529.52 Million. *Analytics India Magazine.* https://analyticsindiamag.com/indian-ai-startup-funding-total-global-investment-in-india-touched-usd-529-52-million/

Bigman, Y. E., & Gray, K. (2018). People are averse to machines making moral decisions. *Cognition*, *181*, 21–34. doi:10.1016/j.cognition.2018.08.003 PMID:30107256

Birhane, A. (2021). The impossibility of automating ambiguity. *Artificial Life*, *27*(1), 44–61. doi:10.1162/artl_a_00336 PMID:34529757

Blanchard, E. G. (2012). On the weird nature of ITS/AIED conferences. In *International Conference on Intelligent Tutoring Systems* (Vol. 7315, pp. 280–285). Springer. 10.1007/978-3-642-30950-2_36

Boase, J. (2008). Personal networks and the personal communication system: Using multiple media to connect. *Information Communication and Society*, *11*(4), 490–508. doi:10.1080/13691180801999001

Bolukbasi, T., Chang, K. W., Zou, J. Y., Saligrama, V., & Kalai, A. T. (2016). *Man is to Computer Programmer as Woman is to Homemaker?* Debiasing Word Embeddings. In Advances in Neural Information Processing Systems.

Bommasani, R., Hudson, D. A., Adeli, E., Altman, R., Arora, S., von Arx, S., & Liang, P. (2021). On the opportunities and risks of foundation models. *arXiv preprint arXiv:2108.07258.*

Bonderud, D. (2019). *Artificial intelligence, authentic impact: How education AI is making the grade.* EdTech. https://edtechmagazine.com/k12/article/2019/08/artificialintelligence-authentic-impact-how-educational-ai-making-grade-perfcon

Borenstein, J., & Howard, A. (2021). Emerging challenges in AI and the need for AI ethics education. *AI and Ethics, 1*(1), 61–65. doi:10.100743681-020-00002-7

Borenstein, J., Mahajan, H. P., Wagner, A. R., & Howard, A. (2020). Trust and pediatric exoskeletons: A comparative study of clinician and parental perspectives. *IEEE Transactions on Technology and Society, 1*(2), 83–88. doi:10.1109/TTS.2020.2974990

Borokini, F., Wakunuma, K., & Akintoye, S. (2023). The Use of Gendered Chatbots in Nigeria: Critical Perspectives. In *Responsible AI in Africa: Challenges and Opportunities* (pp. 119–139). Springer International Publishing. doi:10.1007/978-3-031-08215-3_6

Bortoló, G. M., Valdés, J. Á., & Nicolas-Sans, R. (2023). Sustainable, technological, and innovative challenges post Covid-19 in health, economy, and education sectors. *Technological Forecasting and Social Change, 190*, 122424. doi:10.1016/j.techfore.2023.122424 PMID:36811031

Bouchrika, I. (2023, June 28). *College dropout rates: 2023 Statistics by race, gender & income.* Research.com. https://research.com/universities-colleges/college-dropout-rates

Bozkurt, A. (2020). Educational technology research patterns in the realm of the digital knowledge age. *Journal of Interactive Media in Education, 2020*(1), 18. doi:10.5334/jime.570

Bozkurt, A. (2023). Generative artificial intelligence (AI) powered conversational educational agents: The inevitable paradigm shift. *Asian Journal of Distance Education, 18*(1).

Bozkurt, A., Xiao, J., Lambert, S., Pazurek, A., Crompton, H., Koseoglu, S., Farrow, R., Bond, M., Nerantzi, C., & Honeychurch, S. (2023). Speculative Futures on ChatGPT and Generative Artificial Intelligence (AI): A collective reflection from the educational landscape. *Asian J. Distance Educ, 18*, 50–130.

Bozkurt, A., Xiao, J., Lambert, S., Pazurek, A., Crompton, H., Koseoglu, S., & Jandrić, P. (2023). Speculative futures on ChatGPT and generative artificial intelligence (AI): A collective reflection from the educational landscape. *Asian Journal of Distance Education, 18*(1).

Brekelmans, M., Wubbels, T., & Den Brok, P. (2002). Teacher experience and the teacher–student relationship in the classroom environment. In S. C. Goh & M. S. Khine (Eds.), *Studies in educational learning environments: An international perspective* (pp. 73–99). World Scientific Publishing. doi:10.1142/9789812777133_0004

Breucker, P., Cointet, J., Hannud Abdo, A., Orsal, G., de Quatrebarbes, C., Duong, T., Martinez, C., Ospina Delgado, J. P., Medina Zuluaga, L. D., Gómez Peña, D. F., Sánchez Castaño, T. A., Marques da Costa, J., Laglil, H., Villard, L., & Barbier, M. (2016). *CorTexT Manager (version v2).* Cortext. https://docs.cortext.net

Brown, A., Chouldechova, A., Putnam-Hornstein, E., Tobin, A., & Vaithianathan, R. (2019). *Toward algorithmic accountability in public services.* Paper presented at the CHI Conference on Human Factors in Computing Systems, Glasgow, Scotland. https://doi.org/10.1145/3290605.3300271https:// desc.12747

Bulger, M., Ciancio, A., Faulkner, D., Stobart, G., & Deterding, S. (2019). *Ethical AI in Education.* Nesta.

Burrell, J., & Fourcade, M. (2021). The society of algorithms. *Annual Review of Sociology, 47*(1), 213–237. doi:10.1146/annurev-soc-090820-020800

Campedelli, G. M. (2021). Where are we? Using Scopus to map the literature at the intersection between artificial intelligence and research on crime. *Journal of Computational Social Science*, *4*(2), 503–530. doi:10.100742001-020-00082-9

Carter, L., Liu, D., & Cantrell, C. (2020). Exploring the intersection of the digital divide and artificial intelligence: A hermeneutic literature review. *AIS Transactions on Human-Computer Interaction*, *12*(4), 253–275. doi:10.17705/1thci.00138

Casas-Roma, J., & Conesa, J. (2021). A literature review on artificial intelligence and ethics in online learning. *Intelligent Systems and Learning Data Analytics in Online Education*, 111-131. . doi:10.1016/B978-0-12-823410-5.00006-1

Castellar, A. A., & Looy, V. J. (2021). Digital Game-Based Learning effectiveness assessment: Reflections on study design. *Computers & Education*, *2021*(167), 104160.

Castillo-Segura, P., Fernández-Panadero, C. Alario-Hoyos,C P.J. Muñoz- Merino, C.PJ., Kloos C.D. (2021). Objective and automated assessment of surgical technical skills with IoT systems: A systematic literature review *Artificial Intelligence in Medicine, 1*, 1-17. . artmed. 2020.102007 10200. doi:10.1016/j

Celik, I. (2023). Towards Intelligent-TPACK: An empirical study on teachers' professional knowledge to ethically integrate artificial intelligence (AI)-based tools in education. *Computers in Human Behavior*, *138*, 107468. doi:10.1016/j.chb.2022.107468

Celik, I., Dindar, M., Muukkonen, H., & Järvelä, S. (2022). The promises and challenges of artificial intelligence for teachers: A systematic review of research. *TechTrends*, *66*(4), 616–630. doi:10.100711528-022-00715-y

Chaowicharat, E., & Dejdumrong, N. (2023). A step toward an automatic handwritten homework grading system for mathematics. *Information Technology and Control*, *52*(1), 169–184. doi:10.5755/j01.itc.52.1.32066

Chassang, G., Thomsen, M., Rumeau, P., Sèdes, F., & Delfin, A. (2021). An interdisciplinary conceptual study of Artificial Intelligence (AI) for helping benefit-risk assessment practices. *AI Communications*, *3*(4), 1–26. doi:10.3233/AIC-201523

ChatGPT and generative AI in the classroom. (n.d.). University of Toronto. https://www.viceprovostundergrad.utoronto.ca/strategic-priorities/digital-learning/special-initiative-artificial-intelligence/

ChatGPT and other AI tools: Challenges, opportunities, and strategies for teaching. (2023, February 14). Boston University. https://www.bu.edu/dli/2023/02/14/chat-gpt-and-other-ai-tools-challenges-opportunities-and-strategies-for-teaching/

Chattopadhyay, S., Shankar, S., Gangadhar, R. B., & Kasinathan, K. (2018). Applications of artificial intelligence in assessment for learning in schools. In J. Keengwe (Ed.), *Handbook of research on digital content, mobile learning, and technology integration models in teacher education* (pp. 185–206). IGI Global. doi:10.4018/978-1-5225-2953-8.ch010

Chaudhry, M. A., & Kazim, E. (2022). Artificial Intelligence in Education (AIEd): A high-level academic and industry note 2021. *AI and Ethics*, *2*(1), 157–165. doi:10.100743681-021-00074-z PMID:34790953

Chen, Y., Chen, Y., & Heffernan, N. (2020). Personalized math tutoring with a conversational agent. arXiv preprint arXiv:2012.12121.

Chen, C., Chen, Y.-M., Hsu, C.-L., & Yu, C.-H. (2021). Effects of a chatbot on student engagement and satisfaction in an online course. *Computers & Education*, *157*, 103951.

Cheng, L., Varshney, K. R., & Liu, H. (2021). Socially responsible AI algorithms: Issues, purposes, and challenges. *Journal of Artificial Intelligence Research*, *71*, 1137–1181. doi:10.1613/jair.1.12814

Chen, J., Chen, Y., Ou, R., Wang, J., & Chen, Q. (2022). How to Use Artificial Intelligence to Improve Entrepreneurial Attitude in Business Simulation Games: Implications From a Quasi-Experiment. *Frontiers in Psychology*, *13*, 856085. doi:10.3389/fpsyg.2022.856085 PMID:36467165

Chen, J., Sun, J., & Wang, G. (2022). From unmanned systems to autonomous intelligent systems. *Engineering (Beijing)*, *12*, 16–19. doi:10.1016/j.eng.2021.10.007

Chen, L., Chen, P., & Lin, Z. (2020). Artificial intelligence in education: A review. *IEEE Access : Practical Innovations, Open Solutions*, *8*, 75264–75278. doi:10.1109/ACCESS.2020.2988510

Chennattuserry, J. C., Varghese, B., Elangovan, N., & Sandhya, H. (2022). Pandemic Recovery Strategies: A Disaster Management Tourism Framework. In *Tourism Through Troubled Times (Tourism Security-Safety and Post Conflict Destinations)* (pp. 133–149). Emerald Publishing Limited. doi:10.1108/978-1-80382-311-920221008

Chen, T. J. (2023). ChatGPT and other artificial intelligence applications speed up scientific writing. *Journal of the Chinese Medical Association*, *86*(4), 351–353. doi:10.1097/JCMA.0000000000000900 doi:10.1097/JCMA.0000000000000900 PMID:36791246

Chen, X., Xie, H., Zou, D., & Hwang, G. J. (2020). Application and theory gaps during the rise of artificial intelligence in education. *Computers and Education: Artificial Intelligence*, *1*, 100002. doi:10.1016/j.caeai.2020.100002

Chen, X., Zou, D., Xie, H., & Cheng, G. (2021). Twenty years of personalized language learning. *Journal of Educational Technology & Society*, *24*, 205–222.

Chounta, I. A., Bardone, E., Raudsep, A., & Pedaste, M. (2022). Exploring teachers' perceptions of artificial intelligence as a tool to support their practice in Estonian K-12 education. *International Journal of Artificial Intelligence in Education*, *32*(3), 725–755. doi:10.100740593-021-00243-5

Clarizia, F., Colace, F., Lombardi, M., Pascale, F., & Santaniello, D. (2018). Chatbot: An education support system for students. In *the International Symposium on Cyberspace Safety and Security* (pp. 291–302). Springer.

Clark, D. (2018). *The Fallacy of "Robot" Teachers*. Donald Clark Plan B. https://donaldclarkplanb. blogspot.com/search?q=10+uses+for+Chatbots+in+learni ng+(with+examples)

Clarke, S. (2019). Ethical Considerations for AI in Education. In *Proceedings of the 25th International Conference on Computers in Education* (pp. 38–43). IEEE.

Colaner, N. (2022). Is explainable artificial intelligence intrinsically valuable? *AI & Society*, 1–8.

Conati, C., Barral, O., Putnam, V., & Rieger, L. (2021). Toward personalized XAI: A case study in intelligent tutoring systems. *Artificial Intelligence*, *298*, 103503. doi:10.1016/j.artint.2021.103503

Coniam, D. (2020). Ethical Issues in Using AI for Language Learning: A Perspective from CALL. *Computer Assisted Language Learning*, *33*(1-2), 53–71.

Connolly, N., & McGuinness, C. (2018). Towards digital literacy for the active participation and engagement of young people in a digital world. In M. Magkou, R. Schwalbach, & B. Spruyt (Eds.), *Perspectives on youth: Young people in a digitalised world* (Vol. 4, pp. 77–92). Council of Europe. https://book.coe.int/en/perspectives-on-youth/7597-perspectives-on-youth-vol-4-young-people-in-a-digitalised-world.html

Cools, H., Van Gorp, B., & Opgenhaffen, M. (2022). Where exactly between utopia and dystopia? A framing analysis of AI and automation in US newspapers. *Journalism*, 14648849221122647. doi:10.1177/14648849221122647

Cooper, G. (2023). Examining science education in ChatGPT: An exploratory study of generative artificial intelligence. *Journal of Science Education and Technology*, *32*(3), 1–9. doi:10.100710956-023-10039-y

Cope, B., & Kalantzis, M. (2019). Education 2.0: Artificial intelligence and the end of the test. *Beijing International Review of Education*, *1*(2-3), 528–543. doi:10.1163/25902539-00102009

Costas-Jauregui, V., Oyelere, S. S., Caussin-Torrez, B., Barros-Gavilanes, G., Agbo, F. J., Toivonen, T., Motz, R., & Tenesaca, J. B. (2021, October). Descriptive analytics dashboard for an inclusive learning environment. In 2021 IEEE Frontiers in Education Conference (FIE) (pp. 1-9). IEEE. doi:10.1109/FIE49875.2021.9637388

Crawford, K., Dobbe, R., Fried, G., Joon, M., Lewis, D., & West, S. M. (2019). The AI Now Report 2018. AI Now Institute. Retrieved from https://ainowinstitute.org/AI_Now_2018_Report.pdf

Dai, C., & Ke, F. (2022). Educational applications of artificial intelligence in simulation-based learning: A systematic mapping review. *Computers and Education: Artificial Intelligence*, *3*, 100087. doi:10.1016/j.caeai.2022.100087

Dan, A. (2020, March 4). Unleashing the power of AI for education. Microsoft. Retrieved from https://www. technologyreview.com/2020/03/04/905535/unleashing-thepower-of-ai-for-education/

Darling-Hammond, L. (2017). *AI in Education: Automatic Teaching?* Stanford University. https://edpolicy.stanford.edu/sites/default/files/publications/ai-in-education-report.pdf

Darling-Hammond, L. (2017). *AI in Education: Automatic Teaching?* Stanford University. Retrieved from https://edpolicy.stanford.edu/sites/default/files/publications/ai-in-education-report.pdf

Dauvergne, P. (2021). The globalization of artificial intelligence: Consequences for the politics of environmentalism. *Globalizations*, *18*(2), 285–299. doi:10.1080/14747731.2020.1785670

Davis, H. A. (2006). Exploring the contexts of relationship quality between middle school students and teachers. *The Elementary School Journal*, *106*(3), 193–223. doi:10.1086/501483

Dawson, P., Henderson, M., Mahoney, P., Phillips, M., Ryan, T., Boud, D., & Molloy, E. (2019). What makes for effffective feedback: Staffff and student perspectives. *Assessment & Evaluation in Higher Education*, *44*(1), 25–36. doi:10.1080/02602938.2018.1467877

De Angelis, L., Baglivo, F., Arzilli, G., Privitera, G. P., Ferragina, P., Tozzi, A. E., & Rizzo, C. (2023). ChatGPT and the rise of large language models: The new AI-driven infodemic threat in public health. *Frontiers in Public Health*, *11*, 1567. doi:10.3389/fpubh.2023.1166120 PMID:37181697

De Bruijn, H., Warnier, M., & Janssen, M. (2022). The perils and pitfalls of explainable AI: Strategies for explaining algorithmic decision-making. *Government Information Quarterly*, *39*(2), 101666. doi:10.1016/j.giq.2021.101666

De Saint Laurent, C. (2018). In defence of machine learning: Debunking the myths of artificial intelligence. *Europe's Journal of Psychology*, *14*(4), 734–747. doi:10.5964/ejop.v14i4.1823 PMID:30555582

Deane, P. (2013). On the relation between automated essay scoring and modern views of the writing construct. *Assessing Writing*, *18*(1), 7–24. doi:10.1016/j.asw.2012.10.002

Deho, O. B., Zhan, C., Li, J., Liu, J., Liu, L., & Duy Le, T. (2022). How do the existing fairness metrics and unfairness mitigation algorithms contribute to ethical learning analytics? *British Journal of Educational Technology*, *53*(4), 822–843. doi:10.1111/bjet.13217

Del-Moral-Pérez, M. E., Villalustre-Martínez, L., & Neira-Piñeiro, M. D. R. (2019). Teachers' perception about the contribution of collaborative creation of digital storytelling to the communicative and digital competence in primary education schoolchildren. *Computer Assisted Language Learning, 32*(4), 342–365. doi:10.1080/09588221.2018.1517094

Devlin, J., Chang, M.-W., Lee, K., & Toutanova, K. (2018). Bert: Pre-training of deep bidirectional transformers for language understanding. In *Proceedings of the 2018 Conference of the North American Chapter of the Association for Computational Linguistics: Human Language Technologies,* (pp. 4171–4186).

Digital Curation Centre Report. (2020). *Global Partnership on Artificial Intelligence*. DCC. https://www.dcc.ac.uk/consultancy/GPAI

Dixon, J. H. B. Jr. (2023). Artificial intelligence— "What hath God wrought.". *The Judges' Journal*, *62*(3), 37–39.

Domenech, J. (2023). ChatGPT in the Classroom: Friend or Foe? *9th International Conference on Higher Education Advances (HEAd'23)*. IEEE. 10.4995/HEAd23.2023.16179

Döring, H. (2019). Public perceptions of the proper role of the state. In *The State in Western Europe Retreat or Redefinition?* (pp. 12–31). Routledge. doi:10.4324/9781315037479-2

Druga, S., Vu, S. T., Likhith, E., & Qiu, T. (2019). Inclusive AI literacy for kids around the world. *Proceedings of FabLearn, 2019*, 104–111. doi:10.1145/3311890.3311904

Duignan, P. A. (2020). *Navigating the future of learning: the role of smart technologies. Leading Educational Systems and Schools in Times of Disruption and Exponential Change: A Call for Courage, Commitment and Collaboration.* Emerald Publishing Limited., doi:10.1108/978-1-83909-850-520201012/full/html

Dwivedi, Y. K., Hughes, L., Ismagilova, E., Aarts, G., Coombs, C., Crick, T., Duan, Y., Dwivedi, R., Edwards, J., Eirug, A., Galanos, V., Ilavarasan, P. V., Janssen, M., Jones, P., Kar, A. K., Kizgin, H., Kronemann, B., Lal, B., Lucini, B., & Williams, M. D. (2021). Artificial Intelligence (AI): Multidisciplinary perspectives on emerging challenges, opportunities, and agenda for research, practice and policy. *International Journal of Information Management*, *57*, 101994. doi:10.1016/j.ijinfomgt.2019.08.002

Eaton, S. E. (2023, March 4). Artificial intelligence and academic integrity, post-plagiarism. *University World News*. https://www.universityworldnews.com/post.php?story=20230228133041549

Eicher, B., Polepeddi, L., & Goel, A. (2018). Jill Watson doesn't care if you're pregnant: Grounding AI ethics in empirical studies. *Proceedings of the 2018 AAAI/ACM Conference on AI, Ethics, and Society* (pp. 88-94). ACM. 10.1145/3278721.3278760

El-Hamamsy, L., Chessel-Lazzarotto, F., Bruno, B., Roy, D., Cahlikova, T., Chevalier, M., Parriaux, G., Pellet, J. P., Lanares, J., Zufferey, J. D., & Mondada, F. (2021). A computer science and robotics integration model for primary school: Evaluation of a large-scale in-service K-4 teacher-training program. *Education and Information Technologies, 26*(3), 2445–2475. doi:10.100710639-020-10355-5 PMID:33162777

Elliott, A. (2019). *The culture of AI: Everyday life and the digital revolution.* Routledge. doi:10.4324/9781315387185

Elsevier. (2022). How Scopus works, Scopus contents. Elsevier. https://www. elsevier.com/solutions/scopus/how-scopus-works/content

Elshafey, A. E., Anany, M. R., Mohamed, A. S., Sakr, N., & Aly, S. G. (2021). Dr. Proctor: A multi-modal AI-based platform for remote proctoring in education. In *International Conference on Artificial Intelligence in Education* (pp. 145-150). Springer, Cham. 10.1007/978-3-030-78270-2_26

Elshani, L., & Nuçi, K. P. (2021). Constructing a personalized learning path using genetic algorithms approach. *ArXiv. /abs/2104.11276*

Erbil, D. G. (2020). A review of flipped classroom and cooperative learning method within the context of Vygotsky theory. *Frontiers in Psychology*, *11*, 1157. doi:10.3389/fpsyg.2020.01157 PMID:32655437

Essel, H. B., Butakor, P. K., & Nortey, S. (2019). Summative e-examination for high stake assessment in higher education: A case of undergraduate students at the Kwame Nkrumah University of Science and Technology. *Global Journal of Human-Social Science: Arts & Humanities-Psychology, 19*, 03.

Essien, A., Chukwukelu, G., & Essien, V. (2021). Opportunities and challenges of adopting artificial intelligence for learning and teaching in higher education. In M. B. Ali & T. Wood-Harper (Eds.), *Fostering communication and learning with underutilized technologies in higher education* (pp. 67–78). Information Science Reference/IGI Global., doi:10.4018/978-1-7998-4846-2.ch005

European Commission Report (2021). The EU in 2021. EC. https://op.europa.eu/webpub/com/general-report-2021/en/

European Commission Report. (2018). *Annual Activity Report.* EC. https://commission.europa.eu/publications/annual-activity-reports-2018_en

European Commission. (2021). *Ethics Guidelines for Trustworthy AI.* EC. https://ec.europa.eu/digital-single-market/en/news/ethics-guidelines-trustworthy-ai

European Commission. (2021). *Ethics Guidelines for Trustworthy AI.* European Commission. https://ec.europa.eu/digital-single-market/en/news/ethics-guidelines-trustworthy-ai

European Parliament. (2021). Report on artificial intelligence in education, culture and the audiovisual sector (2020/2017(INI)). Committee on Culture and Education. https://www.europarl.europa.eu/ doceo/document/A-9-2021-0127_EN.html

Fadhil, A., & Villafiorita, A. (2017). An Adaptive Learning with Gamification & Conversational UIs: The Rise of CiboPoliBot. In *25th Conference on User Modeling, Adaptation and Personalization* (pp. 408–412). 10.1145/3099023.3099112

Fahimnia, B., Sarkis, J., & Davarzani, H. (2015). Green supply chain management: A review and bibliometric analysis. *International Journal of Production Economics*, *162*, 101–114. doi:10.1016/j.ijpe.2015.01.003

Farrokhnia, M., Banihashem, S. K., Noroozi, O., & Wals, A. (2023). A SWOT analysis of ChatGPT: Implications for educational practice and research. *Innovations in Education and Teaching International*, •••, 1–15. doi:10.1080/14703297.2023.2195846

Farrow, E. (2021). Mindset matters: How mindset affects the ability of staff to anticipate and adapt to Artificial Intelligence (AI) future scenarios in organisational settings. *AI & Society*, *36*(3), 895–909. doi:10.100700146-020-01101-z PMID:33223620

Faulconer, E., Griffiffiffith, J., & Gruss, A. (2021). the impact of positive feedback on student outcomes and perceptions. *Assessment & Evaluation in Higher Education*, *47*(2), 1–10.

Federspiel, F., Mitchell, R., Asokan, A., Umana, C., & McCoy, D. (2023). Threats by artificial intelligence to human health and human existence. *BMJ Global Health*, *8*(5), e010435. doi:10.1136/bmjgh-2022-010435 PMID:37160371

Felix, C. V. (2020). The role of the teacher and AI in education. In E. Sengupta, P. Blessinger, & M. S. Makhanya (Eds.), *International perspectives on the role of technology in humanizing higher education* (Vol. 33, pp. 33–48). Emerald Publishing., doi:10.1108/S2055-364120200000033003

Fernando, A. F. L., David, R. H. T., & Roque, M. M. (2023). Personalized tutoring: Chatgpt as a virtual tutor for personalized learning experiences. *Przestrzen Spoleczna*, *23*(1), 292–312.

Finkel, M., & Krämer, N. C. (2022). Humanoid robots–artificial. Human-like. Credible? Empirical comparisons of source credibility attributions between humans, humanoid robots, and non-human-like devices. *International Journal of Social Robotics*, *14*(6), 1397–1411. doi:10.100712369-022-00879-w

Fleming, M. (2018). Streamlining student course requests using chatbots. [Conference Session]. *29th Australasian Association for Engineering Education Conference 2018 (AAEE 2018).* Engineers Australia. https://search.informit.org/doi/epdf/10.3316/ informit.166919861347542

Floridi, L., & Cowls, J. (2022). A unified framework of five principles for AI in society. *Machine learning and the city: Applications in architecture and urban design*, 535-545

Floridi, L. (2018). Soft ethics and the governance of the digital. *Philosophy & Technology*, *31*(1), 1–8. doi:10.100713347-018-0303-9 PMID:30322997

Floridi, L. (2021). Translating principles into practices of digital ethics: Five risks of being unethical. In *Ethics, Governance, and Policies in Artificial Intelligence* (pp. 81–90). Springer. doi:10.1007/978-3-030-81907-1_6

Floridi, L., & Cowls, J. (2019). A unified framework of five principles for AI in society. *Harvard Data Science Review*, *1*(1).

Floridi, L., Cowls, J., Beltrametti, M., Chatila, R., Chazerand, P., Dignum, V., & Luetge, C. (2018). AI4People—An Ethical Framework for a Good AI Society: Opportunities, Risks, Principles, and Recommendations. *Minds and Machines*, *28*(4), 689–707. doi:10.100711023-018-9482-5 PMID:30930541

Font de la Vall, R. R., & Araya, F´. G´. (2023, January). Exploring the benefits and challenges of AI-language learning tools. *International Journal of Social Sciences and Humanities Invention*, *10*(01), 7569–7576. doi:10.18535/ijsshi/v10i01.02

Fontes, C., Hohma, E., Corrigan, C. C., & Lütge, C. (2022). AI-powered public surveillance systems: Why we (might) need them and how we want them. *Technology in Society*, *71*, 102137. doi:10.1016/j.techsoc.2022.102137

Fox, R. (2001). Constructivism examined. *Oxford Review of Education*, *27*(1), 23–35. doi:10.1080/03054980125310

Fuchs, K. (2023, May). Exploring the opportunities and challenges of NLP models in higher education: Is chat GPT a blessing or a curse? *Frontiers in Education*, *8*, 8. doi:10.3389/feduc.2023.1166682

Ganapini, M. B., Campbell, M., Fabiano, F., Horesh, L., Lenchner, J., Loreggia, A., & Venable, K. B. (2023). Thinking fast and slow in AI: The role of metacognition. In *Machine Learning, Optimization, and Data Science: 8th International Conference, LOD 2022,* (pp. 502-509). Cham: Springer Nature Switzerland.

Gang-Hoon, K., Trimi, S., & Ji-Hyong, C. (2014). Big-data applications in the government sector. *Communications of the ACM*, *57*(3), 78–85. doi:10.1145/2500873

Garcia Brustenga, G., Fuertes-Alpiste, M., Molas-Castells, N. (2018). *Briefing paper: chatbots in education.* Barcelona: eLearn Center. Universitat Oberta de Catalunya., doi:10.7238/elc.chatbots.2018

García-Peñalvo, F. J. (2023). The perception of Artificial Intelligence in educational contexts after the launch of ChatGPT: Disruption or Panic? .

Gardner, J., O'Leary, M., & Yuan, L. (2021). Artificial intelligence in educational assessment: 'Breakthrough? Or buncombe and ballyhoo?'. *Journal of Computer Assisted Learning*, *37*(5), 1207–1216. doi:10.1111/jcal.12577

Gedrimiene, E., Silvola, A., Pursiainen, J., Rusanen, J., & Muukkonen, H. (2020). Learning analytics in education: Literature review and case examples from vocational education. *Scandinavian Journal of Educational Research*, *64*(7), 1105–1119. doi:10.1080/00313831.2019.1649718

General Data Protection Regulation (GDPR). (2019). *Home.* GDPR. https://gdpr-info.eu/

Germain, T. (2023, January 20). The CEO behind ChatGPT says schools need to get over their cheating fears. Some experts agree. *Gizmodo.* https://gizmodo.com/chatgpt-openai-ceo-sam-altman-schools-cheating-1850011314

Ghajargar, M., Bardzell, J., & Lagerkvist, L. (2022, November). A redhead walks into a bar: Experiences of writing fiction with artificial intelligence. In *Academic Mindtrek 2022: Proceedings of the 25th International Academic Mindtrek Conference* (pp. 230–241). Association for Computing Machinery. 10.1145/3569219.3569418

Gilson, A., Safranek, C. W., Huang, T., Socrates, V., Chi, L., Taylor, A., & Chartash, D. (2023). How does ChatGPT perform on the United States medical Licensing examination? The implications of large language Models for Medical Education and knowledge Assessment. *JMIR Medical Education*, *9*, e45312. doi:10.2196/45312 PMID:36753318

Gocen, A., & Aydemir, F. (2021). Artificial intelligence in education and schools. *Research on Education and Media*, *12*(1), 13–21. doi:10.2478/rem-2020-0003

Gondwe, G. (2023). *CHATGPT and the Global South: How are journalists in sub-Saharan Africa engaging with generative AI?* Online Media and Global Communication.

González-Calatayud, V., Prendes-Espinosa, P., & Roig-Vila, R. (2021). Artificial intelligence for student assessment: A systematic review. *Applied Sciences (Basel, Switzerland)*, *11*(12), 5467. doi:10.3390/app11125467

Goralski, M. A., & Tan, T. K. (2020). Artificial intelligence and sustainable development. *International Journal of Management Education*, *18*(1), 100330. doi:10.1016/j.ijme.2019.100330

Göschlberger, B., & Brandstetter, C. (2019, December). Conversational AI for corporate e-learning. In *Proceedings of the 21st International Conference on Information Integration and Web-based Applications & Services* (pp. 674-678). IEEE.

GPTChat. (2023, July 12). *ChatGPT: The Most Advanced AI Chatbot By OpenAI* [Video]. ChatGPT Pro. https://chatgpt.pro/

Gruber, T. R. (1993). A translation approach to portable ontology specifications. *Knowledge Acquisition*, *5*(2), 199–220. doi:10.1006/knac.1993.1008

Guilherme, A. (2017). AI and education: The importance of teacher and student relations. *AI & Society*, *34*(1), 47–54. doi:10.100700146-017-0693-8

Gupta, S., & Chen, Y. (2022). Supporting inclusive learning using chatbots? A chatbot-led interview study. *Journal of Information Systems Education*, *33*(1), 98–108.

Gutnik, L., Hakimzada, A. F., Yoskowitz, N. A., & Patel, V. L. (2006). The role of emotion in decision-making: A cognitive neuroeconomic approach towards understanding sexual risk behavior. *Journal of Biomedical Informatics*, *39*(6), 720–736. doi:10.1016/j.jbi.2006.03.002 PMID:16759915

Hakami, E., & Hernández Leo, D. (2020). How are learning analytics considering the societal values of fairness, accountability, transparency and human well-being: A literature review. In Martínez-Monés A, Álvarez A, Caeiro-Rodríguez M, Dimitriadis Y (Eds.), Learning Analytics Summer Institute Spain 2020 (pp. 121-41). Aachen: CEUR. Valladolid, Spain.

Haluza, D., & Jungwirth, D. (2023). Artificial Intelligence and Ten Societal Megatrends: An Exploratory Study Using GPT-3. *Systems*, *11*(3), 120. doi:10.3390ystems11030120

Han, V. (2017). Are Chatbots the Future of Training? *TD: Talent Development, 71*(9), 42-46. https:// www.td.org/magazines/td-magazine/are-chatbots-the-futureof-training

Haneda, M. (2017). Dialogic learning and teaching across diverse contexts: Promises and challenges. *Language and Education, 31*(1), 1–5. doi:10.1080/09500782.2016.1230128

Hanna, R., & Kazim, E. (2021). Philosophical foundations for digital ethics and AI ethics: A dignitarian approach. *AI and Ethics, 1*(4), 405–423. doi:10.100743681-021-00040-9 PMID:34790944

Han, X., Hu, F., Xiong, G., Liu, X., Gong, X., Niu, X., Shi, W., & Wang, X. (2018, November). Design of AI+ curriculum for primary and secondary schools in Qingdao. In *2018 Chinese Automation Congress (CAC)* (pp. 4135–4140). IEEE. 10.1109/CAC.2018.8623310

Harper, R. H. (2021). AI: The social future of intelligence. In *Routledge Handbook of Social Futures* (pp. 52–58). Routledge. doi:10.4324/9780429440717-4

Hassani, H., & Silva, E. S. (2023). The role of ChatGPT in data science: How ai-assisted conversational interfaces are revolutionizing the field. *Big Data Cogn. Comput., 7*(2), 62. doi:10.3390/bdcc7020062

Hatherley, J. J. (2020). Limits of trust in medical AI. *Journal of Medical Ethics, 46*(7), 478–481. doi:10.1136/medethics-2019-105935 PMID:32220870

Haug, C. J., & Drazen, J. M. (2023). Artificial intelligence and machine learning in clinical medicine, 2023. *The New England Journal of Medicine, 388*(13), 1201–1208. doi:10.1056/NEJMra2302038 PMID:36988595

Heikkilä, A., & Kankaanranta, M. (2020). Ethical Perspectives on Learning Analytics: A Systematic Review. *Educational Technology Research and Development, 68*(2), 461–494.

He, J., Baxter, S. L., Xu, J., Xu, J., Zhou, X., & Zhang, K. (2019). The practical implementation of artificial intelligence technologies in medicine. *Nature Medicine, 25*(1), 30–36. doi:10.103841591-018-0307-0 PMID:30617336

Helm, J. M., Swiergosz, A. M., Haeberle, H. S., Karnuta, J. M., Schaffer, J. L., Krebs, V. E., Spitzer, A. I., & Ramkumar, P. N. (2020). Machine learning and artificial intelligence: Definitions, applications, and future directions. *Current Reviews in Musculoskeletal Medicine, 13*(1), 69–76. doi:10.100712178-020-09600-8 PMID:31983042

Hendrycks, D., Carlini, N., Schulman, J., & Steinhardt, J. (2021). Unsolved problems in ML safety. *arXiv preprint arXiv:2109.13916.*

Henin, C., & Le Métayer, D. (2021). Beyond explainability: Justifiability and contestability of algorithmic decision systems. *AI & Society,* •••, 1–14.

Heo, J., & Lee, J. (2019, July). CiSA: An inclusive chatbot service for international students and academics. In *International Conference on Human-Computer Interaction* (pp. 153-167). Springer, Cham. 10.1007/978-3-030-30033-3_12

Hephzibah, T. (2020). Critical Literature Review on Chatbots in Education. [ijtsrd]. *International Journal of Trend in Scientific Research and Development, 4*(6), 786–788. https://tinyurl.com/2wpc3jv8

He, Q., Zheng, H., Ma, X., Wang, L., Kong, H., & Zhu, Z. (2022). Artificial intelligence application in a renewable energy-driven desalination system: A critical review. *Energy and AI, 7*, 100123. doi:10.1016/j.egyai.2021.100123

Hernández-Sellés, N., Muñoz-Carril, P., & González-Sanmamed, M. (2019). Computer-supported collaborative learning: An analysis of the relationship between interaction, emotional support and online collaborative tools. *Computers & Education, 138*, 1–12. doi:10.1016/j.compedu.2019.04.012

Herwix, A., Haj-Bolouri, A., Rossi, M., Tremblay, M. C., Purao, S., & Gregor, S. (2022). Ethics in information systems and design science research: Five perspectives. *Communications of the Association for Information Systems*, *50*(1), 589–616. doi:10.17705/1CAIS.05028

Hickman, E., & Petrin, M. (2021). Trustworthy AI and corporate governance: The EU's ethics guidelines for trustworthy artificial intelligence from a company law perspective. *European Business Organization Law Review*, *22*(4), 593–625. doi:10.100740804-021-00224-0

Hien, H. T., Cuong, P. N., Nam, L. N. H., Nhung, H. L. T. K., & Thang, L. D. (2018, December). Intelligent assistants in higher-education environments: The FIT-EBot, a chatbot for administrative and learning support. In *Proceedings of the Ninth International Symposium on Information and Communication Technology* (pp. 69–76). IEEE. 10.1145/3287921.3287937

High-Level Expert Group on Artificial Intelligence (AI HLEG). (2019). *Ethics guidelines for Trustworthy AI.* European Commission. https://ec.europa.eu/futurium/en/ai-alliance-consultation.1.html

Hill, P., & Barber, M. (2014). *Preparing for a renaissance in assessment.* Pearson.

Hill, S., & Grinnell, C. (2014). Using digital storytelling with infographics in STEM professional writing pedagogy. In *2014 IEEE International Professional Communication Conference (IPCC)* (pp. 1–7). IEEE. 10.1109/IPCC.2014.7020367

Hoekstra, A., & Kaptein, M. (2021). The integrity of integrity programs: Toward a normative framework. *Public Integrity*, *23*(2), 129–141. doi:10.1080/10999922.2020.1776077

Holmes, W., Porayska-Pomsta, K., Holstein, K., Sutherland, E., Baker, T., Shum, S. B., ... Koedinger, K. R. (2021). Ethics of AI in education: Towards a community-wide framework. *International Journal of Artificial Intelligence in Education*, 1–23.

Holstein, K., Wortman Vaughan, J., Daumé, H. III, Dudík, M., Wallach, H., & Heller, S. (2019). Improving fairness in machine learning systems: What do industry practitioners need? In *Proceedings of the 2019 CHI Conference on Human Factors in Computing Systems* (p. 666). ACM. 10.1145/3290605.3300830

Honorlock. (2023). *Preventing AI content tools in higher.* Issuu. https://issuu.com/honorlockonlineproctoring/docs/preventing_ai_content_tools_in_higher_education

Hooda, M., Rana, C., Dahiya, O., Rizwan, A., & Hossain, M. D. S. (2022). Artificial Intelligence for Assessment and Feedback to Enhance Student Success in Higher Education Mathematical Problems in Engineering. doi:10.1155/2022/5215722

Hosseini-Asl, E., Chen, X., Bos, J., & Hovy, E. (2020). Few-shot dialogue gen-eration with pre-trained language models. In *Proceedings of the 58th Annual Meeting of the Association for Computational Linguistics*, (pp. 6878–6888). IEEE.

How ChatGPT and other AI tools can maximize the learning potential of your case-based classes. (2023, June 1). HBSP. https://he.hbsp.harvard.edu/how-chat-gpt-can-maximize-your-case-based-classes.html

Howlett, N. (2017). How machine learning is developing to get more insight from complex voice-of-customer data. *Applied Marketing Analytics*, *3*(3), 250–254.

Ho, Y.-R., Chen, B.-Y., & Li, C.-M. (2023). Thinking more wisely: Using the socratic method to develop critical thinking skills amongst healthcare students. *BMC Medical Education*, *23*(1), 173. doi:10.118612909-023-04134-2 PMID:36941597

Hsu, Y.-C., & Ching, Y.-H. (2023). Generative artificial intelligence in education, part one: The dynamic frontier. *TechTrends*, *67*(4), 603–607. doi:10.100711528-023-00863-9

Hu, W., Huang, Y., Jia, Y., & Ma, N. (2021). Exploring the relationship between socio emotional process and collaborative problem solving. *2021 13th International Conference on Education Technology and Computers*. ACM. 10.1145/3498765.3498834

Huang, X., & Lajoie, S. P. (2023). Social emotional interaction in collaborative learning: Why it matters and how can we measure it? *Social Sciences & Humanities Open*, *7*(1), 100447. doi:10.1016/j.ssaho.2023.100447

Hughes, A. (n.d.). *ChatGPT: Everything you need to know about OpenAI's GPT-4 tool*. Science Focus. https://www.sciencefocus.com/future-technology/gpt-3/

Humble, K. (2023). Artificial Intelligence, International Law and the Race for Killer Robots in Modern Warfare. In *Artificial Intelligence, Social Harms and Human Rights* (pp. 57–76). Springer International Publishing. doi:10.1007/978-3-031-19149-7_3

Hu, Q., & Rangwala, H. (2020). Towards fair educational data mining: A case study on detecting at-risk students. In *Proceedings of the 13th International Conference on Educational Data Mining (EDM 2020)* (pp. 431–437). ERIC.

Hussar, W. J., & Bailey, T. M. (2020). Projections of Education Statistics to 2028 (NCES 2020-024). U.S. Department of Education, Washington, DC: National Center for Education Statistics.

Hwang, G. J., & Chien, S. Y. (2022). Definition, roles, and potential research issues of the metaverse in education: An artificial intelligence perspective. *Computers and Education: Artificial Intelligence*, 100082.

Hwang, G. J., & Chang, C. Y. (2021). A review of opportunities and challenges of chatbots in education. *Interactive Learning Environments*, 1–14. doi:10.1080/10494820.2021.1952615

Hwang, G. J., & Tu, Y. F. (2021). Roles and Research Trends of Artificial Intelligence in Mathematics Education: A Bibliometric Mapping Analysis and Systematic Review. *Mathematics*, *9*(6), 584. doi:10.3390/math9060584

Hwang, G. J., Xie, H., Wah, B. W., & Gašević, D. (2020). Vision, challenges, roles and research issues of Artificial Intelligence in Education. *Computers and Education: Artificial Intelligence*, *1*, 100001. doi:10.1016/j.caeai.2020.100001

Hwang, H., & Park, M. H. (2020). The Threat of AI and Our Response: The AI Charter of Ethics in South Korea. *Asian Journal of Innovation & Policy*, *9*(1).

IEEE. (2019). *Ethically aligned design*. IEEE. https://ethicsinaction.ieee.org/

Ifenthaler, D. (2020). Ethical Considerations for AI in Education. Technology. *Knowledge and Learning*, *25*(3), 333–336.

Igna, I., & Venturini, F. (2023). The determinants of AI innovation across European firms. *Research Policy*, *52*(2), 104661. doi:10.1016/j.respol.2022.104661

Inside Higher Ed. (2023). Emerging technology and AI. *Inside Higher Ed*. https://www.insidehighered.com/sites/default/files/2023-06/2023-IHE-Emerging-Technology-and-AI_.pdf

Iseke-Barnes, J. M. (1996). Issues of educational uses of the Internet: Power and criticism in communications and searching. *Journal of Educational Computing Research*, *15*(1), 1–23. doi:10.2190/FLYP-YNQC-9T55-MKB5

Islam, S. R., Russell, I., Eberle, W., & Dicheva, D. (2022). Instilling conscience about bias and fairness in automated decisions. *Journal of Computing Sciences in Colleges*, *37*(8), 22–31.

Ison, D. C. (2018). An empirical analysis of differences in plagiarism among world cultures. *Journal of Higher Education Policy and Management*, *40*(4), 291–304. doi:10.1080/1360080X.2018.1479949

Ivanović, M. (2021). E-learning Personalization Systems and Sustainable Education. *Sustainability (Basel), 13*(12), 6713. doi:10.3390u13126713

Jain, V., & Shetty, A. S. (2022). Digital competence among schoolteachers across gender. *Turkish Online Journal of Qualitative Inquiry, 13*(1), 1083–1089.

Jalal, S., Parker, W., Ferguson, D., & Nicolaou, S. (2021). Exploring the role of artificial intelligence in an emergency and trauma radiology department. *Canadian Association of Radiologists Journal, 72*(1), 167–174. doi:10.1177/0846537120918338 PMID:32309989

Jalil, N. A., Hwang, H. J., & Dawi, N. M. (2019). Machine learning trends, perspectives, and prospects in the education sector. In *Proceedings of the 3rd International Conference on Education and Multimedia Technology* (pp. 201-205). ACM. 10.1145/3345120.3345147

Jeffs, T., Morrison, W. F., Messenheimer, T., & Rizza, M. G. (2008). A retrospective analysis of technological advancements in special education. *Computers in Schools, 20*(1), 129–152. doi:10.1080/07380560801972961

Jeong, S., Lee, I. Y., Jun, B. O., Ryu, Y., Sohn, J. W., Kim, S., Woo, C., Koo, J. W., Cho, I., Oh, U., Kim, K., & Suh, P. (2019). Korea Brain Initiative: Emerging Issues and Institutionalization of Neuroethics. *Neuron, 101*(3), 390–393. doi:10.1016/j.neuron.2019.01.042 PMID:30731064

Johansen, V., & Schanke, T. (2013). Entrepreneurship Education in secondary education and training. *Scandinavian Journal of Educational Research, 57*(4), 357–368. doi:10.1080/00313831.2012.656280

Johnson, A. (2019). *5 ways AI is changing the education industry.* eLearningIndustry. https://elearningindustry.com/ai-is-changing-the-education-industry-5-ways

Johnson, M., Schuster, M., Le, Q., Krikun, M., Wu, Y., Chen, Z., & Chen, Y. (2016). Google's neural machine translation system: Bridging the gap between human and machine translation. *arXiv pre.*

Jomah, O., Masoud, A. K., Kishore, X. P., & Aurelia, S. (2016). Micro learning: A modernized education system. *BRAIN. Broad Research in Artificial Intelligence and Neuroscience, 7*(1), 103–110.

K, M., K, M., & K, M. (2022). What is ChatGPT? Best use cases for ChatGPT. *Aalpha.* https://www.aalpha.net/blog/what-is-chatgpt-best-use-cases-for-chatgpt/

Kabudi, T., Pappas, I., & Olsen, D. H. (2021). AI-enabled adaptive learning systems: A systematic mapping of the literature. *Computers and Education: Artificial Intelligence, 2,* 100017. doi:10.1016/j.caeai.2021.100017

Kaimara, P., Fokides, E., Oikonomou, A., & Deliyannis, I. (2021). Potential Barriers to the Implementation of Digital Game-Based Learning in the Classroom: Pre-service Teachers' Views. *Technol. Knowl. Learn., 26*(4), 825–844. doi:10.100710758-021-09512-7

Kallio, J. M., & Halverson, R. (2020). Distributed leadership for personalized learning. *Journal of Research on Technology in Education, 52*(3), 371–390. doi:10.1080/15391523.2020.1734508

Kamita, T., Ito, T., Matsumoto, A., Munakata, T., & Inoue, T. (2019). A chatbot system for mental healthcare based on SAT counseling method. *Mobile Information Systems, 2019,* 2019. doi:10.1155/2019/9517321

Kane, D. (2020). *Analyzing an interactive chatbot and its impact on academic reference service.* Association and college research libraries conference, Cleveland, OH2019.

Kapetanaki, A., Krouska, A., Troussas, C., & Sgouropoulou, C. (2021). A novel framework incorporating augmented reality and pedagogy for improving reading comprehension in special education. In *Novelties in Intelligent Digital Systems* (pp. 105–110). IOS Press. doi:10.3233/FAIA210081

Karthika, J., & Selvam, V. (2022). Accessible and engaging voices: Teaching English to adult second-language learners with visual impairment using WhatsApp voice notes in India. *British Journal of Visual Impairment.* doi:10.1177/02646196211070929

Kasneci, E., Sessler, K., K¨uchemann, S., Bannert, M., Dementieva, D., Fischer, F., Gasser, U., Groh, G., G¨unnemann, S., H¨ullermeier, E., Krusche, S., Kutyniok, G., Michaeli, T., Nerdel, C., Pfeffer, J¨., Poquet, O., Sailer, M., Schmidt, A., Seidel, T., & Kasneci, G. (2023). Chatgpt for good? on opportunities and challenges of large language models for education. *Learning and Individual Differences*, *103*, 102274. doi:10.1016/j.lindif.2023.102274

Kassymova, G. K., Malinichev, D. M., Lavrinenko, S. V., Panichkina, M. V., Koptyaeva, S. V., & Arpentieva, M. R. (2023). Ethical Problems of Digitalization and Artificial Intelligence in Education: A Global Perspective. *Journal of Pharmaceutical Negative Results*, 2150–2161.

Kaufman, G., & Flanagan, M. (2015). A psychologically "embedded" approach to designing games for prosocial causes. *Cyberpsychology (Brno)*, *9*(3). doi:10.5817/CP2015-3-5

Kengam, J. (2020). Artificial intelligence in education. *Research Gate*, *18*, 1–4.

Khairy, D., Alkhalaf, S., Areed, M. F., Amasha, M. A., & Abougalala, R. A. (2022). An algorithm for providing adaptive behavior to humanoid robot in oral assessment. *International Journal of Advanced Computer Science and Applications*, *13*(9). doi:10.14569/IJACSA.2022.01309119

Khan, A. A., Badshah, S., Liang, P., Waseem, M., Khan, B., Ahmad, A., & Akbar, M. A. (2022, June). Ethics of AI: A systematic literature review of principles and challenges. In *Proceedings of the International Conference on Evaluation and Assessment in Software Engineering 2022* (pp. 383-392). ACM. 10.1145/3530019.3531329

Khan, A. A., Wagan, A. A., Laghari, A. A., Gilal, A. R., Aziz, I. A., & Talpur, B. A. (2022). State-of-the-Art Consortium Serverless Network Architecture for Healthcare System Using Blockchain Smart Contracts. *IEEE Access : Practical Innovations, Open Solutions*, *10*, 78887–78898. doi:10.1109/ACCESS.2022.3194195

Khan, N., Muhammad, K., Hussain, T., Nasir, M., Munsif, M., Imran, A. S., & Sajjad, M. (2021). An Adaptive Game-Based Learning Strategy for Children Road Safety Education and Practice in Virtual Space. *Sensors (Basel)*, *21*(11), 3661. doi:10.339021113661 PMID:34070237

Khensous, G., Labed, K., & Labed, Z. (2023). Exploring the evolution and applications of natural language processing in education. *Romanian Journal of Information Technology and Automatic Control*, *33*(2), 61–74.

Khogali, H. O., & Mekid, S. (2023). The blended future of automation and AI: Examining some long-term societal and ethical impact features. *Technology in Society*, *73*, 102232. doi:10.1016/j.techsoc.2023.102232

Khosravi, H., Demartini, G., Sadiq, S., & Gasevic, D. (2021, April). Charting the design and analytics agenda of learnersourcing systems. In *LAK21: 11th International Learning Analytics and Knowledge Conference* (pp. 32-42). ACM. 10.1145/3448139.3448143

Khosravi, H., Sadiq, S., & Gasevic, D. (2020, February). Development and adoption of an adaptive learning system: Reflections and lessons learned. In *Proceedings of the 51st ACM Technical Symposium on Computer Science Education* (pp. 58-64). ACM. 10.1145/3328778.3366900

Khosravi, H., Shum, S. B., Chen, G., Conati, C., Tsai, Y. S., Kay, J., & Gašević, D. (2022). Explainable artificial intelligence in education. *Computers and Education: Artificial Intelligence*, *3*, 100074.

Kiennert, C., De Vos, N., Knockaert, M., & Garcia-Alfaro, J. (2019). The influence of conception paradigms on data protection in e-learning platforms: A case study. *IEEE Access : Practical Innovations, Open Solutions*, *7*, 64110–64119. doi:10.1109/ACCESS.2019.2915275

Kile, F. (2013). Artificial intelligence and society: A furtive transformation. *AI & Society*, *28*(1), 107–115. doi:10.100700146-012-0396-0

Kim, J. H., Baek, J., Hwang, C., Bae, C., & Park, J. (2021, June). Condensed discriminative question set for reliable exam score prediction. In *International Conference on Artificial Intelligence in Education* (pp. 446-450). Springer, Cham. 10.1007/978-3-030-78270-2_79

Kim, S., Park, J., & Lee, H. (2019). Automated essay scoring using a deep learning model. *Journal of Educational Technology Development and Exchange*, *2*(1), 1–17.

King, M. R. (2023). A conversation on artificial intelligence, chatbots, and plagiarism in higher education. *Cellular and Molecular Bioengineering*, *16*(1), 1–2. doi:10.100712195-022-00754-8 PMID:36660590

Klinger, J., Mateos-Garcia, J., & Stathoulopoulos, K. (2020). A narrowing of AI research? *arXiv preprint arXiv:2009.10385.*

Koh, J., Cowling, M. A., Sim, K. N., & Jha, M. (2022b, June 22). Ways AI will change teaching and learning. *Campus Morning Mail.* https://campusmorningmail.com.au/news/ways-ai-will-change-teaching-and-learning

Koh, J., Cowling, M., Jha, M., & Sim, K. N. (2022a). Collaborating with AIed for better student-teacher reconnection. In *ASCILITE 2022 Conference Proceedings*, Article e22126. ASCILITE. 10.14742/apubs.2022.126

Kong, S. C., Cheung, W. M. Y., & Zhang, G. (2021). Evaluation of an artificial intelligence literacy course for university students with diverse study backgrounds. *Computers and Education: Artificial Intelligence*, *2*, 100026. doi:10.1016/j.caeai.2021.100026

Kooli, C. (2023). Chatbots in education and research: A critical examination of ethical implications and solutions. *Sustainability (Basel)*, *15*(7), 5614. doi:10.3390u15075614

Kramer, A. D., Guillory, J. E., & Hancock, J. T. (2014). Experimental evidence of massive-scale emotional contagion through social networks. *Proceedings of the National Academy of Sciences of the United States of America*, *111*(24), 8788–8790. doi:10.1073/pnas.1320040111 PMID:24889601

Kučak, D., Juričić, V., & Đambić, G. (2018). Machine Learning In Education-A Survey Of Current Research Trends. *Annals of DAAAM & Proceedings, 29.*

Kumar, V., & Boulanger, D. (2020, October). Explainable automated essay scoring: Deep learning really has pedagogical value. [). Frontiers Media SA.]. *Frontiers in Education*, *5*, 572367. doi:10.3389/feduc.2020.572367

Kung, C., & Yu, R. (2020). Interpretable models do not compromise accuracy or fairness in predicting college success. In *Proceedings of the Seventh ACM Conference on Learning@ Scale* (pp. 413–416). ACM. 10.1145/3386527.3406755

Lakshmi, Y. (2022). Chatbots in Education System. *University News: A Weekly Journal of Higher Education, 60*(8), 15-18. https://ssrn.com/abstract=4039535

Lankshear, C., & Knobel, M. (Eds.). (2008). *Digital literacies: Concepts, policies and practices* (*Vol. 30*). Peter Lang. https://www.peterlang.com/document/1104560

Larson, D. B., Harvey, H., Rubin, D. L., Irani, N., Justin, R. T., & Langlotz, C. P. (2021). Regulatory frameworks for development and evaluation of artificial intelligence–based diagnostic imaging algorithms: Summary and recommendations. *Journal of the American College of Radiology, 18*(3), 413–424. doi:10.1016/j.jacr.2020.09.060 PMID:33096088

Last, M., & Danon, G. (2020). Automatic question generation. *Wiley Interdisciplinary Reviews. Data Mining and Knowledge Discovery, 10*(6), e1382. doi:10.1002/widm.1382

Lateef, F. (2010). Simulation-based learning: Just like the real thing. *Journal of Emergencies, Trauma and Shock, 3*(4), 348–352. doi:10.4103/0974-2700.70743 PMID:21063557

Latham, A., & Goltz, S. (2019, June). A survey of the general public's views on the ethics of using AI in education. In *International Conference on Artificial Intelligence in Education* (pp. 194-206). Springer, Cham. 10.1007/978-3-030-23204-7_17

Lean, J., Moizer, J., Derham, C., Strachan, L., & Bhuiyan, Z. (2021). *Real World Learning: Simulation and Gaming*. Applied Pedagogies for Higher Education. doi:10.1007/978-3-030-46951-1_9

Lee, J. S. (2012). The effects of the teacher–student relationship and academic press on student engagement and academic performance. *International Journal of Educational Research, 53*, 330–340. doi:10.1016/j.ijer.2012.04.006

Lee, M., Liang, P., & Yang, Q. (2022, April). Designing a human-AI collaborative writing dataset for exploring language model capabilities. In *CHI 2022: Conference on Human Factors in Computing Systems* (pp. 1–19). Association for Computing Machinery. 10.1145/3491102.3502030

Lee, S. H., Maenner, M. J., & Heilig, C. M. (2019). A comparison of machine learning algorithms for the surveillance of autism spectrum disorder. *PLoS One, 14*(9), 1–11. doi:10.1371/journal.pone.0222907 PMID:31553774

Lee, Y.-J., Lim, C.-G., Choi, Y., Lm, J.-H., & Choi, H.-J. 2022. PERSONACHATGEN: Generating Personalized Dialogues using GPT-3. In *Proceedings of the 1st Workshop on Customized Chat Grounding Persona and Knowledge*, pages 29–48, Gyeongju, Republic of Korea. Association for Computational Linguistics.

Lei, H., Chiu, M. M., Wang, D., Wang, C., & Xie, T. (2022). Effects of Game-Based Learning on Students' Achievement in Science: A Meta-Analysis. *Journal of Educational Computing Research, 60*(6), 1373–1398. doi:10.1177/07356331211064543

Leiter, C., Zhang, R., Chen, Y., Belouadi, J., Larionov, D. Y., Fresen, V., & Eger, S. (2023). ChatGPT: A Meta-Analysis after 2.5 Months. *arXiv (Cornell University)*. https://doi.org//arxiv.2302.13795 doi:10.48550

Leitner, M., Greenwald, E., Wang, N., Montgomery, R., & Merchant, C. (2022). Designing Game-Based Learning for High School Artificial Intelligence Education. *International Journal of Artificial Intelligence in Education*. Advance online publication. doi:10.100740593-022-00327-w

Lepori, B., Becker, M., & Cattaneo, A. (2020). Ethical Challenges of Artificial Intelligence and Big Data in Education. In Ethical Technology and Digital Competence (pp. 227-247). Springer.

Lepri, B., Oliver, N., Letouzé, E., Pentland, A., Vinck, P., & de Montjoye, Y. A. (2018). Fair, transparent, and accountable algorithmic decision-making processes. *Philosophy & Technology, 31*(4), 611–627. doi:10.100713347-017-0279-x

Leslie, D. (2019). Understanding artificial intelligence ethics and safety. *arXiv preprint arXiv:1906.05684.*

Levin-Banchik, L. (2018). Assessing Knowledge Retention, with our without simulations. *Journal of Political Science Education, 14*(3), 341–359. doi:10.1080/15512169.2017.1405355

Li, J., Chen, W., Chen, D., & Li, K. (2021). Gpt-3 for personalized language learning. *arXiv preprint arXiv:2103.05874.*

Limna, P., Jakwatanatham, S., Siripipattanakul, S., Kaewpuang, P., & Sriboonruang, P. (2022). A review of artificial intelligence (AI) in education during the digital era. *Advance Knowledge for Executives, 1*(1), 1–9.

Lim, T., Gottipati, S., & Cheong, M. (2022). Authentic Assessments for Digital Education: Learning Technologies Shaping Assessment Practices. *Proceedings of the 30th International Conference on Computers in Education (ICCE 2022),* Kuala Lumpur, Malaysia.

Lim, W. M., Gunasekara, A., Pallant, J. L., Pallant, J. I., & Pechenkina, E. (2023). Generative AI and the future of education: Ragnarök or reformation? A paradoxical perspective from management educators. *International Journal of Management Education, 21*(2), 100790. doi:10.1016/j.ijme.2023.100790

Lin, P. Y., Chai, C. S., Jong, M. S. Y., Dai, Y., Guo, Y., & Qin, J. (2021). Modeling the structural relationship among primary students' motivation to learn artificial intelligence. *Computers and Education: Artificial Intelligence, 2,* 100006. doi:10.1016/j.caeai.2020.100006

Lipko, H. (2016). Meet Jill Watson: Georgia Tech's first AI teaching assistant. GA Tech. https://pe.gatech.edu/blog/meet-jill-watson-georgia-techs-first-ai-teaching-assistant

Litman, D., Zhang, H., Correnti, R., Matsumura, L. C., & Wang, E. (2021, June). A fairness evaluation of automated methods for scoring text evidence usage in writing. In *International Conference on Artificial Intelligence in Education* (pp. 255-267). Springer, Cham. 10.1007/978-3-030-78292-4_21

Liu, H., Wang, Y., Fan, W., Liu, X., Li, Y., Jain, S., Liu, Y., Jain, A., & Tang, J. (2022). Trustworthy AI: A computational perspective. *ACM Transactions on Intelligent Systems and Technology, 14*(1), 1–59. doi:10.1145/3546872

Liu, L., Subbareddy, R., & Raghavendra, C. G. (2022). AI intelligence chatbot to improve students' learning in the higher education platform. *Journal of Interconnection Networks, 22*(Supp02), 1–17. doi:10.1142/S0219265921430325

Liu, M., & Hu, X. (2020). Ethical Issues of AI in Education: An Empirical Study. *International Journal of Emerging Technologies in Learning, 15*(23), 39–54.

Liu, X., Qiu, X., Chen, W., & Liu, S. (2020). Multilingual pre-training for neu-ral machine translation. In *Proceedings of the 58th Annual Meeting of the Association for Computational Linguistics,* (pp. 6296–6311). IEEE.

Li, W., Sun, K., Schaub, F., & Brooks, C. (2021). Disparities in students' propensity to consent to learning analytics. *International Journal of Artificial Intelligence in Education.* doi:10.100740593-021-00254-2

Lo, C. K. (2023). What is the impact of ChatGPT on education? A rapid review of the literature. *Education Sciences, 13*(4), 410. doi:10.3390/educsci13040410

Loftus, M., & Madden, M. G. (2020). A pedagogy of data and Artificial intelligence for student subjectification. *Teaching in Higher Education, 25*(4), 456–475. doi:10.1080/13562517.2020.1748593

Luan, H., Geczy, P., Lai, H., Gobert, J. H., Yang, S. J., Ogata, H., Baltes, J., Guerra, R., Li, P., & Tsai, C. (2020). Challenges and Future Directions of Big Data and Artificial Intelligence in Education. *Frontiers in Psychology, 11,* 580820. doi:10.3389/fpsyg.2020.580820 PMID:33192896

Lucey, B. (n.d.). *ChatGPT: our study shows AI can produce academic papers good enough for journals – just as some ban it.* The Conversation. https://theconversation.com/chatgpt-our-study-shows-ai-can-produce-academic-papers-good-enough-for-journals-just-as-some-ban-it-197762

Luckin, R. (2017). Towards artificial intelligence-based assessment systems. *Nature Human Behaviour, 1,* 0028. . doi:10.1038/s41562-016-0028

Luckin, R., & Cukurova, M. (2019). Designing educational technologies in the age of AI: A learning sciences-driven approach. *British Journal of Educational Technology, 50*(6), 2824–2838. doi:10.1111/bjet.12861

Luckin, R., Holmes, W., Griffiths, M., & Forcier, L. B. (2016). *Intelligence Unleashed: An Argument for AI in Education.* Pearson Education.

Lund, B., & Wang, T. (2023). Chatting about ChatGPT: How may AI and GPT impact academia and libraries? *Library Hi Tech News, 40*(3), 26–29. doi:10.1108/LHTN-01-2023-0009

Luo, N., Zhang, M., & Qi, D. (2017). Effects of different interactions on students' sense of community in e learning environment. *Computers & Education, 115*, 153-160. https://doi.org/. 006 doi:10.1016/j.compedu.2017.08

Lu, X. (2019). An empirical study on the artificial intelligence writing evaluation system in China CET. *Big Data, 7*(2), 121–129. doi:10.1089/big.2018.0151 PMID:31074642

Madhav, A. S., & Tyagi, A. K. (2022). The world with future technologies (Post-COVID-19): open issues, challenges, and the road ahead. *Intelligent Interactive Multimedia Systems for e-Healthcare Applications*, 411-452.

Magomadov, V. S. (2020). The application of artificial intelligence and Big Data analytics in personalized learning. *Journal of Physics: Conference Series, 1691*(1), 012169. doi:10.1088/1742-6596/1691/1/012169

Maher, D. (2023). Video conferencing and authentic learning in the primary school classroom. In M. Leask & S. Younie (Eds.), *Teaching and learning with technologies in the primary school* (3rd ed.). Routledge.

Mahona, P., & Pacho, T. (2021). Reshaping Education in the Post-COVID-19 Pandemic in Africa. *African Research Journal of Education and Social Sciences (ARJESS), 8*(3), 13-26. http://arjess.org/education-research/reshaping-education-in-the-post-covid-19-pandemic-in- africa-.pdf

Makira, J., & Owino, E. (2021). The Use of Technology for Learning during the Covid-19 Pandemic Season: A Case of Rural Schools in Kenya. *International Journal of Innovative Science and Research Technology, 6*.https://ijisrt.com/assets/upload/files/IJISRT21JAN172.pdf

Makridakis, S. (2017). The forthcoming Artificial Intelligence (AI) revolution: Its impact on society and firms. *Futures, 90*, 46–60. doi:10.1016/j.futures.2017.03.006

Malinka, K., Peresíni, M., Firc, A., Hujnák, O., & Janus, F. (2023, June). On the educational impact of ChatGPT: Is Artificial Intelligence ready to obtain a university degree? In *Proceedings of the 2023 Conference on Innovation and Technology in Computer Science Education* V. 1 (pp. 47-53). IEEE. 10.1145/3587102.3588827

Malle, B. F., Bello, P., & Scheutz, M. (2019). Requirements for an artificial agent with norm competence. In *Proceedings of the 2019 AAAI/ACM Conference on AI, Ethics, and Society*, (pp. 21–27). ACM. 10.1145/3306618.3314252

Mantello, P., Ho, M. T., Nguyen, M. H., & Vuong, Q. H. (2023). Bosses without a heart: Socio-demographic and cross-cultural determinants of attitude toward Emotional AI in the workplace. *AI & Society, 38*(1), 97–119. doi:10.100700146-021-01290-1 PMID:34776651

Manyika, J., Lund, S., Chui, M., Bughin, J., Woetzel, J., Batra, P., Ko, R., & Sanghvi, S. (2017). *Jobs lost, jobs gained: Workforce transitions in a time of automation.* McKinsey Global Institute. http://hdl.voced.edu.au/10707/444873

Marino, M. T., Vasquez, E., Dieker, L., Basham, J., & Blackorby, J. (2023). The future of artificial intelligence in special education technology. *Journal of Special Education Technology, 38*(3), 404–416. doi:10.1177/01626434231165977

Marr, B. (2018, July 25). How is AI used in education--Real world examples of today and a peek into the future. *Forbes.* https://www.forbes.com/sites/bernardmarr/2018/07/25/how-is-ai-used-in-education-real-world-examples-of-today-and-a-peek-into-the-future

Martin Nunez, J. L., & Diaz Lantada, A. (2020). Artificial intelligence aided engineering education: State of the art, potentials and challenges. *International Journal of Engineering Education, 36*(6), 1740–1751.

Martinez-Maldonado, R., Gaševic, D., Echeverria, V., Fernandez Nieto, G., Swiecki, Z., & Buckingham Shum, S. (2021). What Do You Mean by Collaboration Analytics? A Conceptual Model. *Journal of Learning Analytics, 8*(1), 126–153. doi:10.18608/jla.2021.7227

Masakowski, Y. R. (2020). Artificial intelligence and the future global security environment. In *Artificial Intelligence and Global Security* (pp. 1–34). Emerald Publishing Limited. doi:10.1108/978-1-78973-811-720201001

Masters, K. (2023). Ethical use of artificial intelligence in health professions education: AMEE Guide No. 158. *Medical Teacher, 45*(6), 574–584. doi:10.1080/0142159X.2023.2186203 PMID:36912253

Mayfield, E., Madaio, M., Prabhumoye, S., Gerritsen, D., McLaughlin, B., Dixon-Román, E., & Black, A. W. (2019, August). Equity beyond bias in language technologies for education. In *Proceedings of the Fourteenth Workshop on Innovative Use of NLP for Building Educational Applications* (pp. 444-460). Association for Computational Linguistics. 10.18653/v1/W19-4446

McBride, C. (2015). *Children's literacy development: A cross-cultural perspective on learning to read and write* (2nd ed.). Routledge. doi:10.4324/9781315849409

McEwen, R. (2023, January 22). Academic papers written by AI get a solid B — but is it cheating? *The Toronto Star.* https://www.thestar.com/opinion/contributors/2023/01/22/academic-papers-written-by-ai-get-a-solid-b-but-is-it-cheating.html

McGlashan, A. (2018). A pedagogic approach to enhance creative ideation in classroom practice. *International Journal of Technology and Design Education, 28*(2), 377–393. doi:10.100710798-017-9404-5

McKendrick, K. (2019). Artificial intelligence prediction and counterterrorism. London: The Royal Institute of International Affairs-Chatham House, 9.

McLaren, B. M., & Nguyen, H. A. (2023). Chapter 20: Digital learning games in artificial intelligence in education (AIED): a review. In Handbook of Artificial Intelligence in Education. Cheltenham, UK: Edward Elgar Publishing. doi:10.4337/9781800375413.00032

Megahed, N. A., Abdel-Kader, R. F., & Soliman, H. Y. (2022). Post-pandemic education strategy: Framework for artificial intelligence-empowered education in engineering (AIEd-Eng) for lifelong learning. In *International Conference on Advanced Machine Learning Technologies and Applications* (pp. 544-556). Springer, Cham. 10.1007/978-3-031-03918-8_45

Mele, C., & Russo-Spena, T. (2023). Artificial Intelligence in Services. Elgar Encyclopedia of Services, 356.

Mena-Guacas, A. F., Urueña Rodríguez, J. A., Santana Trujillo, D. M., Gómez-Galán, J., & López-Meneses, E. (2023). Collaborative learning and skill development for educational growth of artificial intelligence: A systematic review. *Contemporary Educational Technology, 15*(3), ep428. doi:10.30935/cedtech/13123

Merikko, J., Ng, K., Saqr, M., & Ihantola, P. (2022). To opt in or to opt out? Predicting student preference for learning analytics-based formative feedback. *IEEE Access : Practical Innovations, Open Solutions, 10*, 99195–99204. doi:10.1109/ACCESS.2022.3207274

Meyer, J. G., Urbanowicz, R. J., Martin, P. C. N., O'Connor, K., Li, R., Peng, P.-C., Bright, T. J., Tatonetti, N., Won, K. J., Gonzalez-Hernandez, G., & Moore, J. H. (2023). Chatgpt and large language models in academia: Opportunities and challenges. *BioData Mining, 16*(1), 20. doi:10.118613040-023-00339-9 PMID:37443040

Mhlanga, D. (2023). Open AI in education, the responsible and ethical use of ChatGPT towards lifelong learning. *Education, the Responsible and Ethical Use of ChatGPT Towards Lifelong Learning.*

Mikalef, P., Conboy, K., Lundström, J. E., & Popovič, A. (2022). Thinking responsibly about responsible AI and 'the dark side'of AI. *European Journal of Information Systems, 31*(3), 257–268. doi:10.1080/0960085X.2022.2026621

Milano, S., McGrane, J. A., & Leonelli, S. (2023, March). Large language models challenge the future of higher education. *Nature Machine Intelligence, 5*(4), 333–334. doi:10.103842256-023-00644-2

Miller, G. J. (2022, March). Artificial Intelligence Project Success Factors—Beyond the Ethical Principles. In *Information Technology for Management: Business and Social Issues: 16th Conference, ISM 2021, and FedCSIS-AIST 2021 Track,* (pp. 65-96). Cham: Springer International Publishing.

Miller, F. A., Katz, J. H., & Gans, R. (2018). AI x I = AI2: The OD imperative to add inclusion to the algorithms of artificial intelligence. *OD Practitioner, 50*(1), 6–12.

Mirbabaie, M., Brünker, F., Möllmann, N. R., & Stieglitz, S. (2022). The rise of artificial intelligence–understanding the AI identity threat at the workplace. *Electronic Markets, 32*(1), 1–27. doi:10.100712525-021-00496-x

Mishra, P., & Koehler, M. J. (2006). Technological pedagogical content knowledge: A framework for teacher knowledge. *Teachers College Record, 108*(6), 1017–1054. doi:10.1111/j.1467-9620.2006.00684.x

Mogaji, E. (2020). More Nigerian banks are using chatbots to serve customers, but with mixed results. *The Conversation.*

Mogavi, R. H., Deng, C., Kim, J. J., Zhou, P., Kwon, Y. D., Metwally, A. H. S., & Hui, P. (2023). Exploring user perspectives on chatgpt: Applications, perceptions, and implications for AI-integrated education. arXiv preprint arXiv:2305.13114.

Moher, D., Liberati, A., Tetzlaff, J., & Altman, D. G.Prisma Group. (2009). Preferred reporting items for systematic reviews and meta-analyses: The PRISMA statement. *PLoS Medicine, 6*(7), e1000097. doi:10.1371/journal.pmed.1000097 PMID:19621072

Mok, A. (2023, January 19). CEO of ChatGPT maker responds to schools' plagiarism concerns: 'We adapted to calculators and changed what we. *Business Insider.* https://www.businessinsider.in/tech/news/ceo-of-chatgpt-maker-responds-to-schools-plagiarism-concerns-we-adapted-to-calculators-and-changed-what-we-tested-in-math-class/articleshow/97147698.cms

Mollick, E. (2022, December 14). *ChatGPT is a tipping point for AI.* Harvard Business Review. https://hbr.org/2022/12/chatgpt-is-a-tipping-point-for-ai

MollickE. R.MollickL. (2023) Using AI to implement effective teaching strategies in classrooms: Five strategies, including prompts. doi:10.2139/ssrn.4391243

Molnár, G., & Szüts, Z. (2018, September). The role of chatbots in formal education. In *2018 IEEE 16th International Symposium on Intelligent Systems and Informatics (SISY)* (pp. 000197-000202). IEEE. 10.1109/SISY.2018.8524609

Morley, J., Floridi, L., Kinsey, L., & Elhalal, A. (2020). From what to how: An initial review of publicly available AI ethics tools, methods and research to translate principles into practices. *Science and Engineering Ethics, 26*(4), 2141–2168. doi:10.100711948-019-00165-5 PMID:31828533

Morocco-Clarke, A., Sodangi, F. A., & Momodu, F. (2023). The implications and effects of ChatGPT on academic scholarship and authorship: A death knell for original academic publications? *Information & Communications Technology Law*, 1–21. doi:10.1080/13600834.2023.2239623

Mougiakou, E., Papadimitriou, S., & Virvou, M. (2018, July). Intelligent tutoring systems and transparency: The case of children and adolescents. In *2018 9th International Conference on Information, Intelligence, Systems and Applications (IISA)* (pp. 1-8). IEEE.

Müller, V. C. (2020). *Ethics of Artificial Intelligence and Robotics*. Stanford. https://plato.stanford.edu/entries/ ethics-ai/

Nader, K., Toprac, P., Scott, S., & Baker, S. (2022). Public understanding of artificial intelligence through entertainment media. *AI & Society*, 1–14. doi:10.100700146-022-01427-w PMID:35400854

National Science and Technology Council. (2016). *Preparing for the Future of Artificial Intelligence*. The White House. https://obamawhitehouse.archives.gov/sites/default/files/whitehouse_files/microsites/ostp/NSTC/preparing_for_the_future_of_ai.pdf

National Science and Technology Council. (2016). *Preparing for the Future of Artificial Intelligence*. White House. https://obamawhitehouse.archives.gov/sites/default/files/whitehouse_files/microsites/ostp/NSTC/preparing_for_the_future_of_ai.pdf

Nazaretsky, T., Cukurova, M., & Alexandron, G. (2022). An instrument for measuring teachers' trust in AI-based educational technology. In *LAK22: 12th International Learning Analytics and Knowledge Conference* (pp. 56-66). ACM. 10.1145/3506860.3506866

NBC. (2023, January 5). *ChatGPT banned from New York City public schools' devices and networks*. NBC News. https://www.nbcnews.com/tech/tech-news/new-york-city-public-schools-ban-chatgpt-devices-networks-rcna64446

Ndukwe, I. G., Daniel, B. K., & Amadi, C. E. (2019). A Machine Learning Grading System Using Chatbots. In S. Isotani, E. Millán, A. Ogan, P. Hastings, B. McLaren, & R. Luckin (Eds.), Lecture Notes in Computer Science: Vol. 11626. *Artificial Intelligence in Education. AIED 2019*. Springer. doi:10.1007/978-3-030-23207-8_67

Ng, D. T. K., Leung, J. K. L., Chu, S. K. W., & Qiao, M. S. (2021). Conceptualizing AI literacy: An exploratory review. *Computers and Education: Artificial Intelligence*, *2*, 100041. doi:10.1016/j.caeai.2021.100041

Ng, D. T. K., Luo, W., Chan, H. M. Y., & Chu, S. K. W. (2022). Using digital story writing as a pedagogy to develop AI literacy among primary students. *Computers and Education: Artificial Intelligence*, *3*, 100054. doi:10.1016/j.caeai.2022.100054

Nguyen, A., Ngo, H. N., Hong, Y., Dang, B., & Nguyen, B. P. T. (2022). Ethical principles for artificial intelligence in education. *Education and Information Technologies*. Advance online publication. doi:10.100710639-022-11316-w PMID:36254344

Nichols, R. (2022). The cultural evolution of Chinese morality, and the essential value of multi-disciplinary research in understanding it. In The Routledge International Handbook of Morality, Cognition, and Emotion in China (pp. 19-37). Routledge. doi:10.4324/9781003281566-3

Nicolopoulou, A. (1993). Play, cognitive development, and the social world: Piaget, Vygotsky, and beyond. *Human Development*, *36*(1), 1–23. doi:10.1159/000277285

Nigam, A., Pasricha, R., Singh, T., & Churi, P. (2021). A systematic review on AI-based proctoring systems: Past, present, and future. *Education and Information Technologies*, *26*(5), 6421–6445. doi:10.100710639-021-10597-x PMID:34177348

Nobre, G. (2020). Artificial Intelligence (AI) in communications: Journalism, public relations, advertising, and propaganda. https://doi.org/doi:10.13140/RG.2.2.33598.31040

Novelli, C., Taddeo, M., & Floridi, L. (2023). Accountability in artificial intelligence: What it is and how it works. *AI & Society*, 1–12. doi:10.100700146-023-01635-y

NSW Education Standards Authority. (2017). *Digital literacy skills and learning report*. NSW. https://www.nsw.gov.au/education-and-training/nesa/about/research/reports/digital-literacy-skills-and-learning-report

O'Connor, K. E. (2008). "You choose to care": Teachers, emotions and professional identity. *Teaching and Teacher Education*, *24*(1), 117–126. doi:10.1016/j.tate.2006.11.008

O'Neil, C. (2016). *Weapons of math destruction: How big data increases inequality and threatens democracy*. Penguin Books.

Ochieng, V. O., & Ngware, M. W. (2022). Adoption of Education Technologies for Learning During COVID-19 Pandemic: The Experiences of Marginalized and Vulnerable Learner Populations in Kenya. *International Journal of Educational Reform, 10567879221076081*. doi:10.1177/10567879221076081

OECD. (2019). *AI in Education: Tertiary Education, Skills, and Lifelong Learning*. OECD Publishing.

Ogden, C. R., & Richards, I. A. (1923). *The Meaning of Meaning: A Study of the Influence of Language upon Thought and of the Science of Symbolism*. Routledge & Kegan Paul.

Oke, A., & Fernandes, F. A. P. (2020). Innovations in teaching and learning: Exploring the perceptions of the education sector on the 4th industrial revolution (4IR). *Journal of Open Innovation*, *6*(2), 31. doi:10.3390/joitmc6020031

Okewu, E., Adewole, P., Misra, S., Maskeliunas, R., & Damase-vicius, R. (2021). Artificial neural networks for educational data mining in higher education: A systematic literature review. *Applied Artificial Intelligence*, *35*(13), 983–1021. doi:10.1080/08839514.2021.1922847

Olusegun Oyetola, S., Oladokun, B. D., Ezinne Maxwell, C., & Obotu Akor, S. (2023). Artificial intelligence in the library: Gauging the potential application and implications for contemporary library services in Nigeria. *Data & Metadata*, *2*, 36. doi:10.56294/dm202336

Olusegun, S., Oladokun, B. D., Maxwell, C. E., & Akor, S. O. (2023). *Artificial intelligence in the library: Potential implications to library and information services in the 21st Century Nigeria*.

Opondo, J. O., & Paschal, M. J. (2023). Blended Learning: An Emerging Pedagogy for Learning in Higher Education. In O. S. Ambili & M. Omanaseelan (Eds.), *Metamorphosis in Education* (pp. 47–59). Taran Publication.

Oracle. (2020). *Artificial Intelligence and Chatbots in Higher Education*. Oracle. http://www.oracle.com/us/ industries/education-and-research/he-artificial-intelligencer-5180773.pdf

Oregon State University. (2023, March 22). *ChatGPT and other AI tools: Implications for teaching and learning*. Center for Teaching and Learning. https://ctl.oregonstate.edu/chatgpt-and-other-ai-tools-implications-teaching-and-learning

Ouyang, F., Zheng, L., & Jiao, P. (2022). Artificial intelligence in online higher education: A systematic review of empirical research from 2011 to 2020. *Education and Information Technologies*, *27*(6), 1–33. doi:10.100710639-022-10925-9

Owe, A., & Baum, S. D. (2021). Moral consideration of nonhumans in the ethics of artificial intelligence. *AI and Ethics*, *1*(4), 517–528. doi:10.100743681-021-00065-0

Owoc, M. L., Weichbroth, P., & Sawicka, A. (2021). Artificial Intelligence Technologies in Education: Benefifits, Challenges and Strategies of Implementation. Artificial Intelligence for Knowledge Management (pp.37-58). doi:10.1007/978-3-030-85001-2_4

Pallathadka, H., Sonia, B., Sanchez, D. T., De Vera, J. V., Godinez, J. A. T., & Pepito, M. T. (2022). Investigating the impact of artificial intelligence in education sector by predicting student performance. *Materials Today: Proceedings*, *51*, 2264–2267. doi:10.1016/j.matpr.2021.11.395

Palomares, I., Martínez-Cámara, E., Montes, R., García-Moral, P., Chiachio, M., Chiachio, J., Alonso, S., Melero, F. J., Molina, D., Fernández, B., Moral, C., Marchena, R., de Vargas, J. P., & Herrera, F. (2021). A panoramic view and swot analysis of artificial intelligence for achieving the sustainable development goals by 2030: Progress and prospects. *Applied Intelligence*, *51*(9), 6497–6527. doi:10.100710489-021-02264-y PMID:34764606

Pandemic, E. L. (2021). Induced remote learning increases need for mobile game-based learning to engage learners. *Educational Technology Research and Development*, *69*(1), 185–188. doi:10.100711423-020-09861-7

Panigrahi, C. M. A., & Joshi, V. (2020). Use of artificial intelligence in education. *Management Accountant*, *55*(5), 64–67. doi:10.33516/maj.v55i5.64-67p

Papa, R., & Jackson, K. M. (2021). Enduring questions, innovative technologies: Educational theories interface with AI. In *Intelligent Computing* (pp. 725–742). Springer. doi:10.1007/978-3-030-80126-7_51

Paschal, M. J., & Gougou, S. A.-M. (2022). Promoting 21st Century Skills in English Language Teaching: A Pedagogical Transformation in Ivory Coast. *Global Journal of Educational Studies*, *8*(2), 50–74. doi:10.5296/gjes.v8i2.20333

Paschal, M. J., & Mahama, M. (2023). Performance-Based Assessments: Redefining Teacher-Trainees Evaluation. In O. S. Ambili & M. Omanaseelan (Eds.), *Metamorphosis in Education* (pp. 23–46). Taran Publication.

Paschal, M. J., & Mkulu, D. G. (2020). Online Classes during COVID-19 Pandemic in Higher Learning Institutions in Africa. *Global Research in Higher Education*, *3*(3), 1–21. doi:10.22158/grhe.v3n3p1

Paschal, M. J., & Mkulu, D. G. (2020a). Teacher- Students' Relationship and Students 'Academic Performance in Public Secondary Schools in Magu District, Tanzania. *Journal of Research in Education and Society*, *11*(1), 20–23. http://www.icidr.org/jresv11no1-content.php

Paschal, M. J., Pacho, O. T., & Adewoyin, O. (2022). Teaching methods applied in higher education during COVID-19 pandemic in Africa. *International Journal of Educational Policy Research and Review.*, *9*(1). Advance online publication. doi:10.15739/IJEPRR.22.003

Peeters, M. M., van Diggelen, J., Van Den Bosch, K., Bronkhorst, A., Neerincx, M. A., Schraagen, J. M., & Raaijmakers, S. (2021). Hybrid collective intelligence in a human–AI society. *AI & Society*, *36*(1), 217–238. doi:10.100700146-020-01005-y

Peña-Ayala, A. (2018). Learning analytics: A glance of evolution, status, and trends according to a proposed taxonomy. *Wiley Interdisciplinary Reviews. Data Mining and Knowledge Discovery*, *8*(3), e1243. doi:10.1002/widm.1243

Pereira, J. (2016). Leveraging chatbots to improve self-guided learning through conversational quizzes. *Proceedings of the Fourth International Conference on Technological Ecosystems for Enhancing Multiculturality* (pp. 911-918). ACM. 10.1145/3012430.3012625

Pereira, L. M. (2019). Should I kill or rather not? *AI & Society*, *34*(4), 939–943. doi:10.100700146-018-0850-8

Petersen, K., & Gencel, C. (2013). Worldviews, research methods, and their relationship to validity in empirical software engineering research. In *2013 Joint Conference of the 23rd International Workshop on Software Measurement and the 8th International Conference on Software Process and Product Measurement* (pp. 81-89). IEEE. 10.1109/IWSM-Mensura.2013.22

Petersen, K., Vakkalanka, S., & Kuzniarz, L. (2015). Guidelines for conducting systematic mapping studies in software engineering: An update. *Information and Software Technology, 64*, 1–18. doi:10.1016/j.infsof.2015.03.007

Pianta, R. C., Steinberg, M. S., & Rollins, K. B. (1995). The first two years of school: Teacher–child relationships and deflections in children's classroom adjustment. *Development and Psychopathology, 7*(2), 295–312. doi:10.1017/S0954579400006519

Pizzi, M., Romanoff, M., & Engelhardt, T. (2020). AI for humanitarian action: Human rights and ethics. *International Review of the Red Cross, 102*(913), 145–180. doi:10.1017/S1816383121000011

Pocock, K. (2023). What is ChatGPT and how can you use it? *PC Guide*. https://www.pcguide.com/apps/what-is-chat-gpt/

Pontual Falcão, T., Lins Rodrigues, R., Cechinel, C., Dermeval, D., Harada Teixeira de Oliveira, E., Gasparini, I., ... Ferreira Mello, R. (2022, March). A Penny for your Thoughts: Students and Instructors' Expectations about Learning Analytics in Brazil. In *LAK22: 12th International Learning Analytics and Knowledge Conference* (pp. 186-196). 10.1145/3506860.3506886

Popper, K. (1979). *Three worlds*. University of Michigan.

Prem, E. (2023). From ethical AI frameworks to tools: A review of approaches. *AI and Ethics, 3*(3), 1–18. doi:10.100743681-023-00258-9

Project, P. E., & Peirce, C. S. (1998). *The essential peirce* (Vol. 2). Indiana University Press.

Qiao-Franco, G., & Bode, I. (2023). Weaponised artificial intelligence and Chinese practices of human–machine interaction. *The Chinese Journal of International Politics, 16*(1), 106–128. doi:10.1093/cjip/poac024

Rachha, A., & Seyam, M. (2023). Explainable AI In Education: Current Trends, Challenges, And Opportunities. *SoutheastCon, 2023*, 232–239. doi:10.1109/SoutheastCon51012.2023.10115140

Rahayu, S., Rahmadani, E., Syafitri, E., Prasetyoningsih, L. S. A., Ubaidillah, M. F., & Tavakoli, M. (2022). Teaching with Technology during COVID-19 Pandemic: An Interview Study with Teachers in Indonesia. *Education Research International, 2022*, 1–9. doi:10.1155/2022/7853310

Rahman, M. & Watanobe, Y. (2023). Chatgpt for education and research: Opportunities, threats, and strategies. *Applied Sciences (Switzerland), 13*(9).

Raji, I. D., Scheuerman, M. K., & Amironesei, R. (2021, March). You can't sit with us: Exclusionary pedagogy in ai ethics education. In *Proceedings of the 2021 ACM Conference on Fairness, Accountability, and Transparency* (pp. 515-525). ACM. 10.1145/3442188.3445914

Ramachandran, P., Liu, S., Lasecki, W., & Riedl, M. (2021). Creating educational materials using gpt-3. *arXiv preprint arXiv:2103.05874*, .

Rambe, P. (2020). A Framework for Ethical Integration of AI in Education: Core Components and Approaches. In Artificial Intelligence in Education (pp. 295-299). Springer.

Ranganathan, S. R. (1931). The five laws of library science. Madras Library Association (Madras, India) and Edward Goldston (London, UK).

Ranganathan, S. R. (1931). *The five laws of library science. Madras Library Association (Madras, India) and Edward Goldston.* Assessing U.S. Higher Education Sector's AI Adoption and Capabilities. https://edudownloads.azureedge.net/msdownloads/FutureReadyBusiness_HigherEducation_AI_US_Design_v2.pdf?azure-portal=true

Regan, P. M., & Jesse, J. (2019). Ethical challenges of edtech, big data and personalized learning: Twenty-first century student sorting and tracking. *Ethics and Information Technology, 21*(3), 167–179. doi:10.100710676-018-9492-2

Rehman, S. (2022, June 29). *Challenges in chatbot development.* IDETA. https://www.ideta.io/blog-posts-english/challenges-in-chatbot-development-chatbot-strategy

Rivas, P.; Zhao, L. Marketing with chatgpt: Navigating the ethical terrain of gpt-based chatbot technology. *AI* **2023**, *4*, 375–384.

Robin, B. R. (2008). Digital storytelling: A powerful technology tool for the 21st century classroom. *Theory into Practice, 47*(3), 220–228. doi:10.1080/00405840802153916

Rodrigues, S. P., van Eck, N. J., Waltman, L., & Jansen, F. W. (2014). Mapping patient safety: A large-scale literature review using bibliometric visualisation techniques. *BMJ Open, 4*(3), e004468. doi:10.1136/bmjopen-2013-004468 PMID:24625640

Rogoff, B. (1998). Cognition as a Collaborative Process. In D. Kuhn & R. S. Siegler (Eds.), Handbook of Child Psychology: Vol. 2. *Cognition, Perception, and Language* (5th ed., pp. 679–744). Wiley.

Rojas-Sánchez, M. A., Palos-Sánchez, P. R., & Folgado-Fernández, J. A. (2023). Systematic literature review and bibliometric analysis on virtual reality and education. *Education and Information Technologies, 28*(1), 155–192. doi:10.100710639-022-11167-5 PMID:35789766

Romero, C., & Ventura, S. (2020). Educational data mining and learning analytics: An updated survey. *Wiley Interdisciplinary Reviews. Data Mining and Knowledge Discovery, 10*(3), e1355. doi:10.1002/widm.1355

Rudra, S. (2023, March 30). *ChatGPT in education: The pros, cons and unknowns of generative AI.* Technology Solutions That Drive Education. https://edtechmagazine.com/k12/article/2023/03/chatgpt-in-education-generative-ai-perfcon

Russell & Norvig. (2023). Mission AI, Research for Policy. Springer. https://doi.org/ doi:10.1007/978-3-031-21448-6_215-39

Sabzalieva, E., & Valentini, A. ChatGPT and Artificial Intelligence in Higher Education: Quick Start Guide. 2023. Available online: https://eduq.info/xmlui/handle/11515/38828

Sadler, D. R. (1989). Formative assessment in the design of instructional systems. *Instructional Science, 18*(2), 119–144. doi:10.1007/BF00117714

Safii, M. (2019, February). Redefining the five laws of library science in the digital age. In *2nd Internasional Conference on Culture and Language in Southeast Asia (ICCLAS 2018)* (pp. 24-27). Atlantis Press. 10.2991/icclas-18.2019.7

Salahuddin, Z., Woodruff, H. C., Chatterjee, A., & Lambin, P. (2022). Transparency of deep neural networks for medical image analysis: A review of interpretability methods. *Computers in Biology and Medicine, 140*, 105111. doi:10.1016/j.compbiomed.2021.105111 PMID:34891095

Säljö, R. (1996). Mental and physical artifacts in cognitive practice. In P. Reimann & H. Spada (Eds.), *Learning in humans and machines: Towards an interdisciplinary learning science* (pp. 83–96). Pergamon.

Sallam, M. (2023). ChatGPT utility in healthcare education, research, and practice: Systematic review on the promising perspectives and valid concerns. *Health Care, 11*, 887. PMID:36981544

SallamM. (2023). *The utility of ChatGPT as an example of large language models in healthcare education, research and practice: Systematic review on the future perspectives and potential limitations*. medRxiv. doi:10.1101/2023.02.19.23286155

Salomon, G., Perkins, D. N., & Globerson, T. (1991). Partners in Cognition: Extending Human Intelligence with Intelligent Technologies. *Educational Researcher*, *20*(3), 2–9. doi:10.3102/0013189X020003002

Samuel, J. (2023). *Response to the March 2023 'Pause Giant AI Experiments: An Open Letter.'*

Sánchez-Prieto, J. C., Gamazo, A., Cruz-Benito, J., Therón, R., & García-Peñalvo, F. J. (2020). AI-driven assessment of students: Current uses and research trends. In P. Zaphiris & A. Ioannou (Eds.), *Learning and Collaboration Technologies. Design, Experiences*. Springer Nature. DOI: 10.1007/978-3-030-50513-4_22

Sánchez-Prieto, J. C., Cruz-Benito, J., Therón Sánchez, R., & García Peñalvo, F. J. (2020). Assessed by machines: Development of a TAM-based tool to measure ai-based assessment acceptance among students. *International Journal of Interactive Multimedia and Artificial Intelligence*, *6*(4), 80–86. doi:10.9781/ijimai.2020.11.009

Sandhya, H. (2021). The Survival of Travel and Tourism Industry amidst the Covid 19 Pandemic-Challenges and Opportunities of the Indian Tourism Sector. *Atna Journal of Tourism Studies, 16*(1).

Sandhya, H., & Varghese, B. (2023). Big Data and Artificial Intelligence: Creative Tools for Destination Competitiveness. In Multidisciplinary Approaches in AI, Creativity, Innovation, and Green Collaboration (pp. 155-166). IGI Global.

Sandhya, H., & Varghese, B. (2023). The Emerging Role of Innovative Teaching Practices in Tourism Education in the Post-COVID-19 Era. In Innovative Digital Practices and Globalization in Higher Education (pp. 286-299). IGI Global.

Sandoval, Z. V. (2018). Design and implementation of a chatbot in online higher education settings. *Issues in Information Systems*, *19*(4).

Sauer, F. (2021). Lethal autonomous weapons systems. In *The Routledge Social Science Handbook of AI* (pp. 237–250). Routledge. doi:10.4324/9780429198533-17

Schiff, D. (2021). Out of the laboratory and into the classroom: The future of artificial intelligence in education. *AI & Society*, *36*(1), 331–348. doi:10.100700146-020-01033-8 PMID:32836908

Schneider, B., Dowell, N., & Thompson, K. (2021). Collaboration analytics—Current state and potential futures. *Journal of Learning Analytics*, *8*(1), 1–12. doi:10.18608/jla.2021.7447

Schopenhauer, A., Aquila, R., Carus, D., & Kolak, D. (2016). *Arthur Schopenhauer: The World as Will and Presentation* (Vol. I). Routledge.

Seldon, A., & Abidoye, T. R. (2018). The Ethics of AI in Education: A Research Agenda. *Journal of Learning Analytics*, *5*(3), 169–183.

Selwyn, N. (2018). *Six reasons AI technology will never take over from human teachers*. Monash University. https://lens.monash.edu/@education/2018/06/15/1352383/ai-technology-will-never-take-over-from-human-teachers

Selwyn, N. (2019). Should We Be Worried About... Artificial Intelligence in Education? *Learning, Media and Technology*, *44*(1), 1–4.

Seo, K., Tang, J., Roll, I., Fels, S., & Yoon, D. (2021). The impact of artificial intelligence on learner–instructor interaction in online learning. *International Journal of Educational Technology in Higher Education*, *18*(1), 1–23. doi:10.118641239-021-00292-9 PMID:34778540

Shabaninejad, S., Khosravi, H., Abdi, S., Indulska, M., & Sadiq, S. (2022, June). Incorporating explainable learning analytics to assist educators with identifying students in need of attention. In *Proceedings of the Ninth ACM Conference on Learning@ Scale* (pp. 384-388). ACM. 10.1145/3491140.3528292

Shah, M., & Sarker, M. H. (2020). Ethical Considerations of Artificial Intelligence and Intelligent Tutoring Systems in Education. In *Proceedings of the 2020 IEEE Technology and Engineering Education Conference (ITEEA)* (pp. 1-10). IEEE.

Shapiro, J., & Blackman, R. (2020). Four steps for drafting an ethical data practices blueprint. *TechCrunch.* https://techcrunch.com/2020/07/24/four-steps-for-an-ethical-data-practices-blueprint/

Sharma, U., Tomar, P., Bhardwaj, H., & Sakalle, A. (2021). Artificial intelligence and its implications in education. In Impact of AI Technologies on Teaching, Learning, and Research in Higher Education (pp. 222-235). IGI Global. doi:10.4018/978-1-7998-4763-2.ch014

Shaw, C., & Switky, B. (2018). Designing and Using Simulations in the International Relations Classroom. *Journal of Political Science Education, 14*(4), 523–534. doi:10.1080/15512169.2018.1433543

Shaw, J., Rudzicz, F., Jamieson, T., & Goldfarb, A. (2019). Artificial intelligence and the implementation challenge. *Journal of Medical Internet Research, 21*(7), e13659. doi:10.2196/13659 PMID:31293245

Shemshack, A., & Spector, J. M. (2020). A systematic literature review of personalized learning terms. *Smart Learning Environments, 7*(1), 1–20. doi:10.118640561-020-00140-9

Shen, L., & Su, A. (2020). The changing roles of teachers with AI. In M. K. Habib (Ed.), *Revolutionizing education in the age of AI and machine learning* (pp. 1–25). IGI Global. doi:10.4018/978-1-5225-7793-5.ch001

Shneiderman, B. (2020). Bridging the gap between ethics and practice: Guidelines for reliable, safe, and trustworthy human-centered AI systems. [TiiS]. *ACM Transactions on Interactive Intelligent Systems, 10*(4), 1–31. doi:10.1145/3419764

Shridhar, K. (2017). *How Close Are Chatbots to Passing the Turing Test?* Chatbots Magazine.

Shweta. (2022, August 21). What is a chatbot? Everything you need to know. *Forbes.* https://www.forbes.com/advisor/business/software/what-is-a-chatbot/

Siau, K., & Wang, W. (2020). Artificial intelligence (AI) ethics: Ethics of AI and ethical AI. *Journal of Database Management, 31*(2), 74–87. doi:10.4018/JDM.2020040105

Sibai, F. N. (2020, June). AI crimes: a classification. In *2020 International Conference on Cyber Security and Protection of Digital Services (Cyber Security)* (pp. 1-8). IEEE.

Siegel, D., Acharya, P., & Sivo, S. (2017). Extending the Technology Acceptance Model to Improve Usage & Decrease Resistance toward a New Technology by Faculty in Higher Education. *The Journal of Technology Studies, 43*(2), 58–69. doi:10.21061/jots.v43i2.a.1

Siepmann, C. A. (1941). Further thoughts on radio criticism. *Public Opinion Quarterly, 5*(2), 308–312. doi:10.1086/265500

Sievert, C., & Shirley, K. E. (2014). A method for visualizing and interpreting topics. *Proceedings of the Workshop on Interactive Language Learning, Visualization, and Interfaces* (pp. 63–70). Baltimore, Maryland, USA. 10.3115/v1/W14-3110

Skavronskaya, L., Hadinejad, A., & Cotterell, D. (2023). Reversing the threat of artificial intelligence to opportunity: A discussion of ChatGPT in tourism education. *Journal of Teaching in Travel & Tourism, 23*(2), 253–258. doi:10.1080/15313220.2023.2196658

Skerrett, D. (2017). Seven reasons why most chatbots launched in 2017 are dead on arrival. *EContent (Wilton, Conn.), 40*(4), 14–15.

Skinner, B., Leavey, G., & Rothi, D. (2019). 'Managerialism and teacher professional identity: Impact on well-being among teachers in the UK'. *Educational Review*. doi:10.1080/00131911.2018.1556205

Smith, M. T., & Evans, J. J. (2018). Storytelling as transdisciplinarity: An experiment in first-year composition and communication. In B. Hokanson, G. Clinton, & K. Kaminski (Eds.), Educational technology and narrative: Story and instructional design (pp. 103–112). Springer International Publishing.

Smith, B., & Welty, C. (2001). *Ontology: Towards a new synthesis. Formal Ontology in Information Systems*. ACM Press.

Smith, H. (2021). Clinical AI: Opacity, accountability, responsibility and liability. *AI & Society, 36*(2), 535–545. doi:10.100700146-020-01019-6

Smyrnaiou, Z., Georgakopoulou, E., & Sotiriou, S. (2020). Promoting a mixed-design model of scientific creativity through digital storytelling—The CCQ model for creativity. *International Journal of STEM Education, 7*(1), 1–22. doi:10.118640594-020-00223-6

Solutions, A. (2020). Chatbots Statistics. *Artificial Solutions.* https://www.artificial-solutions.com/ chatbots#12

Sönmez, V. (2021). Ethical Issues in AI-Based Educational Technologies: A Systematic Literature Review. *Journal of Educational Computing Research, 59*(7), 1144–1175.

Spilt, J. L., Koomen, H. M., & Thijs, J. T. (2011). Teacher wellbeing: The importance of teacher–student relationships. *Educational Psychology Review, 23*(4), 457–477. doi:10.100710648-011-9170-y

Stachowicz-Stanusch, A., & Amann, W. (2018). *Artificial intelligence at universities in Poland*. Organizacja i Zarządzanie: kwartalnik naukowy.

Stahl, B. C., Timmermans, J. O. B., & Mittelstadt, B. D. (2016). The ethics of computing: A survey of the computing-oriented literature. *ACM Computing Surveys, 48*(4), 1–38. doi:10.1145/2871196

Stahl, B. C., & Wright, D. (2018). Ethics and privacy in AI and big data: Implementing responsible research and innovation. *IEEE Security and Privacy, 16*(3), 26–33. doi:10.1109/MSP.2018.2701164

Stark, L., & Hoey, J. (2021). The ethics of emotion in artificial intelligence systems. In *Proceedings of the 2021 ACM Conference on Fairness, Accountability, and Transparency* (pp. 782-793). ACM. 10.1145/3442188.3445939

Steinbauer, G., Kandlhofer, M., Chklovski, T., Heintz, F., & Koenig, S. (2021). A differentiated discussion about AI education K-12. *Kunstliche Intelligenz, 35*(2), 131–137. doi:10.100713218-021-00724-8 PMID:34007103

Stern, J. (2022, December 16). Five chats to help you understand ChatGPT. *The Atlantic*. https://www.theatlantic.com/technology/archive/2022/12/openai-chatgpt-chatbot-messages/672411/

Stringer, R. (2018). Realist ethical naturalism for ethical non-naturalists. *Philosophical Studies, 175*(2), 339–362. doi:10.100711098-017-0870-0

Suh, S., & An, P. (2022, March). Leveraging generative conversational AI to develop a creative learning environment for computational thinking. In *27th International Conference on Intelligent User Interfaces* (pp. 73–76). Association for Computing Machinery. 10.1145/3490100.3516473

Sunilkumar, S. R. (2023, January 21). ChatGPT co-authors research papers; Is it even ethical, academia debates. *Hindustan Times*. https://www.hindustantimes.com/technology/chatgpt-co-authors-research-papers-is-it-even-ethical-academia-debates-101674303574136.html

Sun, L., Tang, Y., & Zuo, W. (2020). Coronavirus pushes education online. *Nature Materials, 19*(6), 687–687. doi:10.103841563-020-0678-8 PMID:32341513

Sunstein, C. R. (2018). *Republic: Divided democracy in the age of social media.* Princeton University Press.

Suresh Babu, C. V., & Padma, R. (2022) "Technology Transformation Through Skilled Teachers in Teaching Accountancy." Advancing STEM Education and Innovation in a Time of Distance Learning, edited by Roberto Alonso González-Lezcano, IGI Global, 2023, pp. 211-233. doi:10.4018/978-1-6684-5053-6.ch011

Suresh Babu, C. V. (2022). *Artificial Intelligence and Expert Systems.* Anniyappa Publications.

Suresh Babu, C. V., & Rohan, B. (2023). Evaluation and Quality Assurance for Rapid E-Learning and Development of Digital Learning Resources. In M. Santally, Y. Rajabalee, & R. Rajputh (Eds.), *Implementing Rapid E-Learning Through Interactive Materials Development* (pp. 139–170). IGI Global., doi:10.4018/978-1-6684-4940-0.ch008

Sweeney, P. (2022). Trusting social robots. *AI and Ethics*, 1–8. PMID:35634257

Tan, S. C., Lee, A. V. Y., & Lee, M. (2022). A systematic review of artificial intelligence techniques for collaborative learning over the past two decades. *Computers and Education. Artificial Intelligence, 3*, 100097. doi:10.1016/j.caeai.2022.100097

Tapalova, O., & Zhiyenbayeva, N. (2022). Artificial Intelligence in Education: AIEd for Personalised Learning Pathways. *The Electronic Journal of e-Learning, 20*(5). www.ejel.org

Tapalova, O., Zhivenbaveva, N., & Gura, D. (2022). Artificial intelligence in education: AIEd for personalised learning pathways. *Electronic Journal of e-Learning, 20*(5), 639–653. doi:10.34190/ejel.20.5.2597

Taylor, K. (2019). Ethical Principles for AI and Education. In *Proceedings of the 9th International Conference on Learning Analytics & Knowledge* (pp. 479-480). IEEE.

Teal, M. (2023, April 18). *The ethics of college students using ChatGPT.* Ethics and Policy. https://ethicspolicy.unc.edu/news/2023/04/17/the-ethics-of-college-students-using-chatgpt/

Tetzlaff, L., Schmiedek, F., & Brod, G. (2021). Developing personalized education: A dynamic framework. *Educational Psychology Review, 33*(3), 863–882. doi:10.100710648-020-09570-w

Tharp, R. G., & Gallimore, R. (1988). *Rousing Minds to Life: Teaching, Learning, and Schooling in Social Context.* Cambridge University Press.

The Institute for Ethical AI in Education. (n.d.). *The Ethical Framework for AI in Education.* Buckingham. https://www.buckingham.ac.uk/wp-content/uploads/2021/03/The-Institute-for-Ethical-AI-in-Education-The-Ethical-Framework-for-AI-in-Education.pdf

The Open University. (2014). *Policy on Ethical use of Student Data for Learning Analytics.* The Open University. https://help.open.ac.uk/documents/policies/ethical-use-of-student-data/files/22/ethical-use-of-student-data-policy.pdf

Tlili, A., Essalmi, F., Jemni, M., & Chen, N. S. (2018). A complete validated learning analytics framework: Designing issues from data preparation perspective. [IJICTE]. *International Journal of Information and Communication Technology Education, 14*(2), 1–16. doi:10.4018/IJICTE.2018040101

Tlili, A., Essalmi, F., Jemni, M., & Chen, N. S. (2019). A complete validated learning analytics framework: Designing issues from data use perspective. [IJICTE]. *International Journal of Information and Communication Technology Education, 15*(3), 42–59. doi:10.4018/IJICTE.2019070104

Today, I. (2023, February 8). ChatGPT and its impact on education sector. *India Today*. https://www.indiatoday.in/education-today/featurephilia/story/chatgpt-and-its-impact-on-education-sector-2331895-2023-02-08

Topsakal, O., & Topsakal, E. (2022). Framework for A Foreign Language Teaching Software for Children Utilizing AR, Voicebots and ChatGPT (Large Language Models). *The Journal of Cognitive Systems*.

Tsyhaniuk, D., & Akenten, W. N. (2021). Examining budgeting and fund allocation in higher education. *Financial Markets, Institutions and Risks*. https://doi.org/ doi:10.21272/fmir.5(4).128-138.202

Tucker, C. R. (2020). *Balance With Blended Learning: Partner With Your Students to Reimagine Learning and Reclaim Your Life*. Corwin.

Tuomi, I. (2018). *The impact of artificial intelligence on learning, teaching, and education. Policies for the future. M. Cabrera Giraldez* (R. Vuorikari & Y. Punie, Eds.). Publications Office of the European Union., doi:10.2760/12297

UNESCO. (2019). *Artificial intelligence in education: Challenges and opportunities for sustainable development*. UNESCO. http://repositorio.minedu.gob.pe/bitstream/handle/20.500.12799/6533/Artificial%20intelligence%20in%20education%20challenges%20and%20opportunities%20for%20sustainable%20development.pdf

UNESCO. (2020). Artificial Intelligence in Education: Challenges and Opportunities for Sustainable Development. Retrieved from https://unesdoc.unesco.org/ark:/48223/pf0000374845

UNESCO. (2020). *Artificial Intelligence in Education: Challenges and Opportunities for Sustainable Development*. UNESCO. https://unesdoc.unesco.org/ark:/48223/pf0000374845

UNESCO. (2020a). *International forum on AI and education 2022. Steering AI to empower teachers and transform teaching* [Concept note]. UNESCO. https://en.unesco.org/sites/default/files/ai-in-education-forum-2022-cn-en.pdf

UNESCO. (2021). AI *in Education: Ethics Guidelines for UNESCO Member States*. UNESCO. https://en.unesco.org/ai-edu-ethics

UNESCO. (2022b). *Recommendations on the ethics of artificial intelligence*. UNESCO. https://unesdoc.unesco.org/ark:/48223/pf0000381137

UNESCO. (2023). *ChatGPT and Artificial Intelligence in higher education: quick start guide*. United Nations Educational, Scientific and Cultural Organisation.

UNICEF. (2020, August 24). Wh*at will a return to school during the COVID-19 pandemic look like?* UNICEF. https://www.unicef.org/coronavirus/what-will-return-school-during-covid-19- pandemic-look

United Nations Educational, Scientific and Cultural Organization (UNESCO). (2021). Recommendation on the ethics of artificial intelligence. UNESDOC Digital Library. https://unesdoc.unesco.org/ark:/48223/pf0000380455

United Nations. (2020, August). *Policy Brief: Education during COVID-19 and beyond*. United Nations. https://www.un.org/development/desa/dspd/wp-content/uploads/sites/22/2020/08/sg_policy_brief_covid-19_and_education_august_2020.pdf

Urquidi-Martín, A. C., Tamarit-Aznar, C., & Sánchez-García, J. (2019). Determinants of the Effectiveness of Using Renewable Resource Management-Based Simulations in the Development of Critical Thinking: An Application of the Experiential Learning Theory. *Sustainability (Basel)*, *11*(19), 5469. doi:10.3390u11195469

Uunona, G. N., & Goosen, L. (2023). Leveraging Ethical Standards in Artificial Intelligence Technologies: A Guideline for Responsible Teaching and Learning Applications. In Handbook of Research on Instructional Technologies in Health Education and Allied Disciplines (pp. 310-330). IGI Global. doi:10.4018/978-1-6684-7164-7.ch014 van Otterlo, M. (2017). From algorithmic black boxes to adaptive white boxes: Declarative decision-theoretic ethical programs as codes of ethics. *arXiv preprint arXiv:1711.06035.*

Vandewaetere, M., Cornillie, F., & Desmet, P. (2020). Ethical Guidelines for Using Artificial Intelligence in Education: Teachers' Perspectives. *International Journal of Artificial Intelligence in Education, 30*(4), 526–561.

Varghese, B., & Pratyusha, Y. B. V. L. (2022). *Tools and Technologies for the Governance of Knowledge Management.* Understanding, Implementing, and Evaluating Knowledge Management in Business Settings. doi:10.4018/978-1-6684-4431-3.ch008

Vargo, C., & Hopp, T. (2023). *Incivility on Popular Politics and News Subreddits: An Analysis of In-groups.* Community Guidelines and Relationships with Social Media Engagement.

Vaswani, A., Shazeer, N., Parmar, N., Uszkoreit, J., Jones, L., & Aidan, N. (2017). Gomez, Lukasz Kaiser, and Illia Polosukhin. Attention is all you need. *Advances in Neural Information Processing Systems*, 5998–6008.

Verleger, M., & Pembridge, J. (2018, October). A pilot study integrating an AI-driven chatbot in an introductory programming course. In IEEE frontiers in Education Conference (FIE), (pp. 1–4). IEEE Publications.

Vinay, S. B. (2023). Application of artificial intelligence (AI) in school teaching and learning process - Review and analysis. *International Journal of Information Technology and Management Information Systems, 14*(1), 1–5. doi:10.17605/OSF.IO/AERNV

Vincent, J. (2023, January 5). ChatGPT and AI language tools banned by AI conference for writing papers. *The Verge.* https://www.theverge.com/2023/1/5/23540291/chatgpt-ai-writing-tool-banned-writing-academic-icml-paper

Vincent-Lancrin, S., & Van der Vlies, R. (2020). *Trustworthy artificial intelligence (AI) in education: Promises and challenges.*

Visvizi, A. (2021). *Artificial intelligence (AI): Explaining, querying, demystifying.* Artificial Intelligence and Its Contexts: Security, Business and Governance, 13-26.

Voigt, R., Von dem Bussche, A., & Even, M. (2019). Artificial Intelligence in Education: A Critical Look Beyond the Hype. *Journal of Educational Technology, 16*(2), 41–52.

Wagan, A. A., Khan, A. A., Chen, Y., Yee, P. L., Yang, J., & Laghari, A. A. (2023). Artificial Intelligence-Enabled Game-Based Learning and Quality of Experience: A Novel and Secure Framework (B-AIQoE). *Sustainability (Basel), 15*(6), 5362. doi:10.3390u15065362

Waltzer, T., Cox, R. L., & Heyman, G. D. (2023). Testing the ability of teachers and students to differentiate between essays generated by ChatGPT and high school students. *Human Behavior and Emerging Technologies, 2023*(1), 1–9. doi:10.1155/2023/1923981

Wampler, M. (2023, January 5). The technology behind Chat GPT-3. *ClearCOGS.* https://www.clearcogs.com/post/the-technology-behind-chat-gpt-3

Wang, M., & Zheng, X. (2021). Using Game-Based Learning to Support Learning Science: A Study with Middle School Students. *The Asia-Pacific Education Researcher, 30*(2), 167–17. doi:10.100740299-020-00523-z

Wang, X., & Hovy, E. (2020). Automatic feedback generation for student writing using pre-trained language models. In *Proceedings of the 58th Annual Meeting of the Association for Computational Linguistics*, (pp. 6835–6846).

Wang, X., Li, L., Tan, S. C., Yang, L., & Lei, J. (2023). Preparing for AI-enhanced education: Conceptualizing and empirically examining teachers' AI readiness. *Computers in Human Behavior, 146*, 107798. doi:10.1016/j.chb.2023.107798

Wang, Y., Liu, C., & Tu, Y.-F. (2021). Factors affecting the adoption of AI-based applications in higher education: An analysis of teachers' perspectives using structural equation modeling. *Journal of Educational Technology & Society*, *24*(3), 116–129.

Watty, K., McKay, J., & Ngo, L. (2016). Innovators or inhibitors? Accounting faculty resistance to new educational technologies in higher education. *Journal of Accounting Education*, *36*, 1–15. doi:10.1016/j.jaccedu.2016.03.003

Weitzman, M. L. (1993). What to preserve? An application of diversity theory to crane conservation. *The Quarterly Journal of Economics*, *108*(1), 157–183. doi:10.2307/2118499

Welding, L. (2023, March 13). Half of college students say using AI is cheating. *Best Colleges*. https://www.bestcolleges.com/research/college-students-ai-tools-survey/

Wen, J., & Wang, W. (2023). The future of ChatGPT in academic research and publishing: A commentary for clinical and translational medicine. *Clinical and Translational Medicine*, *13*(3), 1207. doi:10.1002/ctm2.1207 PMID:36941774

Werthner, H., Stanger, A., Schiaffonati, V., Knees, P., Hardman, L., & Ghezzi, C. (2023). Digital Humanism: The Time Is Now. *Computer*, *56*(1), 138–142. doi:10.1109/MC.2022.3219528

Wertsch, J. V. (1991). *Voices of the Mind: A Sociocultural Approach to Mediated Action*. Harvard University Press.

Wetcho, S., & Na-Songkhla, J. (2022). An investigation of pre-service teachers using mobile and wearable devices for emotion recognition and social sharing of emotion to support emotion regulation in mCSCL environments. *Contemporary Educational Technology*, *14*(2), ep359. doi:10.30935/cedtech/11668

White, J. P., Dennis, S., Tomko, M., Bell, J., & Winter, S. (2021). Paths to social licence for tracking-data analytics in university research and services. *PLoS One*, *16*(5), e0251964. doi:10.1371/journal.pone.0251964 PMID:34019592

White, M. C., & Bembenutty, H. (2013). Not all avoidance help seekers are created equal: Individual differences in adaptive and executive help seeking. *SAGE Open*, *3*(2), 2158244013484916. doi:10.1177/2158244013484916

Whittlestone, J., Nyrup, R., Alexandrova, A., Dihal, K., & Cave, S. (2019). *Ethical and societal implications of algorithms, data, and artificial intelligence: A roadmap for research*. Nuffield Foundation.

Williamson, B. (2021). Psychodata: Disassembling the psychological, economic, and statistical infrastructure of 'social-emotional learning.'. *Journal of Education Policy*, *36*(1), 129–154. doi:10.1080/02680939.2019.1672895

Wogu, I. A. P., Misra, S., Assibong, P. A., Olu-Owolabi, E. F., Maskeli¯unas, R., & Damasevicius, R. (2019). Artificial intelligence, smart classrooms, and online education in the 21st century: Implications for human development. *Journal of Cases on Information Technology*, *21*(3), 66–79. doi:10.4018/JCIT.2019070105

Wolla, S., Schug, M. C., & Wood, W. C. (2019). The economics of artificial intelligence and robotics. *Social Education*, *83*(2), 84–88.

Wong, J. (2020, October 25). Post-secondary students call for changes to online exam rules as cheating concerns rise. *CBC*. https://www.cbc.ca/news/canada/post-secondary-assessment-integrity-proctoring-1.5767953

Woo, J. H., & Choi, H. (2021). Systematic review for AI-based language learning tools. *Journal of Digital Contents Society*, *22*(11), 1783–1792. doi:10.9728/dcs.2021.22.11.1783

Wu, F., Lu, C., Zhu, M., Chen, H., Zhu, J., Yu, K., Li, L., Li, M., Chen, Q., Li, X., Cao, X., Wang, Z., Zha, Z., Zhuang, Y., & Pan, Y. (2020). Towards a new generation of artificial intelligence in China. *Nature Machine Intelligence*, *2*(6), 312–316. doi:10.103842256-020-0183-4

Xu, Z., Wijekumar, K., Ramirez, G., Hu, X., & Irey, R. (2019). The effectiveness of intelligent tutoring systems on K-12 students' reading comprehension: A meta-analysis. *British Journal of Educational Technology*, *50*(6), 3119–3137. doi:10.1111/bjet.12758

Yamin, M. M., Ullah, M., Ullah, H., & Katt, B. (2021). Weaponized AI for cyber attacks. *Journal of Information Security and Applications*, *57*, 102722. doi:10.1016/j.jisa.2020.102722

Yan, L., Sha, L., Zhao, L., Li, Y., Martinez-Maldonado, R., Chen, G., & Gašević, D. (2023). Practical and ethical challenges of large language models in education: A systematic literature review. arXiv preprint arXiv:2303.13379.

Yan, L., Sha, L., Zhao, L., Li, Y., Martinez-Maldonado, R., Chen, G., Li, X., Jin, Y., & Gasevic, D. (2023). Practical and ethical challenges of large language models in education: A systematic scoping review. *British Journal of Educational Technology.*

Yang, Z., Dai, Z., Yang, Y., Carbonell, J., & Le, Q. (2019). Evaluating automated essay scoring with bert. *arXiv preprint arXiv:1902.08531.*

Young, A. T., Amara, D., Bhattacharya, A., & Wei, M. L. (2021). Patient and general public attitudes towards clinical artificial intelligence: A mixed methods systematic review. *The Lancet. Digital Health*, *3*(9), e599–e611. doi:10.1016/S2589-7500(21)00132-1 PMID:34446266

Young, K., & Maher, D. (2023). Generative AI technology to support high school students experiencing writing challenges. In R. E. Ferdig, R. Hartshorne, E. Baumgartner, R. Kaplan-Rakowski, & C. Mouza (Eds.), *What PreK-12 teachers should know about educational technology in 2023: A research-to-practice anthology* (pp. 123–132). Association for the Advancement of Computing in Education., http://hdl.handle.net/10453/171654

Yu, H. (2023). Reflection on whether Chat GPT should be banned by academia from the perspective of education and teaching. *Frontiers in Psychology*, *14*, 2156. doi:10.3389/fpsyg.2023.1181712 PMID:37325766

Zajda, J., & Vissing, Y. (Eds.). (2022). *Discourses of globalisation, ideology, and human rights* (Vol. 14). Springer. doi:10.1007/978-3-030-90590-3

Zawacki-Richter, O., Marín, V. I., Bond, M., & Gouverneur, F. (2019). Systematic review of research on artificial intelligence applications in higher education – where are the educators? *International Journal of Educational Technology in Higher Education*, *16*(1), 39. Advance online publication. doi:10.118641239-019-0171-0

Zellers, R., Bau, D., Neelakantan, A., Holtzman, A., Rashkin, H., Yatskar, M., & Farhadi, A. (2019). Defending against neural fake news. *arXiv preprint arXiv:1905.12616.*

Zeng, J. (2020). Artificial intelligence and China's authoritarian governance. *International Affairs*, *96*(6), 1441–1459. doi:10.1093/ia/iiaa172

Zhai, X., Chu, X., Chai, C. S., Jong, M. S. Y., Istenic, A., Spector, M., Liu, J. B., Yuan, J., & Li, Y. (2021). A Review of Artificial Intelligence (AI) in Education from 2010 to 2020. Complexity. doi:10.1155/2021/8812542

Zhang, C., Zhang, C., Li, C., Qiao, Y., Zheng, S., Dam, S. K., Zhang, M., Kim, J. U., Kim, S. T., & Choi, J. (2023). One small step for generative ai, one giant leap for agi: A complete survey on chatgpt in aigc era. *arXiv*.2304.06488.

Zhang, Q., Lin S., Liu, J & Jin, Y. (2022). A game perspective on collaborative learning among students in higher education. *Cogent Education.* doi:. 2022.2115617 doi:10.1080/2331186X

Zhang, B., Zhu, J., & Su, H. (2023). Toward the third generation artificial intelligence. *Science China. Information Sciences*, *66*(2), 1–19. doi:10.100711432-021-3449-x

Zhang, S., Chen, J., Wen, Y., Chen, H., Gao, Q., & Wang, Q. (2021). Capturing regulatory patterns in online collaborative learning: A network analytic approach. *International Journal of Computer-Supported Collaborative Learning, 16*(1), 37–66. doi:10.100711412-021-09339-5

Zhang, Y., Wu, M., Tian, G. Y., Zhang, G., & Lu, J. (2021). Ethics and privacy of artificial intelligence: Understandings from bibliometrics. *Knowledge-Based Systems, 222*, 106994. doi:10.1016/j.knosys.2021.106994

Zhao, Y. (2020). Tofu Is Not Cheese: Rethinking Education Amid the COVID-19 Pandemic. *ECNU Review of Education, 3*(2), 189–203. doi:10.1177/2096531120928082

Zuiderwijk, A., Chen, Y. C., & Salem, F. (2021). Implications of the use of artificial intelligence in public governance: A systematic literature review and a research agenda. *Government Information Quarterly, 38*(3), 101577. doi:10.1016/j.giq.2021.101577

About the Contributors

Jared Sagini Keengwe is a Professor at the University of North Dakota (UND) and serves as the Director of the Undergraduate Elementary Education program. He is the editor-in-chief of two IGI Global Book Series: Advances in Higher Education and Professional Development (AHEPD) and Advances in Early Childhood and K-12 Education (AECKE). Prof. Keengwe has published several books and manuscripts in refereed journals. His work was honored with the UND Foundation/McDermott Faculty Award for Excellence in Academic Advising. He was a recipient of the North Dakota Spirit Faculty Achievement Award in recognition of significant contributions in teaching, research, and service. At the national level, Prof. Keengwe was a recipient of the International Institute of Education Fellowship under the Carnegie African Diaspora Fellowship Program (CADFP) – a scholar fellowship program for educational projects at African higher education institutions. The program is funded by a grant from Carnegie Corporation of New York (CCNY).

* * *

Luanne Amato currently serves as an Associate Professor at Holy Family University in Philadelphia, PA where she teaches quantitative subjects and concepts in management marketing. She holds a Doctor of Education degree in Curriculum, Teaching, and Learning from Northeastern University, Boston, MA and received an MBA in International Business from Rosemont College, Bryn Mawr, PA. Student engagement and best practices in instruction are the main focus of her research, presentations, and published works. Luanne has contributed three chapters to textbooks published by IGI Global Publications in The Handbook of Research on Active Learning; The Handbook of Research on Adult Education and the Development of Lifelong Learners and The Handbook of Research on Social Inequality and Education. She resides with her husband in Pennsylvania and has 5 children and 4 grandchildren.

C.V. Suresh Babu is a pioneer in content development. A true entrepreneur, he founded Anniyappa Publications, a company that is highly active in publishing books related to Computer Science and Management. Dr. C.V. Suresh Babu has also ventured into SB Institute, a center for knowledge transfer. He holds a Ph.D. in Engineering Education from the National Institute of Technical Teachers Training & Research in Chennai, along with seven master's degrees in various disciplines such as Engineering, Computer Applications, Management, Commerce, Economics, Psychology, Law, and Education. Additionally, he has UGC-NET/SET qualifications in the fields of Computer Science, Management, Commerce, and Education. Currently, Dr. C.V. Suresh Babu is a Professor in the Department of Information Technology at the School of Computing Science, Hindustan Institute of Technology and Science (Hindustan University) in Padur, Chennai, Tamil Nadu, India. For more information, you can visit his personal blog at .

Oluwabunmi Bakare is an Information Professional/Researcher in the Department of Information Management, Faculty of Communication & Information Sciences, Lead City University. Her research interest covers emerging technologies, digital & virtual libraries, information use and user communities, bullying and mobile bullying, etc. She is passionate about emphasizing the significant roles of Librarians in solving different societal issues with the arsenal of information at their disposal. She is a fellow of the Council for the Development of Social Science Research in Africa and a Queen Elizabeth Scholar in the Advanced Scholars West Africa (QES-AS-WA) program, Carleton University, Canada.

Michelle Cheong is the Professor of Information Systems (Education) and Associate Dean of Postgraduate Professional Education at the School of Computing & Information Systems (SCIS) at the Singapore Management University (SMU). Michelle has won several teaching awards at SMU and she also bagged the inaugural Teradata University Network (TUN) Teaching Innovation Award 2013, which recognizes excellence in the teaching of Business Intelligence and Business Analytics at the undergraduate, graduate and/or executive education levels. Her research interests are in Data and Decision Analytics, and data driven pedagogical research including Technology-Enhanced Learning, Learning Analytics, and AI in Education. She publishes in journals and conferences including Education and Information Technology, Decision Sciences Journal of Innovative Education, Informs Transactions on Education, International Conference on Computers in Education, and International Conference on Teaching, Assessment and Learning for Engineering.

Swapna Gottipati is an Associate Professor of Information Systems (Education) and the Associate Dean of Undergraduate Education at the School of Computing and Information Systems, Singapore Management University. Her research interests include text mining, natural language processing, educational analytics, opinion mining, AI, and business process innovation. Her current research focuses on AI for education and healthcare projects. She has published around 80 papers in highly ranked conferences such as EMNLP, COLING, ICCE, EDUCON, and ASE. She is also a recipient/nominee of several best paper awards at conferences and the Innovative Teacher Awards at SMU. Prior to joining SMU, she worked as a consultant for banking, financial, health, and mobile projects, where she designed, developed, and supported various software systems.

Sandhya H. is pursuing PhD in Tourism Management from Christ University Bangalore. She successfully completed her Mphil and Masters in Tourism Administration (MTA) from Christ University Bangalore by securing the first rank. She has industry experience of one year having worked with one of the leading multinational tour operations companies, Kuoni SOTC, Bangalore and teaching experience of over 6 years having associated with some of the prestigious academic institutions and colleges in Kerala. She has worked as Research Associate of the Major Research Project on the lines of Destination Management Organisations. She is a very passionate and keen researcher and her research interests include Destination Management, Destination Branding and Smart Tourism. She is currently working as Academic Auditor and Deputy Academic Coordinator at Kairos Institute, Cochin, Kerala.

Catherine Hayes is Professor of Health Professions Pedagogy and Scholarship at the University of Sunderland, UK. She is a UK National Teaching Fellow and Principal Fellow of the UK Higher Education Academy. As a graduate of Podiatric Medicine in 1992, Catherine was a Founding Fellow of the Faculty of Podiatric Medicine at the Royal College of Physicians and Surgeons (Glasgow) in 2012 and was awarded

Fellowship of the Royal College of Podiatry (London) in 2010. She is currently Programme Leader of the University of Sunderland's Professional Doctorate pathways for the DBA, EdD, DPM and DProf.

Temitope Oluwatofunmi Idowu-Davies is an educational expert who is passionate about instilling core religious and theological values in learners in addition to promoting equity within the gender ecosystem which is fundamental in the SDGs. She is presently working on contemporary technological trends that scholars should toe in order to be able to effectively discharge their duties to learners.

Mary Kanja is Marriage and Family Therapist (MFT)/ and a counseling Psychologist, she is a Research Mentor with Eider Africa and research supervisor with Pan Africa Christian University. Competent in Family Negotiation and Mediation. Qualified as a Clinical Supervisor, HIV Counsellor, Trauma Mitigation and Management Counselor. She has a passion for promoting family's mental and spiritual health and wellbeing especially of the caregivers of children with special needs. She is PhD holder in Marriage and Family Therapy (MFT) at Pan Africa Christian University (PACU), a Master of Arts in Counselling Psychology at International Leadership University (ILU) formerly NIST, Bachelor in counseling psychology (Arts) at Pan Africa Christian University, Diploma in Community Development and Social Work at Rural Aid Kenya Training Institute, and a Diploma in Christian Ministry at Nairobi International School of Theology (NIST) She has publishes two Journal articles as indicated below on the effects of caregiving of children with autism spectrum disorder on the caregivers' psychological wellbeing in selected integrated primary schools in Nairobi County, Kenya. She is affiliated to Kenya Association of Marriage and Family Therapist (KAMFT) professional body. Her hobbies are Reading, travelling, swimming, visiting with friends, knitting

Tristan Lim is a Lecturer at the School of Business Management, and a member of the Institutional Review Board at Nanyang Polytechnic. In the realm of technology-enabled education, Tristan is particularly intrigued by how assessment drives learning. His research focus has been on the implications of AI on assessment design and the ethical considerations accompanying the implementation of AI in assessments. Tristan was honored with 2 teaching excellence awards in 2020 and 2021, and he was the faculty advisor for 7 award-winning student teams in regional to global industry and academic competitions. Tristan has served on 46 conference technical program committees and journal editorial boards since 2020, including 1 associate editorship. He was also a winner for the IEOM Best Paper Award 2021 (Runner up).

Damian Maher is senior lecturer in in the School of International Studies and Education at the University of Technology Sydney (UTS). Damian has a long history of researching in schools and started teaching at a point where computers were being introduced in a significant way. He is now training pre-service teachers and incorporates the use of digital technologies into his teaching. Damian has conducted numerous research projects looking at the use of digital technologies from kindergarten through to the tertiary level. One of Damian's current research focuses is examining AI in education.

Kiran L Maney currently working as Associate Professor and Programme Coordinator for BBA Branding and Advertising, Sub task force - NEP, and Course Facilitator in the arena of Marketing at CMS, JAIN (Deemed-to-be University). Entrepreneur and consultant to start-up companies. Tutor and mentor for students pursuing CIM UK. She has over 25 years of work experience (15 years of corporate experience in the area of sales and marketing and 10 years of teaching experience). Continuous mentoring, and training students on developing entrepreneurial skills. Teaching and Interfacing with CIM (UK) for the dual course, over 500+ students completed Applied Marketing Course from CIM under her guidance. Guided 200+ students in minor and major projects. Networking with resource persons from different fields for bridging the gap between educators and corporate requirements. Successfully organized and coordinated for ATAL AICTE 5-day FDP 2021. She has contributed as a resource person at AICTE ATAL FDP and delivered a session on LMS, she has been a session speaker at Christ College, Ramiah College, and Jain University in the area of marketing. She has conducted workshops with hands-on experience on Tableau, Customer analytics, Personality development, and Team building. Developed and designed the course delivery, and practical assignments. Founded student clubs – GrahaQ CMS Marketing Club. Having worked in esteemed organizations like Onida Savak and Featherlite. Started her own venture in home interiors and is currently a consultant to NovoTree Minds Consulting Pvt Ltd, Bangalore, and Mark Enterprises Pvt Ltd, Bangalore. Mentor and Consultant for a Start-up company from inception for building a strong marketing platform. Dr. Kiran has authored the books Game of Cases: Case Analysis and Methodology, Corporate Trends, Advertising and Media Management, Entrepreneurship in Emerging Economies, Marketing & Event Management, and Marketing Management (new CBCS 2020-21 BCom). She holds M.B.A., B.Sc, and B.Ed from Karnataka University, Dharwad, India, and Ph.D. from JAIN University. Completed Chartered Institute of Marketing, UK Level, Marketing Management from IIMBx, Indian Institute of Management, Bangalore. Online Certificate Short-term courses from Yale University, IE Business School, University of California, University of Illinois, University of Mexico, Yonsei University, and ISB.

Beatrice Akoth Owino is from Nairobi, Kenya and is currently affiliated with United States International University – Africa. She holds a Master of Science Degree in Information Systems Technology (Cyber Security) and is currently pursuing her Ph.D. in Information Systems Technology, in Computing Department, in the School of Science and Technology, USIU-Africa. Her research interests include Cyber Security and Forensics, AI & Ethics, Information Systems Management and Security. She holds various Certifications including Certified Ethical Hacker (CEH), MCITP, ITIL, and Microsoft Azure. She works at MSF Spain as Service Operations Manager, E-Learning.

Mahona Joseph Paschal is a Professional Teacher, Interdisciplinary Scholar who is skilled in Teaching, Supervision, Creative writing, Leadership and Management in Education. He is a graduate of St Augustine University with a Master of Education Management and Planning. He also holds a Bachelor' of Arts with Education from Kampala International University. He enjoys teaching and really inspired to assist students in building positivity and excitement and empower them to complete their ambitions. Mahona is the author of Responsive Classroom: Student's Relationship and Academic Performance in Tanzania (2020), several Peer Reviewed Articles, Book Chapters in Edited Volumes and Learning Models. He is always looking to learn new skills, techniques and approaches himself over the best experience to his students and he is dedicated to getting the most out of everything he does. Mahona's passion for teaching and learning is evident in the deep investments he makes in helping learners confidently and skillfully engage in Academic works, become bolder writers and better communicators

Chris Schoettle currently serves as an Associate Dean for the School of Business and Technology at Holy Family University in Philadelphia, PA. She holds a Doctorate of Education degree in Educational Leadership from Gratz College, Melrose Park, PA and received an M.Ed. in Math Education from Aracadia University, Glenside, PA and an M.Ed. in Sport and Recreation Administration from Temple University, Philadelphia, PA. Best practices in teaching and utilizing new technologies in teaching are her research interests. She resides with her husband and two sons in Philadelphia, PA.

Bindi Varghese has a Doctorate in Commerce, specializing in Tourism. She is affiliated with Christ University, as an Associate Professor and is the Research Coordinator at School of Business Studies and Social Sciences. She has served many educational institutions in South India and has served as a national and international expert for a decade among the educational institutions of India. Currently, she is actively associated with Indian Tourism Congress (ITC) and Kerala Development Society (KDS), New Delhi. Dr. Bindi completed a major research project on the title "Strategic Intervention of Destination Management Organizations to Enhance Competitiveness of Tourism Destinations– A Model for Karnataka" funded by Christ University. She has authored one book; on Medical Tourism in India: by an international publisher in Germany, and has also contributed chapters to edited books and has published several articles in areas of Destination Management, Governance, Medical Tourism, and E-Tourism.

Index

A

B

C

D

E

F

G

H

I

L

M

N

P

R

S

T

U

V

www.ingramcontent.com/pod-product-compliance
Lightning Source LLC
LaVergne TN
LVHW062152300926
849161LV00010B/2648